MW01194732

NATIONALIZING FRANCE'S ARMY

Winner of the Walker Cowen Memorial Prize
for an outstanding work of scholarship
in eighteenth-century studies

NATIONALIZING FRANCE'S ARMY

FOREIGN, BLACK, AND JEWISH TROOPS
IN THE FRENCH MILITARY, 1715–1831

CHRISTOPHER J. TOZZI

University of Virginia Press

CHARLOTTESVILLE AND LONDON

University of Virginia Press
© 2016 by the Rector and Visitors of the University of Virginia
All rights reserved
Printed in the United States of America on acid-free paper

First published 2016

1 3 5 7 9 8 6 4 2

LIBRARY OF CONGRESS CATALOGING-IN-PUBLICATION DATA

NAMES: Tozzi, Christopher J., 1986– author.
TITLE: Nationalizing France's Army : foreign, Black, and Jewish troops in the
French military, 1715–1831 / Christopher J. Tozzi.
OTHER TITLES: Foreign, Black, and Jewish troops in the French military, 1715–1831
DESCRIPTION: Charlottesville : University of Virginia Press, [2016] | Series:
Winner of the Walker Cowen Memorial Prize for an outstanding work of scholarship
in eighteenth-century studies | Includes bibliographical references and index.
IDENTIFIERS: LCCN 2015035152| ISBN 9780813938332 (cloth : alk. paper) |
ISBN 9780813938349 (ebook)
SUBJECTS: LCSH: France—History, Military—1789–1815. | France. Armée—
History—18th century. | Jewish soldiers—France—History. | Soldiers, Black—
France—History. | Mercenary troops—France—History. | Foreign enlistment—
France—History. | Napoleonic Wars, 1800–1815—Participation, Foreign. | France.
Armée—History—19th century. | France—History, Military—1715–1789.
CLASSIFICATION: LCC DC152.5 .T66 2016 | DDC 355.00944/09033—dc23

LC record available at http://lccn.loc.gov/2015035152

CONTENTS

Acknowledgments vii

Introduction 1

ONE The Army before the Nation: Foreign Troops
in Old Regime France 17

TWO Nationalizing the Army 49

THREE Foreign Legions from the Old Regime
to the Terror 86

FOUR The Limits of Pragmatism: Foreign Soldiers
and the Terror 115

FIVE Constitutionalism and Innovation: Foreign Troops
under the Directory and the Consulate 140

SIX Revolutionary Continuities: Napoleon's
Foreign Troops 170

SEVEN Jews, Soldiering, and Citizenship in
Revolutionary and Napoleonic France 198

Conclusion: Foreign Soldiers and the
Revolutionary Legacy 217

APPENDIX A Places of Birth for Troops in
Foreign Regiments 221

APPENDIX B The Foreign Regiments in 1789 226

Notes on Archival Sources 229

Notes 233

Bibliography 279

Index 301

ACKNOWLEDGMENTS

In contrast to my colleagues in the "hard" sciences, I work in a discipline in which little scholarship appears under coauthorship. That is a pity, because this book is hardly the fruit of my labors alone. Accordingly, it is with great pleasure that I acknowledge in the space below some of the colleagues, friends, and organizations whose assistance and encouragement made this project possible. I regret only that, for want of unrestricted space, many names of those who deserve credit will remain absent from these pages.

In Paris, Bernard Gainot, Florence Gauthier, Jennifer Heuer, and Marie-Jeanne Rossignol offered guidance while I was performing the research that laid the foundation for this book. From the United States, Rafe Blaufarb, François Furstenberg, and Richard Kagan read early drafts of chapters that made their way into the manuscript. Wilda Anderson, Steven David, Michael Kwass, and John Marshall provided comments on the project as a whole, which proved invaluable as I revised the manuscript for publication.

I received feedback on separately published book chapters and journal articles, in which some of the ideas that made their way into this book had their first incarnations, from Reynald Abad, Mary Ashburn Miller, Vicki Caron, Hilary Footitt, Eddie Kolla, Khalid Kurji, David Moak, Kenneth Moss, Alyssa Sepinwall, David Woodworth, and a still-anonymous reader for the *Journal of Modern History.* The anonymous reviewers of my manuscript for the University of Virginia Press helped enormously to sharpen the arguments and flesh out the substance of this book during the final stages of revision.

I am grateful, too, to the staff of the University of Virginia Press, especially Angie Hogan and Mark Mones, for making the preparation and production of this book a remarkably smooth and enjoyable process.

Generous material support for research came from the Social Sciences Research Council (with funding provided by the Andrew W. Mellon Foundation); a *bourse* Chateaubriand from the embassy of France in the United States; a Massachusetts Fellowship from the Society of the Cincinnati; a Jane L. Keddy Memorial Fellowship from the John Carter Brown Library; the Institut Français d'Amérique; a Carl J. Ekberg research grant from the

Center for French Colonial Studies; a Leonard and Helen R. Stulman Jewish Studies Award from Johns Hopkins University; a research grant from John Hopkins funded by J. Brien Key; and an award from the Singleton Center for the Study of Pre-Modern Europe at Johns Hopkins.

Howard University provided a research grant, as well as a reduction of my teaching load, that supported the completion of this book. I owe much, too, to my colleagues at Howard, especially Ana-Lucia Araujo, Jeffrey Kerr-Ritchie, and Edna Greene Medford, for their mentorship while I worked on the manuscript.

I have been extraordinarily lucky to have the support of a host of friends who, on both sides of the Atlantic, made the years I spent researching and writing this book such rich ones for mind and soul. Will Brown, Sara Damiano, Cole Jones, and Jessica Walker were particularly supportive colleagues and companions in Baltimore. Anne-Lise Guignard provided a futon, and some excellent *tarte flambée,* during research in Strasbourg. In Paris, Nimisha Barton, Philippe Florentin, Lucy Gellman, Kelly Jakes, Michael Kozakowski, Vanessa Lincoln, Anton Matytsin, Malgorzata Przepiórka, Katherine McDonough, Laura Sims, Kelly Summers, and Karen Turman helped me to make the very most of days inside the archives, as well as evenings on quai de la Tournelle.

I am profoundly grateful to David A. Bell, whose boundless generosity, unfailing encouragement, and exceptional direction not only assured the success of this book, but also did very much to make possible the rewarding life I now lead as a teacher and researcher.

Some material in chapter 7 is adapted from my essay "Jews, Soldiering, and Citizenship in Revolutionary and Napoleonic France," in *The Journal of Modern History* 86 (June 2014). © 2014 by the University of Chicago 0022-2801/2014/8602-0001$10.00. All rights reserved. Some material that appears in chapters 1, 4, and 6 on languages spoken by foreign troops is adapted from my essay "One Army, Many Languages: Foreign Troops and Linguistic Diversity in the Eighteenth-Century French Military," in Hilary Footitt and Michael Kelly, eds., *Languages and the Military: Alliances, Occupation and Peace Building,* 2012, Palgrave Macmillan, reproduced with permission of Palgrave Macmillan. I am grateful to the publishers of both of these works for allowing me to adapt parts of these contributions for use in this book.

MORE PERSONALLY, I remain deeply indebted to my parents, Barbara, Anthony, and Carole Tozzi, for their unflagging support during the years I worked on this project, even when it was not at all clear how a terminal degree in French history would translate into gainful employment. My grandmothers, Dorothy Schatzle and Mary Ann Tozzi, will not see these pages in print, but their love is inscribed onto each one of them. So, too, is that of my grandfathers, Robert Schatzle and Antonio Tozzi—sons of immigrants, soldiers in their time—who made their livings with their hands, yet are proud that I have not. I dedicate this book to my grandparents, who gave so much to assure the privileged life I live.

Finally, I owe more than I can say to Kate Sohasky. Her love and companionship were, by far, my luckiest finds in the course of working on this book, and they sustained me through much of it. (Her role in acquainting me fully with the stimulative power of caffeine did not hurt, either.) I am endlessly blessed to be able to look forward to a lifetime and more with her.

NATIONALIZING FRANCE'S ARMY

INTRODUCTION

THE TURBULENT YEARS BETWEEN 1789 and 1815 saw more than a half-dozen regimes rise and fall in France. Isidore Lynch, whose career as a soldier and army administrator spanned more than four decades, served nearly all of them. He first enlisted in 1770, when he became a sous-lieutenant in the Regiment of Clare. His service in the French expeditionary forces in North America a decade later, during the American Revolution, helped to secure him promotion to colonel of the Regiment of Walsh in 1784. In 1792, after the outbreak of the French revolutionary war, Lynch commanded the vanguard of the French army at the pivotal battle of Valmy, where he "distinguished himself most brilliantly, leading his troops with great tranquility and guiding them firmly under fire for more than twelve hours," according to a superior officer. His subsequent suspension and imprisonment during the Reign of Terror in 1793 did not dispel his taste for service in the army, in which he reenlisted in June 1795. Reservations about fighting fellow Catholics in the Vendée prompted him to retire a few months later, but he reenlisted in 1800 as an inspector in Napoleon Bonaparte's army. It was not until 1815, when a Bourbon king sat once again upon the throne of France, that Lynch definitively ended his military career.[1]

Lynch's long decades of service were hardly unique in an era during which near-constant warfare and the introduction of universal male conscription funneled millions of men into the ranks of the army in France. But what distinguished Lynch from most of his comrades in arms was his nationality. Born in London to a family from County Galway, Ireland, but having lived in France since childhood, Lynch found himself described variously as English, Irish, or French.[2] The complexity of these national origins was of little significance prior to the French Revolution, when modern conceptualizations of nationality did not yet exist and the Bourbon monarchy imposed few meaningful distinctions between its native subjects and those of foreign origin, particularly if they served in the army. Beginning in 1789, however, Lynch's failure to fall cleanly into any of the categories of nationality that evolved during the Revolution became an issue of signal importance. Most of all, it helped to legitimate his suspension and imprisonment during the Terror on the grounds that he was a foreigner, notwithstanding his protest that "France has been my *patrie* since the age of nine."[3]

Lynch was only one of tens of thousands of men who served in the French army during the revolutionary era, yet whose status as French nationals and citizens was subject to contestation because they had not been born in France or they belonged to minority racial or religious groups. Like Lynch, many of these men pursued long careers in the French army despite the political upheavals of the period and the emergence early in the Revolution of the principle that only French citizens should bear arms in defense of the nation. Their presence beneath French battle-standards, and the significance of their role in defending the nascent French nation-state, reveal deep contradictions within the nation-building project that, beginning in 1789, transformed the corporatist society and absolutist monarchy of Old Regime France into a modern nation-state that prioritized clearly defined geographic and demographic boundaries. Their experience also helps to explain the origins of one of the core tensions that has affected France since the Revolution, namely, French society's inability to realize fully the ideal of forging a national community based solely on common political principles, in which cultural, linguistic, religious, and racial differences play no role.

FROM THE VIEWPOINT of most people in Old Regime Europe, where the presence of large numbers of foreigners within the armies of France and other major powers was commonplace, bearing arms for a foreign sovereign was unremarkable. Far from constituting roving bands of "mercenaries," an anachronistic term that some historians have inappropriately applied to these forces, most foreign troops before the revolutionary era served in permanent "foreign regiments," which their host countries maintained for the express purpose of recruiting soldiers born abroad. For their part, European sovereigns usually tolerated the service of their subjects in foreign armies so long as the men were not deserters from the forces of their native states. Some monarchs went so far as to encourage the practice as a way of strengthening diplomatic ties with allies.[4] The phenomenon of service for foreign powers extended even beyond Europe's borders; Bonaparte, for instance, considered an appointment in the Ottoman army prior to his rise to power in France, and troops of non-European descent born in Asia, Africa, and the Americas, such as the black cavaliers of France's Volontaires de Saxe Regiment, served in the European metropole despite the French monarchy's nominal prohibition against the entry of blacks into France.[5] Such practices introduced a substantial degree of demographic, linguistic, religious, and cultural difference within the ranks of eighteenth-century armies.

In many European countries, the impetus for reorganizing the army into a more homogeneous institution, in which only citizens could serve, arose slowly. In France, however, where the Revolution of 1789 prompted the proclamation of a radically new vision of the polity, this was not the case. For the revolutionaries, who discarded the Old Regime society of orders and, with it, the notion that only a monarch endowed with absolute authority could effectively govern the diverse conglomeration of corporations, estates, and jurisdictions that existed in France prior to 1789, the "nation" emerged powerfully and singularly at the outset of the Revolution as the essential source of sovereignty.[6] Because France's leaders reconceptualized the armed forces as a vital expression of the national will, and even as a microcosm of the nation itself, they became deeply committed to "nationalizing" the army from a very early date.

To the revolutionaries, "nationalization," a term they employed frequently, meant not only placing the army at the disposal of the nation as a whole rather than of the king, but also restricting participation in the army to French citizens who formed part of the newly sovereign national community. It was this principle that led the deputy Louis de Noailles to proclaim before the National Assembly in September 1789 that "in the future there will be no more foreign troops" in French service. His colleague Edmond-Louis-Alexis Dubois de Crancé similarly declared three months later, "I take it as a basic principle that in France every citizen must be a soldier, and every soldier a citizen."[7] Such statements reflected a fundamentally new conceptualization of the French army and its relation to the society it served, one starkly at odds with the Old Regime model.

The impulse to nationalize the revolutionary army, however, proved tremendously difficult to reconcile with the new nation's pragmatic needs. For several decades after 1789, successive French regimes grappled with a vexing set of contingencies and tensions that rendered the total elimination of foreigners from the armed forces impossible. Chief among them was the difficulty of defining the difference between French nationals and foreigners in an era when both the theoretical and practical meanings of nationality and citizenship, especially for soldiers, remained indeterminate and fluid. In the corporate society of Old Regime France, where an individual's geographic place of birth mattered much less than his or her social status, foreigners in the royal army routinely declared themselves French on the basis of their military service. For its part, the Crown effectively treated its foreign troops as French subjects even though very few of them underwent formal naturalization procedures.

As a result, many foreigners in the Old Regime army, unlike their civilian counterparts, enjoyed special immunities from such obligations as the *droit d'aubaine,* a heavy tax that the Crown levied on the estates of non-naturalized foreigners after their deaths. The monarchy also often invited retired soldiers and their families to settle permanently in France, another policy that blurred the line separating them from native-born French subjects. These practices conferred on foreign troops prior to 1789 a status tantamount to French citizenship *avant la lettre.*[8] They also provided a precedent upon which foreign troops during the Revolution claimed French nationality in order to remain eligible for service in the army even after the revolutionaries moved to purge it of noncitizens.

Thus, the very task of determining who in the armed forces was French, and who was not, was anything but simple as the nationalization process proceeded during the Revolution. These difficulties, which the considerable vagueness of the word for foreigner, *étranger,* during the Revolution did nothing to help, persisted well after the Constitution of 1791 formally codified definitions of French nationality and naturalization procedures for the first time.[9]

The revolutionary and Napoleonic armies' constant demand both for simple manpower and for skilled, experienced military leaders also complicated efforts to nationalize military personnel. From the beginning of the revolutionary war on April 20, 1792, through the Waterloo campaign of 1815, foreigners constituted a vital asset for French generals struggling to fill the ranks of their regiments and battalions. This was particularly true in an era when efforts to enlist French natives, via either voluntary or compulsory means, often proved considerably less effective than French leaders hoped.[10] Foreign troops were also especially valuable to the French state because many of them had gained long decades of experience serving in the regiments of the Old Regime. Their military expertise distinguished them during the Revolution from native French recruits, few of whom had borne arms prior to 1789.[11] In addition, the desertion and emigration of vast numbers of aristocratic French officers, amounting to more than two thousand between September and December 1791 alone, further increased the pragmatic importance of veteran foreigners who could fulfill leadership roles in an army short on seasoned commanders.[12]

Historiographical Context

Despite the importance of foreigners to the revolutionary army, few historians have appreciated the extraordinary tensions and contradictions that arose during the endeavor to transform France's army into a purely national institution. Scholars have devoted some study to foreigners in French military service during the eighteenth and early nineteenth centuries, with the Swiss and the Irish in particular receiving appreciable attention, albeit primarily from their own compatriots. Yet most such literature belongs to the field of operational military history and includes relatively little consideration of the political, social or ideological stakes of soldiering by foreigners during the revolutionary era.[13] Meanwhile, existing work on the phenomenon of citizen-soldiering during the Revolution almost entirely ignores the issue of foreigners in the military.[14] For its part, the substantial literature on nationality and citizenship during the eighteenth century, which includes several studies that focus specifically on civilian foreigners in revolutionary France, also affords little systematic attention to their counterparts who served in the army.[15] Nor does it consider the ways in which military service presented unique opportunities for foreign men, and sometimes their families, to nuance and challenge their political status in France.

Yet the story of the nationalization of the French army offers an incisive and novel perspective for understanding not only the history of revolutionary France, but also the development of the "national" institutions that are a cornerstone of modern states. In most societies today, especially those organized according to democratic or republican precepts, the principle that state institutions should be composed of members of the nation they serve, as well as mirror that nation's character and values, is a sine qua non of political sovereignty and legitimacy. This concept also structured the thinking of the French revolutionaries and their successors as they endeavored to remake France's army, which constituted one of the country's largest and arguably most important institutions, into a national organization by purging it of noncitizens. Yet the chronic failure of French regimes to achieve this goal, from the beginning of the Revolution through the Bourbon Restoration, proved that the construction of the modern nation-state, founded upon national institutions drawn from the same body of citizens they serve, was much more halting and complicated in one of the world's first modern democracies than the simple pronouncements of the French revolutionaries in 1789 suggested, and than many scholars have taken for granted when crediting the Revolution with having "invented both the nation-state and the modern institution and ideology of national citizenship."[16] It was one thing to declare the primacy of the French nation and conceptualize an ideology of national citizenship. It was quite another to establish a state that was actually consonant with the "nation-form" and free of the tensions emanating from racial, cultural, religious, and linguistic difference that thwarted efforts to nationalize the revolutionary army, and which persist in France today.

This book illuminates the deep complexities and contradictions of the effort to forge the French army into a national institution by examining both the high-level official sources that have comprised the basis of most existing scholarship related to this topic and, especially, archival material that has been subject to less study. It deals in large part with the policies of the state, but with careful attention to how those policies translated into actual action, as well as the way they influenced, and were influenced by, nonofficial actors in France and abroad. In so doing, the book engages several key issues that are vital to understanding how the army of a major European society slowly and imperfectly morphed into a modern, national institution, and how its development both reflected and helped to shape the political, social, and ideological tenets of that society.

Reconsidering the French Revolution and Foreigners

First, the treatment of foreign troops highlighted the extent to which nationalist sentiment, and a commitment to excluding outsiders from the nascent national community regardless of their political sympathies, conditioned conceptualizations of the French nation and state from the very first moments of the Revolution. Even prior to the storming of the Bastille, suspicion and animosity toward foreign troops in the service of France, due primarily to the simple fact that they were not French natives but exacerbated by differences of culture and language, emerged unambiguously among reform-minded thinkers. This sentiment built to a certain extent upon philosophical traditions that questioned the effectiveness of foreign recruits, but it mostly reflected the new conceptualization of France as a nation-state that rapidly took hold at the outset of the Revolution. Calls to disband France's foreign regiments appeared not only in several *cahiers de doléances,* the lists of grievances that French subjects submitted to the king on the eve of the Revolution, but also in such nationalist declarations as the comte de Sanois's pronouncement in April 1789 that "I believe it necessary to request the total dissolution of the foreign troops so that we can place children of the *patrie* in the service of the *patrie.*"[17] Many of France's revolutionary leaders shared these views, and as early as the fall of 1789 they began formulating legislation to eliminate foreigners from the army.

The efforts very early in the Revolution to purge foreigners from the ranks, which persisted despite the enthusiastic declarations by many foreign troops of their loyalty to the revolutionary regime, repudiate the myth that the French nation-state in its earliest incarnation embodied universalist ideals and welcomed the participation of every man who professed allegiance to revolutionary political principles, regardless of his creed, language, culture, or place of birth. Previous studies of foreigners in revolutionary France, which focus on civilians, show that by the Reign of Terror in 1794, xenophobia had emerged. These studies offer varying interpretations of the reasons for and precise chronology of that outcome. Yet none of these works questions the ostensible predominance of a "cosmopolitan" spirit during the first several years of the Revolution. Albert Mathiez's classic study of foreigners in revolutionary France pointed to setbacks in the revolutionary war, especially the disillusioning rejection of French armies by foreign populations, to argue that xenophobic sentiment emerged by the spring of 1793.[18] Sophie Wahnich's sophisticated study of revolutionary language and rhetoric attributed the retreat from universalism, which she dated to the summer of 1793, to the revolutionaries' conceptualization of sovereignty and citizenship, which they defined in ways that fundamentally contradicted their universalist pronouncements.[19] Her conclusions regarding the treatment of foreigners are consistent with a broader body of scholarship, including classic theoretical work by Hannah Arendt and François Furet, as well as Dan Edelstein's excellent, more recent research on Jacobin interpretations of "natural right," that emphasized the contradiction between the lofty political ideals the revolutionaries proclaimed in 1789 and other core components of revolutionary political thinking, especially conceptualizations of sovereignty that restricted political legitimacy to men who were uncontested members of the nation.[20] And while Michael Rapport, in the most comprehensive examination to date of the lived experience of foreigners during the revolutionary decade, emphasized the extent of the "gap between what the revolutionaries said and what they actually did," his empirically rich study did not dispute the portrayal of the French attitude toward foreigners as welcoming and cosmopolitan prior to the Terror.[21]

Yet the eagerness of the revolutionaries to exclude foreign and minority troops from the army at all points in the revolutionary chronology reveals a different story. It indicates that the universalist ideals that ostensibly flowered during the first several years of the Revolution, and the model of nation building they supposedly instated, in fact were riddled by nationalist exclusivity from the outset. French society did not descend from cosmopolitanism into xenophobia during the Terror as a result of the war, as Mathiez claimed, or because of fundamental contradictions within revolutionary thought, as more recent scholarship contends. Xenophobia was instead a feature of the Revolution from its earliest moments.

On the basis of this evidence, it is necessary to discard not only portrayals of the revolutionaries in 1789 as genuine cosmopolitans but also, more important, the suggestion that the nation-state model in France, in contrast to its counterpart in countries such as Germany, was founded purely upon the notion that political rights alone, regardless of differences in race, language, religion, or culture, could form the basis for the national community.[22] Moreover, the endurance of hostility toward noncitizen soldiers throughout the entire course of the revolutionary decade and beyond, a trend that previous scholarship missed by focusing on the reprieves granted to foreign civilians after the Reign of Terror ended, showed that the exclusionary model of nation building in France remained firmly in place during the revolutionary decade and, indeed, through the Napoleonic and Restoration eras.

Citizenship in Theory and Practice

If historians have traditionally failed to appreciate the significance of the anti-foreign sentiment that prevailed in France from the very beginning of the Revolution, they have also rarely taken into account the enormous difficulty of enforcing official policies on citizenship and nationality. These policies were central to the project of nationalizing the army and building a nation-state, since restricting military service to French citizens required that the state first make clear who was and who was not French. Yet while issuing decrees on nationality was easy enough, executing those laws often proved tremendously complicated. This was especially true within the context of the army, where foreign troops, as noted above, had traditionally been able to stake claims to French nationality that were unavailable to their civilian counterparts.

Existing scholarship on the Revolution has done little to untangle French revolutionary theories on citizenship from actual practice. With a few notable exceptions, scholars have most often approached questions of citizenship and nationality during the revolutionary era from the angle of legislation and official political discourse.[23] Such studies tend to overlook the tremendous complications that arose when French administrators sought to execute decrees that were often rife with contradictions and ambiguities. Yet by examining not only the published minutes of parliamentary debates and other high-level official sources but also archival records of individual cases, this book highlights the frequent divergence between the ways in which the French revolutionaries defined citizenship in theory and how it functioned in practice.

Indeed, the very notion that citizenship in revolutionary France was fundamentally dichotomous—that however one defined "foreigner," the category had a clear and consistent opposite in the form of French citizens—becomes problematic when one measures it against the experiences of foreigners in the army. Because of their military service, many foreign troops, as well as similar groups of "others"—especially Jews and blacks, who also feature centrally in this book—fell cleanly into no category of national belonging. The ways they identified themselves, and the status French authorities assigned to them, shifted constantly. Their experiences were hardly consonant with either contemporary discourses or modern scholarship whose authors take for granted that an individual is always fully French or fully foreign, depending on the changing criteria for drawing the distinction. Foreigners serving in the army often fell somewhere between these poles, effectively treated as less French than white, Christian natives of France but, because of their participation in the army, more French than foreign civilians and members of other marginal groups who did not perform military service. These factors helped to ensure that the nationalization of the army, and the coalescence of the nation-state it served, proved terrifically more difficult than French leaders envisioned.

Ideology and Pragmatism in Revolutionary France

Alongside the fluidity and ambiguity of citizenship practices, an enduring tension between the ideological goals and the pragmatic needs of the French nation also rendered efforts to nationalize France's army much less neat and simple than many French patriots hoped and than official rhetoric that centered on the supremacy of the nation implied. On the one hand, the political tenets that the revolutionaries adopted early in the Revolution, which succeeding regimes also embraced, left no room for the participation of foreigners in the army. Yet on the other hand, France's unrelenting need during decades of near-continuous warfare for every soldier it could muster, as well as for skilled officers, meant that eliminating foreigners from the army came at an enormous practical cost. As a result, military authorities often disregarded laws prohibiting the enlistment of foreigners, and political leaders experimented continuously with different strategies for enrolling foreign troops without compromising political values. From the "foreign legions" that the revolutionaries raised as irregular auxiliary units of the army in 1792 and 1793, to the Directory's outsourcing of foreign recruitment to allied "sister-republics," to Napoleon's vacillating policies on foreign regiments during his final years in power, the French state grappled constantly with the contradictions between the practical benefits of foreign troops and their political incompatibility with the foundational principles of the French nation-state.

The tension between the ideological and pragmatic demands of military policy that emerged during the French Revolution has continued to resonate powerfully in more modern times. It prefigured, for instance, the debates that arose in the more horrific context of Nazi Germany over whether the state should admit Jews into the army to help meet its pressing need for soldiers.[24] It also anticipated ongoing controversy in the United States today concerning the enlistment of homosexuals, which some parties continue to oppose despite the American military's chronic shortages of both recruits in general and personnel with certain skills, such as knowledge of strategically relevant languages, that gay volunteers might help to address.[25] And beyond the specific context of the military, the service of foreigners in the French revolutionary armed forces is comparable to present-day controversies surrounding "guest workers," whom many countries invite within their borders to reduce shortages of economic manpower but who are often less welcome from political, social, and cultural perspectives.[26]

Military Culture and Merit

In addition to highlighting the conflict between the ideological and pragmatic objectives of the French revolutionaries, the treatment of foreigners in the army sheds new light on the related topic of merit in revolutionary France. Through studies primarily of nobles in the eighteenth century, several historians have demonstrated the emergence during the closing decades of the Old Regime of a reconceptualization of the relationship between merit and privilege. Their work has also traced the consequences of this shift after 1789, when the revolutionaries officially abolished feudal privileges and reconfigured military culture to ensure that, at least in theory, the most skilled and experienced soldiers and officers enjoyed priority for promotion, rather than the wealthiest or best bred.[27]

Without a doubt, scores of talented young men of humble birth benefited from the emphasis on merit during the Revolution to pursue military careers in ways that would have been virtually impossible under the Old Regime. Yet the revolutionaries' eagerness to purge even the most militarily effective foreigners from the ranks indicated that the objective of transforming the army into a national institution constricted the culture of merit that ostensibly predominated within the revolutionary armed forces. By showing that the new regime's commitment to reordering society according to categories of national belonging trumped the vision of merit-based equality that French leaders proclaimed, this book shows that the reconceptualization of merit during the Revolution was limited primarily to reacting against aristocratic privilege, rather than assuring equality of opportunity to people of all origins.

The Military and the Forging of Citizens

Efforts to nationalize the army reflected, first and foremost, French leaders' concern with assimilating the armed forces to the political program of the nation-state. At the same time, however, they constituted part of an endeavor to transform the army into a nation-building tool. During the Revolution, military service reinforced the devotion of French citizen-soldiers to the state, and to the national vision that French leaders cultivated. Yet when the state denied the opportunity to bear arms for France to individuals whom it did not recognize as fully French, the army became a powerful tool for delineating the political and social boundaries of the nation. Further still, military service could help to smooth over the ambiguous status of groups whose full integration into the nation was tenuous, as in the case of Jews, blacks, and residents of the peripheral territories that France annexed during the revolutionary wars. In each of these respects, the French military emerged during the late eighteenth century as an instrument not just for defending the nation, but also for constructing the nation by helping to define, even if imperfectly, who belonged to the national community and who did not.

Yet historians have rarely taken into account the significance of the army, and in particular the efforts to purge it of foreigners, in the nation-building project of revolutionary France. The rich literature on the construction of French nationalism and national identity during the era affords surprisingly little attention to the armed forces.[28] Nor has the prominent scholarship on the army's role during the later nineteenth century in transforming "peasants into Frenchmen" considered the crucial precedents for this process that the revolutionaries set.[29]

Organization and Themes

This book examines the role of foreigners and minority groups in the French army from the Old Regime through the Bourbon Restoration period of the early nineteenth century. It also studies the participation of these groups in the navy, although to a lesser extent than it does the army, whose size and centrality to France's defense made it a much more intense area of focus than seaborne forces as the revolutionaries moved to impose their vision of the nation-state on the country's institutions. Traditional, "old" military history—discussion of battles, regiments, and commanders—necessarily factors into this work, but the bulk of the material emphasizes the social, political, and ideological dimensions of the effort to transform the army into a national institution.

The first chapter deals with foreign troops in Old Regime France. It shows that the French Crown, for a variety of reasons, favored the enlistment of foreign soldiers and officers in the army. The Old Regime monarchy also promoted the integration of foreign recruits into French society in ways that largely erased their distinction from French natives. While certain Old Regime theorists issued calls for reorganizing the army into one of "soldier-citizens" in which foreigners had no place, they exerted little influence on Old Regime authorities, who widely accepted and celebrated the participation of foreigners in the army up to the eve of the Revolution.

Chapter 2, which investigates the treatment of foreign troops between the beginning of the Revolution and the onset of the Reign of Terror, highlights the revolutionaries' sharp break with Old Regime policies on foreigners in the army. From the very first moments of the Revolution, suspicion and hostility toward foreign troops became widespread in France. These attitudes persisted during the Revolution's first several years not only among French lawmakers, who abolished all of France's foreign regiments by the fall of 1792 (although they permitted foreigners who had already enlisted to remain in the army), but also throughout a wide portion of French society as a whole. The counterrevolutionary actions of some foreign troops during this period informed this hostility; however, many other foreigners in the army, like their French comrades, overtly sympathized with the revolutionaries. Yet French leaders, in a reflection of the pervasiveness of nationalist thinking, deemed the permanent presence of any foreigners in the armed forces unacceptable simply because these troops were not French.

The third chapter discusses the foreign legions and "free companies" that the revolutionaries raised as auxiliary corps during the first years of the revolutionary war. Levied in an environment of high-minded cosmopolitan rhetoric, these units theoretically provided foreigners sympathetic to the Revolution, even those operating as far away as the frontier of the United States, with a means of bearing arms on France's behalf after the National Assembly had nationalized the regular line army. At the same time, they represented an expedient by which the revolutionaries could capitalize on foreign manpower to advance their military goals without compromising their political commitment to barring foreigners from the line regiments. In practice, however, the relegation of these special corps to the margins of the army rendered them poor substitutes for the foreign regiments they supplanted. The foreign special corps also proved short-lived, with French legislators abolishing the last of them by early 1794 as a result of the same political priorities and ideological pressures that had prompted the dissolution of the foreign regiments a few years earlier.

As chapter 4 demonstrates, the suspicion toward foreign troops that fueled the demise of the foreign legions and free companies only intensified after the Reign of Terror began in 1793.[30] Although it was at this time that the French army's need for every willing soldier and officer it could find was greatest, the revolutionaries enacted a series of laws that strictly limited the freedom of foreigners in the army and navy and even ordered their collective imprisonment, although French generals rarely enforced the most extreme measures. The government also recalled many experienced, high-ranking foreign officers from the battlefield, where the struggling army desperately needed their skills, to answer political charges in Paris, and placed many of them on trial. On the surface, military crisis served as an excuse for the repressive measures of the Terror; at a deeper level, however, the policies stemmed from the revolutionaries' fundamental wariness toward foreign troops and the state's commitment to transforming the army into a purely national institution, tenets that were evident well before the start of the war.

Chapter 5 shows that the leaders who succeeded the Jacobins after the Reign of Terror ended in July 1794 went even further than their predecessors in nationalizing the army by explicitly codifying French citizenship as a prerequisite for army service in the Constitution of 1795. At the same time, however, the overseas campaigns that the Directory pursued during the second half of the 1790s to Ireland, Egypt, and (more ephemerally) Canada made foreign troops particularly valuable as guides or as easily expendable expeditionary forces. The Directorial government also experimented with novel means of enlisting foreigners under the flags of French sister-republics, allied states whose armies were effectively under French control yet which were nominally independent of France. Such attempts to reconcile France's political priorities with its continuing need for foreign troops, however, were rarely as effective as French leaders hoped. By the eve of Bonaparte's Brumaire coup in November 1799, which replaced the Directory with the Consulate, the government once again permitted foreigners to enlist directly in the French army, but it relegated them to obscure units that it consigned mostly to unhappy service overseas. Meanwhile, as this chapter also demonstrates, the Directorial and Consular governments extended special privileges to soldiers from formerly foreign territories that France annexed during the second half of the 1790s. The eagerness with which the state encouraged France's newest citizens on the country's geographic peripheries to enlist, while at the same time marginalizing foreign troops, highlighted the importance that the army had assumed as a tool for defining the national community that French leaders sought to construct.

The penultimate chapter continues the story of foreign troops in France and its overseas possessions into the period of the Napoleonic Empire. Whether they enlisted in the French army itself or in the forces of allied states, foreigners remained a vital source of manpower for Napoleon's expansive campaigns across Europe; indeed, by 1812 they accounted for nearly half the strength of the Grande armée.[31] Napoleon reintroduced foreign regiments to France at the beginning of his reign, but by the closing years of the Empire, political paranoia over foreigners' loyalty to the regime prompted orders to disarm and detain most of the foreign troops serving in French forces. Although Napoleon briefly resurrected the foreign contingent of the army during the Hundred Days as a matter of military necessity, the Restoration monarchs, as chapter 6 and the conclusion explain, quickly did away with these units upon returning permanently to the throne. Afterward, Louis XVIII's brief experiment with a new foreign legion ended in the unit's nationalization shortly after its creation, and the modern French Foreign Legion, which King Louis Philippe I formed in 1831, bore little resemblance to the foreign regiments that had existed in earlier decades. By the end of the revolutionary era, there remained little doubt that the juncture between military service and nationality in France had been permanently reconfigured and that except in special circumstances, bearing arms for France was a privilege and duty available only to those persons whom the state recognized as citizens.

The final chapter, which examines the military service of Jews in France during the revolutionary era, approaches the convergence of citizenship and military service from an angle that in many ways represents the opposite of that of the preceding chapters. While the Old Regime monarchy officially regarded Jews as foreigners, and all but barred them from serving in the army, Jews began enlisting in the army in large numbers after the revolutionaries declared them citizens in 1790 (for Sephardic Jews) and 1791 (for the rest). Although hostility toward Jewish soldiers persisted from some quarters in France during the Revolution and under the Napoleonic Empire, French leaders and Jews themselves deployed soldiering as a tool for reinforcing Jewish integration into French society, laying the foundations of a paradigm of Franco-Jewish republican citizenship that remained central to Jewish life into the later nineteenth and twentieth centuries. In this way, at the same time that foreigners faced exclusion from or marginalization within the army precisely because French authorities did not consider them French, military service helped to forge French Jews into citizens once the government declared its willingness to accept them as such.

The military experience in France and its colonies of men of African, Asian, and Amerindian descent, who also feature in several chapters of this book, was comparable to that of Jews. Having been born in France or its overseas territories, these "people of color," to borrow a common contemporary term, were not foreign in the same sense as individuals who hailed from abroad. Yet their status as full French citizens remained subject to contestation throughout the revolutionary period. By extension, the roles the state permitted them to play in the military also shifted; at times when French leaders sought to encourage racial equality, they promoted the enlistment of troops of color, going so far in 1792 as to levy a special legion for blacks residing in metropolitan France. (Had the legion lasted long enough to see combat, its soldiers may well have been the first black troops to enter the Rhineland, more than a century before Franco-African occupation troops prompted outrage in Germany following the First World War.[32]) Yet at other moments, especially in the wake of Bonaparte's reintroduction of slavery to the French empire in 1802, black troops faced marginalization and prejudice, despite their efforts to seize upon army service as a means of reaffirming their equality with whites.

The experiences of troops of non-European ancestry in the revolutionary army thus shed further light on the army's transformation into a national institution that served as a tool for forging citizens and distinguishing individuals whom the government sought to include in the national community from those who remained outsiders. In addition, the contentious participation of these men in the armed forces anticipated not only the tensions surrounding the deployment of massive numbers of colonial soldiers in metropolitan France during the wars of the twentieth century, but also ongoing debates in many modern societies regarding the integration of racial and religious minorities into the army.[33] And it directly prefigured the difficulty that afflicts the French nation-state today as it seeks to reconcile the presence of large numbers of people of color, many of whom are also culturally and religiously different from the majority population, with the political principle that race plays no role in defining the national community.

ONE

THE ARMY BEFORE THE NATION

FOREIGN TROOPS IN OLD REGIME FRANCE

ONE MIGHT EXPECT the French monarchy of the Old Regime to have had little desire to recruit troops from abroad. As the largest and most populous state in western Europe, the Bourbon polity had no obvious need to invite foreigners within its borders, least of all to serve in its army. And in an era when differences of religion within France presented chronic difficulties for the royal administration, attracting foreign soldiers to France, and with them yet more cultural, religious, and linguistic diversity, might have seemed anathema to the Crown's interests.

In this respect, it was ironic that many thousands of the men who enrolled in the French army under the Old Regime were not natives of the state they served. Nor in many cases did they speak French or adhere to the Catholic Church, an institution that, like the army, was tightly bound to Bourbon absolutism. These troops instead hailed from a wide array of foreign countries representing nearly every corner of Europe, as well as parts of Africa, Asia, and the Americas. By their very presence they defied many of the myths that legitimized the Bourbon state, highlighting the rich racial, religious, cultural, and linguistic variety that characterized France under the Old Regime despite the fictions to which the Crown clung. These soldiers also demonstrated, through the special privileges that the monarchy extended to them, the ease with which one could "become French" before 1789 by bearing arms for the king.

To be sure, it is difficult to speak of becoming French under the Old Regime. Modern notions of citizenship did not begin to emerge in France until the Revolution, and the word *nationalité* did not even enter the language until as late as 1807.[1] Prior to 1789, an individual's country of birth mattered officially only within the context of inheritance procedures associated with the *droit d'aubaine,* or royal right of escheat. Through this precept, the Crown seized the property of deceased foreigners who had resided in the kingdom and had not received *lettres de naturalité* granting them immunity from the *droit d'aubaine.*[2] By the second half of the eighteenth century, however, even this feeble juridical distinction between French natives and foreigners had grown largely obsolete as the result of a series of reciprocal treaties with foreign sovereigns that protected the property of emigrants.[3] Within this context, distinguishing "foreign" from "French" soldiers under the Old Regime can imply a series of anachronistic assumptions that the practices of the time did not at all bear out.

Still, as this chapter makes clear, the tens of thousands of men born abroad who served in the army of Old Regime France were different in numerous respects—linguistic, cultural, racial, political—from their indigenous French counterparts. They also thought of themselves differently, and often embraced identities that placed them somewhere between the societies they had left and that of their host country. Finally and most importantly, the Crown distinguished foreign troops in many important ways from its native subjects. Thus, while foreignness and nativeness in Old Regime France were by no means the black-and-white, dichotomous categories that they theoretically represent in most modern states, they existed nonetheless. Investigating the way in which these notions of national belonging intersected with the Old Regime army, as this chapter does, reveals a wealth of information about the political, social, and military institutions of prerevolutionary France. It also helps to show just how starkly those institutions changed when French leaders endorsed a radically new vision of the national community beginning in 1789.

The Origins of the Foreign Regiments

While units composed partially or fully of foreigners had been present in French military forces since the Middle Ages, it was not until the early seventeenth century that the monarchy institutionalized them by establishing the first permanent foreign regiment of the royal line army.[4] Not all soldiers of foreign origin in Old Regime France served in the foreign regiments; on the contrary, by the 1780s about a third of the foreign personnel of the army belonged to "French" regiments, the term contemporaries used to designate units the state did not consider foreign.[5] Nor was France unique in maintaining units for the express purpose of recruiting foreigners. All other major European states did the same in an era when soldiers and officers, as the introduction to this book noted, routinely enlisted in the armies of foreign sovereigns. The Spanish and Austrian monarchies maintained Irish regiments, for example, and by the later eighteenth century about 40,000 Swiss troops were scattered across the armies not only of France but also of the United Provinces, Naples, Spain, and (as part of a tradition that endures into the present) the papacy.[6] As many as 70,000 French natives, too, served abroad, according to contemporary estimates.[7]

Yet what set France's foreign regiments apart from those of other European states were the political transformations that affected them during the final decades of the eighteenth century. And while these changes became most acute after the start of the Revolution, they represented, in some respects, a continuation of shifting policies on foreign military recruitment that are fully understandable only within the context of the history of France's foreign regiments over the course of the seventeenth and eighteenth centuries.

While the total number of foreign regiments in France varied over time, on the eve of the Revolution the Crown officially designated thirty-two of the royal army's 168 regular regiments as foreign.[8] These included eight cavalry units and twenty-four infantry regiments. Together, these forces nominally represented five different foreign nationalities, with the foreign cavalry comprising two German regiments and six Hungarian hussar units, and the infantry counting twelve Swiss regiments, eight German, three Irish, and one Liégeois. In addition, two other infantry units, the Swiss Guards Regiment and the Company of the Hundred Swiss, formed part of the military reserve of the royal household, where they served as bodyguards for the king and his family and performed ceremonial functions.[9] Two Italian infantry regiments existed as well until 1788, when military reforms on the eve of the Revolution led to their reorganization into infantry battalions that had no foreign designation.[10]

In practice, as the evidence below shows, the countries of origin of troops in these foreign units were much more diverse than their official classifications suggested. In addition, the extent to which foreigners actually comprised the foreign regiments by the latter part of the eighteenth century varied from unit to unit. Nonetheless, the six national groups—Swiss, Germans, Irish, Italians, Liégeois, and Hungarians—that nominally constituted the foreign regiments on the eve of the Revolution were historically central to the evolution of the foreign contingent of the French army of the Old Regime, as well as to the diplomatic and political considerations that conditioned it.

SWISS

The oldest and most important group of foreigners within the French army was the Swiss, whose tradition of soldiering for French monarchs stretched back far enough for the baron of Zurlauben to pen an eight-volume study of the topic in the mid-eighteenth century.[11] The official presence of Swiss soldiers within the French army dated to the Middle Ages, when Charles VII in 1444 formed a company of Swiss troops following the battle of Basel. His son, Louis XI, established the first permanent unit of Swiss soldiers in France when he added the Hundred Swiss to his personal guard in April 1481. This corps existed continuously from the late fifteenth century until the French Revolution.[12] The French began to employ larger Swiss units in the seventeenth century, when Louis XIII in

March 1616 levied the Swiss Guards Regiment as a permanent corps of the French army and as France's first official foreign regiment. The monarchy raised or hired other Swiss regiments on a temporary basis during the Thirty Years' War and the Fronde, but it was not until the personal reign of Louis XIV that most of the permanent Swiss regiments serving in France at the time of the Revolution came into existence.[13]

The French Crown's diplomatic relationship with the cantons of Switzerland, which François I formalized in 1522 by establishing an embassy to the Helvetic Confederation at Solothurn, provided the main artery for enlisting Swiss men in French service.[14] In most cases, the Swiss military units serving in France were governed by "capitulations" (so-called because the documents were divided into chapters, *capitula* in Latin), which the king of France contracted with the governments of particular Swiss states. The agreements obliged the Swiss to supply the French Crown with a certain number of soldiers on a recurring basis in exchange for cash and other favors. According to the terms of the capitulations, the Swiss regiments in French service, together with the men comprising them, remained the property of the states that had raised them and were exempt from French legal jurisdiction.

From the Swiss perspective, the practice of furnishing troops to France offered three key advantages: economically, it was a source of revenue for Switzerland, an overpopulated, landlocked region with few natural resources; diplomatically, it reaffirmed the Swiss cantons' alliance with the French king, an important resource in an era when the region came under frequent threat from the Habsburgs; and militarily, the capitulations afforded a means of maintaining a pool of Swiss men with combat experience whom the cantons could recall from France in the event that they went to war.[15] Some commentators in Switzerland denounced the hiring out of the cantons' regiments to foreign powers as a drain on the region's demographic resources and an affront to the autonomy of the Swiss states; nonetheless, on the eve of the Revolution, about 14,000 Swiss soldiers were serving in France.[16]

GERMANS

Second to the Swiss in numerical significance within the foreign contingent of the royal army were Germans. The Bourbons began levying German regiments during the conflicts of the early seventeenth century, but they initially abolished those regiments when war gave way to peace. The first permanent German corps in France appeared in 1654, when Guillaume de Nassau-Saarbrück levied the Regiment of Alsace, a region that at the time remained independent of France.[17] This unit retained its designation as a foreign infantry corps despite Louis XIV's acquisition of most of the jurisdictions of Alsace by the end of the seventeenth century. The Sun King went on to raise three additional permanent German regiments (including the Regiment of Royal-Suédois, which despite its name contained very few Swedes and was considered a German unit) before his death in 1715, and his successors had established four more by the mid-eighteenth century.[18]

The recruitment of Germans was facilitated in part by the eagerness of many of the petty princes of Germany, in emulation of their neighbors in Switzerland, to rent their subjects to foreign powers in exchange for money. Frederick II of Prussia decried this practice as barbaric and befitting only of nomadic tribes; nonetheless, for German potentates with armies too small to contemplate serious independent military action, loaning troop contingents to more powerful governments was a means not only of acquiring cash but also of gaining some level of influence on the grand stage of European politics.[19] Thus 1,123 of the elector of Mainz's 5,973 soldiers served in the armies of foreign powers between 1786 and 1787, for instance, and the British government employed 29,166 men from German principalities on the left bank of the Rhine in its effort to suppress the American Revolution.[20] French recruiters also enlisted some Germans residing near the frontier during the eighteenth century without the consent of German princes, a practice discussed at greater length below.

IRISH

While formal agreements between German and Swiss sovereigns and the French Crown played an important role in supplying troops from those regions for the French army, the establishment of France's Irish regiments followed a different trajectory. Natives of the British Isles had been present in French armies since the Middle Ages, with Scotland in particular contributing significant numbers of troops via its monarchy's "Auld Alliance" with the French against the English. For some time a company of Scottish Guards, which originated during the reign of France's Charles VII, even served in the royal household alongside the Hundred Swiss and the French Guards, although by the second half of the seventeenth century this unit had ceased to recruit foreigners.[21] Meanwhile, the defeat of rebellious Munster noblemen by the forces of Elizabeth I in 1583, the failure of the Spanish invasion of Ireland at Kinsale in 1602, and the "Flight of the Earls" in 1607, all elements of the process of English subjugation of Ireland that culminated in the Cromwellian conquest of 1649–53, drove large numbers of Irish men to the continent in search of employment in foreign armies.[22] Many of these troops ended up in Spanish or Austrian service, while others fought for the French Crown in the temporary Irish regiments it levied during the wars of the seventeenth century.[23]

The Irish military presence in France became permanent during the

Williamite War that James II of England fought against William of Orange between 1689 and 1691. To support James, a Catholic, in his bid to defend his throne against William and his mostly Protestant supporters (and, at the same time, to prolong the dynastic conflict in the British Isles in order to divert Hanoverian troops from the continent, where the French Crown's real interests lay during the contemporaneous War of the League of Augsburg), Louis XIV deployed 6,000 French troops to Ireland.[24] In exchange, James's Jacobite supporters dispatched five inexperienced Irish regiments to France in 1690. These were joined the next year by fifteen more regiments of Irish troops who emigrated following the capitulation of the Franco-Jacobite forces in Ireland in October 1691. In all, approximately 19,000 Irish soldiers arrived in France during this period, which became known as the "Flight of the Wild Geese."[25] Although these regiments remained nominally under the sovereignty of James II, who had also fled Ireland for France and established a court-in-exile at Saint-Germain-en-Laye, the French Crown pressed them into service against its continental enemies for the remainder of the Nine Years' War, which ended with the peace of Ryswick in 1697. A few months later, in February 1688, Louis XIV reorganized James's Irish troops into five regiments that he formally incorporated into the French army.[26] These units, three of which remained continuously in service until the Revolution, comprised what became known as France's Irish Brigades.

The return of relative political harmony to Ireland by the turn of the eighteenth century meant that Irish regiments after that period no longer emigrated wholesale to France. The Irish Brigades, however, continued to recruit natives of Ireland, and to a lesser extent Scots and Englishmen, through the final years of the Old Regime. The restrictions on the professional opportunities of British Catholics that the Penal Laws imposed during the eighteenth century, combined with the dispossession of many Catholics in Ireland following the Cromwellian conquest and the Revolution of 1688, provided strong incentive for young Catholic men to emigrate abroad. Many of these emigrants sought out careers in the armies of France and other continental powers, although in other cases French officers forcibly impressed Irish and British natives into the Irish regiments.[27] Meanwhile, although the British government officially prohibited French recruiters from operating in Ireland, it tolerated the practice at times as a means of reducing the number of able-bodied Catholics on the island who might participate in a rebellion against British rule. In 1729 the British Crown went so far as to negotiate a covert agreement with the French that granted them the right to enlist 750 men within Ireland over a period of three months, provided their activities remained clandestine.[28]

At other times, particularly when Britain was at war with France, British authorities in Ireland hanged individuals convicted of recruitment operations on behalf of France's Irish regiments.[29] At the outset of the Seven Years' War, Parliament took the further step of collectively condemning to death all British subjects serving in the French army regardless of where or when they had enlisted. From then on, not only Irish officers in French service who returned to Ireland to recruit, but all Irish military personnel in French regiments who became British prisoners of war, faced execution as traitors.[30]

ITALIANS

From the time of the Thirty Years' War and the ministry of Cardinal Mazarin, himself a native of Naples, the Italian peninsula and nearby islands contributed large numbers of troops to the French army. The first permanent Italian units in France appeared slightly later, beginning in 1671 with the Royal-Italien Regiment.[31] During succeeding decades the Crown raised a variety of other regiments to recruit the inhabitants of Italy, Piedmont, Savoy, and Corsica. Besides Royal-Italien, however, the only one of these units to survive up to the eve of the Revolution was the Regiment of Royal-Corse, which the monarchy created in 1739 to enlist refugees fleeing Genoese rule in Corsica. Royal-Corse officially remained a foreign regiment after the island came under French sovereignty in 1770, despite the fact that a majority of its personnel were Corsican natives, and hence French subjects following the annexation.[32] Military reforms in March 1788 converted both Royal-Italien and Royal-Corse into light-infantry battalions that the Crown did not designate as foreign. Although the French state no longer maintained any officially Italian units after this time, most of the Italians who were already in French service during the reforms transferred to other units in France, and natives of Italy continued to enlist in various foreign or national corps of the French army into the revolutionary decade.[33]

LIÉGEOIS

The Regiment of Royal-Liégeois, which Louis XVI established in 1787 with the cooperation of the prince-bishop of Liège, was the youngest of the foreign regiments in existence at the outbreak of the Revolution, but it was not the first of its kind.[34] Infantry and cavalry regiments that drew most of their recruits from the bishopric of Liège had existed during earlier periods of the Old Regime, as had units associated with other independent principalities in the Low Countries.[35] In addition, as the investigation of the *contrôles de troupe* below highlights, by the closing decades of the eighteenth century speakers of Walloon and Flemish accounted for a very significant portion of the personnel of many of the foreign regiments, since the Low Countries provided a fertile and readily accessible recruiting ground when foreigners from further afield became increasingly difficult to enlist.

HUNGARIANS

No national group proved more difficult for the French Crown to recruit by the later eighteenth century than Hungarians, who in theory filled the hussar regiments that represented France's sixth major set of foreign units. These corps traced their origin to 1692, when Louis XIV formed the first hussar regiment from Hungarian deserters from the Austrian cavalry.[36] A total of nine other hussar units appeared during the eighteenth century, some permanently and some only for the duration of a particular war.[37] The enlistment of cavaliers in Austrian-controlled Hungary, however, became difficult not only as a result of the long distances involved but also because it jeopardized French relations with the Austrian monarchy, which became an ally of France after the "diplomatic revolution" of 1756. As a result, recruiters for the Hungarian regiments relied for most of the eighteenth century primarily on cavalry troops who deserted enemy armies, including not only Hungarians but also Germans and some Liégeois.[38]

Nonetheless, some troops for the Hungarian regiments came from as far away as the shores of the Marmara Sea, where Ladislas Bercheny, a Hungarian nobleman who had fled to France following the failure of Francis II Rakoczy's revolt against Austrian rule in Hungary in 1701, traveled during the reign of Louis XV. Bercheny was in search of Hungarian refugees who had followed Rakoczy to his court-in-exile at Rodosto, on Ottoman territory. He returned to France in 1721 with 174 hussars and nine officers, who formed the core of the Regiment of Bercheny, which members of his family commanded until 1791.[39]

Missions such as Bercheny's to far-off lands were not a practical source of steady recruitment, however, and by the end of the Old Regime the hussar regiments, although still nominally Hungarian, counted few foreigners among their ranks. They instead drew most of their personnel from the German-speaking provinces of eastern France—a characteristic that did not, however, prevent the hussars on the eve of the Revolution from retaining a lexicon of curse words in Hungarian.[40]

Global Recruits: Africans, Asians, North Americans

If the Hungarian hussars whom Bercheny embarked on ships in the Marmara and sailed to Marseille in 1721 traveled quite far to serve the French king, other soldiers could boast of yet more remote origins. These included, first, black men who served in several units in Europe during the eighteenth century. The identification of black soldiers can be difficult because contemporary documents most often described them only with the adjective *"nègre,"* an ambiguous term (and a highly pejorative one in modern usage) that the sources rarely clarified.[41] As a result, it is often impossible to know whether a particular "black" soldier was of African, Amerindian, or Asian descent. Nor is it usually clear to what extent he might have had partial European ancestry.

There is nonetheless no doubt that some dark-skinned natives of Africa, Asia, and the Americas served in the royal army. Those in the Regiment of the Volontaires de Saxe represented the most significant example. Levied during the War of the Austrian Succession by Maurice de Saxe, a native of Germany who spent most of his career in French service and attained the highest French military rank of the Old Regime, marshal of France, the regiment drew most of its recruits from among the Polish and Tartar populations of eastern Europe. However, its first company, which numbered approximately one hundred men, was composed almost entirely of black cavaliers born in Africa, the Caribbean, South America, and India.[42]

At the same time, small numbers of soldiers whom the recruitment registers described as *"nègre"* were scattered across various royal regiments in the European metropole during the eighteenth century. For example, Nicolas Palio, a native of Saint-Domingue, served as a drummer in the German Regiment of La Marck from April 1775 to September 1779.[43] Another black North American, François Baptiste, from "Lusignain [Louisiana] en Amérique," enlisted in the Regiment of Bouillon, also nominally a German corps, in 1768.[44] He narrowly missed serving alongside Philippe Mudras, a native of Senegal who enrolled in Bouillon around the same date but died in Lorraine in 1767.[45] Of yet more distant origin were Frantz Balthazard, a native of the Mughal Empire who enlisted in Bouillon as well in 1766 as a drummer, but later passed to the elite grenadier company of that regiment; Mathieu Bartholome, from Madagascar, who joined the Dillon Regiment of the Irish Brigades in 1728; and François Indien, a native (as his name suggested) of India who served in the La Marck Regiment for about a month before deserting in 1784.[46]

Because the contemporary documentation available on black men such as these serving with French regiments on European soil is sparse, it is difficult to ascertain the circumstances that brought them from their places of birth to metropolitan France in an era when the state theoretically prohibited the emigration of blacks to its European possessions, and in which the total black population of the metropole amounted to no more than ten thousand people within a country of twenty million total.[47] Since a majority of the black troops were natives of France's Caribbean colonies, however, and others originated near the French foothold of Pondicherry on the Indian subcontinent, circumstantial evidence suggests that the French colonial empire facilitated the travel of these soldiers to Europe. This is particularly true of the black troops who enlisted during the period of French intervention in the American Revolution, which provided ample opportunities for French officers stationed in the Caribbean to enroll local recruits; nonetheless, the examples above indicate that a small number of blacks found their way into French regiments in Europe beginning many decades before French expeditionary forces sailed for North America in 1779. Whatever their origins, the presence of black soldiers within the line regiments of the royal army in Europe highlighted the truly global scope of France's political and military influence during the eighteenth century.[48]

Indeed, the international reach of French military recruitment in the eighteenth century penetrated even into Britain's overseas colonies themselves. The Irish Regiment of Clare during the era of the War of Austrian Succession included three infantrymen born in New England.[49] All of them enlisted on separate dates and in different companies, suggesting that their enrollments occurred independently of one another. One of these men, Jean Newton, a native of New York who enlisted in November 1744 at the age of twenty-seven, was killed several months later at the battle of Fontenoy. His two American-born comrades in the regiment survived that battle but deserted the French army in early 1747—a fortuitous decision given the staggering casualties that the regiment suffered the following summer at the battle of Lauffeld.[50] The Dillon Regiment enlisted several natives of Britain's North American colonies during the closing decades of the Old Regime as well, including not only men from the mainland but also several from Barbados. The Anglo-Saxon names of all of these individuals, and the absence of descriptions of any of them as black, suggest that they were of European descent.[51]

As with black troops, there is little evidence to explain what motivated or compelled residents of British North America to enroll in the French army. Some may have been prisoners of war whom the French captured and impressed into service; others possibly enlisted by traveling to France's colonies or through contact with French troops present in North America during the American Revolution. The fact that the Irish regiments of the French army appear to have been the only units in which non-black North Americans enrolled during the eighteenth century suggests that Irish expatriate networks may have played a role in their recruitment as well. In any case, the service of these men is further evidence of the global migrations that the French army helped to facilitate during the eighteenth century.

Foreign Troops Overseas

Interactions between people of different national, cultural, and linguistic backgrounds also transpired when foreign troops deployed overseas. The Swiss Regiment of Karrer, a colonial corps that belonged to the ministry of the navy rather than to the army, served for several decades in North America and was among the forces garrisoning the Louisbourg fortress when the British first attacked it in 1745.[52] In addition to helping to defend French possessions overseas, the Karrer corps fulfilled a demographic purpose by endorsing special privileges that the Crown bestowed to encourage the permanent settlement of the Swiss soldiers and their families in the colonies, such as paying their wives to accompany them to the New World.[53] The regiment also introduced Swiss Protestant soldiers to the French colonies despite the official policy banning non-Catholics from New France.[54]

German troops were present in the colonies as well during the wars of the mid-eighteenth century, when they were among the troops defending Louisbourg during the second, successful British assault in 1758.[55] Some of the Germans who arrived in New France to serve in the army settled there permanently.[56] German and Swiss soldiers also served with an expeditionary force that invaded Ireland in 1760 by way of Norway and the Faroe Islands in the far North Sea.[57]

Two decades later, French intervention in the War of American Independence brought a large contingent of foreign troops to North America. These included detachments from the Irish regiments of Walsh, Clare, and Dillon, which fought in the Caribbean and Georgia, and from Royal-Deux-Ponts, a German regiment present at the siege of Yorktown in 1781.[58] One of its members, Georg Daniel Flohr, maintained a journal while in America that provides a rare account of an ordinary enlisted man's experiences in the French army during the American Revolution.[59] A contingent of Italian soldiers from the Royal-Corse Regiment embarked to join the overseas expeditionary force late in the war as well.[60] The duc de Lauzun also levied a corps in March 1780, composed in large part of foreigners and administered by the navy, for service in North America. Known as the Legion of Lauzun, it was present at the engagements of White Plains and Yorktown.[61] Some of its personnel had served previously during French campaigns in Africa.[62] In the years between the American and French revolutions, the French state went on to deploy other foreign troops as far away as India.[63]

With the exception of the soldiers from line regiments deployed to North America between 1779 and 1783, most of the foreign troops who served on the frontiers of European settlement during the eighteenth century belonged to the ministry of the navy. This branch of the French state was responsible under the Old Regime not only for the defense of France's interests at sea, but also for the administration of its colonies. In addition to the corps discussed above, naval administrators created a foreign unit called the Foreign Regiment of Dunkerque in 1762. Although a majority of its personnel were born in metropolitan France, it included a number of recruits from the Low Countries, as well as one native each of Ireland, Martinique, and Quebec.[64]

Meanwhile, other military units of the navy, even those not specifically designated as foreign, contained foreigners. The Jacobite refugees who followed James II to France at the end of the seventeenth century included naval officers who entered French service.[65] This trend continued many decades later as naval commanders such as the Scottish captain Hamilton, who had served for twenty-five years aboard British warships, switched his allegiance to Louis XVI in 1777 and in so doing "sacrificed his estates in his country to devote himself to France."[66] Other naval personnel came from as far away as Russia, from which Peter I, following his tour of western Europe, dispatched a contingent of young sailors to the ports of Brest and Toulon in 1717 in the hope that they would improve their skills as naval officers by serving alongside their French counterparts.[67]

Motivations for Foreign Recruitment

Given the long distances and other challenges involved in recruiting foreigners, one may wonder why the Bourbon polity remained so committed to maintaining foreign regiments for well over a century. Yet in the eyes of many contemporaries, employing a contingent of foreigners of diverse nationalities within the French military was a priority for a number of reasons. The most common argument focused on the demographic expediency of foreign recruits, which Maurice de Saxe summarized most famously during the War of the Austrian Succession when he declared, in a statement repeated by later generations of military officials, that each foreigner in the French army "serves us as three men: he spares one in France, he deprives our enemies of one, and he serves us as one."[68] Such thinking was particularly influential in an era when economic theorists, who tended to underestimate the population of France significantly, linked the prosperity of the kingdom to the number of inhabitants fit to work.[69]

Other advocates of foreign recruitment emphasized its role in promoting France's diplomatic, political, and economic influence abroad. The royal advisor Jules-Louis Bolé de Chamlay wrote in 1711, "We must maintain foreign regiments not only for the service they provide, but also to improve our relationships with the nations from which their officers come."[70] This same argument held true on the eve of the Revolution, when the anonymous author of a treatise advocating the establishment of a corps of Greek soldiers wrote, "The employment of foreign troops expands the political relations of a state with the nations from which the troops come, affirms its influence over them [and] promotes commerce with them."[71] It was reasoning such as this that rendered especially important the recruitment of troops from specific states with which the Crown sought to cultivate close diplomatic relations. The treaties with the Swiss cantons described above were the most prominent example of this practice, but another significant initiative was the largely unsuccessful effort to allow only Swedish nobles to serve as officers in the Regiment of Royal-Suèdois in the interest of forging stronger ties with the Swedish monarchy.[72] Similarly, the marquis de Monteynard celebrated the recruitment of Germans not only because they augmented France's population with foreigners "with whom our officers and soldiers will become familiar, and a great number of whom will adopt our customs and establish themselves in France," but also because it reinforced the Crown's relationship with German princes.[73] In other circumstances, diplomatic breaks with foreign governments could have important ramifications for their subjects enrolled in the French army. Such was the case in 1765, when Louis XV expelled natives of the Swiss canton of Schwyz from all of his regiments as punishment for a diplomatic affront that the canton had committed.[74]

In addition to serving as a boon for French interests abroad, foreign recruitment facilitated the Crown's domestic agenda. Some influential political theorists viewed foreign troops as a safeguard for the regime against its own subjects, who might become unruly if too many of them were trained in the art of war. It was for this reason that the Baron of Montesquieu warned in 1698, "There is no state whose policy permits the arming of all its citizens."[75]

Perhaps more important, foreign recruitment also helped the Crown to affirm its sovereignty over remote parts of the kingdom. The anonymous author of a memorandum from the mid-eighteenth century, observing that Louis XIV had levied German regiments whose command he assigned to the nobles of Franche-Comté in order to help facilitate French annexation of that province, advocated a similar strategy for better incorporating the peripheral province of Lorraine into the realm. Although that territory, according to the writer, was "to some extent already united to the Crown[,] . . . this *pays* cannot be regarded with the same eye as the other provinces of the kingdom; we cannot have the same confidence in the loyalty of the people, and the local nobility does not yet possess the same attachment to the king as that of the rest of the kingdom." The author accordingly recommended that the Crown levy two new "foreign" regiments in Lorraine, with the names Royal-Lorraine and Royal-Barrois, and assign their command to aristocrats from the province in order to reinforce the latter's fidelity to the Bourbon monarchy.[76] Another observer pointed in 1781 to the Regiment of Alsace, which (like the other German regiments) enjoyed the right to recruit a certain proportion of its soldiers and officers from among the king's German-speaking subjects in eastern France, as an essential resource for "providing careers to the Lutheran nobility of Alsace," thereby helping to integrate them into the French polity.[77]

The final major argument in favor of foreign recruitment was the notion that certain countries abroad bred better soldiers than France as a result both of more rigorous military traditions and discipline and of the natural physical superiority of their populations. As one observer wrote, foreign soldiers, who were "better disciplined and trained" than French natives, could serve as a model for the king's other troops.[78] Going further, an anonymous advocate for the creation of a legion of Germans for service in France's colonies advanced not only demographic arguments in favor of the corps, claiming that it would increase the population of the colonies without diminishing the number of French subjects in the metropole, but also made the case that Germans were simply physically superior to French recruits. According to the treatise, which parroted reasoning that first became popular when the French recruited German-speaking settlers to Louisiana earlier in the eighteenth century, Germans represented "an excellent species of men, with a stronger and more robust constitution than our own." They were "consequently in an excellent state for tolerating the harshness of a new climate in which our French suffer fatally."[79]

To be sure, enthusiasm for foreign recruitment was not universal in Old Regime France. Jean-Jacques Rousseau, perhaps informed by Niccolò Machiavelli's condemnation of military forces hired from abroad as "useless and dangerous," suggested that citizen militias were more militarily and politically effective than armies that relied on foreign recruits.[80] The comte de Guibert, an officer and military theorist who played a key role in the military reforms that the monarchy initiated on the very eve of the Revolution, also condemned "mercenary" troops in his *Essai général de tactique* (*General Essay on Tactics*), although he did not specify whether the term, as he used it, referred to foreign soldiers in particular, or merely fickle, self-serving troops of any kind.[81] Finally, the most explicit argument against foreign recruitment under the Old Regime appeared in Joseph Servan's treatise *Le soldat citoyen* (*The Soldier-Citizen*), a broad proposal for reforming the French military that Servan wrote between 1760 and 1771 and published in 1780.[82] Servan, an obscure Old Regime officer and minor nobleman who later served two tenures as war minister during the Revolution, endorsed the argument that foreign soldiers benefited France by sparing some French natives from military service, but suggested that the state should strictly limit the number of foreign troops it employed.[83] Servan based his appeal partially on the pragmatic consideration that foreigners were difficult to enlist. Yet his text prefigured the politically charged nationalist polemic against foreign troops that predominated during the Revolution by deeming them "dangerous to the kingdom in times of peace, and dangerous to the army in times of war."[84]

Religion and Foreign Troops

While proto-nationalist arguments such as Servan's factored into criticism of foreign recruitment, it was perhaps surprising that few observers expressed qualms about the diverse religious practices of foreign troops. Yet the multiplicity of faiths among foreign military personnel belied the religious diversity that characterized Old Regime France in an era when the theoretical underpinnings of Bourbon absolutism lay, in large part, in the monarchy's commitment to the Catholic Church, and when France's enemies seized on this image to denounce the French king as an enemy of Protestantism.[85]

The Crown did not officially recognize Protestants within the kingdom until 1787, but most non-Catholic Christians in the foreign regiments benefited from special privileges that allowed them to practice their faiths freely throughout the eighteenth century. The capitulations of the Swiss regiments explicitly guaranteed freedom of religion to their personnel, and the monarchy granted similar dispensations to Protestant generals who entered French service.[86] In some instances French authorities even emphasized the religious liberties afforded to soldiers in the French army as one of the chief means of attracting foreign military volunteers of non-Catholic faiths to France.[87]

The promise to foreign soldiers of the right to practice their religions freely did not amount to equality with Catholics, however. In most cases the monarch denied Protestants admission into the Hôtel des Invalides, the institution that Louis XIV established for retired or wounded soldiers in Paris.[88] Non-Catholics also faced exclusion from the Order of Saint-Louis, an honorary society that the state established in 1693 to reward soldiers who completed long tours of duty in the French army. In addition, while the Crown provided Catholic chaplains for most regiments of the army, it did not supply Protestant pastors for units with large numbers of Calvinist or Lutheran troops. As a result, many Swiss officers grudgingly hired the pastors with their own funds, a practice that the comte de Guibert decried as unfair in 1789.[89]

Gradually, however, the situation for non-Catholics in the military improved. Louis XIV lifted the ban on admission to the Invalides for Swiss

Protestants late in his reign, and in 1759, Louis XV established the Order of Military Merit, an honorary society that was similar to the Order of Saint-Louis but in which only Protestant veterans could enlist. It existed until the revolutionaries abolished it in 1791 as part of broader reforms to promote religious equality.[90] By the 1770s the monarchy even permitted within the kingdom a military academy in which only Protestant pupils could enroll.[91] Reforms such as these, even if they reflected a separate-but-equal approach to providing parity between soldiers of different religions rather than a commitment to actual equality, meant that by the eve of the Revolution a career in the French army posed few obstacles to foreigners who were not Catholic.

Such religious toleration notwithstanding, some foreigners chose to convert to Catholicism while serving in the French army. Louis-Fréderic Arbonnier de Disy, a Swiss native who enlisted in French service in 1716 and eventually became a colonel, renounced Protestantism eight years later, a decision that made it possible for him to join the Order of Saint-Louis in 1740.[92] Geoffrey O'Connell, a Protestant Irish soldier, converted to Catholicism at Angers around the same time as Disy.[93] Similarly, it was not uncommon for Swiss soldiers garrisoned in villages outside of Paris to abjure Protestantism in the days before their deaths, and a smaller number converted to Catholicism at the time of their marriages to local French women.[94]

Given not only the spiritual but also the worldly ramifications that such conversions could present for the men who undertook them, they were not choices to be taken lightly, as the case of Daniel Humbert Droz made clear. In 1776 Droz, a Swiss soldier in the Courten Regiment, "abjured the Calvinist heresy in which he had been raised" and became a Catholic, a decision that he said made it impossible ever to return again to his home in Switzerland.[95] The motives behind Droz's conversion were not clear; nonetheless, the decisions by soldiers like him to forswear the confessions of their countries of birth highlighted the role that the army played in diffusing different spiritual values among the men of diverse backgrounds who bore arms for the French king.

There is no evidence of the segregation of Protestant from Catholic soldiers within individual corps, or of the barring of entry of any individual to a foreign regiment because of his religion. In most cases Catholics represented a majority of the personnel of the Swiss and German units, but the Protestants serving alongside them constituted substantial minorities. The Royal-Deux-Ponts Regiment, which was 50.1 percent Catholic at the end of the Seven Years' War, probably contained the highest proportion of Protestant soldiers.[96] The number of Protestants in other units was lower; of 127 troops who served in the German Regiment of La Marck between

1776 and 1786 and whose religious affiliations were noted in the unit's enlistment registers, only 19.6 percent were Protestant. These included sixteen Lutherans, of whom five were French subjects from Alsace, and nine Calvinists, all of them of German or Austrian origin. The rest of the troops in La Marck, including nine Germans, six Austrians, and a large number of Alsatians and Lorrainers, were Catholic.[97] Statistics were similar in the German cavalry Regiment of Royal-Nassau.[98] These proportions held true among officers within the foreign regiments as well; in the German Regiment of Bentheim (known as Salm-Salm during the Revolution), twenty-four officers were Catholic, eight Lutheran, and one Calvinist in 1754.[99] The situation was no different in the Swiss regiments, which readily amalgamated Catholics and Protestants.[100]

If Protestants comprised a significant minority among the troops of the Swiss and German regiments, they were less prevalent within the Irish Brigades.[101] This trend is unsurprising, since escaping exclusion from the officer corps of the British army and other repressions to which the Penal Laws subjected Catholics in Ireland was one of the chief motivations for Irish military emigration to France. Indeed, France's role as a refuge for Catholic clerics from Ireland dated to the earliest years of the Protestant Reformation and Elizabethan persecutions in Ireland, when sympathy for the oppression that Irish refugees had suffered because of their religion helped to facilitate their gradual acceptance by French natives.[102] Irish soldiers consequently forged strong conceptual associations between Catholicism and their military service in France.[103] This trend held even during the Napoleonic period, when an Irish veteran of the French army responded to an attempt by a Spanish priest to compare the history of France with that of Spain by declaring that "there could be no comparison, as in [Spain], at that moment the inhabitants were not persecuted and deprived of their civil rights on account of the religion they professed . . . whilst in poor Ireland the millions of unemancipated catholic serfs were kept in bondage by a protestant ascendency of a few hundred thousand individuals."[104] Thus, even after the British government began easing the Penal Laws in the late eighteenth century, Catholic identity remained paramount for many Irish military emigrants to France.

The vast majority of non-Catholic foreign soldiers in the French army under the Old Regime, including many of the black troops from Africa, Asia, and the Americas whose names occasionally appeared on regimental rosters, were Protestants. Nonetheless, small numbers of non-Christians served as well. Among the most notable examples were the Muslim cavaliers whom Maurice de Saxe, who expressed a fascination with Islam, sought for his Volontaires de Saxe Regiment.[105] The total number of Muslim troops whom Saxe was able to enlist was not clear, but it is certain that at least the captain of the unit's first company practiced Islam, prompting Saxe to quip of French military forces that "the accusations made against us that we are a little like the Turks are not unjust."[106] The recruitment of Muslims not only contributed to the religious diversity of the Old Regime army, but also anticipated the Muslim hussar unit that served the Napoleonic Empire.[107]

Some Jews also enlisted in the royal army, despite the special tax that the Crown levied on France's Jewish communities in exchange for exemption from compulsory military service in the unpopular *milice*. Names suggestive of Jewish origins occasionally appeared on *contrôles de troupe* during the eighteenth century, and in at least one case from 1702, French officials attempted to conscript Jews for military service, although there is no evidence that this was a systematic practice.[108] André Simon Moïse, a Jew who converted to Catholicism in 1689 and whose baptismal certificate described him as a "soldier in the Regiment of Champagne," is another example of the presence of Jews in the Old Regime army.[109] Whether Moïse had enlisted prior to his conversion was unclear, and the number of Jews who enrolled in the army before the Revolution was by all indications very small. There is also no evidence that Jews associated themselves in any particular way with the foreign regiments, although the Yiddish language that many Jews from eastern France spoke might presumably have attracted the few Jewish troops who existed to the German regiments. What is certain, as chapter 7 shows, is that military service by Jews became much more widespread, and assumed enormous political importance, after the beginning of the Revolution.

Foreign Troops and Linguistic Diversity

Of yet greater variety than the religions practiced by troops within the foreign regiments were the languages they spoke. Alongside the German dialects of soldiers from Germany, Switzerland, and eastern France were the Gaelic and English tongues of troops from Ireland, Dutch and Walloon among natives of the Low Countries, and variants of Italian within the Royal-Corse and Royal-Italien regiments. In addition, the languages introduced by recruits from eastern Europe and overseas, as well as the dialectic variations of French itself under the Old Regime, meant that the army was home to a truly expansive medley of different tongues during the eighteenth century. And because many of the foreign regiments by the final decades of the Old Regime amalgamated soldiers from a large range of national backgrounds, interactions between native speakers of different languages was likely an everyday phenomenon within those corps.

Politically, this linguistic diversity was of little concern to France's rulers, who beginning in the sixteenth century had replaced Latin with Parisian French as the official language of state bureaucracy but who exhibited little concern with the languages their subjects spoke.[110] Within the army, however, the failure of personnel to understand orders effectively in whichever language an officer issued them could be deadly. As a result, military officials over the course of the Old Regime period pursued various strategies for ensuring that officers and soldiers in the foreign regiments could communicate both with French speakers outside their units and with one another. In general, these solutions centered on the employment of multilingual personnel to overcome language barriers. Some of the foreign corps, beginning with the Hundred Swiss in 1626, maintained special ranks for interpreters who were fluent in both French and the language of the national group with which their regiment was nominally associated.[111] At the same time, other multilingual officers, even those not officially employed as interpreters, helped to ensure smooth communication within the foreign regiments. Foreign-born generals such as Ulrich Frédéric Woldemar, Count of Lowendal, who spoke Latin, Danish, German, English, Italian, Russian, and French, went a long way toward bridging language barriers within the army.[112] Not all foreign officers could boast such linguistic talents, however; David Ogilvy, a Scot who commanded the regiment of his name from 1747 to 1752, was not fluent enough in French even to write simple correspondence with the war ministry after his retirement.[113] The Crown also undertook efforts to enlist multilingual French natives in the foreign regiments by exempting them from regulations that prohibited French subjects from enrolling in most of the foreign corps.[114]

Employing polyglot personnel remained the monarchy's chief solution to the challenge of linguistic diversity within the army for most of the duration of the Old Regime. Toward the middle of the eighteenth century, however, an initiative aimed at regulating the language of command for the French army as a whole added a new imperative to language policy within the foreign regiments. On May 6, 1755, Louis XV issued a decree that ordered all of the non-foreign regiments to adopt an official list of commands for drills and maneuvers, with the goal of improving the interchangeability of detachments from different units in the army.[115] Although the decree itself concerned only commands issued in French and did not mention those of the foreign regiments, officers within those units soon produced their own official translations of the instructions into German, Italian, and English.[116]

While these officers experienced little difficulty developing lists of official commands in different languages, convincing their comrades and superiors to agree upon the translations proved more problematic than many translators anticipated. It was at this juncture that the inherent difficulties of regulating commands within a multilingual army during the eighteenth century became clearest. For one, French military authorities were suspicious of many of the translations and questioned their accuracy. In many cases, such concerns apparently stemmed from a total lack of familiarity on the part of military administrators with languages other than French; thus one French officer complained, after reviewing the English translations, that "the word *your* appears to be employed indifferently in place of *le, la, vostre* [and] *vos,* and *the* is used to translate both *le* and *la*."[117] The German article *die* perplexed another French officer because it appeared in the German translations before both singular and plural nouns, a fact that seemed suspect to him because of the notion that all noun markers should be unambiguous with regard to number, as they are in French.[118]

At the same time, several of the individuals involved in the translation project of 1755 recognized the inherent ambiguity of language itself as a factor that inevitably rendered their work imperfect. The officer who created the English translations declared to his superiors that he had undertaken every effort to ensure that as many English-speaking troops as possible would understand the orders, but he cautioned nonetheless that "a single thing can be translated from one language into another in any number of different fashions, according to the particular expressions of different individuals. An officer commanding several detachments will therefore be understood perfectly only by his own troops." Similarly, Major Settiers, the Swiss officer who produced the German translation of the commands for use within the Swiss regiments, suggested that some of his work might be adaptable for the German regiments as well, but warned, "I think it would be inappropriate to subject them to the same phrases because some of their words are different, as are ours."[119]

Finally, the fact that the native tongues of soldiers in the foreign units, particularly by the decades preceding the Revolution, corresponded only loosely with the nominal national designations of the units called into question the effectiveness of the entire translation initiative. Even if all officers within the Irish regiments adopted a standardized set of commands in English, for example, their usefulness for the numerous speakers of Walloon and Dutch serving under them—to say nothing of Irish recruits whose native language was not English but Irish Gaelic—would almost certainly have been limited.[120] Conditions may have been better in the somewhat more nationally homogeneous German and Swiss regiments, but even in those units communication remained a problem. The duc de Bouillon, colonel of the German regiment of his name, addressed a memorandum to the secretary of war in 1789 observing that as a result of the unit's recruitment of many officers and soldiers from Dutch-speaking Flanders, the regiment's personnel "speak the German language very poorly." He suggested that French replace German as the official language of command of the regiment.[121] The war ministry never acted upon Bouillon's pragmatic suggestion, yet as chapter 4 shows, the political imperatives of the Revolution later resulted in radical attempts to reconfigure linguistic practices within the army.

Special Privileges of Foreign Troops

Like differences of religion and language, the special favors that the Crown bestowed upon foreign troops under the Old Regime further distinguished them from most native-born French subjects. The privileges that the state extended to foreign troops varied from regiment to regiment but were particularly remarkable for the Swiss corps. The capitulations for the Swiss regiments exempted them from the unpopular tasks of serving at sea and in the colonies.[122] In some cases Swiss troops also enjoyed exemption from having to fight against certain powers on the European continent; for example, the Crown could not deploy the Reinach Regiment against the forces of the pope, the Holy Roman Emperor, or any states belonging to the Helvetic Confederation.[123] Like French nobles, soldiers in the Swiss regiments enjoyed the additional privilege of immunity from the *taille* and other taxes imposed on most residents of France.[124] Later in the eighteenth century they gained exemption from the *capitation* and *vingtième* taxes as well, a particularly notable privilege given that even French aristocrats were subject to those financial duties.[125] At the same time, although the Crown obliged the Swiss troops to swear loyalty to the Bourbon monarch, their oaths included the qualification that the soldiers were ultimately answerable only to the Swiss cantons.[126] But the most significant privilege of the Swiss troops, and the most egregious in the eyes of the revolutionaries, was their immunity from French justice via clauses in the capitulations mandating that only the officers of the Swiss regiments, not French authorities, could try and punish Swiss soldiers accused of committing crimes in France, even if they involved French civilians.[127]

Such privileges provoked resentment among French subjects, who contested the special rights of foreign soldiers. The accidental murder by a Swiss soldier of the owner of a house who billeted troops from the Castella Regiment in Aix in 1712, for instance, prompted local authorities to protest that in cases involving the deaths of civilians, "the privilege that the Swiss regiments have should perhaps not prevail over the ordinary laws, which provide local judges authority in these affairs."[128] In a similar vein, municipal authorities argued in 1714 that clauses in the Swiss regiments' capitulations that exempted them from paying local customs duties should not apply to the Swiss garrison of Landau. Their reasoning was that the city, although under the control of the French Crown since the seventeenth century, retained some of the rights it had previously enjoyed as an imperial free city of the Holy Roman Empire, invalidating the privileges of Swiss soldiers serving there. A similar dispute arose in nearby Haguenau several decades later.[129] In Paris, where the municipality was responsible for supplying housing and provisions for the Swiss Guards Regiment, resources that the unit's capitulation guaranteed to it for free, property owners in 1770 addressed a letter to the king complaining that such obligations presented a burden "alarming by its nature and overwhelming by its excess. It endangers their property rights."[130] The sexual assault of a local girl by an Irish soldier in Brittany provoked similar outrage when the attacker's foreign origin spared him from serious punishment.[131]

For their part, foreign troops were quick to defend themselves against efforts to curtail their special privileges. In 1676 the author of a book defending the privileges of the Hundred Swiss declared that since the company's origin in the fifteenth century, it had enjoyed juridical autonomy and had "never answered to the king" of France.[132] Officers of the Swiss Guards, responding to criticism of their immunity from French courts, authored similar pamphlets during the eighteenth century advocating their right to exercise justice on their own terms among their troops.[133] Ultimately, the special privileges that the capitulations guaranteed to Swiss troops, although frequently subject to contestation, remained intact until the dissolution of the Swiss regiments during the Revolution.

A different sort of privilege that foreign troops enjoyed was higher pay. The remuneration of foreign soldiers varied from regiment to regiment and between peacetime and wartime, but foreign soldiers and officers almost always received more money for their services than French natives, reflecting the value that the Crown placed on foreign troops. On average, it cost Louis XV 122 livres 11 deniers to raise a French soldier in the time of the War of the Austrian Succession. In contrast, putting a man from Ireland, Scotland, or Italy under arms required an average of 160 livres, while Germans and Swiss, who were renowned for their reliability in battle and their precision in military drilling, fetched more than 178 livres per soldier.[134] These differing rates reflected not only the difficulty of recruiting troops across France's borders, but also the higher enlistment bonuses and rates of pay that foreigners demanded to enroll in French service. These pay differentials dated back at least a century; in 1632, it had cost the state 763,776 livres to maintain 4,000 men in the French Guards Regiment, but 613,583 livres for only 2,000 in the Swiss Guards.[135] The extraordinary expense associated with foreign troops prompted complaints from French authorities. The duc de Belle-Isle, for example, warned the secretary of war in the mid-eighteenth century that the cost of Swiss and German troops was "exorbitant."[136] The marquis de Puységur similarly protested that "a German or Swiss battalion costs as much as two French ones," a fact he deemed all the more egregious because foreign soldiers tended to desert more frequently while on campaign.[137]

At the same time that legal and financial privileges set foreign troops apart from other inhabitants of the kingdom, all soldiers in Old Regime France, whether French or foreign, occupied a peculiar position that separated them from the rest of society. As the historian André Corvisier wrote, men who enlisted in the army "no longer belonged to the Third Estate, but to a different social order" with its own laws and regulations that included, for instance, prohibition against marrying without the permission of superior officers. For foreign soldiers in particular, the special status of military personnel sometimes proved beneficial, since it exempted them from many of the restrictions that applied to foreigners in general, such as expulsion from France in time of war.[138] At the same time, however, soldiers of the Old Regime suffered isolation from the institutions of the family, religion, and village or neighborhood that formed the core of eighteenth-century life.[139]

Meanwhile, civilians tended to hold soldiers in general in low esteem, a fact that did nothing to help the hostility foreign troops faced in France because of their regiments' privileges. Even the comte de Saint-Germain, who served as minister of war from 1775 to 1777, complained that "armies can only be composed of the slime ['bourbe'] of the nation and of all that is useless to society."[140] On the whole, animosity toward soldiers gradually attenuated over the course of the eighteenth century, due in no small part to the state's enforcement of stricter discipline among its troops and the retreat from practices, such as billeting in civilian homes, that had fueled much of the resentment.[141] The transformation was complete by the first years of the Revolution, which witnessed unprecedented levels of enthusiasm for citizen-soldiers who made patriotic sacrifices for the nation. For the duration of the Old Regime, however, the notion that men in the army had little in common with the king's civilian subjects, and lingering hostility toward military institutions, rendered yet wider the conceptual divide separating foreign soldiers from their host country.

Changing Recruitment Trends after 1750

Critics of the foreign regiments' special privileges enjoyed another opportunity for questioning the Crown's policies on the units during the final decades of the Old Regime, when it became increasingly apparent that they were enlisting large numbers of soldiers who did not hail from the countries from which the state expected them to recruit, or who were not foreign at all. It was not until 1791 that the foreign corps lost their official designations as such, but practical obstacles to acquiring volunteers from the specific national groups with which the regiments were associated meant that, by the eve of the Revolution, most of the foreign units amalgamated soldiers from a wide range of countries, including significant numbers of native French subjects.

The *contrôles de troupe,* regimental rosters that recorded the name, place of birth and other basic biographical data of every soldier who enlisted in the French army during the eighteenth century, provide an excellent opportunity for studying changes in recruitment patterns among the foreign regiments during the final decades of the Old Regime. To be sure, these primary documents were not free of imperfections; for one, the places of birth they recorded did not always reliably indicate a soldier's nationality, since some recruits lied about their origins or enlisted under false names and because the locality in which a soldier was born was not a definite indicator of his language, race or political affiliation. In addition, the identities of some localities cited in the *contrôles* were ambiguous, particularly for foreigners who originated in distant areas unfamiliar to the officers responsible for maintaining regimental records.[142] Thus John Dixon of the Irish Regiment of Berwick was described as a native of "Lisbon in Ireland ['*Lisbon en Irlande*']," and the *contrôle* for the Volontaires de Saxe Regiment listed the birthplace of one cavalier as "Mozambique in Portugal ['*Mosambique en Portugal*']."[143] The records for Frantz Balthazard, one of the black troops described above, similarly identified him as a native of the "empire of the Great Mughal in Africa," not India, where the Mughal dynasty actually ruled.[144] In addition, several *contrôles* reportedly disappeared during the Revolution, depriving historians of data on certain regiments, especially the Swiss.[145]

Despite these shortcomings, the *contrôles* make clear (and the tables in appendix A illustrate further) that the national composition of most of the foreign regiments grew much more diverse between the 1740s and the eve of the Revolution. For example, of 408 soldiers enlisted in the Irish Regiment of Dillon between 1708 and 1731, 270 were natives of Ireland, 36 of England, and 11 of Scotland, meaning that 77 percent of the unit's personnel came from the British Isles. Most of the remaining troops were natives of various German states, and only 9, or about 2 percent, were born in France.[146] In contrast, of 916 entries in the *contrôle* for the same regiment dating from between 1776 and 1784, only 62 were for natives of Ireland, 17 of England, and 5 of Scotland, bringing the proportion of British and Irish recruits to 9 percent. The vast majority of the regiment's personnel during the later period, 407 men, were born in the Low Countries; the rest were divided into smaller contingents of soldiers from locations as diverse as Portugal, Bohemia, and Malta.[147]

Similar changes affected the German regiments. In the Regiment of La Marck, 48 percent of the men who enlisted between 1746 and 1748 were natives of German states or of the Holy Roman Empire. A further 20 percent were French subjects from Alsace, where the Crown permitted limited recruitment for the German regiments.[148] By the decade 1776–86, the proportion of Alsatians and Lorrainians in La Marck had risen to 38.5 percent, while troops from German-speaking territories outside France accounted for less than one quarter of total personnel.[149] The Swiss regiments were unique for continuing to draw a strong majority of their recruits from Switzerland up until their dissolution in 1792; nonetheless, by the eve of the Revolution, around one-fourth of the men in even the Swiss regiments were natives of Germany or France.[150]

Changing recruitment trends for the foreign corps during the second half of the eighteenth century prompted disapproval from most quarters. The Count of Clermont complained to the secretary of war in August 1758 that the Legion of Clermont, an auxiliary corps intended to recruit only foreigners, had levied "all of its men in the kingdom, including in Paris itself."[151] Similarly, the anonymous author of a treatise from January 1763 lamented that French subjects comprised one-third of the personnel of the German regiments. "Hidden behind false names and false descriptions," he declared, these French natives had pretended to be foreign in order to enlist in German units. The writer added that the Irish regiments were in an even worse state, containing "only a very few soldiers of their nation, with the rest composed of French deserters and of Flemish or German foreigners."[152] An officer in one of the Irish regiments, Daniel O'Conor, also complained bitterly in 1756 of the replacement of Irish natives in the corps with "robbers and criminals from all parts of the world." Because of the lack of Irish recruits, he wrote, "I look upon myself as in a society of foreigners; perhaps there is not a tenth part of us Irish, and our national enthusiasm is no more."[153]

Throughout the eighteenth century, the Crown undertook efforts to address such complaints. It routinely issued edicts forbidding the foreign regiments from recruiting inside France and providing harsh penalties for officers who failed to respect the regulations. (As noted above, the monarchy made exceptions for the German regiments, which it allowed to recruit partially in Alsace and Lorraine.) An ordinance of 1763 was the harshest, establishing breaking on the wheel as the punishment for recruiters with the rank of captain or higher found guilty of enlisting French subjects, as well as foreigners who had resided in France for more than three years, within foreign regiments. Noncommissioned officers convicted of the same offense were subject to the somewhat lighter penalty of condemnation to the galleys. The same ordinance ordered the military governors of cities in which foreign regiments were garrisoned to purge those corps of French subjects, suggesting that the Crown did not trust the officers of the foreign regiments themselves to undertake such tasks faithfully. The decree of 1763 also assigned to the foreign regiments specific territories beyond France's border in which each was allowed to recruit, forbidding the recruiters of one regiment from operating in the zone reserved for another.[154]

The state only sporadically enforced regulations such as these, however. Moreover, even when recruiters respected royal directives, they did not guarantee that true foreigners filled the foreign regiments, since French subjects such as Jean-Baptiste-Noël Bouchotte, a native of Lorraine who served as war minister during the Revolution, still found ways to enlist in foreign corps. Bouchotte naturalized himself in the German principality of Nassau under the Old Regime and adopted the Germanophone name "Bucholz" in order to become eligible for a commission in the hussar Regiment of Esterhazy, one of the French king's foreign corps.[155]

Efforts to restrict recruitment for the foreign regiments to specific national groups were exacerbated by the haphazard practices on which many recruiters relied during the eighteenth century. Some of the foreign units, particularly the Swiss corps that the cantons had loaned to the Crown and certain of the German regiments that allied states "gifted" to the French king, were stocked with troops provided by foreign governments.[156] In addition, during wartime, soldiers captured from enemy armies were sometimes offered the choice of enrolling in a foreign regiment of the French army, a fate that some found preferable to spending the duration of the conflict in a prisoner of war camp, even if it meant fighting against one's former comrades.

The number of foreign recruits acquired in this way, however, was minimal.[157] In most cases, individual officers from the foreign regiments were responsible for filling their ranks with new recruits. To do so they frequently operated on foreign territory without the consent of local sovereigns, a practice that often proved problematic. The British government, as noted above, executed officers in French service who traveled to Ireland to round up volunteers. Recruiters operating across the French frontier on the Continent often fared no better. The marquis de Dallavicini warned a colleague in 1747, for example, that recruitment for the Royal-Corse Regiment was stalling because "the levying of recruits on the territories of the Republic of Genoa," which controlled Corsica at the time, "for foreign powers is entirely at odds with the Republic's laws."[158] Yet perhaps the greatest difficulties befell recruiters such as Georges Klenamer, an officer in the La Marck Regiment whom a band of Prussian officers assaulted on the territory of the prince-bishop of Liège in 1781. The Prussians, according to Klenamer, stabbed him with a sword and left him partially paralyzed in one arm in order to prevent him from enrolling recruits whom they sought for themselves.[159]

Difficulties such as these, which contributed to the chronic failure of the foreign regiments during the second half of the eighteenth century to obtain sufficient numbers of soldiers from among the nationalities with which they were nominally associated, led to a number of new proposals for recruitment strategies during the decades preceding the Revolution. The most ambitious of these plans, which appeared as early as 1742, involved the establishment of diplomatic conventions with various German princes to provide a fixed number of recruits each year from among the inhabitants of their principalities.[160] Royal officials modeled these proposals on the capitulations for the Swiss regiments, whose recruits the Swiss cantons were responsible for furnishing, but the German case differed in that the task of actually rounding up recruits and bringing them to France fell to French authorities. The diplomatic conventions merely ensured the consent of the German princes for allowing French recruiters to operate on their territories.[161] The first of these treaties, which representatives of the king of France and the elector of Bavaria signed on June 3, 1773, permitted the establishment of a recruiting depot for the French army in the town of Wemding and allowed the French to enlist up to 150 of the Bavarian elector's subjects each year. The Bourbons reached similar agreements during the following decade with the Duke of Zweibrücken and the landgrave of Hesse.[162]

To the disappointment of authorities in the war ministry, however, these endeavors proved to be failures. According to one contemporary analysis, the recruitment depot in Bavaria, which the Crown had spent 100,000 livres to establish, remained operational only for twenty-three months and enlisted no more than 123 Bavarians and 229 deserters from various other countries. These included 59 French natives who, after enrolling in the Royal-Bavière Regiment, "had been expelled from the regiment, causing a spirit of desertion and flight" among the recruits who remained.[163] Another report on the Bavarian depot presented a somewhat more positive image, claiming that between August 1775 and September 1777 it had enrolled 402 men, of whom only 19 were deserters from the French army. Nonetheless, the author agreed with other observers that the convention with the Bavarian elector had fallen short of producing the desired results.[164] French authorities also shared the view that the Prussian and Austrian governments were to blame for the failure of the recruitment project in Bavaria and elsewhere. They claimed that the German princes who signed recruitment conventions proved reluctant to honor their obligations with the French king fully for fear of falling out of favor with powerful patrons at the courts of Berlin and Vienna.[165]

Beyond the German capitulations, a range of other proposals for improving foreign recruitment gained the attention of the war ministry during the later eighteenth century. One idea centered on purchasing regiments from German princes wholesale during times of war, as the governments of Britain and the United Provinces of the Netherlands did.[166] A more far-fetched scheme involved the levying of German men via obligatory conscription on territory occupied by French armies during the Seven Years' War, then shipping them to western France for coastal defense. This plan, inspired by the practices of the king of Prussia on occupied Saxon territory, anticipated the revolutionary government's deployment of Germans to suppress rebellion in the Vendée several decades later.[167] In the event, the monarchy never acted on either of these propositions, and despite the intense focus beginning in the mid-eighteenth century on strategies for developing more uniform and steady avenues of recruitment for the foreign regiments, the Old Regime never found an effective solution to the problem before the Revolution erupted.

Foreigners into Frenchmen: Integrating Foreign Soldiers into French Society

While recruiting foreign soldiers often proved difficult, cultivating a strong relationship between them and their host state and society was surprisingly less so. Despite the differences of religion, language, and privilege that distinguished foreign troops from French natives, many foreigners in the army developed a remarkable degree of attachment to their host country. They perceived themselves as French, established strong bonds with the French monarchy, and, through extraordinary measures that applied only to foreign military personnel, often became naturalized subjects of the French Crown.

The integration of foreign troops into French society began with the erasure of legal measures distinguishing them from French natives. As early as 1602, more than a century before the *droit d'aubaine* lapsed for most foreign civilians in France, royal *lettres patentes* exempted the Hundred Swiss from the tax by elaborating upon a decree of Louis XI from 1483 that declared that Swiss soldiers in French service, "although natives of the country of Switzerland, are nonetheless regarded as good and natural subjects" of the French monarch.[168] In 1687 Louis XIV extended this privilege to foreigners serving in the French navy, and a royal decree of 1715 granted to all foreign soldiers and sailors who served at least ten years in

France the right to bequeath their property to heirs of their choice, as well as recognition in all other respects as natural subjects of the French king.[169] This privilege was subject to contestation by French natives throughout the eighteenth century, but the Parlement of Paris and the Crown consistently upheld it.[170] It was through these measures that Michel Reilly, an officer of Irish origin with forty-seven years of service in the Irish Brigades, successfully defended his property in France in the 1760s against attempts by British authorities to seize it by convincing French legal magistrates that his "*naturalité* in France cannot be questioned; if military honors do not suffice to confer this privilege, everyone is familiar with the declaration of the king of 1715, registered by the court, which regards as naturalized French subjects those who have served ten years in the army."[171] Similarly, it was with the Crown's recognition of foreign soldiers as naturalized subjects in mind that the Count of Clare, colonel of the Irish regiment of the same name, declared during the 1750s that Irish and Scottish troops "should be regarded less as foreigners and more as nationals, since the king has allowed them on different occasions to enjoy the same rights and privileges as his subjects, without requiring *lettres de naturalité.*"[172] Arthur Dillon, colonel of another of the Irish regiments, later cited Louis XIV's naturalization of foreign troops to argue during the Revolution that the Irish corps were not foreign, as the next chapter notes.[173]

At the same time that legal distinctions between foreign soldiers and French subjects were disappearing, foreign troops also integrated socially into French society through close contact with civilians. In an age before the French state provided barracks for all of its regiments, foreign soldiers often lodged within civilian households. They also married French women in numbers significant enough for natives to complain that "they leave no possibility of marriage to the men from this country."[174] In the eyes of contemporaries, marriage in France, combined with the conversions to Catholicism that some foreign soldiers undertook, constituted a renunciation of their native countries in favor of definitive integration into French society.[175]

Also notable was that the foreign origins of officers such as Thomas Lally did not factor into debates even in instances where their loyalty to the Crown was in doubt. Lally, who was born in France to Irish parents who had emigrated there in the late seventeenth century, faced charges of sedition after suffering defeats in India at the hands of the British during the Seven Years' War. Yet his detractors did not even mention his family's Irish origins during his trial before the Parlement of Paris in 1766, which ended in his condemnation to death despite spirited public appeals in his defense by prominent French elites.[176]

In addition, many foreign soldiers retired permanently to France after completing careers in the French army, when the state generally afforded them the option either of staying in the kingdom or returning to their countries of origin. In a typical example, of fourteen foreign-born officers who retired from the German Regiment of Nassau in 1763, twelve planned to remain in France.[177] Similarly, many foreign officers spent their semi-annual semester leaves in France rather than returning to their native countries. This trend, which was particularly true in the case of the Irish regiments, where British-born veterans of the French army could risk their lives by returning home, suggested that in many cases these officers had definitively severed ties with their places of birth.[178]

To be sure, not all foreign soldiers willingly embraced France as their new home. Daniel O'Conor, an Irish officer disillusioned by what he viewed as libertine French culture and the presence within the Irish regiments of "banditti" lacking authentic ties to Ireland, was not unique in his views when he declared in the mid-eighteenth century, "Determined I am to leave this debauched country of France for the rest of my days. I stare and look round me as in a wilderness where nothing like honesty and sincerity appears." Yet it was telling that this same officer never made good on his promise to quit France; instead, O'Conor remained in the French army until 1793, when he died in combat in Guadeloupe.[179]

Given the remarkable extent to which foreign troops forged permanent ties to France, it is inaccurate to characterize them as "mercenaries," as historians have frequently done. Although few scholars who have used this term to refer to foreign troops in revolutionary-era France have defined exactly what it means in their usage, it carries the implication for modern readers that foreigners fought for the French king in exchange for money but otherwise exhibited no particular attachment to France, ostensibly in contrast to native-born French troops.[180]

Yet attempts to distinguish Frenchmen from foreigners in the army by labeling the latter mercenaries are problematic for several reasons. First, while it was certainly the case that economic considerations were the primary motive of most foreigners for enlisting in the royal army, this was equally true for their native French counterparts, as it was for virtually all non-conscript troops in Old Regime Europe. Although troops in the *milice*, which conscripted most of its recruits, usually enlisted forcibly, French soldiers in the line regiments chose to enroll chiefly because the army guaranteed wages and sustenance to men who often had few other means of earning a living; indeed, it was not by chance that recruitment rates were highest during the winter months, when fear of starvation provided a strong impetus to enlist for laborers lacking permanent employment.[181] Beyond economic considerations, the other major factors that drove Old Regime soldiers to enlist, including a desire to escape the monotony of village life and the camaraderie of the army, applied to foreigners as much as they did to French natives.[182] Even patriotic sentiment, which occasionally motivated some soldiers to serve prior to the Revolution, affected foreigners as well as French troops, as the statements and actions of foreign soldiers during the revolutionary crisis of 1789, detailed in the following chapter, indicated. In light of this evidence, it is not accurate to distinguish foreign troops from French-born soldiers on the basis of the notion that the former served solely for reasons of economic self-interest and had no attachment to their host country.

It was also true that certain of the foreign regiments, especially the Swiss corps, bore a strong resemblance to what present-day observers tend to regard as mercenary units because the French Crown essentially rented them from foreign states. By the standards of the time, however, even the Swiss troops had little in common with the opportunistic, rootless soldiers whose image the term "mercenary" conjures. The true mercenaries of early-modern Europe were the roving bands of poorly disciplined, irregularly equipped men whom sovereigns recruited through what historians have called the contract system. These soldiers extended loyalty only to the particular officer paying them at a given moment, and they rarely hesitated to switch sides if more fruitful opportunities presented themselves. It was the mutinying and pillaging by these troops during conflicts such as the Thirty Years' War that earned early-modern soldiers such unforgiving disrepute in the eyes of contemporaries. And it was precisely in response to the political and military unreliability of these loosely regulated forces that the French Crown, emulating other states, began constructing the professional royal army in the mid-1600s as a replacement for the contract system. By the eighteenth century, that project was complete and all of the royal army's soldiers, whether born in France or elsewhere, served in permanent regiments where the state provided them with food, clothing, and pay in exchange for loyalty to the sovereign, rather than to their individual officers.[183] Despite the peculiar juridical status of some of the foreign regiments, and the fact that they were often under the command of foreign aristocrats who owed fealty to monarchs beyond France's borders, there is no evidence that foreign troops under the Old Regime resembled the capricious recruits produced by the contract system any more than native French soldiers did, or that they were any less obedient to the French Crown.

It is also telling that French speakers prior to the Revolution had no term equivalent to "mercenary" in present-day usage.[184] The word *mercenaire*, whose etymological evolution parallels that of its English cognate, *mercenary*, has existed in French since at least the thirteenth century. In the centuries preceding the Revolution, however, it referred only to individuals who performed an activity in exchange for money, often but not always with the connotation of selfishness or opportunism. It bore no specific conceptual connection to either foreigners or the military until 1789, when the revolutionaries first employed the word derogatorily to denounce foreign soldiers. Dictionaries began defining *mercenaires* as "foreign troops whose services one purchases" only in the 1790s.[185] Thus, to describe the foreign soldiers and officers of the Old Regime as mercenaries represents not only a failure to appreciate their strong relationship with the French state and society, but also an anachronism.

HOWEVER ONE CHOOSES to label them, the foreign troops of Old Regime France played a decisive role both on and off the battlefield. In a testament to the diversity that characterized Old Regime France and its colonial empire despite the image of orthodoxy to which the Crown clung, foreign troops traced their origins to a profuse multitude of territories in Europe, Asia, Africa, and the Americas, spoke a rich diversity of languages, practiced a number of religions, and enjoyed unique privileges guaranteed by the French king. Yet many of them nonetheless perceived themselves as French subjects and were effectively treated as such by the Crown. The monarchy not only welcomed them into the French army for the role they played in advancing the military, diplomatic, and political agendas of the absolutist state, but also extended to them a status equivalent to French nationality *avant la lettre*.[186]

The Revolution quickly destabilized the relationship between these foreign soldiers and the French state and society. Although the nation-building myths that the new regime constructed to replace the fictions it discarded after 1789 emphasized cosmopolitanism and universality, the treatment of foreign troops during the Revolution marked a definitive break with the policies of the Old Regime. While many foreign soldiers remained loyal to the French state, the revolutionaries never regarded them in the same light as the absolute monarchy had, nor did they grant them the same privileges or inclusion within French society. Instead, as the following chapter demonstrates, the Revolution from its very outset entailed the marginalization of foreign troops and the denial of their claims to French citizenship. Ultimately, it resulted in their purging from an army that the revolutionaries reconceptualized as one of French citizen-soldiers alone.

TWO

NATIONALIZING THE ARMY

FROM THE TROOPS THAT the monarchy deployed throughout France to maintain order in the wake of initial popular disturbances as the Revolution began, to the mutinous grenadiers whose expertise was key to the capture of the Bastille in July 1789, to the regiments that royalist French generals attempted to march on Paris on several occasions, soldiers were at the heart of early revolutionary events. These troops included not only native French subjects but also many thousands of the foreigners serving in France at the outset of the Revolution.

The experiences of foreign soldiers and officers as France entered into revolution, as well as the political sympathies they espoused, were nuanced and diverse. Some foreign soldiers served as bulwarks of the monarchy as it confronted unruly subjects. Others expressed intense devotion to the revolutionary cause, which they supported not only with words but also with such actions as refusing to attack insurgents and enlisting by the hundreds in the National Guard. And in an era when citizenship and national identity were in flux, many foreign soldiers, building upon the Old Regime precedents that the previous chapter discussed, even claimed French nationality on the basis of their military service and revolutionary enthusiasm.

Yet despite the sympathy of many foreign troops for the revolutionaries, the image of foreign soldiers that most French political leaders constructed, which reflected a view widespread throughout French society as a whole, from the outset of the Revolution was a decidedly negative one. Recalling only moments when foreign troops associated themselves with counterrevolution and forgetting those in which they refused to obey reactionary authorities, contemporaries consistently denounced foreign soldiers as a danger to the nation and its constitutional aspirations. It took some time for these anxieties to translate into legislative action, and at first the new regime took only incremental steps toward purging the army of foreigners. During the summer of 1791, however, the National Assembly decreed the wholesale "nationalization" of the German, Irish, and Liégeois regiments, a move it followed a year later by expelling the Swiss corps in the aftermath of the bloody revolutionary *journée* of August 10, 1792. By the time the Legislative Assembly dissolved in September 1792, service in the professional line army had become, at least in theory, the privilege and duty of French natives alone.

An array of varying considerations informed the development of this policy. It reflected, in part, the revolutionaries' commitment to dispensing with the privileges and inequalities of the Old Regime. It was also informed by the spirit of military experimentation that predominated during the first years of the Revolution, when legislators and theorists continually reformulated proposals for building a new national army. In addition, for several years pragmatic diplomatic and military concerns strongly influenced the government's actions concerning the foreign contingent of the military, particularly as it became clear that France needed every ally and soldier it could muster as royalists and their foreign supporters threatened existential war against the new regime. Yet at a purely ideological level, hostility toward foreign troops stemmed from the belief that, because of the simple fact of their being foreign, these soldiers were fundamentally incompatible with the nascent French nation-state, despite the cosmopolitan pronouncements of French leaders.

To an extent, opposition to foreign recruitment during the first years of the Revolution drew upon the arguments that Old Regime theorists, such as Rousseau, Guibert, and Servan, had advanced, which chapter 1 detailed. But earlier intellectual traditions do not fully account for the invectives that the revolutionaries launched against foreign troops. Critics of the foreign regiments during the Revolution almost never cited Old Regime thinkers directly. Even Machiavelli, whose criticisms of mercenaries within writings on republicanism might have seemed an obvious point of reference for revolutionary leaders, did not figure in any of the major debates on military reform. Instead, the wariness toward foreign troops reflected first and foremost the new political values that the revolutionaries endorsed. In their vision, the nation alone embodied sovereignty and political legitimacy. Rejecting foreigners from the army, an institution that the revolutionaries linked in unprecedented ways to patriotism and citizenship, was a means of excluding them from the national community more generally, thereby helping to reinforce the new modes of political legitimacy that underlay the revolutionary state.

Because the changes that culminated in the Legislative Assembly's elimination of foreign corps from the line army were the product of rigid political thinking but came into force only gradually, they exemplified the complex interplay between ideology and pragmatism that drove revolutionary events. This is a key observation for a field of study in which François Furet's interpretation of the Revolution as the product of an ideologically determined "revolutionary dynamic" has predominated for the last several decades. The extent to which pragmatic concerns influenced policy on foreign troops showed that practical realities amounted to more than mere "circumstances" within the context of revolutionary change.[1] To be sure, principled objection to military service by foreigners emerged from the very start of the Revolution, reflecting broader currents in revolutionary ideology that vested political legitimacy solely in the nation. Yet had political thinking alone shaped the treatment of foreign troops, the government would not, for example, have preserved the Swiss regiments, which were of paramount diplomatic and military importance, after doing away with the other foreign corps. Nor would legislators have incrementally reduced the total number of foreign soldiers they were willing to admit into the army as they debated a string of proposals on military reorganization. For these reasons, a Furetian lens that discards pragmatic objectives in favor of the dynamic at the core of revolutionary thought cannot fully explain the formulation of policies on foreign soldiers between the outbreak of the Revolution and the dissolution of the Legislative Assembly.

A close study of the treatment of foreign troops during the first years of the Revolution is also of vital importance for a full understanding of foreigners' place in revolutionary France, especially the reasons behind the very different policies that the revolutionaries applied toward foreign soldiers and foreign civilians. Focusing on the latter group, historians have traditionally emphasized the revolutionaries' eagerness during the first several years after the storming of the Bastille to cast the Revolution in universal terms, which meant welcoming the participation of individuals whom the new regime did not consider French nationals. As Albert Mathiez wrote in his seminal study of foreigners in revolutionary France, through the end of 1792, French leaders, "as a result of the philosophy of the eighteenth century, were cosmopolitan. A European spirit reigned everywhere."[2] Mathiez bound this conclusion to the notion that non-ennobled French elites at the time shared common aspirations of "class struggle" with their counterparts in other European countries, a thesis at the core of the Marxist "bourgeois-revolution" interpretation of the events of 1789 that most historians today flatly reject.[3] Yet despite its framing within a Marxist dialectic, Mathiez's thesis that the revolutionaries warmly welcomed foreigners into France until the time of the Terror has endured in more recent studies. Although Michael Rapport emphasized the extent to which the actual treatment of foreigners tended to vary on a case-by-case basis, he nonetheless concurred with Mathiez that it was not until the spring of 1793 that, largely as a result of military crisis, xenophobia emerged

in France.[4] Nor did Sophie Wahnich, who traced the repression of foreigners in France during the Terror to the paradoxes inherent in French
revolutionary political language rather than to the war, dispute the view
that foreigners enjoyed hospitable treatment for the first several years
after 1789.[5]

Such conclusions accurately describe the experience in revolutionary
France of foreign civilians. The revolutionaries did little to restrict the
liberties of foreigners residing in or traveling through France before the
outbreak of war in the spring of 1792, and wholesale policies subjecting
foreigners to surveillance and arrest did not appear until the Terror. Some
foreigners, such as the Anglo-American Thomas Paine and the Prussian
Anacharsis Cloots, both of whom served as deputies in the National Convention until their colleagues expelled them in late 1793 because they were
foreign, even assumed prominent roles in the French state.[6] There can be
little denying that cosmopolitan and universalist principles guided the revolutionaries for a significant stretch of time in their policies on foreigners
who did not bear arms.

Yet wholly different principles prevailed within the context of the
army, an institution that the revolutionaries radically reconceptualized by
forging powerful links between military service and citizenship, nationality, and patriotism. These associations, which reflected the new regime's
goal of transforming the corporatist society of Old Regime France into a
nation-state, meant that from the very earliest moments of the Revolution,
the revolutionaries, and French society as a whole, maligned and mar-
ginalized foreign troops regardless of the latter's political attitudes. Even
deserters from foreign armies who wished to offer their services to France
often received cold receptions.

To a limited extent, the policies that the revolutionaries applied toward
foreign troops reflected their effort to justify the dismantlement of the Old
Regime, which relied on foreign regiments heavily during the crisis of 1789.
Yet the chief impetus for hostility toward foreign troops, even at the same
moments in which the revolutionaries were proclaiming their friendship
toward foreigners who did not serve in the army, was ideological in nature.
In this way, the treatment of foreign troops early in the Revolution prefigured the repression of foreigners in general, which reached its apex during
the Terror. It also highlighted the kernel of nationalist xenophobia that was
present within French revolutionary thinking from the very beginning of
the Revolution, despite the cosmopolitan rhetoric that predominated for
several years after 1789. And it underlined the extent to which the image
of the French nation-state as a polity that welcomed sympathizers of all
backgrounds was a fiction, even during the comparatively peaceful period
of the "liberal Revolution" of 1789–92.

Perceptions of Foreign Troops during the Crisis of 1789

Opposition to foreigners serving in the military was widespread in revolutionary France, evident not only among French officials but throughout a wide segment of society. It also predated even the earliest episodes of revolutionary violence that prominently involved foreign troops, suggesting that animosity toward foreign soldiers stemmed not from their actions, but from deeply rooted ideological considerations that deemed foreign soldiers incompatible with the new nation-state that revolutionary reformers envisioned, even if the foreigners endorsed French political ideals. Several of the *cahiers de doléances*, the lists of grievances that each of France's three estates presented to Louis XVI in the spring of 1789, advocated the dissolution of foreign corps while proclaiming, to quote the petition of one community in the Paris region, "that a nation can be best protected and defended against its foreign enemies by itself."[7] Other members of the Third Estate warned in their *cahiers* that foreign troops were dangerous tools in the hands of tyrannical rulers, and that "the task of defending the homeland belongs to the soldier-citizen alone."[8] Even among some members of the aristocracy, who had a greater interest in preserving the status quo of which foreign troops were a part, opposition to the foreign regiments was such that the comte de Sanois declared to an assembly of nobles from the Paris region in April 1789, "I believe it necessary to request the total dissolution of the foreign units so that we can place children of the *patrie* in the service of the *patrie*."[9]

The involvement of foreign soldiers in revolutionary events, beginning with the riot in Grenoble on June 7, 1788, that became known as the Day of the Tiles, propelled such rhetoric further. Swiss troops were among those who, mobilized to quell the unrest in Grenoble that had grown out of discontent over the prospect of new taxes, faced a barrage of roof tiles lobbed by angry townspeople.[10] The selection by military authorities of Swiss soldiers to respond to the crisis was due to the simple fact of the soldiers' proximity to Grenoble at the time rather than a belief that the Swiss would prove more reliable than French troops in a confrontation with civilians. Nonetheless, the Swiss troops' deployment set an example that royal authorities emulated in other disturbances of the period, such as in April 1789, when they dispatched the Swiss Regiment of Diesbach to stop the sacking of merchants' houses in Amiens.[11]

It was in Paris, however, that foreign regiments became most visible as the revolutionary movement gained momentum. Of the 4,000 troops that the Crown had called to the capital by the last week of June 1789, ostensibly for the purpose of maintaining order in the rebellious city but with the inevitable effect of intimidating the nascent National Assembly in Versailles and further provoking the Parisian populace, 2,600 belonged to foreign corps.[12] Not all of these soldiers, who represented two Swiss regiments and detachments from four hussar units, were actually foreign; as chapter 1 noted, many of the recruits in the hussar squadrons, in particular, by 1789 were German speakers native to France's eastern provinces.[13] Nonetheless, the fact that a majority of the troops were nominally foreign was not lost on contemporaries, who accused the king of planning to unleash foreign "mercenaries"—a term that was beginning to acquire a new meaning in the context of the revolutionary crisis—against his own dissenting subjects. These worries only increased as June turned into July and the number of regular troops in and around Paris swelled to 17,000, of which 5,800 belonged to foreign units.[14] Foreigners constituted a major portion of the infantry in particular, with seven Swiss and two German regiments operating alongside only seven French ones.[15]

Given the numerical importance of foreign troops within the forces called to Paris, it was perhaps unavoidable that the most prominent instances of revolutionary violence during the summer of 1789 quickly enveloped them. The attack on a crowd of civilians and mutinous French soldiers in the Vendôme Square and the Tuileries Gardens on July 12, which the German cavalry Regiment of Royal-Allemand spearheaded, represented the first major clash between the populace and royal troops in Paris. The event helped to inflame popular hostility toward the foreign regiments not only as a result of the civilian casualties it produced but also because it dispelled hopes that the army would fully disobey orders to attack civilians.[16]

Two days later, the fear of violent repression that the attack by Royal-Allemand helped to fuel prompted the people of Paris to train their sights on the Bastille and its vast store of gunpowder, which would be a vital asset in case violence against royal forces continued. The permanent garrison of the ancient fortress counted only eighty-two aged or handicapped soldiers no longer fit for regular military duty, but these had been reinforced on July 7 by thirty-two grenadiers from the Swiss Regiment of Salis-Samade, which was camped alongside other royal troops on Paris's outskirts at the Champ de Mars. As the Swiss lieutenant commanding this detachment, Louis de Flue, later detailed in a logbook entry describing the assault on the Bastille and its aftermath, he and his soldiers suffered sanguinary reprisals after the governor of the Bastille surrendered the fortress to assailants, who were led by mutineers from the French Guards Regiment.[17] The victorious attackers murdered at least two Swiss soldiers after taking them prisoner, and Flue saved his own life only by declaring, apparently disingenuously, his fervor for the revolutionary cause.[18]

The role that some foreign troops assumed in attempts to repress revolutionary activity in Paris during the summer of 1789 provided the foundation for an association in the minds of contemporaries between foreign soldiers and counterrevolution that persisted long after control of the military passed from the Crown to the National Assembly. As early as July 8, even before the attack by the Royal-Allemand Regiment in the Tuileries and the storming of the Bastille, the comte de Mirabeau drew a distinction between the national and foreign contingents of the royal forces when he affirmed that the former would never obey orders to attack French patriots, who "form part of the same nation," but expressed no such confidence in the foreign regiments. Mirabeau thus formed a contradistinction between troops whom he described explicitly as "French" on the one hand, and foreign soldiers whom he deemed prone, in the image of slavish automata, to "blind devotion" toward military orders on the other. His pronouncement represented the earliest major example of revolutionary rhetoric that contrasted French citizen-soldiers with supposedly unenlightened foreign troops who uncritically followed orders from their reactionary commanders.[19] Local political leaders in Paris expressed similar views during the summer of 1789 when they warned that foreign troops had historically abandoned and betrayed the peoples who had hired them, and complained that "foreign soldiers, which France maintains and feeds for its defense, threatened its own children."[20]

Even after the resolution of the crisis of the summer of 1789, popular hostility toward foreign troops remained widespread throughout France. "After what happened in the month of July 1789," the retired French diplomat Claude-Charles de Peyssonnel wrote in May 1790, "it is inconceivable that no one disbanded these [foreign] troops immediately."[21] In an address to the Jacobin Club of Paris during the same month, Peyssonnel condemned the Swiss Guards as a "praetorian guard" and demanded that the National Assembly reserve for itself the right to disband the Swiss regiments whenever it deemed necessary, regardless of the diplomatic agreements with the Swiss cantons.[22] During another speech to the Paris Jacobin club in July 1791, the revolutionary leader Jacques-Pierre Brissot, in remarks that anticipated his later pronouncement before the National Assembly that "the army of a free people is itself," drew a sharp distinction between the "armed citizens" who should fill the ranks of the French army and "mercenary soldiers" on whom despots relied.[23] In similar terms, the Jacobins of the town of Chalon-sur-Saône complained in September 1791 that French "regiments of proven patriotism" were being replaced by foreign corps, implying that the latter were less committed to the Revolution simply by the fact of their being foreign rather than because of anything they had done. The radical journalist Jean-Paul Marat also took the disloyalty of foreign regiments as a given, denouncing most of them as invariably attached to the royalist cause and warning of "the danger of having foreigners in one's service. We should not offer to them any public function, however small, especially not in the army."[24] Bitter memories of the presumed role of the foreign regiments in enforcing royal authority at the outset of the Revolution lingered as late as December 1792, when one deputy recalled how the Crown in 1789 had "surrounded the National Assembly with mercenary troops, pawns of the court, foreign regiments."[25]

Foreign Troops as French Patriots

The reductionist association between foreign troops and counterrevolution that emerged during the earliest phases of the Revolution, although ubiquitous in the minds of contemporaries, hardly reflected the behavior of all of the foreign soldiers in France during that period. While the cavaliers of Royal-Allemand exhibited little reluctance to engage in violent reprisals against civilians during the summer of 1789, and a handful of Swiss soldiers participated in the futile defense of the Bastille, other foreign units proved ineffective for putting down disorders or even overtly sympathized with the revolutionaries as the Old Regime collapsed. The soldiers of the Salis-Samade Regiment declared in June 1789 that they would sabotage their weapons if ordered to march against civilians.[26] In the event, the regiment did not prove so obstinate and participated in maneuvers, but its failure to act decisively during the fighting of July 12, when it missed opportunities to secure key sites on the right bank of the city such as the Hôtel de Ville, paved the way for the escalation of the revolt and the capture of the Bastille two days later.[27] Meanwhile, the Swiss troops of the Châteauvieux Regiment, according to a contemporary newspaper report, similarly "promised to abandon their weapons" if pressed to fight against the people of Paris. Their sentiment echoed that which the Baron of Ballatin, a captain in the Châteauvieux corps, had expressed a year earlier when he wrote to his colonel, "I dearly hope, along with everyone else, that we will not be compelled to make war on the king's subjects."[28] Even among the Swiss Guards, one of the oldest and most prestigious of the king's foreign regiments, and the one with the strongest connection to the royal family, officers reported "a nearly universal lack of discipline" among their troops by early August 1789.[29]

Disorder within many of the foreign corps in Paris confirmed the prediction in the last week of June 1789 by the Saxon ambassador at Versailles, lost on most of his French contemporaries, that even the foreign regiments would prove unreliable if the Crown deployed them against the Parisian populace.[30] It also reflected the sentiments of the anonymous author of a pamphlet addressed to the people of Paris on behalf of the foreign troops, who declared in their name that "we dare to call ourselves French" and promised no harm against "the patriotic people who has done us the honor of adopting us."[31]

The high desertion rates of foreign soldiers in Paris during the summer of 1789 further highlighted the receptiveness of many of them to the Revolution. Following the fall of the Bastille, 113 men deserted the Diesbach Regiment to enlist in the Parisian National Guard.[32] Salis-Samade similarly suffered 80 desertions between July 15 and July 28, and the German Regiment of Bouillon, which had camped on the grounds of Versailles in immediate proximity to the royal court, saw 42 soldiers depart without permission between July 14 and the end of the year.[33] The Swiss Regiment of Sonnenberg lost 128 soldiers between October 1788 and August 1789, most of them presumably during or after the events in Paris of that summer.[34] These were staggering figures for units that had total strengths of about 900 soldiers each and typically lost no more than a few dozen men per year to desertion.[35] The numbers were also eminently comparable to the frequency of desertions from the non-foreign units in Paris during the crisis of 1789.[36] To be sure, not all foreign regiments produced so many deserters; Royal-Allemand had only three in July 1789, an unsurprising fact given the popular hostility that developed toward the soldiers of that unit in the wake of the events of July 12. The Swiss infantry regiments of Castella, Châteauvieux, and Reinach also had relatively low desertion rates, losing only ninety men total between September 1788 and September 1789.[37] Nonetheless, the propensity of foreign soldiers in many instances to desert provided further proof that they were hardly as obedient to the Crown as contemporary depictions made them out to be. It also helped to explain why the monarchy chose the national Regiment of Flanders, rather than a foreign unit, in mid-September 1789 to safeguard the Palace of Versailles in the face of continuing popular unrest that culminated in the October Days.[38]

If the revolutionaries tended to overlook foreign soldiers' insubordination to royal authority, they also afforded little attention to the contributions of foreign troops in assuring stability in Paris as the new regime established its foundations. Veterans of the Swiss Guards Regiment in particular, whose purview under the Old Regime had involved general policing tasks in Paris, played a vital role in protecting property and mitigating violence in the city after mutiny decimated the French Guards Regiment, which had also traditionally been responsible for maintaining public order. Swiss troops were thus of crucial importance in preventing collapse into anarchy during the time it took for the nascent Parisian National Guard, which came into existence on July 13, to develop into an effective replacement for the public security structures of the Old Regime.[39]

Foreigners also accounted for a substantial portion of the National Guard itself, an institution that exemplified the ideals of citizen-soldiering like no other.[40] Several hundred foreign troops became national guards after deserting their regiments during the summer of 1789.[41] In many cases these enlistments likely had more to do with the higher pay that the National Guard offered, which at twenty sous per day was approximately 2.5 times greater than the standard rate in the line regiments, than with revolutionary fervor.[42] The service of many foreigners in the National Guard also proved to be short-lived, since on August 14 the Commune of Paris mandated that Swiss Guards who had enrolled in the National Guard return to the line army, an order with which 348 Swiss troops complied.[43] All the same, the contributions of foreign troops to the National Guard were hardly consonant with the depictions of foreign soldiers as servants of counterrevolution that predominated throughout much of French society during the first stages of the Revolution.

The Regiment of Châteauvieux and the Nancy Mutiny, 1790

Foreign troops retained a great deal of public visibility, though not always of a positive nature, as the Revolution progressed. Among the earliest major events that drew attention to foreign soldiers was the mutiny in August 1790 at Nancy, where the Swiss Regiment of Châteauvieux was garrisoned alongside two French corps, the King's Own infantry regiment and the Mestre de Camp cavalry unit. The affair began on August 9 when the soldiers of the King's Own arrested their officers to protest what they perceived as unfair treatment. The commanders secured their release only after handing over large sums of money to the troops. The next day, soldiers from the Châteauvieux Regiment, inspired by the actions of their French comrades, petitioned their officers with complaints about the disciplinary policies to which they were subject. The Swiss commanders responded by arresting and publicly whipping the two soldiers who had presented the petitions. This harsh response rallied many of the French troops in Nancy, as well as local townspeople, to the assistance of the unfortunate Swiss soldiers, whom they forcibly liberated from captivity. Hostility toward the Swiss officers did not end there, however; on August 12 they were taken hostage by soldiers who extorted from them the quite substantial sum of 27,000 livres. The French soldiers of the Mestre de Camp Regiment arrested their officers as well, and those of the King's Own remained in a state of mutiny. Municipal authorities refused to act against the soldiers because of the popular support for their actions among civilians in the city.

The National Assembly intervened in the Nancy affair on August 16, when the deputies issued a decree ordering the soldiers to submit to their officers or face charges of high treason. They also dispatched the marshal de Malseigne to the city to restore order. His berating of the Swiss soldiers for their behavior, however, only inflamed matters further. It led the mutinous troops to attempt to arrest the marshal despite a declaration they had signed on August 20 promising obedience to their superiors. Malseigne escaped to the nearby town of Lunéville, but all of the other officers in the city, including the commandant, General de Noue, found themselves under arrest as the mutineers raided the royal arsenal. By this time Nancy had effectively become a city in revolt against the national government, with a regiment of Swiss troops at the core of the rebellion.

The crisis finally ended on August 31, when François Claude Amour, marquis de Bouillé, marched on the town with a force of 4,500 troops. These included a large contingent of foreigners, including the entire regiments of Castella and Vigier and detachments from Royal-Liégeois and Royal-Allemand. Pitting his Swiss, German, and Liégeois troops, as well as some national guards, against the Châteauvieux mutineers and their French comrades, Bouillé fought his way into the town. His soldiers suffered more than one hundred casualties but eventually suppressed the mutiny. In the aftermath of the Nancy affair, the officers of the Châteauvieux Regiment, exercising their prerogative of imposing justice upon their men independent of the French state, sentenced one of the Swiss mutineers to be broken on the wheel, twenty-two to hang, forty-one to three decades of hard labor as galley slaves in Brest, and seventy-four to imprisonment.[44]

Reactions to the Swiss soldiers' participation in the Nancy rebellion varied widely, reflecting the diversity of conceptualizations at this early point in the revolutionary chronology of the role that foreign troops, and foreigners in general, might play in the Revolution. In the immediate aftermath of the affair, Swiss expatriates residing in Paris harshly condemned the Châteauvieux Regiment, whose insubordination they attributed to the influence of the "scum" of non-Swiss soldiers whom unscrupulous recruiters had admitted into the corps.[45] For these Swiss expatriates, who were probably political dissidents from the cantons, the mutiny of the Châteauvieux soldiers represented an embarrassment that threatened hopes that the Revolution in France might spread to Switzerland. At the same time, however, other leading voices lamented the fate of the Swiss mutineers. Comparing Châteauvieux's personnel to the German troops of the Royal-Allemand Regiment, one of the units that had participated in Bouillé's suppression of the Nancy mutiny, Marat praised the former for having ostensibly been the first regiment in the days preceding the storming of the Bastille "that, on the Champ de Mars[,] . . . declared itself in favor of the cause of liberty, and the first that swore not to shed the blood of citizens." Marat exaggerated the extent to which the Châteauvieux troops had demonstrated solidarity with Parisian patriots during the summer of 1789, but his praise of the Swiss soldiers served to amplify his vilification of Royal-Allemand, which, Marat reminded his readers, had "been the first to serve the cause of tyranny" during the summer of 1789 when it attacked civilians in the Tuileries Gardens.[46]

Within the National Assembly, most deputies initially condemned the Nancy mutineers for rebelling against the laws of the state. Later, however, revolutionary leaders retreated from this reproachful stance. The shift stemmed in large part from the identification of Bouillé with counterrevolution in the wake of the royal family's Flight to Varennes in June 1791, which he helped to coordinate and in the aftermath of which he himself emigrated. A few months later, on September 14, 1791, the National Assembly granted amnesty to the soldiers from the two non-foreign regiments that had participated in the rebellion, but it was unable to extend such terms to the Châteauvieux soldiers because of the Swiss troops' immunity from French justice. The best the deputies could do was order French diplomats to pressure the Helvetic Confederation for the release of the Swiss soldiers serving in the galley prisons of Brest.[47] These efforts met with cold rejection from the Swiss cantons, and an independent initiative by private citizens of Brest to travel to Switzerland in order to appeal for the soldiers' liberation never materialized.[48]

Yet the issue of the Châteauvieux soldiers retained the attention of the National Assembly for some time. Although the deputies hesitated at first to risk a diplomatic rupture with the Helvetic Confederation by counteracting the cantons' ruling on the troops, they eventually grew frustrated enough with the intransigence of the Swiss authorities to consider defying them—which was easy enough to do, since the condemned Châteauvieux soldiers remained in France, where the Swiss cantons could not interfere in their fate.[49] Jean-Philippe Garran de Coulon in December 1791 cited legal precedents from the Old Regime for enforcing French sovereignty over the Swiss regiments and argued that the French state should simply liberate the Swiss soldiers whom it detained in its own prisons.[50] Pierre-Edouard Lemontey warned in response that the imposition of French sovereignty upon the Swiss troops would be dangerous because it might undermine the French government's control over its own soldiers in the event that it loaned them to foreign powers at some future date; nonetheless, Lemontey suggested that although it was not within the National Assembly's authority to pardon the Châteauvieux soldiers, France was under no obligation to execute sentences that foreigners had imposed upon the men by punishing them on French territory. "One nation," he declared, "can become the partner of another, but never its jailer; it is not appropriate for a free nation to become the warden of soldiers sent to the galleys by a foreign nation."[51] A majority of the deputies endorsed this view, and on December 24, 1791, the Assembly voted to release the Châteauvieux soldiers in Brest.[52]

After French authorities finally executed this order, forty of the surviving Swiss mutineers traveled to Paris for an audience in April 1792 before the National Assembly. There, the deputies lauded the soldiers' devotion to the French nation even as they underlined their status as foreigners by referring to them consistently as the "Swiss of Châteauvieux."[53] The same week, the city of Paris organized a fête for the soldiers.

The controversy surrounding the celebration, however, highlighted the persistence of hostility toward foreign troops in France, even those who had mutinied alongside French soldiers to protest the excesses that their aristocratic officers committed. While Parisian supporters of the Swiss troops praised them for their fidelity to the Revolution and even suggested that the Châteauvieux Regiment receive the honor of incorporation into the National Guard, others expressed deep anxieties about demonstrating esteem for the soldiers.[54] To be sure, some of this hostility reflected reluctance to praise troops who had mutinied against the laws of the nation, no matter their national origins. Yet certain critics dwelt upon the foreign identity of the Châteauvieux troops. A contingent of Parisian national guards questioned "the virtues of these foreigners," who, in the guards' view, were complete outsiders to the French nation.[55] Members of the Parisian section of the Isle similarly complained that the fête represented an ignominious insult to the legacy of national guards who had been "massacred by the Swiss of Châteauvieux."[56]

The Châteauvieux mutineers enjoyed support from other quarters, including the Jacobin Club of Paris, and the fête in their honor ultimately proceeded on April 15 without incident.[57] Nonetheless, the reluctance within some quarters to celebrate the soldiers of a Swiss regiment who had refused to attack civilians in 1789, and who were at the center of a mutiny that eventually became a point of pride among French patriots, reflected a certain unwillingness within French society to accept foreign troops as members of the French nation regardless of the commitment they demonstrated to revolutionary principles.

Foreign Regiments and Counterrevolution

The antipathy that the Châteauvieux soldiers faced was made worse by widespread beliefs that other groups of foreign troops had caused public disorders or participated in counterrevolutionary plots elsewhere in France. In some cases these charges were valid, as on October 21, 1790, when the officers and soldiers of the Royal-Liégeois Regiment, which was garrisoned in Belfort, marched through the streets shouting "Vive le Roi!"

and "Au diable la Nation!" while threatening civilians with their weapons.[58] Accounts of the incident suggested that overindulgence in alcohol fueled the disorder at least as much as counterrevolutionary sentiment, but the Royal-Liégeois troops exacerbated the situation several days later when they attempted to storm the city hall. The affair ended calmly after the National Assembly ordered the regiment to withdraw from Belfort, which it did, but critics from many quarters took the event as an opportunity to intensify denunciations of foreign troops. The deputy François-Félix-Hyacinthe Muguet de Nanthou called for the expulsion of the Royal-Liégeois troops from France when he declared before the Assembly, "Without a doubt, the nation has the right to say to the Liégeois regiment: 'Foreigners, we thought you were our friends . . . you joined our enemies, attacked us and broke your promises . . . go back to your country.'"[59] Marat in the wake of the incident called for the removal of all foreign "mercenaries" from the army, warning that "what has occurred in Belfort should open the nation's eyes to the dreadful danger of foreign regiments. They must be sent back without exception."[60] The counterrevolutionary behavior that some of the Royal-Liégeois officers and soldiers had exhibited thus served as a basis for the denunciation of all foreigners in the army, without regard for the loyalty to the new regime that many other foreign troops demonstrated.

The implication of foreign regiments in the Flight to Varennes also bolstered arguments that deemed them traitors to the revolutionary cause. Following that event, Marat claimed that large numbers of officers from throughout the army were deserting across the frontier and attempting to take their soldiers with them, but that only the foreign troops who had supported the royals' attempt to flee from France were falling prey to the émigrés' seductions.[61] At the same time, the German Regiment of Nassau found itself unwelcome in each of three cities in which it sought to rest and resupply after the Varennes affair as a result of claims that it had secretly supported the plot. Yet deeper hostility toward foreign troops was evident in the declaration by the leaders of one of the municipalities that denied entry to the Nassau troops, Sedan, who declared, "There is already . . . a hussar regiment composed completely of Germans" inside the city, whose populace "does not want the entirety of its garrison to be composed of German regiments."[62] Popular hostility toward foreign troops was sufficiently widespread in the aftermath of the Varennes incident to motivate the colonel of the Swiss Guards Regiment, d'Affry, whose soldiers also faced charges of complicity in the affair, to obtain an audience before the National Assembly in order to deny his regiment's opposition to the Revolution. He also took the opportunity to declare, in spite of his Swiss birth, "that he regards himself not as a foreigner, but as a French officer."[63]

There were few facts to justify the allegations to which d'Affry felt compelled to respond. Without a doubt, some foreign officers were complicit in the Varennes plot; among these the most notable was the Swedish colonel of the Royal-Suédois Regiment and reputed paramour of Marie Antoinette, Hans Axel von Fersen.[64] It is also true that Bouillé, when making preparations for the royals' flight, selected a large number of foreign corps to cover their escape from Paris, partially because he believed the well-disciplined foreign troops would prove more reliable than their French equivalents.[65] Yet Bouillé later wrote that the foreign regiments he deployed along much of the royal family's route also simply happened to be the only infantry units he was able to procure at the requisite times and locations, indicating that they were selected for logistical reasons as well as for political ones.[66] Moreover, the loyalty of the foreign troops to the king never came to the test, because poor planning prevented the union of most of the foreign regiments with the royal coach as it traveled from Paris.[67] Even if the scheme had proceeded as Bouillé intended, there is no evidence that the foreign soldiers along the road to Varennes in 1791 would have proven any more faithful to the monarchy than their compatriots in Paris had been when they refused to fire on civilians or deserted during the summer of 1789.

Nor did claims by contemporaries such as Marat in the wake of the Varennes affair that foreigners were especially prone to desert to the émigré camp stand up to the evidence. Many foreign aristocratic officers certainly emigrated, as did large numbers of French nobles serving in the army. Yet the rate of emigration among officers in the foreign units was significantly lower than that for the army as a whole. According to a list published in 1793 of officers missing from their posts without leave, the average number of officers who deserted German, Irish, and Liégeois infantry units was 12.4 per regiment. For French corps, in contrast, the figure was more than 16 officers per unit.[68] In addition, records for the émigré army showed that of approximately 2,000 officers present in 1792, no more than 112 had served previously in foreign regiments of the French army. Virtually all of the others had belonged to non-foreign corps prior to emigrating.[69]

Emigration rates among foreign soldiers were also relatively low, despite exaggerated reports to the contrary. The war ministry informed the National Assembly on May 14, 1792, that the men of the Fourth Regiment of Hussars, formerly the foreign German Regiment of Saxe, had deserted to the enemy, along with one company of the corps previously known as the Hungarian Regiment of Bercheny. (As noted below, the government in 1791 ordered foreign line regiments to adopt numerical designations in place of the names they had used under the Old Regime.) Elements of the Fifteenth Cavalry Regiment, formerly Royal-Allemand, also deserted into

Germany that month.[70] In June some of the elite soldiers of the Hundred Swiss company reportedly crossed the frontier into Koblenz, where the émigrés had established their headquarters, and in the fall of 1792 accounts circulated that many of the Swiss troops who had entered the National Guard after the expulsion of the Swiss regiments in August subsequently deserted, possibly to serve the enemy.[71]

But many of these alleged émigrés from foreign regiments either returned to France soon after leaving or had not actually deserted in the first place. By May 25 nearly all of the soldiers from the former Regiment of Saxe who had crossed the Sarre into enemy territory two weeks earlier had come back to France.[72] Meanwhile, there were enough men from the Saxe and Royal-Allemand units remaining in France at the end of the same month for General François-Christophe de Kellermann to propose that they comprise the core of a legion he was levying.[73] And at least 500 men from the Bercheny Regiment remained in French service in May 1793, when they sought incorporation into a different hussar unit whose name would not conjure the treachery of their émigré comrades.[74] Certainly, some foreign troops left France to join the émigré army, and others later served with the rebels in the Vendée or in the Irish Brigade that the British army established during the Revolution to enlist Irish deserters from French service. Yet there is no evidence that foreign soldiers abandoned the French military at the extraordinary rate their critics claimed.[75]

The Affair of the Regiment of Ernest, 1791–1792

Although many foreign troops demonstrated discipline and loyalty toward the new regime as emigration began decimating the army, the troubles that plagued the Swiss Regiment of Ernest (known at the time also as the Regiment of Watteville) at Marseille and Aix-en-Provence between the fall of 1791 and the spring of 1792 created new opportunities for critics of foreign recruitment to demand the purging of foreigners from the military. This affair played a key role in paving the way for the eventual abolition of the Swiss units, whose importance to France's diplomatic relationship with the Swiss cantons tended to exempt them at first from the reforms and official disdain that other foreign regiments faced.[76]

The Ernest Regiment, which was garrisoned in Marseille beginning in August 1789, was involved in minor disturbances there in December 1790 and May and June 1791. The following October, however, matters came to a head when the regiment's officers insulted civilians in a local theater, leading to a brawl between one of the Swiss soldiers and a Marseillais national guard that escalated into a street battle between the Swiss troops and local residents.[77] The political implications of the incident grew worse after the regiment's officers refused to allow French justices to punish the unruly soldiers on the basis of the regiment's immunity from French law. The authorities in Marseille complained that the commanders were unable to produce any specific documentation confirming the soldiers' juridical exemptions, and added that even if they could, "There is no basis to pretend that treaties give them the privilege of not being subject to the laws of the state in which they live and which pays them."[78] The deputies in Paris agreed, with one representative declaring before the Assembly, "It is unseemly for foreigners to reside among us under any laws other than French ones. . . . It is dangerous that the Swiss, for crimes which threaten the public peace, are judged only by other Swiss."[79] Such willingness to disregard the privileges that the French state's treaties with the cantons guaranteed to Swiss soldiers, despite the diplomatic rupture it might provoke, was one of the earliest examples of the thinking that culminated in the Swiss corps' abolition in August 1792.

In response to the troubles in Marseille, military authorities withdrew the Ernest Regiment from the city in November 1791, deploying it first to police Comtat Venaissin and then to garrison Aix-en-Provence. This change did not put an end to the controversies that embroiled the unit, however, or to their significance for Franco-Swiss relations. In February 1792 an armed column of 8,000 Marseillais, supported by six artillery pieces, marched on Aix with the goal of "delivering the city from the tyranny of the aristocrats, supported by a foreign regiment." The Marseillais acted on their own initiative, without the sanction of the government in Paris. Vowing to "clear out the Swiss at all costs," the militia from Marseille engaged the Ernest Regiment in combat for two days. The Swiss commander finally surrendered when a portion of the National Guard troops in Aix, who had been defending the city alongside his soldiers, defected to the camp of the assailants. The attackers disarmed the Swiss soldiers, who feared they might share the fate suffered in 1789 by their compatriots in the Salis-Samade Regiment who had been murdered after laying down their weapons when the Bastille fell; in the event, however, the Ernest Regiment was able to depart Aix unmolested.[80]

Nonetheless, upon learning of the incident, the canton of Bern, to which the Ernest Regiment belonged, recalled the corps to Switzerland. It also addressed a letter to Louis XVI, which deputies in the National Assembly read as well, bitterly denouncing the humiliating treatment that the Marseillais had imposed upon the corps, one of the oldest Swiss line regiments in French service. The deputies in Paris, however, paid little attention to the departure of this foreign unit from the army, exhibiting more concern with the canton of Bern's insulting decision to communicate directly with the king instead of with them.[81] Their laissez-faire attitude notwithstanding, the French ambassador to Switzerland (and future member of the Directory government), François-Marie, marquis de Barthélemy, warned in a letter to the minister of foreign affairs that the Ernest incident had brought Bern to the brink of war with France; the canton, he reported, went so far as to raise 5,000 troops in preparation for hostilities, only to back down at the urging of the officers of the Ernest Regiment.[82] All the same, the corps ended up among France's enemies, since after returning to Bern it passed to the service of the king of Sardinia, who later joined the First Coalition against the French revolutionaries.[83]

"Nationalizing" the Foreign Regiments, 1789–1791

The disturbances that enveloped the Ernest Regiment and other foreign corps during the first years of the Revolution, combined with the widespread perception that foreign troops were tools of counterrevolution, paved the way for French leaders to begin officially phasing out the foreign contingent of the army as they pursued broader military reforms and innovations. The decrees that gradually scaled back the number of foreigners allowed to serve in the army, and ultimately suppressed the foreign regiments altogether, were tempered by pragmatic diplomatic and military considerations that favored the continuing recruitment of foreigners. Nonetheless, the deputies in the Assembly eventually discarded these concerns as they adopted decrees intended to purge all foreigners from all of the regular units of the army.

Wariness among lawmakers toward foreign troops was evident as early as September 1789, when the deputy and general Louis de Noailles presented the Assembly with a broad vision for the reorganization of the army. His extensive proposal covered topics ranging from recruitment practices to the proportions of different types of military units appropriate for France, but he made his views on foreign troops plain enough. Exhibiting only a "blind obedience" to their commanders, he declared, foreign soldiers had no role to play in a free society, and "it shall therefore be established that in the future there will be no more foreign troops in France."[84] Noailles's statement reflected typical concerns that foreign regiments would uncritically follow orders from despots, but his call for the unqualified purging of all foreigners from the army, without regard for those who had clearly not exhibited a blind obedience to royal authority during the summer of 1789, suggested that his opposition to foreign troops stemmed from deep-seated political principles rather than observations of their behavior. The Assembly did not put Noailles's proposed military reforms to a vote, but they became important in shaping further debate on the reorganization of the army.

Not all of Noailles's colleagues shared his views on foreign troops. In October 1789 an anonymous author addressed a treatise to the Military Committee, the group of deputies responsible for formulating legislation on the army, warning of the crucial importance of preserving at least the Swiss regiments for military and diplomatic reasons, even if the Assembly dissolved the other foreign corps.[85] Meanwhile, the war ministry, keenly aware of the importance of the foreign regiments to France's defense, expressed consistent opposition to calls for their elimination. In December 1789 the war minister, Jean-Frédéric de la Tour du Pin-Gouvernet, reported to the Assembly that 24,000 foreign troops were present in the army, and that for "political reasons" their number should not shrink below 22,000. He did not elaborate on the political considerations that made the foreign contingent necessary, but he emphasized the preservation in particular of the Swiss regiments and likely had in mind the foreign regiments' role in cementing France's relationship to allies abroad.[86] La Tour du Pin repeated his insistence on maintaining at least 22,000 foreign soldiers verbatim in a second report to the Assembly in April 1790.[87]

Yet the war ministry's recommendations to the deputies regarding foreign regiments fell largely on deaf ears. Immediately after hearing La Tour du Pin's report on the army in December 1789, Edmond-Louis-Alexis Dubois de Crancé, speaking on behalf of the Military Committee, declared, "I take it as a basic principle that in France every citizen must be a soldier, and every soldier a citizen." He did not address the question of foreign regiments explicitly, but his views on the necessity of their eradication were plainly evident in the plan he proposed for the reorganization of the army, which centered around abolishing all existing regiments and replacing them with units furnished by individual departments in France. This vision left no room for the recruitment of foreigners other than within the Swiss regiments, which Dubois-Crancé's draft decree exempted from the reforms he envisioned for the rest of the army.[88]

While debating Dubois-Crancé's proposals, few deputies expressed opposition to the dissolution of foreign regiments. Their central concern was instead the universal conscription of French citizens that the project entailed, which some lawmakers criticized as dangerous for the economy and ruinous for families dependent on the men whom it would force to enlist. Yet even in the midst of these discussions no one made reference to the traditional maxim that foreign recruits constituted a vital demographic resource because they spared French civilians from military service, freeing them to serve as workers and fathers.[89]

One of the lone voices in the Assembly defending foreign regiments at this time was that of general Adam-Philippe de Custine, who insisted on the importance of preserving not only the Swiss regiments in order to guarantee France's alliance with the Swiss cantons and the manpower they provided in the event of war, but also "five or six" German regiments. These latter units, he argued, might prove useful during campaigns on German territory, as well as for procuring for France skilled German officers who would otherwise serve the Holy Roman Emperor, an opponent of the Revolution.[90] Nonetheless, Custine favored the dissolution of the rest of the foreign regiments. The fact that he based his calls for the preservation of a limited number of Swiss and German units on questions of practical military and diplomatic necessity, rather than a principled commitment to providing avenues by which foreigners could participate in the revolutionary army, reflected French lawmakers' eagerness to define French nationality as a prerequisite for military service and exclude foreigners from the new nation they were building, regardless of their political principles.

Alongside Custine, Georges-Félix de Wimpffen, a native of the German principality of Zweibrücken who served as an officer in the German Regiment of Royal-Deux-Ponts and was a member of the Military Committee, was the other major advocate for preserving a certain number of foreign regiments during early debates on military reform. Like Custine, Wimpffen centered his arguments around the pragmatic expediency of foreign recruits, particularly Germans. Paraphrasing Maurice de Saxe, he declared that "each enemy deserter enrolled in a foreign regiment is worth three men for France." A certain strand of cosmopolitan thinking was present in his arguments as well, since he suggested that foreigners remained eager to serve in the French army because of France's newfound position as "the ally of all peoples desiring liberty."

Yet at the same time, the role that Wimpffen saw fit for foreigners to play in the French army was decidedly limited. He proposed rigid restrictions on the number of foreign troops that the army could retain, and suggested that, outside of the Swiss regiments, no foreigner should serve as an officer. He also insisted on subjecting foreign troops to surveillance by enlisting a certain number of French natives as ordinary soldiers in the foreign regiments, even though French regiments would bar foreigners from enlisting in any capacity. Wimpffen's proposal, which he delivered in February 1790, anticipated the laws that the Convention passed during the Terror to restrict the freedom of foreigners more than it reflected the cosmopolitan ideals that the revolutionaries claimed to espouse during the first years of the Revolution.[91]

If an undercurrent of nationalist thinking was present even in Custine and Wimpffen's arguments for preserving some foreign troops, such reasoning was all the more explicit in calls for suppressing the foreign regiments altogether. A pamphlet written by Peyssonnel, the retired diplomat, in 1790, which the deputy Jean-Xavier Bureau de Pusy distributed to the representatives in the Assembly, exemplified this rhetoric. Peyssonnel condemned the foreign regiments not only for what he viewed as their support of the monarchy during the summer of 1789, but also because of the fundamentally mysterious, foreign nature that he attributed to them. "We know very little about the foreign regiments in France," he wrote. "Their *esprit de corps,* their internal organization, their language, which our troops understand poorly: these are a means of veiling and hiding, even from the generals who command or inspect the regiments, everything they wish to conceal about themselves." France was the only European state, he claimed, that permitted within its army foreign troops with special uniforms and emblems, as well as privileges that exempted them from the laws of the rest of the nation. He also dismissed the arguments of the war minister regarding the political expediency of foreign regiments as "vague and empty words," and denounced as "ministerial charlatanism" the notion that France would suffer diplomatically if it abolished the foreign regiments. Finally, he alluded to the point Wimpffen had made several months earlier regarding the importance of amalgamating foreign troops with French natives when he declared that it was only because the foreign regiments had admitted French citizens from Alsace and Lorraine that military authorities had been able to keep in check the "foreign deserters and vagabonds" who accounted for most of the regiments' personnel. Unlike Wimpffen, however, Peyssonnel envisioned no possibility of preserving any foreign regiments other than the Swiss units, since even if French soldiers and officers were available to supervise foreign recruits, foreign regiments could not enlist French citizens without "subjecting [French] nationals to an anti-national regimen." He accordingly demanded the dissolution of all of the German, Irish, and Liégeois regiments. The exception that he saw fit to grant to the Swiss units was contingent upon their renouncing the privileges they traditionally enjoyed and serving on a footing identical to that of French corps. In his plan, foreigners who had already enlisted would be allowed to remain in the army, but in the future all recruits would be French nationals so that, "in little time," the foreign contingent of the army would evanescence entirely.[92]

Calls such as Peyssonnel's for the elimination of all foreigners from the army proved too extreme for the deputies of the Assembly to adopt during the first years of the Revolution. Nor did the legislators endorse Dubois-Crancé's radical plan for reorganizing the army, which would have abolished foreign recruitment while instituting universal military conscription in France. They did, however, pass laws that strictly limited the military's capacity for recruiting foreigners. A decree of February 28, 1790, mandated that no foreign regiment could serve in France without the explicit approval of the Assembly and the king.[93] A law of June 1790 imposed similar conditions on the navy.[94] In the same month the deputy Jean-Louis Emmery suggested that, with the exception of the Swiss, no more than 6,000 foreigners should serve in the army, and the Military Committee in July 1790 recommended that their number not exceed one-eighth of the 204,619 soldiers it deemed necessary for France's defense.[95] The authors of this proposal went to great lengths to counter the objections they anticipated to the admission of even this limited number of foreigners into the army, making the case that foreign recruitment not only spared French citizens from military service, but also was vital for procuring deserters from despotic enemy states whose services as interpreters would be invaluable for exporting revolutionary ideas to other countries. In this way, the lawmakers for the first time linked foreign soldiers to the mission of extending the Revolution beyond France's borders, by force if necessary, an idea that became important in later debates on the establishment of legions and on the policies France should adopt toward foreign deserters and prisoners of war.[96] These various proposals regarding foreign recruitment, which were part of broader reforms that the deputies envisioned for the army, culminated in the Assembly's approval on August 18, 1790, of a sweeping military reform package that fixed the maximum number of foreigners in the army, including the Swiss, at 26,000, about the size of the foreign contingent already present. The army could exceed this figure only with special legislative approval.[97]

Still, controversy regarding the admission of foreigners into the ranks continued. In February 1791 proposals by Charles-Léon, marquis de Bouthillier-Chavigny, for further military reform sparked an intense debate during which several deputies called for the total elimination of foreigners from the army. Bouthillier himself favored the preservation of some foreign regiments for the purposes of enlisting foreign deserters, but he was emphatic in demanding that only men born on French territory should serve in French regiments. In applying *jus soli* principles to military recruitment, this suggestion excluded from national units even the small number of soldiers and officers who, though born abroad, had formally acquired French citizenship.

Other deputies decried the recruitment of any foreigners at all, with Antoine-Louis-Claude Destutt de Tracy insisting that foreign troops constituted a threat to the political liberty of a free society. He added that foreigners "will never serve with as much loyalty as the soldiers who are children of a *patrie* to whose defense they commit all of their courage and devotion."[98] Tracy's remarks highlighted the influence of the revolutionary conceptualization of patriotism on the question of foreigners' role in the army. In a political culture where devotion to the *patrie* represented citizens' highest calling, Tracy assumed that foreigners would always prove to be inferior soldiers because their patriotism could never match that of French natives. The self-presentations by foreign soldiers as French citizens who were thoroughly committed to France and its people, which are evident in the material discussed later in this chapter, flew in the face of such arguments. Yet they did not prevent the Assembly from adjourning the debate on Bouthillier's proposals to affirm the government's commitment to maintaining foreign regiments, which the deputies never passed.[99]

The reluctance of many legislators to accept the continuing presence of foreigners within the army led to the Assembly's decision in the summer of 1791 to "nationalize" (*"nationaliser"*) the German, Irish, and Liégeois regiments by eliminating the practices and policies that distinguished them from French regiments. At the beginning of that year, the deputies had already taken a first step toward the assimilation of the foreign regiments into the rest of the army when they ordered them, like their French counterparts, to adopt line numbers.[100] On July 12 the Assembly went further after receiving a petition from soldiers of the German Regiment of Alsace who asked for their corps "to be composed exclusively of French officers and soldiers born in the Rhineland departments, to enjoy all the rights of French regiments, to adopt French uniforms and to lose definitively its designation as foreign, which offends the patriotism of the regiment."[101] This demand reflected the desire of the substantial number of Alsatians and Lorrainians who had enrolled in the regiment to serve under the same terms as their French compatriots from other provinces, but it was less clear whether the Germans and other foreigners who comprised nearly two-thirds of the regiment's personnel at the time shared their sentiment.[102] Nonetheless, the Assembly decreed without debate that the Alsace Regiment would lose its designation as a foreign unit, and would adopt the uniforms and regulations of French corps.

Two weeks after the deputies nationalized the Alsace Regiment, reports arrived in Paris that between four and five hundred soldiers of the German Regiment of Nassau had torn the symbols of foreign heraldry from their uniforms and proclaimed "that they no longer wish to serve or follow their regiment so long as it wears a foreign uniform and is regarded as foreign [and that] they were French and wished to serve as Frenchmen."[103] They also swore the civic oath promising fidelity to the nation. It was unclear from the reports whether the hundreds of soldiers who had disavowed the regiment's foreign identity and declared themselves French were natives of France or of German origin. The former, the latter, or both groups may have been involved, since at the time only about half of the Nassau Regiment's approximately one thousand troops had been born in France.[104] The deputies in the Assembly exhibited little concern over the identity of the troops, however; they instead used the incident as grounds for reorganizing all of the units that the army had formerly categorized as German, Irish, or Liégeois into national regiments, and imposing upon them the uniforms, disciplinary policies, pay rates, and other regulations of French troops.[105] The law allowed foreigners who were already serving in these regiments to remain, but the transformation of the units into French corps meant that, with the exception of the Swiss, foreigners no longer constituted an official component of the regular French army and could no longer legally enlist in it.

For several reasons, however, the nationalization of the foreign regiments proved difficult to effect in practice. First, French officials continued to use certain of the formerly foreign regiments as dumping grounds for foreigners whom they ejected from other units of the army because of their nationality; thus Frederic Meyer and Pierre Batchy, for instance, who enlisted initially in the Ninety-Ninth Regiment, "left this unit as foreigners" but reenrolled in the Ninety-Eighth Regiment, previously the German Regiment of Bouillon.[106] More problematically, relations between French natives and foreigners who remained present in formerly foreign regiments often proved turbulent. The most telling illustration of these troubles occurred in February 1792, when twelve soldiers of French origin deserted the former Alsace Regiment and traveled to Paris to complain that despite the Assembly's nationalization of the unit the previous summer, "it seeks to remain German, it speaks German," and most of its officers refused to accept the decree that nationalized it. The deserters claimed to be acting on behalf of not just themselves but "all the Frenchmen" in the army, and they enjoyed the sympathy of deputies who spoke of a "natural opposition that reigns between individuals of different nations" in the ranks. The notion that antagonism between French and foreign soldiers was intrinsic and unavoidable was at odds with revolutionary cosmopolitan rhetoric affirming the fraternity of all peoples, as well as with the ideal of building a national community in which membership was determined by political principles alone. It also highlighted the deputies' fundamental objections to accepting foreigners into the army. The Alsace deserters eventually returned to their regiment, but as the war minister pointed out in his commentary on the affair, it would take a considerable length of time for a unit commanded by German officers, who spoke German and were accustomed to German military discipline, to adopt French practices.[107] He was especially right on the point of language: in 1794 only fifteen of twenty-six officers in the first battalion of the former Regiment of Alsace were literate in French, and as late as 1798 the number for the second battalion was fifteen out of ninety-two. In both battalions, however, almost all officers could read and write in German.[108]

Foreign Deserters and Volunteers

Even as tensions persisted between French and foreign soldiers within the formerly foreign regiments after the summer of 1791, French political leaders remained eager to express in cosmopolitan terms France's willingness to accommodate foreign volunteers for the army, particularly those who deserted hostile states to fight for France. The declaration of war against Austria on April 20, 1792, included a clause guaranteeing that "France adopts in advance those men who desert the flags of its enemies" and join the French camp.[109] In order to create a financial incentive for enemy troops to desert, the war ministry set aside a fund of two million livres for the payment of foreign deserters who arrived in France following the declaration of war.[110] French leaders also promoted the more relaxed disciplinary policies of the French army, which they deemed most "suited to the principles of humanity and liberty," as an additional vehicle for encouraging the defection of foreign soldiers accustomed to the harsh regulations of Prussian and Austrian forces.[111]

Four months later, on August 2, the Assembly reaffirmed its ostensible commitment to welcoming foreign deserters by issuing a proclamation that promised them a monetary award of fifty livres, as well as a yearly pension of one hundred livres. They could then either remain in France as civilians or enlist in any unit of the French army that they wished, and those who chose to fight for France would receive French citizenship.[112] A decree of August 27 extended the terms of this law, which initially applied only to soldiers, to foreign officers as well.[113]

On the surface, the pronouncements of April and August 1792 appeared as clear reflections of the revolutionaries' cosmopolitan principles, and historians have regarded them as such.[114] Yet the timing of the decrees suggests that they were motivated in large part by pragmatic military concerns. French armies during the summer of 1792 were in retreat on all fronts. On July 11 the National Assembly declared the *patrie* in danger, and the Duke of Brunswick at the end of that month issued his menacing "manifesto" promising to obliterate Paris if the royal family suffered harm. On August 1, one day before the Assembly issued the decree on foreign deserters, Prussian troops crossed the Rhine into France. In these circumstances, a law encouraging foreigners in enemy armies to desert represented a political and military expedient as French generals desperately sought to stem the advance of enemy troops, a feat they achieved only after the victory of generals Kellermann and Charles-François Dumouriez at the battle of Valmy on September 20.

Moreover, the meager extent to which French authorities actually enforced policies on foreign deserters cast serious doubt on the deputies' commitment to welcoming these men into France in practice and not merely in principle. Despite the promise at the time of the declaration of war that the French would warmly adopt foreign deserters, the government implemented no practical measures for receiving them once they arrived in France. It was for this reason that on April 27 Marshal Nicolas Luckner, commander of the Army of the Center and a native of Germany, wrote to the war ministry requesting permission to incorporate foreign deserters into his army, since he had received no information on the specific actions to take regarding them. Luckner also implored generals Custine and Kellermann, who commanded France's other main armies, not to treat foreign deserters simply as prisoners of war.[115] Similarly, it took three weeks after the passage of the August 2 decree for the Assembly to delegate the practical powers required to execute the law to local authorities along the frontier.[116]

The government also poorly disseminated its August proclamations on deserters across the border, according to a foreign officer who had abandoned the Prussian army and claimed that few of his former comrades were familiar with the decree.[117] Their ignorance no doubt stemmed in part from the inexplicable decision by the deputies on the day they passed the law to vote down one legislator's suggestion to translate and print it in German, the language that many potential foreign deserters spoke. It was only through the initiative of a private citizen, Professor Jéremie Oberlin of the Protestant University of Strasbourg, that a translation of the legislation appeared more than a month after its adoption.[118] Meanwhile, however, the decree circulated widely enough among French speakers to serve as a pretense for French natives who had enlisted in enemy armies to desert from them, return to France, and attempt to claim the payment bonus that the law awarded. This phenomenon, as the war minister noted in September 1792, stemmed from the failure of the legislators to specify that deserters needed actually to be foreign, and not merely French expatriates, to benefit from the decrees of August 2 and 27.[119]

Ultimately, the number of foreigners who deserted enemy armies to serve France during the first years of the revolutionary war proved modest, despite enthusiastic reports to the contrary early in the conflict.[120] In addition, many of the foreign soldiers who did escape to French lines expecting hospitable treatment sometimes suffered a very different reception. A member of the Military Committee reported to the Assembly in October 1792 that French national guards had murdered four Prussian deserters who had surrendered to them, apparently in the hope of enlisting in the French army.[121] Similarly, in December of the same year, a delegation of Swedish soldiers appeared before the Assembly to register the grievance that the war minister had refused to admit them into the French army "under the pretense that they were foreign."[122] Since Sweden remained neutral in the war against France, these troops were not technically subject to the terms of the laws of August 2 and 27, which applied only to deserters from enemy armies; nonetheless, their exclusion from the army simply because they were not French reflected a lack of willingness on the part of French authorities to put the cosmopolitan spirit of the laws into practice.

Even high-ranking veterans of foreign armies who offered their services to France suffered cold receptions, despite the need for experienced commanders at a time when French aristocratic officers were emigrating by the hundreds.[123] In May 1792, shortly after the outbreak of war, the Assembly only partially and reluctantly granted a request by foreign officers who were known, according to the war minister, "by the reputation they attained in the American war," meaning the American Revolution, to recruit and command corps of foreigners on behalf of France. The deputies decreed that no more than four of the foreign officers could enter French service, and further stipulated that they would command French troops, not foreign recruits.[124] The Naval Committee similarly declined an offer in the same month by Dutch captains to serve aboard French warships. Its representatives claimed that the volunteers lacked experience, but also expressed opposition to the simple idea of accepting foreigners into the French navy because "it is unnatural to think that an officer who has served with honor ... would abandon his country to seek employment with a foreign power."[125] Three officers from the Swedish military who requested commissions in French service in December 1792 fared no better; although the deputy Laurent Lecointre advocated on their behalf before the Assembly, the representatives permanently adjourned his attempt to force a vote granting military appointments to the men.[126]

If behavior such as this called into question French leaders' real commitment to welcoming foreigners into the army, the vague final article of the law of August 2 also highlighted their reluctance to put cosmopolitan rhetoric fully into practice. The article stipulated that "in the case in which France, contrary to its wishes and hopes, should find itself engaged in a war against a free nation, exercising the rights of sovereignty, the citizens of that nation will not be permitted to enjoy the benefits of this decree." The clause most likely anticipated the possibility of war with Great Britain, which until February 1793 remained at peace with France and which the French regarded as a "free" society because of its parliamentary tradition. By denying the benefits of the law on foreign deserters to British troops regardless of the political principles they espoused, this article prefigured later, decidedly uncosmopolitan decrees such as that of 7 Prairial Year II, which ordered French generals to put to death all British prisoners whom their armies captured because British troops, in the words of the deputy Bertrand Barère, were "more guilty" than those of other nations, given that they were "more enlightened" than those who served absolute monarchs.[127]

Foreign Troops and French Nationality

Throughout the first years of the Revolution, even as public opinion turned against foreign troops and French leaders gradually nationalized most of the foreign regiments, many foreign soldiers and officers expressed steadfast devotion to the revolutionary cause. Some deserted foreign regiments to enlist in French corps, claiming that they could better serve France's interests there.[128] Many others, without receiving formal naturalization, declared themselves naturalized French citizens, a claim easy to make at a time when the revolutionaries were in the process of codifying modern nationality for the first time in France.[129] In July 1790, officers from the Irish regiments petitioned the National Assembly to "naturalize as French the Irish officers in the service of . . . France, which we have justly regarded, for more than a century, as our adoptive *patrie*."[130] The Assembly never responded to this request, but Arthur Dillon, colonel of the Irish regiment of his name and a deputy from Martinique, advanced a similar line of argument in a treatise he wrote to counter calls for the abolition of the foreign regiments. Citing Louis XIV's naturalization of Irish troops in 1715, Dillon made the case, in vain, that the Irish soldiers were in fact French and should therefore enjoy exemption from the reforms the government sought to impose on other foreign troops.[131] The Duke of Fitzjames, colonel of the Irish Regiment of Berwick, advanced a comparable claim when he wrote in a letter to the king, "It is rumoured that the Irish troops, being foreigners, are about to be dissolved by the National Assembly, but the blood they have shed for France ought to have secured for them, one thinks, the privilege of being citizens of that kingdom."[132]

The Irish were not alone in staking claims to French nationality in the early 1790s. Charles de Hesse, a German prince born in Frankfurt and a longtime veteran of the French army whose rabid enthusiasm for the Revolution extended to a promise to "Jacobinize" the city of Orléans at the point of the sword, and who styled himself "le général Marat" in homage to the radical journalist, repeatedly described himself as a French national.[133] He declared in May 1792 that "my only wish is to die for the *patrie* I have adopted," and in June he told the Jacobin Club of Paris, "I consider myself as French as if I had been born inside your walls."[134] John Skey Eustace, a native of Flushing, New York, who served under Dumouriez, similarly described himself in 1792 as a "citizen and officer of the French Republic."[135] Swiss veterans of the French army, even after returning to Switzerland, also declared themselves "Frenchmen and good Frenchmen."[136] Many of the volunteers in the foreign legions that appeared during the first years of the revolutionary war, which the next chapter discusses in detail, presented themselves as French as well on the basis of their military service.

In some cases, French authorities accepted the claims foreigners made to having become French through their military service and attachment to the country. Custine suggested, when arguing in 1789 in favor of preserving some foreign regiments, that German officers who resided in France effectively "became French," and that Irish troops were "naturalized in advance" via their military service.[137] Even Peyssonnel, while harshly denouncing the foreign corps, was willing to accept the extension of French citizenship to foreigners who had already enlisted in the army, provided that they swear the civic oath and that foreign recruitment cease in the future.[138] And Lecointre in May 1792 portrayed soldiers from the Hundred Swiss Company who had attempted to leave France as French nationals, although he did so in the belief that many of them had been born in France despite their identification of Switzerland as their *"patrie."* His objective was to have the men punished as émigrés, which was possible only if they counted as French citizens.[139]

In general, however, the Assembly never issued directives that collectively naturalized foreign soldiers in the way the monarchy had under the Old Regime, nor did it afford them the same citizenship privileges as French troops. Drafts of laws for extending the rights of active citizenship to veterans of the military at first mentioned not only French soldiers but also those who "became French." Such language left room for foreigners to benefit from the decrees. By 1792, however, the deputies had eliminated such qualifiers from the legislation, which referred in its final form to French troops alone.[140] In a similar vein, a February 1790 law regulating the salary of military personnel applied only to "French soldiers," engendering ambiguity that forced the Assembly four months later to clarify its intentions regarding the pay for foreign regiments.[141]

At other times deputies expressed opposition to the notion that foreign soldiers could ever become French citizens. Antoine-Louis Albitte declared in February 1792 that German deserters who wished to serve in France were "unworthy of being French."[142] The Assembly also denied Swiss soldiers equality with French citizens in the law of August 20, 1792, which expelled the Swiss regiments in the wake of the Swiss Guards' bloody defense of the Tuileries Palace ten days earlier. Drafts of the decree included a clause that would have granted "all the rights afforded to French citizens" to Swiss soldiers who chose to remain in the French army, but the final version dropped this guarantee.[143] In the minds of most French officials, foreigners serving in the army were at most an afterthought, and sometimes targets of active derision, when debating laws that connected citizenship to military service.

The End of the Swiss Regiments

In addition to its tacit denial of citizenship to Swiss troops, the decree of August 20, 1792, that abolished the Swiss regiments culminated the long trend toward the formal nationalization of the army. It also represented a decision that had been unthinkable in most quarters at the time of the nationalization of the other foreign units in July 1791. To be sure, the Swiss regiments were no less subject than the other foreign corps to popular animosity during the first years of the Revolution. From an early date, radical journalists such as Marat routinely fired invectives at the Swiss corps, calling on French patriots to "expel all the monsters" who commanded Swiss units, for instance.[144] Even the public disavowal of antirevolutionary principles by the Swiss troops garrisoned in Rueil in May 1791, which they accompanied with a declaration "to remain faithful to the law and the nation," did little to sway Marat (who, ironically, had been born in the Swiss principality of Neuchâtel, although the town was under Prussian control at the time) from his entrenched view that Swiss soldiers were dangerous enemies of the people and the Revolution.[145]

Yet despite such perceptions of Swiss troops as reactionary, the Swiss regiments enjoyed exceptions from most official measures affecting other foreign corps in France. The legislation that reorganized the other units of the army in 1791 did not apply to them, and they continued to enjoy special pay rates after the government standardized wages for soldiers in other corps. The Swiss regiments also maintained their immunity from French law, despite mounting challenges to this privilege. The state even allowed Swiss troops, when swearing the oath of loyalty to the National Assembly and constitution that it required of all soldiers in the revolutionary army, to retain the Old Regime practice of acknowledging their fidelity to the Swiss cantons as well.[146]

The revolutionaries were initially willing to preserve the special status of the Swiss regiments for two main reasons. First, the reputation the Swiss enjoyed as being among France's most skilled and reliable troops, especially at a time when insubordination and political radicalization plagued the rest of the line army, meant that they were particularly valuable as military units. A report to the Assembly from Achard de Bonvouloir in June 1790 on insubordination within the army presented Swiss soldiers as models whom their French counterparts, vulnerable to influence from radical political clubs that encouraged indiscipline, would do well to follow.[147] A few months later the moderate deputies of the Military Committee praised the Swiss troops garrisoned in the suburbs of Paris for refusing to accept printed materials that radical Swiss exiles had presented to them, and for warning local French municipal authorities of the presence of political agitators in their town.[148] A September 1791 report from the Diplomatic Committee again reminded the Assembly of the "inviolable respect for military discipline" that the Swiss soldiers exhibited. It also urged the deputies to find a respectable new mission for the Swiss Guards Regiment, which had lost its traditional function in the royal household after the reorganization of the king's personal forces in 1791.[149]

Revolutionary leaders were keenly aware as well of the diplomatic value of the Swiss regiments, which cemented France's relationship to the cantons of the Helvetic Confederation. Some of the other foreign regiments, such as Royal-Liégeois, also reinforced French alliances with foreign states, but none of these were of the same magnitude of importance as the Swiss cantons, which shared a long, weakly fortified border with France. Thus French authorities frequently warned that "infringing . . . on the privileges of the Swiss [regiments] would mean renouncing their alliance," with potentially grave military consequences for France.[150] The imperative of respecting the traditional privileges of the Swiss troops became all the more important as many of the capitulations between the French state and individual Swiss cantons began expiring during the first years of the Revolution. French diplomats were theoretically in the process of renewing the capitulations, but because the contracts had lapsed, the agreements were being maintained only by the good faith of both parties, making Franco-Swiss relations especially delicate.[151]

Over time, however, French leaders became increasingly less willing to uphold the privileged status of the Swiss corps despite their military and diplomatic significance. As noted above, the refusal of the officers of the Ernest Regiment in Marseille in 1791 to turn over their men to French courts provoked strong criticism in Paris of Swiss juridical autonomy. Early the following year, the Assembly took the first step toward eliminating the privileges of Swiss troops altogether when it moved to rein in the special payment bonuses that Swiss colonels received.[152] Four months later the ministry of the interior, in calling for Swiss troops to accept payment in *assignats* rather than the specie they demanded, affirmed that the foreigners "must follow the general laws of the kingdom." At the same time, the ministry of justice asked the deputies to clarify the jurisdiction of French courts over Swiss soldiers.[153] An incident in May 1792 in which twelve soldiers from the Swiss Guards Regiment faced accusations of sporting white cockades prompted additional calls from legislators for more rigorous legal measures to punish Swiss soldiers "who violate the rights of hospitality afforded to them by the Nation."[154]

Growing intolerance for the Swiss troops' privileges was accompanied by gestures toward the assimilation of the Swiss regiments into the rest of the army, which meant abolishing their special status as foreign regiments. In July 1792 the Assembly invited decommissioned Swiss veterans of the royal household guards to enlist in the *gendarmerie nationale,* where they would serve alongside and on the same footing as French troops.[155] In the same month the deputies debated a decree mandating the departure of the Swiss Guards Regiment from Paris, in accordance with a law prohibiting any regiment from camping in the capital. Some representatives took advantage of this discussion to call for the suppression of the Swiss Guards altogether, with Armand Gensonné declaring of the Swiss units that "it is time to put an end [to their special status] and return these regiments to the regular line army."[156] Another deputy questioned why the Swiss Guards had not been deployed to the frontier along with regular French units, expressing sentiment echoed by Marat a few months later when he complained that foreign regiments enjoyed the tranquility of interior garrisons while the patriots of volunteer battalions were "led into the butchery at Mons and Courtrai," on the front.[157] The Assembly ultimately decided to withdraw two-thirds of the Swiss Guards from Paris, leaving it to the Diplomatic Committee to determine the fate of the remainder after studying the consequences of the issue for Franco-Swiss relations.[158]

This decree proved difficult to execute, however, due to the refusal by the colonel of the Swiss Guards, d'Affry, to accept the order without first receiving the Swiss cantons' consent.[159] As a result, many Swiss Guards remained in Paris on the revolutionary *journée* of August 10, 1792, when their bloody defense of the Tuileries Palace against a mob targeting the royal family sealed the fate of all of the Swiss regiments in French service. Despite the departure of the king from the Tuileries prior to the attack, the massively outnumbered battalion of Swiss Guards responsible for the building's defense fought almost to the last, suffering 650 dead and 100 wounded out of a force of about 900 men. Some Swiss soldiers who surrendered to the assailants were murdered in the aftermath of the battle, despite efforts by political authorities to protect them from popular reprisals. Many others were imprisoned and died a month later during the September Massacres in Parisian jails. The day after the attack, the Assembly ordered the arrest and trial of the officers of the Swiss Guards Regiment. The tribunal acquitted d'Affry because he had been sick and not present during the fighting at the Tuileries, but Major Bachmann was guillotined in early September for his role in the affair.[160]

The reactions of French lawmakers to the day of August 10 were at first not entirely unfavorable to the Swiss soldiers who had participated in it. The president of the Assembly affirmed that the Swiss Guards, in a gesture intended to avoid violence against French citizens, had fired into the air as the attackers approached the Tuileries. On August 11 the deputies even invited a detachment of Swiss soldiers into the chambers of the Assembly, where the foreigners cried, "Vive la nation!"[161] Yet such expressions of devotion to France exerted little influence on representatives who, since the beginning of the year, had grown increasingly willing to accept the military and diplomatic risks of purging all Swiss regiments from the French army.

Brissot seized on the affair of August 10 to urge the Assembly to do just that. He made his case with reference to the events of the day of August 10, but his arguments reflected a deeper opposition to foreign troops as he declared that "free men must defend themselves on their own" and "the army of a free people is itself." In addition, he downplayed the importance of preserving peaceful relations with the Swiss cantons by emphasizing that France, with a million men under arms, had nothing to fear from a collection of tiny alpine states "which count barely 1.2 or 1.5 million souls and 50,000 soldiers."[162] He also claimed, with exaggeration, that only half of the troops in the Swiss regiments were actually Swiss.[163]

Such arguments in favor of removing the Swiss regiments from France troubled military authorities outside the Assembly. Marshal Luckner, seeing the writing on the wall when he received orders to move the Swiss troops under his command away from the front, wrote to the war minister on August 18, 1792, warning that if the government planned to disband the Swiss corps, "we will deprive ourselves of some very excellent troops."[164] Two days later General Kellermann urged the war ministry to undertake all possible measures to convince the Assembly to preserve the Swiss regiments, emphasizing that those deployed with his army had remained perfectly loyal to the revolutionary regime and that it would be a dangerous folly to disband them because of the actions of the Swiss Guards in Paris.[165] The next day General Armand Louis de Gontaut-Biron wrote to Kellermann agreeing that the expulsion of the Swiss regiments would be a "truly dangerous misstep," but also suggesting that it was too late to change the deputies' minds.[166]

Biron was right. Persuaded by Brissot's criticisms of the Swiss regiments, the legislators on August 20 approved the decree he had presented ordering that they return to Switzerland, less any Swiss soldiers who wished to continue serving in France by enrolling in other regiments. The only serious point of contention in the law concerned the clause that would have extended French citizenship rights to Swiss soldiers who chose to remain in the French army. As noted above, the deputies struck this article from the final version of the decree.[167] Nonetheless, Swiss political dissidents in Paris hailed the law, celebrating the elimination from French service of "foreign mercenaries" under the command of aristocratic officers.[168]

The law of August 20 was not ungenerous to the Swiss troops whose regiments it expelled from France. The decree guaranteed that those soldiers who chose to remain in the French army by transferring to a different unit could retain their ranks and even receive bonus payments. It also permitted soldiers and officers who wished to return to their native countries the right to do so, and granted bonuses to those who had served in France for considerable lengths of time.[169] In addition, the law promised that the French government would honor its obligations to retired soldiers from the Swiss regiments to whom it owed pensions or other payments, whether or not they opted to remain in France.[170]

The lengths to which revolutionary leaders went to accommodate the Swiss soldiers whom the decree of August 20 affected, however, did not stem simply from French generosity, but also from several practical considerations. First and most obviously, authorities hoped to avoid public disturbances as they informed more than ten thousand armed and potentially disgruntled men that they could no longer serve in their regiments in France. More important for the survival of the French state as it confronted a growing coalition of enemy powers, they sought to preserve amiable relations with the Swiss cantons. The decree of August 20 included a provision ordering French diplomats to impress the Assembly's friendly intentions upon the Swiss despite the expulsion of the regiments.[171] A month later the deputies followed up this stipulation by undertaking negotiations to provide the Swiss cantons with indemnities they might seek as a result of the treatment of the corps they had loaned to France.[172] Ultimately the French government succeeded in avoiding war with the cantons, but diplomatic relations, already strained, worsened when soldiers from the Swiss units returned to Switzerland and faced punishment for their support of the French Revolution.[173]

A third motive behind the generous treatment of Swiss soldiers was the government's desire to keep them in French service, and out of enemy armies, as a matter of military necessity. One observer warned in a memorandum that agents of the kings of Spain and Sardinia had begun negotiations with the Swiss cantons to employ within their own armies the regiments that had formerly served France. The author stressed the prime importance of ensuring pension payments to retired Swiss soldiers, as well as of promoting to higher ranks those Swiss troops who had remained in the French army, in order to set examples to which young Swiss men would look when choosing between serving France or another power. He added that Swiss veterans of the French army would be useful agents of French revolutionary propaganda when they returned to their native country.[174] Another author suggested raising a special unit along France's border with Switzerland in which former members of the Swiss regiments could serve, in the interest of keeping them out of enemy armies.[175] Meanwhile, French leaders in Paris warned the war ministry of the importance of finding satisfactory positions for Swiss soldiers in other regiments of the army, noting that "their experience and skills will be very useful there, and it is vital not to abandon to our enemies individuals well educated" in the military arts.[176] In 1793 some politicians even floated the idea of renewing the military capitulations with the Swiss cantons and inviting the regiments back to France.[177]

Despite these illustrations of the capital importance that the French state assigned to the manpower and military expertise of Swiss soldiers, the government's actual treatment of Swiss troops after August 20 fell far short of its promises. The satisfactory payment of pensions to Swiss soldiers was hampered by a variety of difficulties, ranging from the inflation of French currency to the bureaucratic challenges of delivering payments beyond France's borders.[178] Laws of March 16, 1793, and 29 Germinal Year II reaffirmed the government's commitment to upholding its financial obligations to Swiss troops, but well after that date France stilled owed many Swiss soldiers money.[179] As officials had predicted, French ministers' shortcomings in this regard discouraged Swiss veterans from remaining in French service. The minister of foreign affairs warned his counterpart in the war ministry in April 1793 that in addition to the influence of Catholic clergy in Switzerland, one of the chief factors preventing veterans of the Swiss regiments from reenlisting in French service was their belief "that we are rather indifferent toward their fate." He added that the poor treatment suffered by Swiss officers who had remained in the French military after August 1792 contributed to the negative image of France within Switzerland.[180]

Despite these perceptions, some Swiss soldiers did reenlist in other units of the French army after the government expelled the Swiss regiments. Some entered volunteer battalions as replacements for French troops seeking to escape military service that was not always as voluntary as the government pretended.[181] Others transferred to infantry units of the line army; the Sixty-Second Regiment, for example, enrolled at least ten veterans of the Swiss corps between September 15 and October 26, 1792, accounting for about one quarter of the total troops it enlisted during this period.[182] In other instances Swiss troops transferred to cavalry units despite their lack of experience as horsemen, or enrolled in the legions that, as the next chapter explains, began appearing in 1792.[183] As many as five hundred former members of the Castella Regiment reportedly joined the Legion of Luckner alone.[184]

Despite the military experience that many of these seasoned Swiss veterans offered to their new units, their French comrades did not always welcome them. In one telling example, French soldiers serving in a volunteer battalion under the command of a former member of the Swiss Guards Regiment complained that they "do not want to take orders from a Swiss." Their grievances prompted the war ministry to order local authorities "to put an end to the misplaced hostility toward an individual who represents a people with whom it is to our benefit to preserve friendly relations."[185] In other situations, however, French political leaders were less supportive of Swiss veterans, refusing to approve the transfer of soldiers from the Swiss regiments into other units of the French army.[186]

While tensions such as these were problematic for French authorities intent on maintaining the military's effectiveness, so too was the relatively low proportion of Swiss troops who ultimately remained in French service after August 1792. A law of August 24, 1792, designated fourteen light-infantry battalions in which Swiss soldiers could reenlist, but fewer than a thousand did so, barely enough to fill one battalion.[187] Similarly, a survey of fifty Swiss soldiers to whom the French government still owed pensions or other payments several years after the expulsion of their regiments revealed that forty-seven remained in France, but only seven of those were still in the army.[188] Worse still for the French were men like Joseph Kalbermatten, a veteran with twenty-nine years of experience in the Regiment of Courten who joined the French émigré army after his unit ceased to serve France in the fall of 1792. He reenlisted in Courten in November 1793, but by that time it was in the service of the king of Spain, who was at war with France.[189]

By the end of September 1792, when the last of the Swiss regiments left France, foreign units no longer comprised part of the regular French army. Although many of the foreigners who had enlisted prior to the nationalization of the German, Irish, and Liégeois regiments in 1791 and the expulsion of the Swiss regiments in 1792 remained in French service, the law forbade French recruiters from enrolling any more foreigners in the line army or volunteer battalions. As the next chapter shows, a number of "foreign legions" appeared at this time that enrolled foreign troops, but these were short-lived auxiliary units, plagued by organizational problems and political controversy, that mostly served as expedients through which the state enlisted small groups of foreigners who were already in France. The legions were never comparable in political, military, or diplomatic importance to the foreign regiments of the Old Regime.

In many ways, the path that ended with the nationalization or expulsion of the foreign regiments followed revolutionary events that fueled hostility toward foreign soldiers in French service. Rightly or wrongly, foreign troops faced consistent association with the forces of reaction and counterrevolution. From the presence of foreign soldiers in Paris in the summer of 1789, to their enlistment in Bouillé's plot to spirit the royal family out of France, to the Swiss Guards' actions on the day of August 10, the foreign regiments compiled a record that justified their disbandment in the eyes of contemporaries.

Yet it was not what the foreign troops did that primarily determined their fate. Their treatment instead reflected a combination of what they were—outsiders in a society that placed far greater weight upon its members' national origins than the cosmopolitan claims of the revolutionaries implied—with pragmatic considerations that favored their presence in France. Most foreign troops were not the committed enemies of the Revolution that many French officials and journalists made them out to be, as their expressions of support for the Revolution and disobedience in the face of counterrevolutionary orders showed. And even if they had been, the statements and actions of French revolutionary reformers from as early as the spring of 1789 indicated that foreigners in the army were fundamentally incompatible in the revolutionaries' minds with the nation they sought to cultivate simply because they were foreigners, not because of their behavior. That France's leaders did not do away with the foreign corps entirely until the end of the summer of 1792 shows that revolutionary events, especially the outbreak of war the previous April, the declaration of the *"patrie en danger,"* and the revolt of August 10, played a role in intensifying hostility toward foreign troops and counteracting the pragmatic considerations that favored their preservation. Yet the seeds of that hostility were present from the outset of the Revolution as a result of the revolutionaries' nationalist political goals and reluctance to incorporate men whom they did not consider fully French into the national community.

THREE

FOREIGN LEGIONS FROM THE OLD REGIME TO THE TERROR

PERHAPS NO MILITARY INSTITUTION is more identifiable with France in particular than the foreign legion. Largely because of the prominence of the modern French Foreign Legion, which has featured in works of popular culture as diverse as Edith Piaf songs and *Looney Tunes* episodes, the image of elite and stoic legionnaires remains inseparable from representations of the French army.[1] Historically, this association is well founded; although the Foreign Legion in existence today dates only from 1831, its heritage extends back to the middle of the eighteenth century, when French military planners first introduced the concept of legions as special corps of troops for completing particular military, and sometimes political, missions. None of the legions that French authorities formed prior to 1789 recruited foreigners exclusively, but the early years of the revolutionary war witnessed the creation of a number of officially foreign legions, as well as their miniaturized counterparts, the "free companies." These units cemented a tradition upon which the Directory and Napoleon built later in the revolutionary era by levying their own legions, and which culminated in the creation of France's modern Foreign Legion.

If the image of France's legionnaires today is one of romanticism and valor, however, that which characterized the foreign legions of the revolutionary army was decidedly different. For although the revolutionaries levied these corps in the hope that they might provide an expedient for drawing upon the manpower and revolutionary enthusiasm of foreigners after the foreign regiments ceased to exist, many of the units came up far short of such visions. The troubled history of the foreign legions stemmed in part from overly optimistic planning, problems of internal organization, and a lack of recruits. Ultimately, however, the units fell victim to the same currents of nationalist thinking that had spurred the purging of foreigners from the regular army earlier in the Revolution. Unlike their illustrious successor of the present day, none of the foreign legions that came into existence during the early 1790s survived for longer than two campaigning seasons or saw serious military action.

The negligible contributions of the foreign legions to the revolutionary war effort, combined with the fact that the number of foreign legionnaires never amounted to more than ten thousand men within an army dozens of times that size, help to explain why these corps are virtually absent from existing studies of revolutionary-era France.[2] Yet the history of these units does much to illuminate central aspects of both the experience of foreigners in revolutionary France and the tensions at the core of the nation-building project that the revolutionaries embraced. The legions strengthened the revolutionaries' ties to the communities of foreign political refugees living among them. In some cases, they also offered foreigners the promise of French citizenship in exchange for military service, although the state often failed to honor that guarantee. And most important, they exemplified the unique opportunities that France's military exigencies made available to foreigners, even those half a world away on the American frontier, who wished to participate in the revolutionary project after the regular line army barred foreign recruits. In each of these ways, the legions and other special corps demonstrated the terrific difficulties and contradictions that arose out of the attempt to align the contours of the army with the boundaries of a national community that closed its doors to foreigners.

Old Regime Legions

Like its cognate in modern English, the word *légion* in Old Regime France was a semantically broad one. In its most specific sense it referred to the legions of the ancient Roman army. More generally, the term could signify any body of troops, ancient or modern, comprising either foot soldiers alone or a combination of different types of forces. Beyond the military context, it could also simply mean a large number of people or objects.[3]

Yet toward the middle of the eighteenth century, *légion* began to refer as well to a more specific type of contemporary military unit, defined by particular tactical and political traits. These corps were the brainchild of Maurice de Saxe, the celebrated French marshal of foreign birth who in 1740 proposed the introduction to the French army of a new type of corps that he called legions.[4] In his vision, which reflected studies of the ancient Roman army, each legion would comprise four regiments and total about four thousand men. Regular infantry were to constitute the main body of the unit, but more mobile light infantry and mounted troops would serve alongside them. Saxe conceived of the legions as a replacement for brigades, the loose temporary combinations of different regiments that Old Regime commanders had traditionally formed for tactical purposes while on campaign. Legions, he argued, would prove more effective because they would be permanent units, remaining active in times of both peace and war, and therefore promised to be more maneuverable than brigaded regiments, which had little experience drilling or marching together prior to wartime. In addition, the familiarity of the different regiments comprising a legion with one another would ensure a stronger esprit de corps among the legionnaires.[5] Between 1740 and 1761, the monarchy raised at least seven legions in the image of those envisioned by Saxe, although later authors continued to debate how best to organize and deploy this type of special unit.[6]

While the main impetus behind the formation of legions and other brigades of special troops under the Old Regime was tactical, some writers attached specific social and political imperatives to them. A manuscript attributed to Philippe Joseph, comte de Rostaing, in the 1750s advocated the development of legions as the most innovative and cutting-edge units of the army from not only a strategic perspective but a political one as well. On the battlefield, Rostaing wrote, French generals commanding the legions should emulate Roman tactics and even revive the tripartite formation of *hartaires, principes,* and *triaires* lines into which the Romans had formed their troops. Rostaing also hoped that legionnaires would complement this classically informed military organization by serving as model soldiers for the rest of the army. With reference to the citizen-soldiers of the Roman Republic, he called on the troops of the legions, whom he explicitly described as "citizens," to embrace civic values and devote themselves to serving their state and society. His thoughts on this point anticipated the values that later became central to the image of the citizen-soldier during the Revolution. The treatise also prefigured calls after 1789 to restrict the political power of generals by recommending that legionnaires answer to the civilian authorities of the state rather than to their individual military commanders. And the text denounced venality within the army, with Rostaing declaring that the legions should select officers on the basis of their military talents rather than social status or wealth. He believed this policy would render the legions more effective than regular royal regiments, in which merit played little role in selecting leaders.[7] The innovative practices that Rostaing hoped the legions might pioneer, which were consonant with those promoted by a broader body of literature from Old Regime military reformers, reflected the liberal thinking that contributed to the outbreak of the Revolution, while also anticipating the revolutionaries' embrace of legions as a medium for military and political experimentation.[8]

Despite the novel ideas that Rostaing presented, his vision of legions as brigades of "citizens" who were "linked to their *patrie* by affection for their birthplace, ties of blood, possession of property or commerce" left little room for the enlistment of men born outside France.[9] Proposals for levying certain "foreign" legions did circulate during the decades preceding the Revolution, however, helping to lay the path for the establishment of foreign legions after 1789. As chapter 1 noted, a treatise from the 1770s or 1780s suggested the establishment of several legions of Germans for service in the colonies.[10] Another author proposed a legion of Greek soldiers in order to strengthen France's commercial ties with the eastern Mediterranean and offset Russian and Ottoman influence in that region.[11] Ultimately, no exclusively foreign legions came into being under the Old Regime, but some foreigners did serve as legionnaires prior to the Revolution.[12]

Despite the enthusiasm of many military planners for the legions, they did not enjoy universal favor. The comte de Guibert criticized them as strategically counterproductive in an age when the most important factor in victory, according to the prevailing military thinking of the time, was not mobility but the effective deployment of the entire mass of an army in pitched battle.[13] An anonymous treatise written in response to Rostaing's proposal on legions similarly denounced the units as too large to maneuver effectively or to garrison a single location, a detriment that the author presumed would mitigate the advantages of brigading troops of different types together. Rostaing's critic also attacked the idea that the legions could cultivate civic-minded soldiers, declaring, in words that prefigured the rhetoric of critics of the foreign legions after 1789, that it was the venerable and prestigious regiments of the line army that could best "represent citizens; other [corps] reflect the image of mercenaries."[14] Such criticisms, as well as the reputation that the legions suffered for recruiting desperate men of questionable morals, led Louis XVI's war minister, Claude-Louis, comte de Saint-Germain, to dissolve the seven existing legions of the French army in 1776.[15] This decision prompted outrage from some military theorists, but it effectively ended the Old Regime's experimentation with legions.[16]

National Legions and Free Companies
in the Revolutionary Army

Memories of the Old Regime legions, however, were not lost among the revolutionaries. Military theorists after 1789 revived the concept of special troops as they created a series of both national and foreign legions to augment the regular army during the first years of the Revolution. Like the Old Regime legions, those of the Revolution were the product, in part, of a quest for tactical innovation; in particular, French leaders were eager to form legions in response to the perception that France's enemies employed large numbers of highly mobile light troops that the French army could counter effectively only with other light units.[17] They also envisioned legions as ideal corps for spearheading offensives into enemy territory.[18]

But the revolutionary legions also assumed novel political missions with especially important significance for foreigners. The foreign legions owed their existence in large part to the revolutionaries' quest for using the war as a means of reaffirming France's commitment to defending the natural rights of all peoples, even if invasion and occupation were part of that process.[19] At the same time, French leaders conceived of the legions in general as vital tools for spreading revolutionary principles abroad and inculcating patriotic values within the army. In these respects, the corps provided especially fruitful terrain for experimenting with innovative ways of reconciling the French state's ongoing interest in enlisting foreigners in its military campaigns with the new conceptualizations of citizenship and military service that emerged beginning in 1789.

The first official proposal on the establishment of legions during the Revolution appeared within Dubois-Crancé's project for the reorganization of the military in December 1789. In addition to replacing all existing corps of the army with regiments levied by individual departments in France, Dubois-Crancé envisioned the establishment of "provincial legions" of dragoon troops. He intended for these units to replace the Swiss Guards and other forces serving in the royal household. As such, their tactical utility on the battlefield was of little concern; nonetheless, by envisioning the provincial legions as special troops distinct from the regular army, Dubois-Crancé's proposal helped to set a precedent that remained important in later debates on legions.[20]

Like the rest of Dubois-Crancé's proposal for military reform, the provincial legions never won the Assembly's approval. Still, the concept of legions remained on the minds of military thinkers as the Revolution progressed. In January 1791 a French marshal addressed a letter to the Military Committee proposing the establishment of a "First National Legion."[21] Nothing came of this idea at the time, but a year later deputies in Paris undertook the first serious discussion of legions when the war minister, Louis-Marie-Jacques Amalric, comte de Narbonne-Lara, presented a report recommending the creation of eight units that he labeled legions, each one composed of 1,722 foot soldiers and 832 cavalrymen.[22]

Narbonne envisioned the legions' primary role as a tactical one, suggesting that their main responsibility should be safeguarding the flanks of French armies. Yet his plan was also significant from a political perspective because it was the first to suggest that foreigners might enlist in the legions. The integration of French and foreign legionnaires that the war minister proposed, however, did not stem from a belief that the two groups would serve honorably and patriotically alongside one another; on the contrary, Narbonne conceived of the legions chiefly as a sort of penal corps for enlisting "those soldiers who are worthy of reproach or who have committed errors." The legions would therefore relegate foreigners to dubious service within a disreputable section of the army, in which they would be particularly prone to death or injury because of their deployment on the flanks of French forces. At a time when the Assembly had abolished most of the foreign line regiments (and was moving toward the removal of the Swiss corps, the only remaining foreign units at the time of Narbonne's proposal), the legions as Narbonne conceptualized them amounted to little more than an expedient for capitalizing on the manpower that France's foreign supporters could provide while still denying them entry to the ordinary military institutions that the government closely associated with patriotic citizenship.

The Assembly did not endorse Narbonne's plan, but legislators and theorists continued to debate the political and military merits of legions. A report by the Military Committee in February 1792 portrayed legionnaires as "chosen among the most robust and agile" soldiers, "brave and intrepid men who . . . eager to obtain glory and good fortune, will confront all types of danger."[23] Unsurprisingly, since the deputies of the Military Committee advocated for legions in part by arguing that legionnaires should have a special familiarity with the foreign territory on which they served and by portraying the legions as a means of "sparing the blood" of French citizens, the proposition of February 1792 allowed for the enlistment of foreigners as long as they displayed the requisite military valor.[24] Nonetheless, the authors of the plan viewed foreign legionnaires as somewhat less symbolically fit to fight for revolutionary France than their French comrades, since it was only after foreigners had entered into the legions, they concluded, that, "surrounded by [French] soldiers of a free nation, they will learn from them to recognize the rights of man and to conquer or die for liberty."[25]

While the Military Committee in early 1792 conceived of foreign legionnaires as inferior to French ones, other members of the Assembly were quick to reject the presence of foreigners in the proposed legions altogether. The deputy Claude Basire warned in the Assembly that foreign recruits would blindly follow the instructions of legionary commanders who, invested with too much power over their troops, might seek to turn the corps against the revolutionary government. Albitte went further, declaring, "If German deserters are named as officers, if men whom I consider unworthy of being French command these troops, might they not sacrifice to the interests of the émigrés a country that is not their own *patrie*?" Foreign legionnaires had a defender in Jean-Baptiste Aubert-Dubayet, who expressed confidence that "these foreigners of whom we are so afraid will be the warmest friends of liberty and the most ardent defenders of the Constitution," but his was a lone voice among legislators who otherwise expressed nearly unanimous opposition to enlisting foreigners in the legions.[26]

Levying more troops for the regular army and planning the "Amalgam" of the line regiments with the volunteer battalions, which preoccupied the Assembly in early 1792, prevented the deputies from acting on the proposals from that time for raising national and foreign legions.[27] The declaration of war on April 20, 1792, however, renewed attention for the topic. Yet the issue of admitting foreigners into the legions remained a contentious one, a fact that became evident on April 21, before the deputies had even officially resumed debate on the legions. In the early part of the legislative session of that day, one representative suggested that instead of levying legions, the government should admit deserters from foreign armies into volunteer battalions. There, he argued, they could serve alongside French patriots without stirring fears of counterrevolution. This proposal met with little enthusiasm, however, and the Assembly did not adopt it.[28]

Later on the same day, a member of the Military Committee once more presented a draft law for forming six legions on the same terms as those that the Committee had proposed in February. The decree included an article permitting the entry of foreigners into the units, again prompting concerted dissent from some deputies. The most forceful came from Lazare Carnot, a captain of artillery whose attention to army planning and strategy as a member of the Committee of Public Safety later earned him the title "organizer of victory." Carnot berated the legions as a folly by which French authorities would find themselves "paying 14,000 foreigners, despite the danger of relying for your defense on troops recruited outside your own country."[29] The objections of Carnot and other deputies notwithstanding, the Assembly finally approved the levy of six legions on April 24 and 25. The law did not designate any of the legions as specifically foreign units, but it allowed foreigners as well as French citizens to enlist as legionnaires.[30]

In the event, legislative disorganization prevented the government from actually forming the six legions it approved in April 1792. The Assembly consequently abandoned the plan in favor of new legislation mandating the establishment of one legion in each of the three main armies defending France's eastern frontier. It charged the generals commanding these forces, Kellermann, Luckner, and Custine, with levying these troops and personally commanding the three legions.[31] The new law permitted foreigners to enter the legions, but only after pools of patriotic French recruits had been exhausted.[32] Moreover, the decree offered to foreigners who served in these corps no promise of French citizenship, despite the suggestion by one deputy, which the Assembly essentially ignored, immediately after the law's adoption to append an article granting French citizenship to foreign legionnaires.[33]

At the same time that the Assembly was debating the formation of legions, a parallel discussion emerged among French lawmakers regarding the establishment of *compagnies franches,* or "free companies." These units, which were each about one hundred men strong, were much smaller than the legions. Like the legions, however, the free companies of the revolutionary era, which emulated corps of the same name that had existed in France under the Old Regime, were conceived as special troops that could serve a variety of unique tactical and political purposes.[34] Also like the legions, free companies engendered intense debate regarding the enlistment of foreigners.

Discussion of free companies first began in the Assembly on April 21, 1792, the same day the legislators renewed their debate on the six legions in the aftermath of the declaration of war. It started with a proposal by the deputy Thomas de Treil de Pardailhan for levying free companies that would enlist foreign deserters from enemy armies and grant them French citizenship after three years of service for France. The French government would accommodate the families of these deserters, too, by establishing institutions in which their wives and children could serve the state in exchange for their upkeep. Basire spoke out against this proposition, however, arguing that France did not have the resources to support foreign deserters and their families, and expressing doubt that many soldiers from foreign armies would come to France in the first place. The Assembly never approved the free companies as Treil envisioned them.[35]

Carnot revived discussion of free companies later during the session of April 21. Unlike Treil, Carnot conceived of free companies as explicitly national units that would recruit only French citizens. Their purpose was not to accommodate foreign deserters but to function as a substitute for the legions, to whose formation Carnot remained entirely opposed. Free companies, he argued, could fulfill the tactical objectives that had inspired calls for the legions while mitigating the financial and political liabilities that the legions created.[36] Three days later, Claude Hugau seconded Carnot's recommendations on the free companies, arguing that they were the only means of effectively opposing the mass of highly mobile light troops from the far reaches of eastern Europe that the Austrians, "like a destructive volcano, will vomit across our frontier."[37] It was not until May 28, however, that the Assembly, in the same decree that ordered the establishment of three legions under the direction of generals Kellermann, Luckner, and Custine, finally approved the formation of free companies.[38] The decree permitted these units, like the legions, to enroll foreigners, but only after the supply of French recruits had run dry. While surviving rosters for the free companies are scarce, the available evidence suggests that only a very small minority of their personnel was foreign.[39]

The legions and free companies that the Assembly approved in the spring of 1792 provided foreigners with a path for service in the French military, a significant provision at a time when the regular line army barred them (with the exception of the Swiss, whose regiments the French did not expel until several months later) from enlisting. Yet these special corps enrolled foreigners only as a last resort, after native French manpower proved insufficient. They also did not capitalize on the special talents or resources foreigners might provide. These policies contradicted the views of many military commentators outside of the Assembly, who had advocated vociferously, while the deputies were drafting the laws, for foreigners to play a prominent role within the legions and other special corps. Kellermann on May 17, 1792, wrote to the war minister pressing him to support the formation of a legion composed entirely of foreigners, since deserters from enemy armies could not enroll in any French regiment. He added that such a corps would prove particularly useful in the military circumstances at hand because it would encourage desertion from the Austrian forces massing on the French border.[40] Luckner issued a similar call, going so far as to draft a law for the formation of legions in which the first article, reflecting the importance for the war effort of soldiers who understood foreign languages, stipulated that only "foreign deserters or Frenchmen who can speak German" could enlist.[41] Other officers emphasized the strategic value of foreign legionnaires, whom they presumed to be particularly adept at *"la petite guerre,"* the type of highly mobile warfare at which the light troops of enemy armies excelled.[42] The marquis de Lafayette, who remained an influential commander in France until emigrating after the revolt of August 10, 1792, overthrew the monarchy, also advocated for the creation of free companies composed of Belgian and Liégeois refugees who resided in France. He warned only that the desire of these foreigners for vengeance against the persecutors they had fled in the Low Countries would necessitate special disciplinary policies to prevent excessive acts of retribution when they invaded that territory.[43]

Revolutionary Foreign Legions

Given these calls for the formation of units of special troops that would recruit foreigners specifically, it was unsurprising that pressure remained strong, even after the Assembly had sanctioned the three national legions and the free companies in May 1792, for the creation of explicitly foreign legions. In the months that followed a number of these units came into existence. In most cases, however, these legions were distinct from their

French counterparts in two important respects. First, they were generally the creations of committees of foreign political refugees in Paris working in conjunction with French ministers; the Assembly granted its approval to most of the foreign legions only after they had become facts on the ground. In addition, while the national legions were subject to the same military regulations as the line regiments and volunteer battalions that comprised the bulk of the army, special capitulations governed most of the foreign legions, establishing them on a footing distinct from the rest of the army. These characteristics affirmed the exceptional nature of the foreign legions, which represented a means of "relegating to the margins of the regular army the political question and the military employment" of foreigners, as Bernard Gainot observed in one of the few modern studies of the corps.[44]

LIÉGEOIS, BELGIAN, AND DUTCH LEGIONS

Refugee groups from the Low Countries were the first to establish foreign legions for service in the French revolutionary army, forming some units even before the creation of the national legions. The Liégeois patriots residing in Paris led the way beginning in December 1791, when a delegation of their representatives, headed by Pierre-Henri-Hélène Lebrun-Tondu, a journalist and the future French minister of foreign affairs, requested permission from the Legislative Assembly to recruit a legion from among the members of their community in France. The deputies never approved the petition, but the Liégeois refugees nonetheless organized the legion on their own, with the toleration of Girondin leaders and with financial support for arming and equipping the corps from general Dumouriez. The unit was ready for combat within eight days of the declaration of war in 1792.[45]

Refugees from Austrian-controlled Belgium emulated the example of their Liégeois counterparts. After a request for approval from the Assembly to form Belgian free companies or other special corps in January 1792 received no reply, the Belgians established units on their own initiative in the frontier cities of Lille and Douai. French generals welcomed these troops, who comprised part of the avant-garde of Luckner's army and participated in the campaign of 1792 in the Low Countries, serving most notably during the capture of Kortrijk.[46]

Dutch patriots, who constituted one of the largest refugee groups in France and counted among their ranks many experienced veterans of the failed revolt against the Stadtholder William V of 1787–89, did not lag far behind the Belgians and Liégeois in forming their own special corps. As early as December 1791, members of their community had requested appointments in the French army, and after the outbreak of war in the spring of 1792, the Batavian Committee, which represented the Dutch refugees in Paris, submitted a capitulation to the French war ministry for the formation of a "Batavian Legion."[47] In July the war minister, Pierre August Lajard, presented this request to the Assembly, where he noted that a legion of Dutch soldiers promised to be both militarily and politically expedient. On the battlefield, he argued, the corps would provide more light troops, of which the French army was still in great need despite the creation of the non-foreign legions and free companies; in addition, he believed the legion would strengthen the ties between France and the Dutch refugees while affording them an opportunity to be of greater service to their French hosts. Brissot objected to the idea, however, warning that the open recruitment of Dutch volunteers in France could provoke war with the United Provinces, with which the revolutionaries remained at peace at the time. The Assembly adjourned the issue.[48]

Nonetheless, a few weeks later the deputies became willing to accept Dutch legionnaires so long as they kept a low profile. On July 26 the Assembly approved the formation of a corps it christened the Free Foreign Legion, a name that did not threaten to raise tensions with any foreign government in particular. According to the law on the legion's creation, it could enlist soldiers of any nationality besides French citizens.[49] In practice, however, it was a substitute for the Batavian Legion that the Assembly had earlier rejected, with Dutch refugees comprising a majority of its officer corps and members of the Batavian Committee filling its administrative council.[50] The next year, the declaration of war by France against the Netherlands on February 1, 1793, facilitated the creation a month later of a second Dutch corps, which openly adopted the title of Second Batavian Legion (the Free Foreign Legion being the first Batavian legion). Like the Free Foreign Legion, most of the Second Batavian Legion's officers were veterans of the Dutch Revolt of the late 1780s.[51] Also in March 1793, the Convention approved a plan by a Dutch refugee named Makketros to levy light-infantry battalions of Dutch soldiers for service with French forces in Belgium, although it voted down an attempt by Makketros to form another special corps, presumably composed of foreigners, two months later on the grounds that there were insufficient officers to command it.[52]

If the Dutch legions stood out from the rest of the army because they were the first foreign legions to receive official sanction from the French government instead of merely the tacit approval it had granted to their Liégeois and Belgian precursors, the occupational backgrounds of their officers also distinguished them. At a time when many officers in the French army had had little experience in professional civilian occupations prior to entering the military, those commanding the Free Foreign Legion and the Second Batavian Legion were of decidedly more bourgeois origins.[53] They included several doctors, lawyers, and merchants, as well as a number of university students. Almost none of the Dutch officers were laborers or farmers.[54] Most of them, however, had had military experience prior to the French Revolution.

Despite the enthusiasm of Dutch, Belgian, and Liégeois refugees for forming legions and free companies and the ready availability of officers, filling the ranks of the units with ordinary soldiers proved difficult. Makketros claimed in September 1793 to have 800 men in his light-infantry formations who were eager to march to the front, but administrative records for his corps from two months later showed only about 450 officers and soldiers present.[55] Worse, by the end of 1794, the Second Batavian Legion counted no more than 12 officers and 54 soldiers total in its first battalion, which should have had about ten times as many troops.[56] A prohibition that a French general leveled against accepting Belgians into the Free Foreign Legion exacerbated the manpower shortages of that corps, and efforts by a Scottish captain in the legion named James Nicolson to establish a supplemental recruitment base for the unit in Scotland apparently bore little fruit.[57]

The Belgian Legion, which inherited the Liégeois legion that had appeared earlier, fared no better than the Dutch units. According to one of its officers, it was unable to enlist and retain recruits because of both a severe shortage of supplies and the unstable political and military situation in Belgium, which French troops occupied in 1792, evacuated a few months later, and did not conquer definitively until 1794.[58]

At the same time that the Dutch and Belgian legions and free companies struggled to enlist troops, political intrigues within the refugee communities further diminished the effectiveness of the corps. An engineer and veteran of the Dutch revolution named Henry Egide Valck complained to Luckner that the Belgian Committee, which represented the Belgian refugees in Paris, had passed him over for promotion in the Belgian Legion for political reasons, despite his military experience.[59] Another officer in the Belgian Legion lamented that the corps was "led by a committee that sought to cultivate political favorites instead of procuring enlightened soldiers for France."[60]

ALLOBROGE LEGION

In contrast to the military and political troubles that engulfed the special units of refugees from the Low Countries, the Allobroge Legion, which recruited political dissidents from Savoy, better exemplified for contemporaries the services that foreign legionnaires could offer to France, especially if those foreigners later became French. At the beginning of the Revolution, the territory of Savoy, on France's southeastern frontier, formed part of the kingdom of Sardinia. Savoyards who were hostile to the regime of their ruler, King Victor Amadeus III, had already formed a refugee community in Paris prior to 1789. It grew in the wake of the storming of the Bastille, in which certain of its members participated.[61] In the spring of 1792 the Savoyard refugees, along with some Swiss expatriates who shared their political views, formed a political committee called the Allobroge Club, named in honor of the ancient Celtic tribe that had resisted Roman expansion in the Alps region.[62]

The following summer, members of the Allobroge Club petitioned the Assembly for permission to form a legion to enroll volunteers from their community. The deputies approved the request on August 8 with little debate.[63] The legion, whose theoretical strength totaled 2,157 men, was to be a foreign one for recruiting "Allobroges," a term whose ambiguity allowed the corps to enlist not only Savoyards but also natives of the alpine territories of the Swiss cantons and Piedmont, which were also part of the ancient Allobroge territory. French citizens and small numbers of Germans, Hungarians, and other European nationalities enrolled as well.[64] Like the Liégeois, Belgian, and Dutch special units, the Allobroge Legion included well-educated officers of bourgeois backgrounds.[65] Prior military experience was not a requirement for service in the unit so long as recruits expressed the requisite political sentiments; thus Balthazard Chastel, a native of the Savoyard town of Veigy, entered the Allobroge Legion as a sous-lieutenant in November 1792 after attesting the following:

> I never served in the line army of France or its allies. The only titles that can justify my selection are those of having the honor of being proscribed by the former duchy of Savoy for two years by the king of Jerusalem, because I was one of the friends and zealous defenders of the French Revolution; of having been imprisoned for two years in the abbey of Saint-Germain for having dared expose the behavior of the traitor Lafayette; . . . of being one of the first to enter the residence of the former king on June 20 [1792], [and of having] the satisfaction on August 10 [1792] of killing two Swiss.[66]

Despite the participation of Chastel and several of the founding members of the Allobroge Legion in fighting against the Swiss Guards at the Tuileries on August 10, 1792, the unit enlisted some veterans of the Swiss regiments following their dissolution in the wake of that event.[67]

True to the image of the legions as troops with special skills for spearheading offensives into enemy territory, the Allobroge Legion served first under General Anne-Pierre de Montesquiou in the Army of the Alps, where the legionnaires helped in the fall of 1792 to overrun the territory in which many of them had been born.[68] The legion's officers later attributed this victory partially to their choice of Savoyard recruits adept at navigating the mountainous terrain of the Alps frontier.[69]

Despite its military successes, however, the Allobroge Legion was subject to hostility from both other units of the army and political authorities. A captain of a free company that garrisoned alongside a detachment from the legion complained that his troops' lives were at risk because they served "only with Allobroges who are not familiar with the military and who are not men on whom one can count."[70] The legion also faced charges of recruiting deserters from other units of the French army and of endangering France's diplomatic relationship with the Swiss cantons by enlisting Swiss political dissidents.[71]

Shifts in the geopolitical situation of Savoy, however, dispelled much of the controversy surrounding the legion by transforming it from a foreign into a national unit. On December 15, 1792, when the French Republic annexed Savoy and transformed the territory into the department of Mont-Blanc, its inhabitants became French citizens.[72] Some of the legion's troops, such as the lieutenant colonel Amédée Doppet, who as late as 1796 still referred to Savoy as both his *pays* and *patrie,* were slow to embrace their new national status; nonetheless, since the French government no longer considered most of the soldiers of the Allobroge Legion foreigners, calls mounted for dissolving the corps and integrating its personnel into other units of the army.[73] In the event, the legion remained intact for some time after the annexation of Savoy, serving at the siege of Toulon in 1793 and subsequently along the Spanish frontier, but by the summer of 1794, military authorities began dismantling it.[74] In November 1795, when they amalgamated the remnants of the legion with a volunteer battalion to form the Fourth Light Demi-Brigade, it ceased to exist, although the new corps that incorporated the legion unofficially bore the appellation of the Allobroge Demi-Brigade for some time after its creation.[75]

GERMANIC LEGION

While Savoy's annexation to France eased the assimilation of the Allobroge Legion into the regular French army, such was not the case for the Germanic Legion, whose history was replete with political controversy. The Assembly considered forming a special corps of German troops more than once, first in mid-August 1792, when the deputies ordered the Military Committee to review considerations on levying a "Prussian Legion."[76] Two weeks later another deputy suggested the formation of a "Vandal Legion" for the recruitment of Prussians.[77] Meanwhile, however, plans for the Germanic Legion were already solidifying outside of the legislature through the efforts of the Committee of Federated Germans, which represented German refugees and other emigrants in France. Beginning in July 1792, the group worked with sympathizers in the French government to gain support for a special corps that would operate under its direction. Their initiative bore fruit on August 6, when two of the Federated Germans' leaders, the Prussian-born deputy (and self-styled "orator of the human race") Cloots and the Saxon doctor Jean-Geoffroy Saiffert, signed a capitulation for the Germanic Legion at the home of the war minister, Joseph Servan. The contract established the corps as a special unit of two thousand infantry and one thousand cavalry with armaments and regulations distinct from those of the regular French army.[78] It also stipulated that only "foreigners or children of foreigners" could enlist in the legion, and it granted French citizenship to the unit's officers.

A month later, on September 4, the Assembly gave its stamp of approval to the legion with a decree that was mostly a verbatim reproduction of the capitulation that representatives of the German refugee community had concluded with Servan a month earlier. The official law, however, varied on two important points. First, it omitted any clause regarding the extension of French nationality to the legion's officers or soldiers. It also did not exclude French citizens from serving in the legion so long as they were not deserters from elsewhere in the army.[79] In this way, the Assembly watered down the political and symbolic significance of the legion and its potential for integrating foreigners into the French national community.

If French legislators denied the Germanic Legion special political significance, the corps nonetheless was of particular military value in the eyes of contemporaries, for several reasons. On campaign, its mobility positioned it to raid enemy positions and wreak havoc on the supply lines of opposing armies, making the legionnaires into a force of "land pirates," as one official described them.[80] At the same time, according to Cloots, the corps promised to serve as "the kernel of future German liberty" by spearheading offensives into German principalities.[81] The legionnaires' linguistic skills also represented a special asset for the French army when officers and soldiers from the unit formed a delegation to negotiate with enemy commanders who could not speak French.[82] Finally, the legion's supporters lauded the fact that, at least in theory, none of the foreigners serving in the unit brought with them families whom the state had to support, rendering the corps more efficient from a financial perspective than those of the regular French army.[83]

If lone deserters and refugees from the German states filled the ranks of the Germanic Legion in principle, however, in practice its roster was much more diverse. Its highest-level officers were Frédéric Dambach, a native of Warsaw who had served in various armies in Holland, Germany, and Poland prior to coming to France; Christian-Frédéric Heyden, who had been born in Prussia to a family of Dutch origin; an Austrian named

Prime-Sébastien Schwartz; and Pierre-Louis Beaufort, a native of Landau in Alsace. In addition to Beaufort, the legion enrolled many other soldiers and officers of French birth.[84] Representatives of a wide swath of foreign European territories besides Germany were present in the unit as well, as was at least one probably black or Amerindian soldier born in Guadeloupe.[85] The legion had the further distinction of enlisting the first Jewish officer known to gain a commission in the French army outside of the volunteer battalions, Anselme Nordon.[86]

The Germanic Legion's national diversity notwithstanding, its commanders subjected it to rigid disciplinary policies that emulated those of the Prussian army.[87] These practices further distinguished the legion from regular French regiments and reinforced its identification as a foreign corps, providing the grounds on which French nationalists began attacking the unit only days after its creation. On September 14, 1792, a member of the Jacobin Club of Paris expressed alarm at the concentration of Germans in the Blancs-Manteaux neighborhood of Paris, the site of the legion's barracks, and denounced the corps as an instrument of counterrevolution.[88] Two months later, reports in the press criticized the unit for prioritizing foreign recruits over French ones, even though recruiting foreigners was a core part of the legion's original mission.[89]

These early controversies assumed a stronger tenor the following spring, when a schism developed within the corps between its German commanders and lower-ranking officers who were French natives. On March 28, 1793, the latter appeared before the National Convention claiming that the legion suffered drastic shortages of manpower, with only 887 troops present out of a theoretical strength of 3,000, and that its foreign officers were forging inspection reports and abusing the unit's finances.[90] Marat took up the cause of these French officers in his journal, printing a number of letters denouncing the "Prussian" commanders of the corps and contrasting their dubious behavior with that of the reportedly patriotic French natives in its ranks.[91] Marat was highly critical during this period of special troops in general, denouncing national and foreign legions alike as the creations of counterrevolutionary conspirators; he even proposed cutting off the ears of unpatriotic legionnaires in order to prevent them from ever serving again in the French army.[92] He exhibited a particular rancor for the Germanic Legion, however.[93]

The political affair that enveloped the Germanic Legion centered around the unit's internal administration, which the corps's German commanders had neglected, according to critics. Yet suspicion against foreign legionnaires simply because of their foreign origin undergirded these allegations. One French officer in the unit complained that his superiors did not understand the French language, and the legion's colonel faced similar attacks in the National Convention for not speaking French.[94] Two deputies on mission also denounced the regular soldiers of foreign origin who served in the unit, warning that the bulk of the corps's personnel would prove unfit for integration into the line army because they were "for the most part foreigners" or former royalists.[95]

The commanders of the Germanic Legion worked intensely to refute charges that they had mismanaged the corps. In an appearance before the National Convention and in a number of publications, they denied allegations that their corps was only at half strength and that they had failed to equip their troops properly.[96] They also charged the war ministry with sabotaging the corps by appointing to it French officers who were unfamiliar with both the German language and German military practices; and they blamed desertion among the legionnaires on the decision by French military authorities to deploy the corps along the northeastern frontier, where its troops "could expect no mercy if they were taken prisoner" by the Austrians or Prussians, rather than on a different front.[97] Finally and most significantly, the foreign officers affirmed their commitment to France and staked claims to French nationality. Labeling the French officers who had denounced the legion "triumvirs and dictators," they contrasted the allegedly undemocratic malice of these men with their own republican sentiments.[98] In addition, Colonel Dambach cited his marriage to a French woman and his fathering of French children, as well as his ownership of property in France, to deflect claims that his loyalties lay elsewhere. France was his *patrie,* he wrote, "as much by sentiment as by the numerous links that attach me to it."[99] The legionnaire and Dutch native Henry Van Vessem similarly declared that he would "faithfully serve the French Republic, which I have long regarded as my *patrie.*"[100] Later, the officers cited the article of the legion's capitulation that naturalized its commanders to support claims to formal French nationality, even though this provision never became part of the law regarding the unit, as noted above.[101]

Despite these responses by the legion's foreign officers to the charges against them, their nationalist political adversaries eventually triumphed. In May 1793 deputies on mission imprisoned the foreign commanders of the unit and replaced them with French officers. The commanders won release in July, but successive regimes in Paris denied them reemployment in the French army on the grounds that they were foreign. It was not until 1796 that the Directory finally deemed the officers eligible to serve France again, but by that date few remained willing to do so. In the meantime, after the government suspended the legion's foreign commanders, it deployed the unit to the Vendée in the spring of 1793. Combat and desertion there devastated the force, and in the wake of the disastrous battle of Saumur on June 9, 1793, deputies on mission disbanded the Germanic Legion definitively. They integrated most of its surviving personnel into light-infantry and cavalry units of the regular army, but they left some of the foreigners without active military posts.[102] The dissolution of the legion, combined with the rejection of plans to raise other special corps of German troops, meant that soldiers of German origin no longer retained any official presence in the French army.[103]

AMERICAN LEGIONS

At the same time that the Germanic Legion's brief and troubled service for the French Republic was nearing its end, supporters of the Revolution half a world away were laying the groundwork for the "revolutionary legions" that citizens of the United States raised for France. Although these units existed only on the distant colonial frontier and ultimately disbanded before making serious military contributions to the French war effort, they nonetheless represented one of the most powerful and fascinating examples of the extent to which French authorities experimented with legions as an expedient for advancing France's interests by capitalizing on foreign support.

The legions in North America, which were under the command of Americans who had received nominal commissions as officers in the French military and which recruited from among the population of the United States, formed part of broader visions for expanding French power and revolutionary values in the New World. From the beginning of the revolutionary era, French leaders had clamored to reclaim territories in North America that France had lost under the Old Regime. For Brissot and his circle, such an endeavor was one component of a larger scheme that included the formation of a transatlantic antislavery movement, a French alliance with the United States, and rapprochement with Britain. At the same time, members of the French diplomatic corps developed their own plans for transforming Spanish possessions in the New World into an independent state open to free commerce with all nations.[104]

French designs in North America gained the support of the frontiersmen of the western United States, who were disillusioned by their own government's reluctance to force the Spanish to open the Mississippi Valley to trade and to afford settlers greater freedom in repressing Amerindian populations. Aware of these sentiments, French leaders became eager to capitalize on them by enlisting Americans in the overseas campaigns they hoped to pursue. As early as 1788, Brissot had written that Americans on the western frontier would be willing to invade Spanish-controlled Louisiana, adding that "it would not be in the power of Congress to moderate their ardor."[105] This vision was not lost on Edmond-Charles Genêt when he arrived as ambassador of the French Republic to the United States in April 1793 with a purview that included authorization to engage American frontiersmen in promoting French revolutionary principles in the New World. Genêt also possessed a number of blank certificates for granting commissions in the French military, and although his initial intent was to distribute these to Amerindian leaders, in the event they served to enlist American citizens as official members of the French army.[106]

The first of Genêt's commissions went to George Rogers Clark, the elder brother of the explorer William Clark, whom the ambassador appointed in July 1792 as "commanding general of the revolutionary and independent armies of the Mississippi" in preparation for an expedition Clark intended to lead against Spanish-controlled Louisiana. Clark, who had begun plotting the invasion even before Genêt arrived in the United States, detailed his plans in a letter in which he also expressed frustration with the American government's failure to recognize his services during the American Revolution to his satisfaction.[107] Genêt provided Clark with the support he needed to begin levying troops and promised to confirm his formal appointment as a major-general in the French army. He also dispatched a native of Louisiana and captain of France's Ninety-Second Regiment (formerly the Irish Regiment of Walsh), Auguste Lachaise, to assist Clark in his preparations for the expedition.[108] By early 1794 Clark was referring to himself as a "Major General in the armies of France" and commissioning American citizens to serve under him as officers in his "French Revolutionary Legion of the Mississippi," which comprised at least two regiments of infantry.[109]

While Clark busied himself along the frontier raising what he called the Independent Revolutionary Legion of the Mississippi, William Tate was undertaking a parallel effort deep within the interior of the United States.[110] Tate, who was possibly of Irish birth but had established himself in South Carolina by the time of the American Revolutionary War, served in that conflict as an officer in the Continental Army and afterward joined the Society of the Cincinnati.[111] After 1789 he became an ardent supporter of the French Revolution and was a founding member of the Republican Society of South Carolina, a political club established in Charleston in 1793 by sympathizers with the revolutionaries across the Atlantic.[112] Charleston was a hotbed of support for the French Revolution during the early 1790s, hosting a recruitment post for the French army as well as a public parade, led by the governor of the state, in January 1793 in honor of the National Convention in Paris.[113]

The French consul in Charleston, Michel-Ange-Bernard Mangourit, shared Genêt's enthusiasm for enlisting American citizens for military campaigns against Spanish possessions.[114] He hatched two major schemes in this vein, the first involving the liberation of Florida from Spanish rule and its transformation into an independent sister-republic of France, and the second with the goal of raising an additional body of troops to assist in Clark's invasion of Louisiana.[115] Mangourit selected Tate to head the latter initiative and granted him a commission as colonel in the French army in October 1793.[116] French diplomats instructed Tate to recruit troops outside of the United States in order to avoid raising tensions with American authorities, but he did not respect that stipulation.[117] Instead he and his officers, who affirmed their commitment to the "support of France against the Agregate of European Dispotism," attracted American recruits by promising each soldier three hundred acres of land in the territory they planned to conquer.[118] Probably anticipating the rough frontier fighting that would be central to their campaign, they also placed a premium on enlisting volunteers from the countryside over city dwellers.[119]

Tate claimed to have enrolled 2,000 soldiers in his army, which he called the American Revolutionary Legion, by January 1794.[120] For his part, Mangourit informed the French ministry of foreign affairs that the number was as high as 4,000, well in excess of the 1,500 he deemed necessary for the mission.[121] These optimistic reports, like those of many eager revolutionary leaders, may well have been exaggerations; since no roster of Tate's legion has survived other than a list of sixty-six of its officers, it is difficult to know for certain how successful he actually was in recruiting American legionnaires.[122] Nonetheless, his activities proved sufficiently alarming for the authorities of South Carolina to arrest several of his officers and for the state legislature to condemn the "levying [of troops] within this state by persons under a foreign authority, without the permission and contrary to the express prohibition of the government of the United States." The state government ordered the prosecution of Tate and his followers for treason.[123] At the same time, the recall of Genêt to France and his replacement by Joseph Fauchet, who canceled the plans of his predecessor for invading Spanish territory and revoked Tate's commission in the French army, put an end to the French government's support for the legion.[124]

In order to escape his persecutors in South Carolina (whom he deemed, in classic Jacobin anglophobic fashion, "no other than . . . British & Spanish Partizans"), Tate himself fled to France in 1795, where he continued his military career into the later years of the revolutionary decade.[125] Neither his American Revolutionary Legion nor Clark's army, which like Tate's force had been on the verge of marching on Louisiana when Fauchet and American officials intervened, ever saw action; had the invasion plan gone forward, however, it is likely that these American officers and soldiers operating in the name of republican France would have succeeded in overcoming New Orleans's light defenses.[126] In so doing they may also have established a decidedly different trajectory for the Louisiana territory than the one that ended with its annexation to the United States in 1803.

To be sure, Tate's American Revolutionary Legion and Clark's Independent Revolutionary Legion of the Mississippi were obscure units of whose existence officials in Paris were most likely not even aware until after Genêt's dismissal. Nonetheless, these corps demonstrated the importance of foreign legions to independently minded French diplomats as a vehicle for advancing French interests abroad. They also highlighted the willingness even of foreigners who lived thousands of miles from France, and who had no personal stakes in its conflict with opposing European powers, to offer military services to the Republic. Like their counterparts fighting for France in Europe, Clark and Tate expressed firm commitments to France's republican values. Their support extended to reconfiguring their national identities through their service in the French military, even if that meant, as Clark wrote, being "exiled" from their native *"patrie"* of the United States.[127]

Black Legionnaires

Events in the New World also occasioned the establishment of legions and free companies of black and mulatto soldiers. At a time when the revolutionaries were debating the citizenship rights of racial minorities, the experiences of these men underlined the unique political and symbolic stakes of military service by individuals regarded from many sides as something less than full citizens of France. Soldiers of color born on French territory, of course, were not foreign in the same sense as the natives of other states who fought for France; indeed, traditionally, all freed blacks in metropolitan France had automatically enjoyed recognition as French subjects without undergoing a formal naturalization process.[128] Yet the claims of blacks to French citizenship remained tenuous and subject to contestation even after French legislators formally emancipated mulattos in April 1792 and abolished slavery in February 1794. Under these conditions, military service by black soldiers reinforced their manumission and integration into French society.

BLACK SOLDIERS IN THE COLONIES

The association between enlistment in the army and emancipation for blacks was not novel to the Revolution. Soldiers of African descent had enrolled in provincial militias in France's colonies since the seventeenth century, and some slaves received manumission through such service. During the American Revolution, French commanders even deployed colonial black units alongside regular French regiments at the unsuccessful siege of Savannah in 1779.[129]

The military exigencies of the revolutionary decade, however, combined with political upheavals in France's Caribbean territories, engendered unprecedented demand for blacks to enlist in the army. The first prominent proposal for enlisting blacks in the colonies in the French army in large numbers appeared in October 1792, when Brissot suggested establishing corps of mulatto troops in Saint-Domingue who, in conjunction with regular French regiments and volunteers from the United States, would secure France's ascendancy in the New World.[130] Brissot's quixotic proposal never came to fruition, but the following January, Gaspard Monge, minister of the navy and colonies, lobbied the Convention to levy an unspecified number of legions in the colonies in which "men of color will be admitted alongside whites."[131]

Although the deputies never endorsed Monge's suggestion, French authorities exercising power on the ground in the Caribbean colonies did enroll a number of black and mulatto soldiers in their struggle to secure the colonies against slave revolt and foreign invasion. In Saint-Domingue, the commissioners Léger-Félicité Sonthonax and Etienne Polverel decreed the establishment of a corps called the Legion of Equality, as well as a number of volunteer battalions, in April 1793.[132] They envisioned these units as mirror images of their counterparts in Europe, and opened them to enlistment by all free citizens regardless of race. Jean-Pierre Boyer, a future president of Haiti, commanded one of the Legion of Equality's battalions.[133] Meanwhile, troops of color were vital to the success of Victor Hugues, the Jacobin administrator of Guadeloupe, in recapturing that island from British and royalist forces in 1794.[134]

To be sure, the decision by white French authorities to enlist blacks and mulattos in military operations in the colonies formed part of a calculated strategy for forging a loyal fighting force as they contended with rebel slaves, reactionary white planters, and foreign armies for control of the islands. Polverel and Sonthonax, who in June 1793 issued the first promise of freedom to slaves who fought for the Republic in the Caribbean, did not do so in order to guarantee these men French citizenship, or as a way to emancipate all the slaves on the island. The decision was instead a response to the commissioners' need for soldiers to defend Cap-Français, the capital of Saint-Domingue, against the military governor, Thomas-François Galbaud, who sympathized with white planters.[135] It was not until August that Polverel and Sonthonax took the more meaningful step of declaring the abolition of slavery on the island for all people, not just those who fought in the army. Later, the relegation of black troops in some of the mixed-race forces that republican authorities levied in the Caribbean to positions of inferiority, and the exclusion of others from career advancement, further limited the political significance of military service by freed slaves and disappointed supporters of emancipation in the colonies.[136]

Nonetheless, abolitionist political leaders in Paris were keen to seize on military service by blacks in the Caribbean to advance calls for an end to slavery. The deputy Jean-Jacques Bréard denounced the segregation of white from black soldiers in the Caribbean in May 1793 as he demanded full equality between troops of different races.[137] In June, representatives of the Commune of Paris petitioned the Convention to decree the emancipation of blacks on all French territories, linking manumission to military service by declaring that freed individuals would become "the most ardent and truest defenders of the *patrie.*"[138] Advocates of abolition such as these built upon the precedent the Assembly had set in September 1792, when it levied two battalions in the colonial territory of Pondicherry to integrate white troops alongside indigenous *cipaye* soldiers. Native Indians could hold up to half of the noncommissioned ranks as well, although the law reserved higher appointments for Europeans.[139]

At the same time, blacks themselves who fought for the Republic in the colonies associated their service with emancipation and French citizenship in novel and powerful ways. Bramant Lazzari, a mulatto commander in Saint-Domingue, called on his neighbors to take up arms against counterrevolutionary forces in August 1793 to defend "the good and sweet liberty that France, our *mère patrie,* has given us." Lazzari's remarks echoed those of another commander of African descent on the island named Pierrot, who affirmed during the same period, while leading troops loyal to the Republic, that "we are all French; our devotion to the *mère patrie* is incontestable."[140]

THE LEGION OF THE AMERICANS

If the enlistment of large numbers of black troops alongside whites in the colonies helped to herald new standards of racial equality in the French empire, yet more remarkable was the establishment in metropolitan France of the Legion of the Americans. This special unit, which enlisted black troops exclusively, significantly expanded upon the precedent that Old Regime commanders had set by enrolling small numbers of black and mulatto soldiers within the royal army.[141] The Legion of the Americans provided new opportunities for the refugee community of people of color in the metropole to participate in the revolutionary project, while also allowing blacks to serve as high-ranking officers for the first time in modern European history.[142]

It was on behalf of the black population of metropolitan France that Julien Raimond, a freeborn man of color from Saint-Domingue who had emigrated to the Continent in 1784, addressed the National Assembly on September 7, 1792. Although he reinforced racial stereotypes by noting the "natural" physical differences distinguishing whites from blacks, he averred that the black citizens in the community he represented were as capable and eager as the rest of French society to fight for the Republic.[143] He accordingly requested permission to form a legion of black troops, which the Assembly approved.[144] Shortly thereafter the legion that Raimond envisioned officially came into existence as the Free Mounted Legion of the Americans and of the Midi, a title contemporaries quickly simplified to Legion of the Americans.[145] The "Americans" in its appellation were the blacks from France's colonies in the New World, who comprised a large part of the unit. By November 7 the corps, which was authorized to recruit up to 800 men, had enlisted 400 infantry and 150 cavalry. French generals dispatched these soldiers to Amiens under the command of Joseph-Bologne de Saint-George, the son of a female slave and a white planter from Guadeloupe who had relocated to France in the 1750s. Saint-George himself, although better known for his career as a musician and composer, was the first colonel of African descent to command troops on the European continent.[146] Thomas-Alexandre Dumas, who was also of mixed European and African ancestry and later fathered the author Alexandre Dumas, served as a lieutenant in the legion.[147]

Despite the legion's success in recruiting soldiers and officers, its military role, like that of most of the foreign legions, proved short-lived. On December 6, 1792, before the unit had seen combat, growing political opposition to the legions and special corps prompted the Convention to convert the Legion of the Americans into a cavalry unit of the regular army. Some of the black legionnaires remained in service after this reorganization, but because military authorities amalgamated them alongside whites and contemporary documents, in the egalitarian spirit of the era, rarely noted soldiers' race during the mid-1790s, it is difficult to determine precisely how many black troops who had originally enrolled in the Legion of the Americans continued to fight in Europe as the revolutionary war progressed.[148] Among the officers, however, it is certain that at least Saint-George and Dumas remained in active service, as they helped to foil Dumouriez's plot to march his troops on Paris after he turned against the revolutionary cause in April 1793.[149]

Meanwhile, enough common soldiers from the legion remained in service for the war ministry to attempt to redeploy a detachment of them to the Caribbean, renewing debate on the political significance of military service by racial minorities. The order likely reflected lingering racial prejudice among some French military officials who were reluctant to integrate the troops into the regular army. It met with vigorous resistance from the black soldiers themselves, who were wary of the prospect of fighting against their former neighbors in the colonies and who knew that they stood better chances of promotion if they remained in Europe.[150] They enjoyed the support of deputies in the Convention, where on May 19 Joseph Serre, speaking on behalf of the War Committee (the successor to the Military Committee), praised the black soldiers for their service in Belgium and decried the initiative to dispatch them overseas, where, he warned, the former masters of freed slaves in the unit might try to reclaim them. Serre also emphasized the symbolic significance of the troops in affirming the revolutionaries' commitment to equality, describing their cause as "relevant for all true friends of liberty and humanity"; at the same time, he linked their military service to emancipation and citizenship as he referred to France as the "adoptive *patrie*" of the black soldiers, suggesting that it was not until they had come to the metropole and enlisted in the army that they had truly acquired citizenship.[151]

The petitions of the black soldiers and their supporters in the Convention succeeded in forcing military authorities to abandon plans to ship the troops to the Caribbean. The soldiers instead remained in service with the Army of the North and later transferred to the Vendée. To be sure, their numbers were small and their existence as legionnaires was brief, but of much greater weight than their military contributions was their symbolic role in reinforcing the association between military service and citizenship for racial minorities. They also set an important precedent for the corps of black soldiers that Napoleon later raised, as well as the tens of thousands of colonial troops who fought in France during the twentieth century.[152]

Other Special Corps

While legions of black and mulatto soldiers helped to integrate racial minorities into French society, other legions, like the foreign regiments of the Old Regime, facilitated the integration into France of geographically peripheral populations. Servan, as commander of the Army of the Pyrenees, sought the Convention's approval in 1793 for levying a unit called the Legion of the Mountains to recruit troops from France's southwestern frontier. Carnot celebrated the military value of these soldiers, "the mountain men known as Miquelets, who are accustomed to scaling hills and are uniquely familiar with the summits and gorges; men born in flat country cannot perform their functions." Other deputies, however, expressed opposition to the unit, warning that the enlistment of irregular troops, some of whom were of foreign origin, so near the border would encourage their desertion to enemy armies after they had received arms and equipment at the Republic's expense. Despite such objections, the Convention sanctioned the legion with a decree of January 29, 1793. The unit served along the Pyrenees frontier, where it offered to Catalan populations an opportunity for special service in the French army in exchange for their valuable familiarity with local terrain and language.[153] In a similar vein, the Legion of Belgian and Liégeois Sans-Culottes, which French generals raised in Brussels after capturing the city in 1792, allowed local workers to bear arms for France as the revolutionaries moved toward annexing the territory and transforming its people into French citizens.[154]

Several other legions with important political missions were the subject of proposals, many of them hopelessly quixotic, that never bore fruit. One, the Propaganda Legion, was the brainchild of a German officer named Mayer who presented the Convention with a plan for raising the corps in November 1792. Mayer claimed to have served under the Old Regime first in the armies of Austria, Prussia, Russia, and Britain both in Europe and overseas, where American forces captured him following the defeat of British troops at Saratoga in 1777. Thereafter he entered the French army in the German Regiment of Salm-Salm, which he apparently deserted at the beginning of the Revolution to become a lieutenant in the Parisian National Guard. He also married a French woman and had three children in France. He emphasized "my knowledge of the customs of the various nations that we are fighting, my familiarity with their languages" and his experiences traveling in different parts of the world as key qualifications for raising the Propaganda Legion, which he envisioned as a corps of six hundred infantry "composed of deserters, prisoners of war and all other foreigners who wish to devote themselves to the service of the Republic." The chief task of the legion, as its appellation implied, was to promote French revolutionary ideology among foreign peoples, ensuring the healthy cultivation of "the opinion which must germinate in the heart of every free man."

From a practical perspective, Mayer's plan for the Propaganda Legion was a poor one. He intended to command his legionnaires in French despite their being foreigners unlikely to speak that language. He also expressed a peculiar fixation with arming his men exclusively with muskets from Swabia, which would likely have posed problems because they could be fired only with Swabian powder, a resource not readily available in France. Mayer's corps never received the approval of either the war ministry or the deputies in the Convention, but his scheme nonetheless exemplified the unique contributions that foreigners envisioned making through military channels in order to spread French revolutionary ideology abroad.[155]

Even more impractical than the Propaganda Legion was the idea, which an anonymous sympathizer from Britain proposed to the war minister, for levying a special unit known as the Company of Sharpshooters (Compagnie de Bons-Tireurs). His plan was to raise a brigade of special troops whom he would arm primarily with pikes, although every tenth soldier would receive a firearm "in order to protect the rest of the corps." Combined with blankets that officers would also distribute to the troops, the pikes would double as posts for constructing makeshift tents. This exceptionally light equipment, as well as the unit's reliance on supplies it appropriated from the enemy, would ensure it extraordinary mobility and self-sufficiency. If this vision was perhaps overly optimistic, so was the suggestion that the eight thousand weapons necessary for arming the corps could be secretly manufactured in Birmingham, England, and smuggled into France. Unsurprisingly, there is no indication that the war ministry ever took the plan seriously; circumstantial evidence, however, suggests that its author was the Scottish native John Oswald, in whom the French government put enough faith to award him command of British volunteers who fought for the Republic in the Vendée.[156]

Dismantling the Legions

Despite the variety of special functions that the legions and other non-regular corps fulfilled not only in a military vein but in political and symbolic ones as well, they never outlived the suspicions and criticisms that they had faced since the earliest debates on their formation. Such hostility stemmed from a number of factors. First, Montagnard political leaders feared the special corps because many had evolved as the pet projects of Girondin deputies and ministers, who might conceivably have leveraged the units to support their political goals. At the same time, sans-culottes resented the special privileges that set the legions apart from the regular army.[157] Even the very names of the legions spawned criticism because, beginning in 1791, the state officially identified other army units only by numbers.[158] Rumors that recruiters for the legions were encouraging soldiers who had already enlisted in volunteer battalions to desert in order to enroll in special corps further contributed to sentiments of jealousy and troubled military authorities.[159]

If it was true that the legions plucked recruits out of the ranks of the regular army, such practices did little to resolve the chronic recruitment difficulties that many of them faced, which also fueled calls for their dissolution. As noted above, several of the Dutch special corps struggled to acquire sufficient numbers of volunteers, while the officers of the Germanic Legion faced widespread criticism that their unit was severely undermanned. Such problems were not unique to the foreign legions; the national Legion of the Moselle (also known as the Legion of Kellermann, after its commander) also suffered from a number of vacancies on its roster, as other national legions probably did as well.[160] It was perhaps unsurprising that recruits for the legions were in short supply at a time when the volunteer battalions had already exhausted the reserves of men in France eager for a taste of military life; moreover, unlike the departmental authorities who levied the volunteer battalions, officers responsible for filling the ranks of the legions lacked coercive mechanisms for compelling individuals to enlist.[161] Whatever the excuse, the personnel shortages in many of the special corps undermined their potential as models of patriotism and military prowess. They also ensured that the number of foreigners who served in the legions, although difficult to determine with precision, never surpassed 10,000, a marginal sum within an army whose total strength reached 800,000 by autumn 1794.[162]

Animosity and suspicion toward foreigners also represented a central factor in the decision to disband many of the special corps. The wariness surrounding the enlistment of foreigners that had marked debates on the legions prior to their formation persisted after they came into existence, with opponents of special units singling out the foreign legions, rather than all of the special corps, for criticism. Residents of the Parisian section of Réunion appeared before the Convention in September 1792 to request the abolition of the foreign legions and free companies, but they did not express opposition to national legions.[163] During continuing debates on the legions in May 1793, several deputies also exhibited concern with the simple fact that the foreign legions were under the command of officers who were neither legally nor culturally French; thus Pierre-Louis Prieur de la Marne denounced Colonel Dambach of the Germanic Legion as a "German baron" who "does not understand a word of the French language." He also declared, with reference to the officers of the Germanic Legion, that "the presence of these foreigners in our armies, especially those fighting against the rebels [of the Vendée], is a most serious danger."[164] Georges Couthon similarly attacked Kellermann's Legion because he believed, apparently erroneously, that the unit, although not officially a foreign legion, contained few French natives.[165] He called for its dissolution, along with that of all other foreign special corps.[166]

The Convention's enthusiasm for the Dutch legions and free companies serving in the Low Countries saved the foreign legions from collective dissolution during these debates in May 1793, which coincided with the revolutionaries' abandonment of efforts to present the war as a struggle for the universal liberties of all peoples.[167] It did not, however, prevent the legislators from ruling at that time that foreign deserters could no longer fight against enemy armies from their countries of origin and should instead serve only in the interior of France or along the Spanish frontier, since few legionnaires were from Spain. Nor did the performance on campaign of any of the legions, national or foreign, dissuade the deputies from gradually abolishing them as the revolutionary war progressed and the army assumed a more consistent and stable form. The Germanic Legion, as noted above, disbanded in June 1793. The Batavian Legion, along with special corps of Belgian and Liégeois troops, ceased to exist the following November.[168] A few months later, the sweeping "amalgamation" decree of January 28, 1794, which reorganized all army units into demi-brigades, disbanded the remaining legions and free companies and integrated their personnel into the regular army.[169] As had been the case during the nationalization of the German, Irish, and Liégeois regiments in 1791 and the expulsion of the Swiss regiments in 1792, foreigners already serving in the special corps were allowed to remain in the army. However, the dissolution of the foreign special units, combined with the annulment in December 1793 of the August 1792 decrees inviting foreign deserters to France, meant that the French army as a matter of official policy no longer accepted foreign recruits of any type into any section of its ranks.[170] This remained true until the Directory revived foreign legions as part of a new wave of military reform during the closing years of the revolutionary decade.

INITIALLY, THE LEGIONS and other special corps that the revolutionaries levied during the first years of the revolutionary war provided foreigners an opportunity to bear arms for France after the government had dissolved the foreign regiments. They also opened new opportunities in the army for black troops, who had never before served in large numbers in metropolitan France or received officers' commissions. Yet the legions and free companies ultimately served only to increase the alienation of foreigners and (to a somewhat lesser extent) racial minorities, even those who deeply supported the revolutionary government, from the ideal of citizen-soldiering and from the French national community. As short-lived experiments that aimed to reconcile the revolutionary project of nationalization with the army's pragmatic need for troops of all backgrounds, the special corps relegated noncitizens to the margins of the army and placed them in difficult circumstances once the legions and free companies ceased to exist. The units also gave rise to political controversies that presented new opportunities for French nationalists to denounce foreign soldiers, sapping the units of their potential role as symbols of cosmopolitanism.

The Terror, as the next chapter shows, continued this trend by irrevocably cementing the exclusion of foreigners from the national army. It ensured that regardless of their national origins, political views, or military talents, foreign troops enjoyed no possibility of active participation in the French revolutionary project or membership within the national community.

FOUR

THE LIMITS OF PRAGMATISM

FOREIGN SOLDIERS AND THE TERROR

IN THEORY, the French state had purged foreigners from the army well before the Reign of Terror reached its apex. The nationalization of most of the foreign regiments in 1791, the expulsion of the Swiss corps in 1792 and the dissolution of the last of the foreign legions by early 1794 ensured that official policy reserved army service to citizens alone before the Revolution entered into its most radical phase.

In practice, however, the army during the Terror was by no means devoid of foreigners. Nor had the revolutionaries reconciled their pragmatic need for all the military resources they could muster with the political impetus that restricted service in the army to French natives. Thousands of foreigners continued to fight for France, not only because many of those who had enlisted at earlier dates remained in the army after the disbanding of foreign units but also because recruiters occasionally enlisted new foreign volunteers in contravention of the law.

The persistent presence of foreigners within the ranks during this period highlighted their enduring importance to the French army, which by the second year of the revolutionary war confronted two distinct personnel crises. First, it faced an incessant need for manpower as fighting became protracted and as efforts to levy recruits inside France via compulsory means rarely proved as successful as the state hoped. Second, the army required competent officers who could provide military expertise after the emigration of thousands of aristocratic commanders had decimated the ranks of the officer corps.[1] Foreigners contributed significantly to the resolution of both of these difficulties.

Yet if the Terror exerted little impact on either the official policies on foreign troops or their actual service, it nonetheless exemplified the extreme risks to the nation's security that the revolutionaries were willing to accept in pursuit of forging a linguistically, politically, and culturally homogeneous national community. The persecution of foreigners in the army reached its zenith during the Terror at precisely the same moment that the army's need for foreign manpower and military expertise was greatest, and that foreigners' service was of the highest value. It continued even after the fall of the Jacobin regime in mid-1794 relaxed the repression of men and women whom the government deemed suspect. The extent to which political principles took precedence over practical concerns in fueling the Terror has long been a matter of debate among historians.[2] In the case of foreign troops, however, there can be little doubt that ideology won the day to ensure that throughout the period, including after the Thermidorian Reaction in July 1794 brought the Jacobin Terror to an end, the revolutionaries eagerly persecuted non-citizens who served in the army.

That persecution was made easier by the hardening of conceptualizations of nationality and foreign troops' abandonment of pretensions to French citizenship, another key development that occurred during the Terror. The requirements for seeking naturalization in France remained varied and inconsistent at least until the ratification of the Constitution of 1795.[3] Under these circumstances, foreign troops continued at the outset of the Terror to present themselves as French nationals, as they had in earlier years. They did so especially in situations where they hoped such claims might win them reprieve from the persecutions they suffered because of their foreign origins. Yet as the Terror progressed and hostility toward the service of foreigners in the army converged with the more general xenophobic attitudes that rose to the surface at the time, it became increasingly difficult for foreign troops to straddle multiple nationalities or challenge the categorizations that French authorities imposed upon them. By the end of the Terror, most foreign soldiers and officers had abandoned such efforts altogether. As a result, conceptualizations of nationality within the context of the army emerged from the period considerably hardened, with the delineation between French and foreign soldiers—as well as between the new nation-state and the foreigners it rejected—sharper than ever.

Foreigners in the National Army, 1792–1794

The number of foreigners in active service by the middle of the revolutionary decade was lower than it had been at any point since the beginning of the Revolution. Still, foreign troops retained a visible presence within both the officer corps of the army and among the ordinary rank-and-file. Their importance to the army, moreover, was greater than their total numbers suggested, since in many instances foreigners fulfilled vital leadership roles in an army as desperate for experienced troops as it was for simple manpower.

FOREIGN OFFICERS

Nowhere were foreigners' military contributions in the era of the Terror more evident than within the officer corps, which included a number of foreign commanders hailing from as far away as Poland and Venezuela. The highest-ranking of these men was marshal of France Nicolas Luckner, who enjoyed a long and distinguished military career in France. Unlike most of his colleagues in the royal army of the Old Regime, Luckner was of humble origins, having been born the son of a brewer in the Bavarian village of Cham in 1722.[4] He began military life at the age of fifteen, when he enlisted in an infantry regiment of the elector of Bavaria and fought against the Turks. Although he reportedly expressed rancor early in his career for soldiers who passed from the service of one sovereign to another, such views did not dissuade him in 1745 from abandoning the Bavarian military to enter the Dutch army.[5] Twelve years later he changed employers again when he used his own funds to raise a Hanoverian hussar regiment, which he commanded for the king of Prussia during the Seven Years' War. Renowned for his skills as a leader of light troops, Luckner rose to the rank of lieutenant general and won distinction for his contributions to the decisive Prussian defeat of French forces at the battle of Rossbach in 1757.[6]

Shortly after the conclusion of the Seven Years' War in 1763, the French Crown enticed Luckner to its camp by offering the lucrative salary of 36,000 livres, along with the promise that he could practice Protestantism freely in France.[7] In May 1763 he entered French service as a lieutenant general. Nonetheless, even while serving the king of France, Luckner retained ties to foreign powers, acquiring properties through marriage in the Danish principality of Holstein and undergoing naturalization as a Danish subject in 1778.[8] Thus Luckner, a Protestant born in Bavaria, veteran of the armies of four different European powers and nominally a Dane, boasted a decidedly cosmopolitan background when Louis XVI in December 1791 promoted him to marshal of France, the highest military rank in the country at the time. Along with the comte de Rochambeau, the hero of France's *Expédition particulière* during the American Revolutionary War, who became a marshal of France on the same date, Luckner was the last officer ever to obtain the rank in the eighteenth century.[9] He was also one of only eight men who held the title during the French revolutionary war.[10]

Luckner, who was reportedly barely able to communicate in French upon his arrival in the kingdom in 1763, had apparently not improved his language skills by the time of the Revolution, when he submitted an address praising the National Assembly in September 1792 in German.[11] The marshal's linguistic background notwithstanding, the war minister, Narbonne, assured the Legislative Assembly on the eve of the revolutionary war that Luckner's "heart was more French than his accent" and expressed confidence that he would prove "more adept at winning a battle than delivering a speech."[12] Luckner accordingly received command of troops along the Ardennes frontier as the French prepared for war. Shortly afterward he assumed the more prominent command of the Army of the North, the main body of forces defending France.[13] In late August 1792, following the defection of the marquis de Lafayette to the Austrian camp (in the wake of his failed attempt to march on Paris and restore the king), the government extended to Luckner the further title of *généralissime* of the armies of the North, Center, and Rhine.[14] By this time he had effectively become the most powerful military commander in France, a position he retained until the government suspended him from his post during the Terror.

Luckner was far from the only high-ranking officer of foreign origin in the French army during this period. Of the fifty men serving in 1793 in the regular army as lieutenant generals, the third most powerful position in France's military hierarchy, eight were foreign. These included the Irishmen Arthur Dillon, Jacques O'Moran, and Dominique Sheldon; the Germans Georges-Michel Vietinghoff, Charles de Hesse, Georges-Félix de Wimpffen, and François-Louis de Wimpffen de Bournebourg; and Francisco de Miranda, a native of Caracas, in present-day Venezuela, and later Latin American revolutionary.[15] In addition, a diverse contingent of foreign generals of lesser rank served under these men, ranging from the American brigadier general John Skey Eustace to Joseph Miaczynski, a field marshal from Poland who had fled to France in 1780. A number of generals of foreign descent who had been born in France to recently emigrated families also served as field commanders. Among the most prominent were Jacques Macdonald, the son of a Jacobite refugee from Scotland, and Thomas O'Meara, who was born into the Irish expatriate community in Dunkirk.[16]

FOREIGN SOLDIERS

Foreigners retained a significant presence among the rank-and-file as well even after the foreign regiments, legions, and free companies had ceased to exist. Their continuing existence within the ranks stemmed from two main factors. First, a large number of troops who had enlisted in foreign corps at earlier dates chose to remain in French service after the reorganization or dissolution of their original units. They did so despite revolutionary leaders' hope that following the nationalization of the foreign regiments, "by the ordinary course of things, these corps would find themselves in little time composed of French nationals," in the words of one politician.[17] At the same time, other foreigners continued to enroll in both line regiments and volunteer battalions despite official regulations against recruiting men who were not French citizens. In some cases officers turned foreign volunteers away; Joseph Dielvard, for example, was rejected from the Sixteenth Regiment in March 1792 "because he is foreign," according to the curt summary of a French recruiter.[18] But in other instances officers readily enlisted foreigners, particularly in units that had formerly been foreign corps. In the Ninety-Fourth Regiment, which had been the German Regiment of Royal-Hesse-Darmstadt until 1791, at least twenty-two foreigners, most of them German, enlisted between July and October 1792.[19] Similarly, in the Seventy-Seventh Regiment, formerly the German Regiment of La Marck, two of the eight men who enrolled between the months of April and May 1792 were foreign.[20] To be sure, the enlistment of foreigners in the line army generally dropped off sharply after the nationalization of the foreign regiments in 1791. Still, the fact that some foreign recruits continued to trickle in made clear that military authorities operating in the field were often willing to disregard decrees restricting enrollment to French citizens as they strove to fill the ranks of the line regiments.

The volunteer battalions, which represented an increasingly important supplement to the line regiments as the revolutionary war progressed, also enlisted foreigners after the Assembly had theoretically nationalized the army. This practice was especially remarkable because the volunteer units had emerged early in the Revolution for the ostensible purpose of recruiting patriotic French citizens. They embodied the ideals of citizen-soldiering more than any of revolutionary France's other military units, and they never received official authorization to recruit foreigners.[21] Nonetheless, some foreigners, including those well versed in the military arts, had enlisted in volunteer corps early in the Revolution. Fidel Antoine Schnÿder de Warensée, for example, a native of Lucerne in Switzerland who had served in several of France's Swiss regiments under the Old Regime until retiring from the army in 1767, reenlisted in 1789 as a lieutenant colonel in the National Guard corps of Landrecy. The Irishman Robert Keary followed a similar path. He retired from the Irish Regiment of Berwick after thirty-nine years of service in 1784 only to take up arms again as a national guard in 1789.[22]

The enrollment of foreign veterans in volunteer battalions continued as the Revolution progressed.[23] In March 1792 Parisian *sans-culottes* called on the government to offer all patriotic soldiers from the foreign line regiments the honor of integration into volunteer battalions.[24] The Assembly did not act on this request, but on a smaller scale some foreigners serving in line regiments deserted to reenlist in the volunteer corps.[25] Between 3,000 and 4,000 veterans of the Swiss regiments also enrolled in these battalions and other units of the army following the dissolution of their regiments in August 1792.[26] The years of experience that these foreigners brought with them when they joined the volunteers were undoubtedly invaluable for corps that were otherwise composed largely of French natives who had performed little or no military service prior to the Revolution.[27]

Quantitatively, foreigners in volunteer units did not constitute a very large group. A survey of 7,505 entries in the *contrôles de troupe* for ten volunteer battalions and companies formed in Paris between January 1792 and September 1794 revealed only 116 recruits who were not born in France.[28] The numbers of foreigners in volunteer units levied in most localities outside the capital, where there were no large concentrations of foreign refugees or similar groups, were almost certainly even less substantial. In frontier departments such as the Haut-Rhin, however, the proportion of men of foreign origin serving in volunteer units could be as high as nearly 10 percent, indicating that in some regions foreigners continued to comprise an important source of manpower for the revolutionary army at a time when French citizenship had theoretically become a prerequisite for enrollment.[29]

It is possible, of course, that some of the apparently foreign men who enlisted in volunteer battalions and line regiments after the theoretical nationalization of the army were actually naturalized French citizens. Since recruitment rosters usually recorded only enlistees' places of birth, not their nationality at the time of enrollment, it is difficult to clarify this point with certainty. In some cases, however, French military officials undertook special efforts to make clear that the soldiers of foreign origin serving in volunteer battalions lacked French nationality. Such was the case for Joseph Stranier, a German who enlisted in the First Battalion of Paris on May 12, 1793, and whom the unit's roster described explicitly as a foreigner; and of Jean Ourea and François Manck, natives of Sardinia who served in the Eighth Battalion of the Bas-Rhin from the time of its creation until November 1796, when each of them was "discharged as a foreigner by order of the war minister."[30] Examples such as these reflected the sharpening of nationality categories among the personnel of the army by the time of the Terror, as well as the increasing difficulty foreigners faced in blending in among French natives.

The eagerness of French authorities to delineate strict boundaries between French nationals and foreigners within the context of the army also became clear in debates in October 1793 regarding whether foreigners might be eligible for conscription.[31] These discussions stemmed from the failure of legislators in the Convention to specify whether the *levée en masse* decree of August 1793, which had placed all of France's demographic and material resources at the disposal of the desperate French army, applied to foreigners residing in France as well as to French citizens. The deputies ruled that only French nationals could be requisitioned for service. Their decision came as a relief for the foreigners who had requested clarification of the August decree in the hope of avoiding compulsory military service. Yet it also highlighted the priority that the government, even at a moment of intense military peril, afforded to distinguishing French citizens from foreigners within the context of the army.[32]

Language, Foreigners, and the Revolutionary Army

If foreigners represented an afterthought in legislation requisitioning individuals for the war effort, they fared even worse as French leaders formulated policies on language and the army. As chapter 1 showed, military authorities before the Revolution developed a variety of strategies for facilitating communication within polyglot forces. In contrast, the Jacobin revolutionaries who controlled France by mid-1793, and who bricked the linguistic homogenization of the country into their political program, abandoned initiatives to accommodate soldiers who did not speak French. To be sure, foreigners were not the only troops in the revolutionary army who faced difficulty communicating in French; many soldiers native to France had grown up speaking Breton, Basque, Flemish, German, or Italian, none of which was mutually intelligible with French. (The dialects of southern France, most notably Occitan, were generally similar enough to Parisian French to pose less of a problem.[33]) For foreign troops in particular, however, failure to communicate in the national language contributed to doubts over their loyalty to the new regime and further isolated them from their French-born counterparts.

La Grillade, ou Les Suisses Aux Enfers, a satirical play that appeared following the violence of August 10, 1792, exemplified these suspicions. It depicted soldiers of the Swiss Guards Regiment as incompetent brutes barely capable of communicating in French.[34] The grammatical faults and inconsistencies that ran throughout lines assigned to the vilified Swiss troops stood in sharp contrast to the words of other characters, who communicated in perfect French. Indeed, the only Swiss soldier speaking in valid French declared himself to be of mixed nationality, the son of a Swiss citizen and a French woman. In eloquent verses he expressed profound remorse for the actions of his foreign comrades. The irony was lost on the play's anonymous author that among the most laudable heroes of the *journée* of August 10, at least in the eyes of French radicals, were the *fédérés* from Marseille, who themselves spoke with heavy Provençal accents. Nonetheless, by associating the Swiss Guards' lack of competence in the French language with their role in the bloodshed of the day of August 10, *La Grillade* and similar texts pointed to linguistic diversity within the army as a political danger to the nation.[35]

Such sentiments reinforced the government's failure to acknowledge or accommodate the linguistic heterogeneity of the military. This negligence posed pragmatic problems by rendering command and administration more difficult, a reality most clearly illustrated by the decree of 27 Pluviôse Year II (February 2, 1794). Passed after many of the aristocratic officers of the Old Regime had emigrated, opening the way for less well educated soldiers of more humble origins to fill their positions, the law required all officers with the rank of corporal or higher to display basic literacy skills in order to ensure the efficient administration of their units. The legislation, however, did not specify in which language reading and writing skills were necessary, the lawmakers having assumed that there were no more foreigners in the military. As a result of the decree, most of the officers in the second battalion of the Fifty-Third Regiment, formerly the German Regiment of Alsace, learned to read and write, skills that a majority of them had not previously possessed.[36] As chapter 2 noted, however, the language in which they became literate was German, not French. As late as 1798, only fifteen of the ninety-two officers in the battalion exhibited any ability to read or write in the latter tongue. Of these fifteen officers, moreover, the most competent was far from an expert in French, able only to "write some words" in that language. Other units of the army displayed similar characteristics, with fifteen of twenty-six officers in the first battalion of the Fifty-Third Regiment and seven of forty in the first battalion of the Ninety-Eighth literate only in German in 1794.[37] Nonetheless, these men retained their commissions because of the ambiguity in the decree regarding which language officers had to be able to read and write. Oversights such as these posed a variety of difficulties for officers in regiments with large numbers of foreign personnel, since a lack of French literacy skills left them unable to perform administrative tasks adequately.[38]

It was not until the rise to power of Napoleon, who restored policies that eased communication between troops who spoke different languages, that the French army resolved linguistic challenges among its personnel. In the meantime, these difficulties underlined the extent to which the ideological commitments of the revolutionary regime compromised the practical priorities necessary to build an effective army and win the war by mobilizing all of the resources at France's disposal, which included foreigners who did not understand the national language.

Xenophobia and the Repression of Foreign Troops

At the same time that foreign troops came under attack for their linguistic deviance, they faced derision from a variety of quarters as plainly xenophobic attitudes replaced the cosmopolitan rhetoric that had predominated during the first years of the Revolution. The Jacobin regime eventually codified these sentiments in a series of laws that restricted the liberties of soldiers and other individuals of foreign origin in France, culminating in orders for the arrest and detention of all foreigners in the army.

Not all episodes of hostility toward foreign troops during the radical period of the Revolution resulted purely from xenophobia. For example, there is little evidence that the murder of Théobald Dillon in April 1792, one of the earliest and most widely publicized attacks against a foreign officer during the revolutionary war, stemmed primarily from the fact that he was not French. Dillon, who had been born in Dublin in 1745 and emigrated the following year with his family to Orléans, had served since 1765 in the regiment of the Irish Brigades that his cousin, Arthur Dillon, commanded.[39] He earned distinction for his performance during the War of American Independence and held the rank of field marshal at the beginning of the French revolutionary war, when he received orders to lead a diversionary attack against the Austrian garrison of Tournai, in Belgium, on April 29, 1792.[40] With instructions to avoid attempting to take the town, Dillon ordered his troops to withdraw after a brief battle with Austrian forces.[41] Many of the raw French soldiers serving under him, however, interpreted the command to disengage as an effort to foil an impending victory. The troops consequently assassinated their general as they returned in disorder to their stronghold at Lille, and later flung his body on a bonfire.[42] Although commentators such as Marat praised Dillon's murder as one of the "great examples of popular justice that can save the *patrie*," the event elicited outrage from many quarters in Paris.[43] The National Assembly ordered an investigation, and Arthur Dillon engaged in a successful effort to clear his cousin's name of treason charges.[44]

Despite Arthur Dillon's keenness, when speaking before the Assembly about his cousin's murder, to emphasize his family's long attachment to France, "which the Dillons have adopted as their *patrie*," there is no indication that Théobald Dillon's foreign birth contributed in an important way to his death. Marat denounced him as a royalist, and some residents of Lille alleged that he had close ties to the monarchy, but neither of these parties mentioned his Irish origins.[45] It was also telling that a contingent of Swiss soldiers present in Lille at the time of Dillon's murder remained free from harm, which would likely not have been the case if hostility toward foreigners was rampant among Dillon's troops.[46] By all indications, Dillon fell victim to a combination of anti-aristocratic sentiment, political radicalism, and the inexperience of many of the soldiers serving under him, who, like the troops that Biron commanded in another diversionary attack that coincided with Dillon's, panicked in the face of orders to withdraw.[47]

Yet if Dillon's foreign origins played no appreciable role in his unfortunate fate, the same did not hold true for many other foreign officers who suffered verbal or physical attacks as the Revolution radicalized, even if they enjoyed victory on the battlefield. As early as October 1792 one critic of foreign officers asked in a public letter, "Why should we retain in France foreign generals, such as Luckner, Kellermann, Arthur Dillon, and others? Can we not be more certain of the loyalty of known patriots?"[48] Kellermann (who was in fact a native of French Alsace, not a foreigner) and Dillon suffered such animosity despite their signal contributions to the French triumph at the battle of Valmy a month earlier. Thus, it was not due to what these generals had done, but rather the simple fact that their critics regarded them as foreign, that they came under suspicion.[49]

O'Meara, despite his birth on French soil and his prominent victory at Dunkirk against besieging British forces in 1793, faced similar attacks from a French colleague who complained in a letter to Maximilien Robespierre, "General O'Meara . . . is Irish and it is actually such a man who is placed in Dunkirk to defend it against his fellow [British] citizens."[50] Thomas Ward, another Irish general who served in the Army of the North, likewise faced denunciations in the spring of 1793 from Marat. In a face-to-face confrontation, Marat denounced Ward as an Englishman, and therefore an enemy of France. When Ward answered that he was in fact Irish and did not regard himself as a British subject, Marat responded simply that "the French are very foolish to allow foreigners to live among them; they ought to cut off their ears and let them bleed for some days and then cut off their heads."[51] Marat failed to appreciate the irony that, as a native of the Prussian territory of Neuchâtel, he himself was of foreign origin, as Ward had pointed out. Nor did Marat's background prevent him during the same period from publicly lambasting Miranda for his alleged ineptitude as a military commander, adding that "we should not entrust the fate of the country to a foreigner."[52]

Such animosity toward foreign officers evolved into legislation restricting their liberties. Some of these laws targeted all foreigners residing in France, while others applied to foreign military personnel specifically. They had their roots in suggestions such as Carnot's on May 18, 1792, that France should not allow a foreigner to bear arms unless two active citizens attested to his patriotism.[53] It was not until February and March of 1793, however, that the deputies adopted the first legislation for reining in the freedom of foreigners with decrees requiring them to declare their presence in France.[54] In the same month, the deputy Albitte called on the Convention to bar foreigners from commanding French armies, complaining that there were too many foreign generals at the head of French troops: "Here one sees Miranda, a Spaniard; over there, a German; somewhere else, a Pole."[55] A month later, Robespierre similarly demanded the expulsion of "all foreign generals to whom we have unwisely confided the command of our armies."[56] The government did not adopt such a policy at the time, but on May 19, 1793, the Executive Council banned all deserters of German origin who were serving with French forces from fighting along the border with Germany, suggesting instead that they transfer to the navy.[57]

Matters worsened for foreigners in France on August 1, 1793. On that date, just short of the one-year anniversary of the decree inviting foreign deserters to France that chapter 2 discussed, the Convention ordered the collective arrest of residents of the country who lacked French citizenship and had arrived later than July 14, 1789.[58] This provision applied to all foreigners regardless of their occupation, but the legislators' special concern for those in the army became clear two days later when the radical deputy Garnier de Saintes, in the course of advocating yet stricter policies against foreigners, suggested amending the law to ensure that the arrest orders would apply to Austrian and Prussian deserters who had fled to France to take up arms, since they might otherwise have evaded the decree by citing the law of August 1792 on foreign deserters. He concluded his speech by casting military service in decidedly national terms, declaring, "To arms, citizens! May all of France be a battlefield, may every Frenchman be a soldier."[59] The deputy Jean-François Delacroix warned in response that it would be unjust to arrest foreign soldiers whom the French government had encouraged a year earlier to rally beneath its flags, but suggested nonetheless that deserters from enemy armies should serve only on fronts opposite those from which they had come, in order "to prevent them from detracting from our cause and to employ them in a manner that might even be useful."[60] The Convention never adopted Garnier's proposed amendment of the August 1 decree, but a month later, on September 6, he succeeded in pushing through another law that placed under arrest all foreigners who were natives of countries with which France was at war, regardless of how long they had lived in France.[61] With the needs of the war effort in mind, the authors of the new legislation provided exemptions for workers and other individuals whom authorities deemed sufficiently patriotic, but foreigners serving in the army received no such dispensation.[62]

Thus, by the fall of 1793, no foreigner in France was safe from repression. Yet the situation became worse still during succeeding months, particularly for foreigners in the army. In October the Convention, in a decree that partially duplicated the terms of the law on enemy subjects from a month earlier, ordered the arrest of all British subjects in France. This policy proved especially problematic for the numerous Irish soldiers and officers whom the French government often officially regarded as British despite the deep-seated aversion of many of them toward the Hanoverian crown.[63] In November, Merlin de Thionville took the further step of suggesting the explicit barring of all foreigners from the army.[64] His vision became reality the next month, when the deputies finally nullified the decrees of August 1792 inviting foreign deserters to France, which had already lost much of their vigor the preceding spring.[65] In theory, up to one-fortieth of the personnel in the navy could still be foreign at this time, but even this policy came under attack in late 1793 by radicals who demanded that "the navy of the Republic . . . be composed of citizens born or naturalized as French."[66]

In case there remained any doubt regarding the government's intentions toward foreign troops, the Executive Council on December 20, 1793, instructed French generals to march the foreign deserters serving in their armies to the interior, where it would place them under the surveillance of local authorities while they performed labor on public or private projects.[67] In February 1794, even as France's military situation remained highly uncertain and the government continued to requisition masses of French citizens in the hope of winning the war through sheer numbers, the Committee of Public Safety once again ordered officials to round up foreign deserters in Paris and dispatch them to the interior, declining an opportunity to augment the ranks of the French army.[68] By July, just before the Thermidorian Reaction, the government instituted further repressive policies against foreign deserters and prisoners of war, forbidding them, under penalty of death, from participating in political clubs or bearing arms in any capacity.[69]

Like most decrees of the revolutionary government, the laws that came into effect during this period concerning foreign troops did not receive uniform or universal enforcement. There is no evidence that French commanders, in the midst of war, complied wholesale with orders to purge the ranks of their armies of foreign deserters. But on individual bases the legislation did affect many foreign soldiers and officers. For example, a Polish cavalryman named Pierre Ham, who had come to France at the beginning of the Revolution and enlisted in the Ninth Hussar Regiment, was ejected from the army in accordance with the laws against foreigners. He eventually returned to Poland to fight the Prussians there, but never again served in the French army.[70] Brigadier General Charles Jennings Kilmaine, an Irish native, similarly lost his post in August 1793, despite his warning to the war ministry that "you have need of a man like me to lead the advance guard of your army," after facing denunciations for his aristocratic and, especially, foreign background.[71] Matters became worse for Kilmaine the following October, when the law ordering the incarceration of British subjects led to the arrest of him and his wife.[72]

The persecution of Kilmaine as a foreigner was particularly notable because the general, although born in Dublin to a mother who had emigrated to France at an early age but returned briefly to Ireland in 1751 for the express purpose of giving birth on Irish soil, had spent virtually his entire life in France.[73] Still, in an example of the sharpening of distinctions between French nationals and foreigners serving in the army, Robespierre plainly derided Kilmaine as English and denounced him as a spy for the émigrés, while Saint-Just also refused to recognize him as anything other than English.[74] In contrast, the commissioner and deputy Edme-Bonaventure Courtois distinguished Kilmaine as an Irishman, but only to conclude that he was unfit to command French troops "because of his status as a foreigner. He is Irish, and republicanism does not fix itself easily inside Irish heads."[75]

Irish origins likewise created difficulties for *chef-de-bataillon* O'Shee. His request for promotion in September 1793 was denied by François-Xavier Audouin, a high-level official in the war ministry who was responsible for officer appointments, on the grounds that "in a moment when the law orders the arrest of foreigners, we cannot entrust the armies of the Republic to them."[76] In the same month, the government suspended Lieutenant General Dominique Sheldon, a Catholic native of England who had served in the French army since entering the Dillon Regiment in 1771, for reasons that, in his own estimation, one could "attribute only to his status as a foreigner," since "his birth was not sullied by nobility."[77]

Foreign Officers Face the Guillotine

Yet Ham, Kilmaine, and O'Shee fared better than many other foreign officers, who after dismissal from their posts suffered the further misfortune of trial before the revolutionary tribunal, often resulting in sentences of death. The foreign origins of these men were rarely the sole source of charges against them, and in some cases they played only a negligible role in their prosecutions. Nonetheless, foreign identity served frequently as at least a pretext for the denunciations that led to the arrests of foreign officers, who in many instances were quick to portray themselves as French citizens in the hope of winning exoneration.

Such was the case for Jacques O'Moran, an Irish native who served as a lieutenant general in the Army of the North until political enemies suspended him from his post on August 6, 1793, assisted by the anti-foreign legislation in vigor at the time.[78] Placed under arrest a few days later after the Convention ordered the detention of all foreigners from enemy states, O'Moran petitioned the Committee of Public Safety for assistance by affirming that, although he had been "born Irish, France has been my *patrie* for forty-one years."[79] This was not the first time O'Moran had presented himself as a French national; a year earlier, in a letter welcoming deputies on mission who had arrived to supervise his troops, he had similarly styled himself French when he wrote of the "zeal and devotion that I profess for the service of the *patrie*."[80] His reaffirmation of this position as he faced persecution during the Terror suggested that he attributed his arrest at least in part to his foreign nationality, and was eager to exploit the fluidity of his national identity that stemmed from his services in the French army.

O'Moran's claims to French nationality did not suffice, however, to spare him from trial before the revolutionary tribunal, which on March 6, 1794, found him guilty of military ineptitude and conspiring with the enemy. He was guillotined the same day.[81] During his final hours, perhaps feeling a sense of betrayal by France, O'Moran abandoned the self-presentations as a French national that he had cultivated earlier and instead expressed a strong identification with Ireland. As he wrote in a letter to the French war minister on the evening before his execution, he regretted being unable to realize "the cherished dream that I shall some day be able to give my life to free my own native land from the tyrannical oppression of the savage English government."[82]

Ward, the Irish general whom Marat had denounced as an Englishman, unsuccessfully adopted a strategy similar to O'Moran's to escape execution. Arrested in October 1793 during a wave of suspicion against British subjects in the wake of the capture of the seaport of Toulon by British and royalist forces, Ward emphasized the close association with the French national community that he had forged through his military services. As he wrote in an appeal to the war minister to secure his release from prison:

> I have been deprived of my freedom in the name and through the authority of a people whose esteem I dare to say I deserve for hav-ing fought for their liberty and glory. . . . Is this the reward I should have expected from the republic for which I abandoned my original *patrie*, where I made myself an outlaw for having fought for the cause of the French Republic? . . . I should not be counted among suspect foreigners.[83]

Despite efforts to distance himself from foreigners, Ward was denounced by the prosecutor of the revolutionary tribunal, Antoine Quentin Fouquier-Tinville, as an "Irishman, former general under Dumouriez and his accomplice." On July 23, 1794, the revolutionary tribunal found Ward guilty of involvement in an alleged prison conspiracy. He was executed the same day, along with his servant and fellow Irish native John Malone.[84]

Ward's colleague Arthur Dillon suffered a similar fate despite a long political and military career in France.[85] As commander of the right wing of the Army of the North, with 25,000 troops under his orders, Dillon was one of the highest-ranking foreign officers in the French army at the outbreak of the revolutionary war. He enjoyed that status only briefly, however; beginning in August 1792 he faced a string of denunciations that resulted in his arrest on more than one occasion, as well as his suspension from his post in October of the same year. In the spring of 1794, when the revolutionary tribunal finally brought him to trial, it found him guilty of involvement in a prison conspiracy. He was executed on April 14.[86] The reasons behind Dillon's persecution were mostly political and stemmed especially from his hostile reaction to the overthrow of the monarchy on August 10, 1792. Yet his foreign origins nonetheless played some role in his trial, when the prosecution cited his connections with General O'Moran as a point against him. One contemporary also reportedly declared that Dillon should "go to his own country; we have little need for his help. Go, you are Irish to the depths of your soul, and I am French, and I hate you!"[87]

Like Dillon, Luckner fell victim to the revolutionary tribunal for reasons that, while largely political in nature, were also informed by his foreign origins. Although Luckner cultivated an image as a committed military man by declaring himself "a stranger to all political affairs," he first fell out of favor with some revolutionary leaders for expressions of loyalty to the king as the monarchy became increasingly unpopular.[88] He complained in the wake of the attack on June 20, 1792, on the Tuileries Palace, which imperiled the royal family, that the "scandalous" threat against the monarch, "who is as dear as the constitution," had caused disorder in his army.[89] Luckner was not overly zealous in his fidelity to the Crown, however; a month later, while answering questions about a plot that Lafayette had allegedly concocted to deploy troops against the anti-royalist faction in Paris, Luckner promised several deputies that "Lafayette is free to do what he wants, but if he marches on Paris I will march on him."[90] Nonetheless, Luckner's opposition to the participation of soldiers in political clubs, a practice he blamed for fomenting indiscipline among the troops and compromising military secrecy, contributed to his poor image in the eyes of some political leaders and did not win him any powerful friends in the national government.[91] He thus had little cause for surprise when an officer in a volunteer battalion warned him on June 26, 1792, that six national guards, "all of them open partisans of the Jacobin faction," had left Paris to infiltrate his army and foment insubordination against its commander.[92]

Luckner's enemies initially contented themselves with condemning him as a royalist. They later became keen, however, to seize on his foreign origins as an additional vector of attack, despite the marshal's self-styling as a "good Frenchman" who was eager to defend "our common *patrie.*"[93] Marat had denounced Luckner since 1791 for attaching himself too closely to the royal court and for alleged military incompetence, but in July 1792 he demeaned him for his Bavarian roots as well, denigrating the general as a "Germanic hypocrite."[94] Luckner also faced claims, probably false, that two of his sons fought in enemy armies, casting doubt upon his loyalty to France.[95] Nonetheless, it was on the basis of official charges that Luckner was "accustomed to sojourning in the courts of tyrants, having two sons in the service of foreign powers [and] appearing to accept the command of the army in the name of liberty only in order to facilitate the triumph of despotism" that the Bavarian native, after being suspended from his military post and arrested in September 1793, was brought to trial before the revolutionary tribunal in the first days of 1794.[96] His condemnation and execution came on January 3.[97]

Miaczynski, the Polish field marshal, fared no better than Luckner. Born in Warsaw in 1750, Miaczynski was a close associate of Dumouriez, whom he had first met when both men participated in the rebellion of the Bar Confederation against Russian domination of Poland in 1768.[98] Miaczynski fled to France after the failure of the revolt. Early in the French Revolution the minister of foreign affairs praised him for his "attachment to France, which he has adopted as his *patrie*," and at the beginning of the revolutionary war Dumouriez secured him a commission in the French army.[99] Miaczynski gained particular recognition on the battlefield as a leader of light cavalry and received command of the Legion of the Ardennes, a national legion he had helped to fund with his personal resources.[100] He also expressed devotion to the cause of spreading republican government throughout Europe and retained a fervent desire to deliver Poland from foreign control, declaring to the war minister in 1792, "While I shed my blood to defend liberty and equality in France, I have not given up hope that I might defend them soon in Poland" as well.[101] Despite his military services and republican sentiments, however, Miaczynski came under political suspicion following the defection of Dumouriez to the Austrians in April 1793. On May 17 the revolutionary tribunal sentenced him to death for charges of conspiring with Dumouriez. He was executed on May 25.[102]

Not all foreign generals whom the government arrested during the Terror suffered fates as unhappy as those of O'Moran, Ward, Dillon, Luckner, and Miaczynski. Miranda, who like the latter faced accusations of assisting Dumouriez in counterrevolutionary activities, managed to exonerate himself before the revolutionary tribunal. Born to a family of Basque origin in 1756 in Caracas, then a part of Spain's colonial empire, Miranda boasted the most remote origin of any general who served in the French revolutionary army, and in fact he appears never to have intended to serve in France at all. His primary commitment throughout his life was to wresting Latin America from Spanish control, and it was only reluctantly that he accepted, at the urging of Servan and other French leaders, a commission as a field marshal in France in September 1792.[103] He rose quickly through the ranks to become second in command of the Army of the North the following March, answering only to his close ally Dumouriez.[104]

Miranda's attachment to the Girondins made him unpopular with Montagnard leaders in Paris, however, and French soldiers serving under him demanded to know how it had come about that "a foreigner has command of the army."[105] Even Cloots, despite his own foreign origins and professions of commitment to universal liberty, denounced Miranda as a "Peruvian" who had attained prominence in France only through the undue influence of Lafayette and Brissot.[106] It was perhaps because Miranda's enemies maligned his foreign origins in these ways that he tempered orders for monitoring the activities of foreign civilians at the front by insisting that the surveillance applied to them "should not be too rigorous, as they have done nothing wrong."[107]

Yet questions of nationality aside, it was the military disaster suffered by the Army of the North at the battle of Neerwinden on March 18, 1793, that provided Miranda's enemies with an opportunity to remove him from power. Six days after the battle, they placed him under arrest, and the defection of Dumouriez early the next month added to suspicion against Miranda. The revolutionary tribunal first interrogated him on April 20. On May 10 it formally accused him of treason for military misconduct at the battle of Neerwinden, as well as at the failed siege of Maastricht that he had overseen the preceding February.[108] His long trial included testimony from a variety of prominent figures. Among them was the American poet Joel Barlow, who attested to Miranda's popularity in the United States, which Miranda had toured in the 1780s; and Thomas Paine, who declared him "a friend of liberty and a good man."[109] Ultimately, probably thanks to the influence that some of Miranda's political allies continued to wield before the purging of the Girondins from the government in June 1793, the jury of the revolutionary tribunal unanimously acquitted him on May 16.[110] This outcome sharply displeased Jacobin radicals; Marat declared nine days later, in the course of celebrating the condemnation of Miaczynski, that Miranda had doubtless been a conspirator in Dumouriez's emigration plot and should have been executed as well.[111] These continuing attacks, combined with the purging of Miranda's political allies from the Convention, led the Committee of Public Safety to incarcerate him once again in July. He remained in detention "for unknown reasons," according to prison records, until January 1795, when the Convention finally decreed his release.[112]

Like Miranda, Henry Christian Stengel also prevailed before the revolutionary tribunal. Born in the Palatinate in 1744, Stengel had served in the forces of the elector-palatine for two years before enlisting in the French army in 1760. By the beginning of the revolutionary war he was colonel of the Ninth Regiment of Dragoons, and on September 13, 1792, he became a field marshal in the Army of the North.[113] Seven days later, Kellermann attested in the wake of the battle of Valmy that Stengel had played a decisive role in that engagement; the following January, however, as it became clear that the elector of Bavaria would likely join the coalition against France, Stengel requested a new assignment away from the eastern frontier because, "born in the Palatinate, I do not wish to bear arms against a prince who has never done anything other than good by me and my family." He added that if he marched against Bavarian troops, the French soldiers serving under him might lose faith in their commander.[114] The war ministry acquiesced to this request and transferred Stengel to the Army of the Pyrenees, but authorities in Germany nonetheless confiscated his property there because of his service in the French army.[115]

In the event, Stengel served only briefly on the Spanish frontier before returning to the main theater of war in the east. There, a defeat in the spring of 1793 near Aix-la-Chapelle prompted his suspension from his post on March 10 with orders that he travel to Paris to answer charges of military misconduct.[116] Arrested and imprisoned in the Conciergerie on April 22, he defended himself with reference to his long history of service in the French army, which he presented as proof of his loyalty to the Republic. In contrast to several other high-ranking foreign officers who went on trial during the Terror, however, he did not claim to be French himself.[117] This strategy proved successful, and on May 28 the revolutionary tribunal unanimously acquitted Stengel.[118] His liberty proved short-lived, as the Commune of Paris arrested him a second time on June 1, but he never again faced trial and ultimately regained his liberty after six more months of incarceration. His suspension from the army, however, remained in effect until 1795.[119]

Hesse, the German prince who enthusiastically expressed his devotion to the Revolution as he commanded French troops, was similarly fortunate in suffering only imprisonment during the Terror. As both a nobleman and a foreigner, he was suspect on two counts that neither his professions of rabid republicanism nor his claims to French nationality could nullify.[120] Thus the French general Jean Antoine Rossignol complained to the war minister, after Hesse had received permission to levy troops in Orléans, "I am shocked that a foreign prince is charged with organizing at Orléans an army that should be commanded by a *sans-culotte*."[121] The deputies Pierre Choudieu and Nicolas Maure similarly denounced the German prince as unfit for commanding French troops, partially on the basis of his foreign origins.[122] Combined with his aristocratic background, radical political views, and adeptness at leveraging populist fervor to advance his agenda, Hesse's foreign origins prompted Robespierre to order the war ministry to suspend the German prince from the army in October 1793.[123]

Matters became worse for "General Marat," as Hesse styled himself, a month later, when on November 11 he was arrested and placed by the *Comité de sureté générale* in the Luxembourg prison on charges of false patriotism.[124] He avoided trial before the revolutionary tribunal, however, perhaps in part because of his eagerness to testify against other suspects. These included Luckner, whom Hesse formally denounced to Fouquier-Tinville several times for military misconduct, conspiring with France's enemies and simple drunkenness.[125] Notably, the public prosecutor appeared eager to conceal the German prince's foreign and aristocratic origins from the revolutionary tribunal when Hesse provided his depositions against Luckner, suggesting that he feared the judges might afford less weight to Hesse's testimony if they knew the latter was not French.[126] Although Robespierre proscribed Hesse on the very eve of Thermidor, the latter's fall facilitated Hesse's survival and eventual release from prison.[127]

The Army after Thermidor

Thermidor brought similar reprieve to most other foreign officers whom the government had imprisoned during the Terror. Almost all of them were free by early 1795. Yet it did nothing to reverse the nationalization of the army that French leaders had pursued since the beginning of the Revolution. Nor did it slacken the sharp delineation between foreign and French troops that had emerged during the Terror. It is true that the period after the Terror witnessed the speedy repeal of draconian legislation against foreigners and the revival of cosmopolitan rhetoric, a trend some historians have cited to portray the repression of foreigners during the Terror as a legitimate reaction to pragmatic concerns that the military victories of the spring of 1794 alleviated.[128] Such interpretations of post-Thermidor France, however, do not explain the rigid exclusion from the army that foreigners continued to face even before the Constitution of 1795 explicitly forbade their recruitment.[129]

The lingering wariness toward foreign troops after Thermidor became particularly clear through the government's reluctance to reintegrate foreign generals into the army after they were politically exonerated. With few exceptions, foreign officers who had lost their commissions during the Terror obtained new posts only after great delays, or never at all. Kilmaine, whose incarceration ended in December 1794, remained unemployed until the government granted him a new commission in June 1795, shortly after he helped defend the government against a revolt in Paris.[130] Thomas Keating, another Irish general who had been arrested in August 1793, regained his liberty at the same time as Kilmaine but secured reappointment in the army only six months later, after emphasizing to the government the victories he had overseen earlier in the war.[131] A similar fate befell Isidore Lynch, the general of Irish descent who was born in London and spent most of his life in France. He was suspended from his command in the fall of 1793 and remained barred from the army until the summer of 1795.[132] Yet more unfortunate was Sheldon, who despite his protest in December 1794 that "twenty-six years of service [in the French army] . . . should earn him the title of French citizen" was dismissed by French bureaucrats as a "foreigner" and never received a favorable response to his request for reintegration into the army.[133]

Stengel and Hesse fared no better than their Irish counterparts. The Committee of Public Safety exonerated the former in January 1795 but prohibited him at that time from reentering the French army. It instead offered him the option only to retire. It was not until the following May, after vociferously petitioning the government, that Stengel obtained an active commission.[134] Hesse, meanwhile, was freed from prison in November 1794 and allowed back into the army two months later. Yet despite the Committee of Public Safety's affirmation at that time that he had "always stuck to the path of the Revolution," his reemployment proved short-lived. Six months after receiving his new post, he learned that the government had revoked the commission and ordered him to retire. Despite prolonged protests against this decision, he never again served in the French army. He spent the remainder of his time in France as a journalist until Bonaparte expelled him from the country in 1803.[135]

To be sure, the unfavorable treatment of foreign officers after Thermidor resulted, in part, from the availability by that time of sufficient numbers of competent and politically reliable commanders of French origin, who had been in short supply following the emigration of large numbers of aristocratic officers earlier in the Revolution.[136] By 1794, enough talented, young officers native to France had risen through the ranks to assure effective leadership for the army, with the result that foreign commanders whose service history dated back to the Old Regime were less important from a strategic perspective. Yet the cold responses that formerly high-ranking foreigners received after requesting new commissions following Thermidor was also a sign of the state's wariness toward placing foreigners once again at the head of its armies. The xenophobic political thinking that had contributed to the suspension of foreign commanders from their posts during the Terror, and to the dissolution of France's foreign corps before that, remained in full vigor after Thermidor.

For foreign officers themselves, the experience of the Terror and the harsh treatment they received in its wake led many to reformulate the terms through which they described their relationship with France. While generals such as O'Moran had claimed French nationality to defend themselves during the Terror, and a handful attempted after Thermidor to style themselves as French citizens as a means of seeking new military posts, many other foreign generals markedly retreated from these pretensions after their experiences of suspension and arrest. In several petitions for reintegration into the army after Thermidor, for example, Hesse emphasized his long career in the French army and the proscription he had suffered in Germany because of his support for the Revolution. Yet he avoided describing himself as a French citizen in the way he had routinely and vociferously done prior to the Terror.[137] Similarly, as chapter 3 noted, the officers of the Germanic Legion had responded to charges of sedition in 1793 by fervently declaring France their *patrie* because marriage, property, and military service bound them to the country. They abandoned such rhetoric by October 1794, however, when in correspondence with the government they described themselves unambiguously as "foreigners" and representatives only of the "German nation."[138] The following June they altered this stance, once again claiming French citizenship while petitioning the war ministry for reintegration into the army; in that instance, however, their argument for French nationality was fundamentally different in that they based it on the specific clause in the legion's capitulation granting citizenship to the legion's officers, rather than on the notion that their citizenship derived from their general military service for France.[139]

Eustace, the officer from the United States, similarly retreated after Thermidor from claims that his military service made him French, an identity he had frequently embraced before the Terror. Shortly after receiving a commission as colonel in the French army in the spring of 1792, Eustace had requested formal naturalization by the National Assembly. Although French authorities never acted on this petition, he did not hesitate to use his rank in the army as grounds for appropriating the title of French citizen for himself.[140] In July 1792 he referred to Louis XVI as "our good king."[141] A month later he described himself as an "adopted citizen" of France and affirmed his willingness to "exist for no other purpose than to share in the triumphs and glories of the French."[142] Similarly, while directing municipal affairs on occupied Belgian territory, he declared that his authority derived from his standing as a "citizen and officer of the French Republic," even as he also took the liberty of renaming local streets in a conquered town in honor of himself and George Washington.[143]

Eustace's eagerness while serving in the army to present himself as a devoted citizen of France stood in sharp contrast to his statements after Dumouriez suspended him from his command in late 1792 on charges that he had corresponded with émigrés. Eustace threatened shortly thereafter to offer his services to Spanish or Dutch authorities because he had suffered "too much ingratitude for being in the service of the French Republic."[144] By September of 1793 he had reverted to signing his correspondence only as a citizen of the United States, rather than a French national.[145] But it was not until after the Terror that Eustace, who remained in France until the Directory expelled him in 1797, gestured most strongly toward his resentment of the French Republic's treatment of foreigners who had served in its armies. In a pamphlet published in 1796, he complained bitterly that the American government had not been more generous in its policies toward French soldiers and officers who had assisted the Continental Army during the American Revolution. The pamphlet implied that foreigners who had fought for revolutionary France had been similarly mistreated. Although Eustace did not mention his own experiences in France, he hinted tellingly at his disillusionment with the French state's refusal to grant him citizenship or to reintegrate him into the army at a rank he found satisfactory as he complained of the fate of foreign "heroes forced to abandon the country they had saved."[146]

Eustace's sentiments at this time were comparable to those of Miranda, who neither sought nor was offered reintegration into the French army after his release from prison in early 1795. Although the South American general remained active on the French political scene after the Terror, he sharply modified his perception of his relationship with France as it became clear to him that the fluidity that had at one time allowed foreigners to claim French citizenship by serving in the army was a thing of the past.[147] He was particularly disillusioned by the Constitution of 1795, which, as the next chapter notes, explicitly forbade foreigners from enlisting in the French army and offered no provision for granting French citizenship to those who had already served. Commenting on drafts of the constitution while legislators were debating it, he complained that according to its terms,

> service in the army or navy of the Republic does not suffice for providing a foreigner with the right of citizenship [*"droit de cité"*], despite the fact that any man who lives for seven years on French soil becomes a citizen without being subject to military service. The most resounding and incontestable proof of attachment to the cause of liberty is the act of spontaneously taking up arms for its defense, which is what the foreigner who fights for the Republic does.[148]

Miranda went on to lament that drafts of the constitution promised full political rights to French citizens who served in at least one military campaign, while denying the same privilege to foreign volunteers fighting alongside them.[149] "If a national who has served in the army," he wrote, "is exempt from all the other requirements necessary to be an active French citizen, would it not make even more sense for this policy to apply as well to a [foreign] individual who of his own volition engages in military service, which for natives is compulsory?" Continuing in this vein, he held up as a model for France the government of Britain, which, despite being "of all free countries the most parsimonious with regard to granting naturalization," conferred citizenship on foreigners who served in its armed forces at sea or in the colonies.[150] Miranda did not mention his personal situation in this commentary on French naturalization policies and military service in the wake of the Terror. Still, his biting resentment of the government's unwillingness to grant special privileges to foreigners who, like him, had risked their lives for France on the battlefield was plain enough.

THE DISILLUSIONING AND SOMETIMES HARROWING experiences of Miranda and many other foreign officers during the Terror and after, as well as the repression of foreigners in general in the same period, stemmed from a variety of factors. Xenophobia was only one of them. Like the numerous military officers of non-foreign origin who faced persecution during the Terror, most of the foreign commanders whom the revolutionary tribunal sentenced to death were the victims first and foremost of political intrigues, often combined with poor fortune on the battlefield.[151] O'Moran went to trial because of the machinations of deputies on mission who became his personal enemies; Arthur Dillon and Luckner made the mistake of criticizing Jacobin revolutionaries; and Miaczynski and Miranda came under suspicion for their association with Dumouriez. The foreign origins of these men were not the primary cause of their condemnations, and, indeed, in most cases prosecutors mentioned the birthplaces of foreign officers only cursorily during trial proceedings.

Yet if hostility toward foreigners played little role in the trials of foreign officers before the revolutionary tribunal, it nonetheless constituted an important component of the broader experience of foreign troops in France during the period. By the fall of 1793, revolutionary leaders had enacted an array of laws against foreign soldiers and officers alike that targeted them purely because they were not French, not on the basis of what they said or did. To be sure, in the cases of rank-and-file soldiers, these laws, which the deputies had decreed in the name of defending the nation from external threats, received minimal enforcement. Still, the legislation facilitated the suspension and arrest of numerous foreign generals, including virtually all of the highest-ranking foreign commanders, many of whom the government only slowly or never at all reintegrated into the army after the Terror ended. In addition, foreigners in the army were subject to plainly xenophobic attacks in a variety of contexts outside the courtroom. Finally, efforts by many foreign officers to style themselves as French as a defense against their persecutors, even if such strategies rarely proved successful, indicated that the officers believed their foreign origins to account in significant part for the suspicions that had led to their arrests.

The persecution of foreign troops during the Terror despite the valuable contributions they offered as a source of both manpower and military expertise showed that their repression was not merely a reaction to the exigencies of the war, or the product of revolutionary political thought. To be sure, military conflict and the radicalization of the state played important roles in intensifying bias against foreign troops, and they help to explain why hostility toward foreigners expanded during the Terror to affect civilians as well as foreigners in the army.[152] Yet the systematic persecution of foreign troops proceeded independently of both France's military fortunes and the political radicalization of the country. The earliest suggestions for categorically prohibiting foreigners from serving in the army, such as Carnot's statement of May 18, 1792, emerged before military setbacks in the summer of 1792 and the spring of 1793 cast legitimate doubt over the survival of the revolutionary regime. They also preceded the triumph of radical political factions, which did not begin to take hold of the reins of the state until the autumn of 1792. Later, the persecution of foreign officers continued even after French victories in the spring of 1794 all but assured the triumph of the Republic. And the reorientation of the country toward a moderate political position after Robespierre's fall in the summer of 1794 ushered in only incremental improvements to the situation of foreign officers in France, rather than the total reversal of xenophobic policies that would have applied if the war and political goals alone had determined their formulation.

Attempts to explain the repression of foreign troops as a side effect of the war or radical politics also do not account for the continuity with earlier phases of the Revolution that marked the revolutionaries' policies on foreign troops during the Terror. In many respects, the terrorist legislation that facilitated the arrest and persecution of foreigners serving in the army was simply the culmination of a process that had begun at the outset of the Revolution, when French leaders had issued the first calls for the nationalization of the military, setting the stage for the dissolution and expulsion of the foreign regiments that followed in 1791 and 1792. Thus, just as there was "no difference in kind between Marat in 1789 and Marat in 1793," so too was there no fundamental distinction between the drive to nationalize the army at the beginning of the Revolution and the continuation of that process in bloodier terms during the Terror.[153]

During the Terror and following Thermidor, the number of foreigners in the army grew smaller than ever. At the same time, the boundaries of the national community were sharpened to a far greater extent than they had been during any preceding period of the Revolution, making it much more difficult for foreign troops to claim French citizenship. Yet neither of these developments put an end to the state's unrelenting demand for either the military manpower or the leadership skills that foreigners offered the army, especially as France pursued campaigns on ever more distant fronts during the later 1790s. On the contrary, as the next chapter shows, these exigencies inspired French leaders under the Directory and Consulate to experiment with new strategies for deploying foreigners in support of the French army. They did so, however, in ways that they hoped would nullify the political consequences of accepting the military services of foreigners, seeking thereby to resolve the contradiction between the state's need for foreign troops and the goal of forging a national community in which foreigners played no role.

FIVE

CONSTITUTIONALISM AND INNOVATION

FOREIGN TROOPS UNDER THE DIRECTORY AND THE CONSULATE

BY THE TIME THE DIRECTORY ASSUMED power in November 1795, France and Europe looked markedly different than they had just a few years prior. In Paris, the ratification of the Constitution of 1795 and the installation of a new regime promised to moderate the excesses that had fueled the extreme political violence of the Jacobin Reign of Terror. Beyond France's borders the revolutionary war continued, but since the summer of 1794, French armies had emerged triumphant, rendering the existential military crises of earlier years a thing of the past. With the survival of the French Republic no longer in question, warfare under the Directory extended to new geographical extremes, reaching the periphery of Europe and beyond. The success of French armies also sharply reconfigured the European diplomatic climate, with France either annexing many of the states with which it had been at war or reorganizing them as "sister-republics" that, although nominally autonomous, were subject to dictates from Paris.

These changes gave rise to several new trends that sharpened the relationship between military service and nationality, which the Convention defined more rigidly than ever by codifying it in the new constitution. For one, the government's pursuit of expeditions to remote locations such as Ireland, Egypt, and Canada ensured foreigners unprecedented importance for the army as guides, translators, and political mediators on distant territory where French troops had rarely or never before ventured. Meanwhile, the constellation of sister-republics covering much of Europe presented French leaders with opportunities to enlist foreigners in military campaigns as part of allied forces rather than in the French army itself, a novel expedient for avoiding the political complications of recruiting foreign troops for France proper. Finally, the annexation of large stretches of formerly foreign land to France, combined with the government's increasing reliance on conscription to fill the army's ranks, added a new facet to military service, which the Directory and later the Consulate deployed as a crucial tool for facilitating the integration into the Republic of populations that had previously lacked French citizenship.

Military Service and the Constitution of 1795

While preceding regimes had excluded foreigners from the military with legislative decrees, the nationalization of the army was a matter of constitutional principle for the Directory. Article 287 of the Constitution of 1795, which the Convention ratified on August 22 of that year, mandated that "no foreigner who has not acquired French citizenship can be admitted into the French army unless he has participated in one or more campaigns for the defense of the Republic."[1] From a practical perspective, the consequences of the legislation were minor: it did not eject from the army those foreigners already serving in it, nor did it introduce any truly novel policies, since by 1795 no unit of the army could legally recruit foreigners in the first place. In addition, the ambiguous clause in the constitution allowing for the enlistment of foreigners who had fought in defense of the Republic, without requiring them to have done so within the French army, left open the possibility that men who had served with allied forces might legally enlist in French service, as indeed many did as the Directory annexed foreign territories. Nonetheless, for the first time the Constitution of 1795 codified at the supreme level of French law, with a clarity never before expressed in regulations on the recruitment of foreigners, the policy that French nationality was a prerequisite for service in the army.

The constitutional article was also important because it generally received broad enforcement for most of the duration of the Directory's rule, at least within Europe. Whereas recruiters earlier in the revolutionary war, as chapter 4 showed, had in many instances continued to enroll foreigners even after decrees forbade them from doing so, such deviance from official policy became more difficult in post-Thermidor France. Even before the Constitution of 1795 took effect, French authorities routinely turned away foreigners seeking appointments in the army, including those who had fought for France previously. For example, Henri Nagtglas, a native of Holland and former captain in the Germanic Legion who lost his commission when military authorities dissolved that corps, petitioned the Committee of Public Safety only days after Robespierre's fall for permission either to reenlist in the army or to return to the Netherlands. When the government finally responded to his request in May 1795, it concluded that "this officer, as a foreigner, cannot be admitted" into the army.[2] Similarly, Joseph Joost, a native of the Swiss city of Lucerne who had served in the French army's Swiss regiments from 1783 until their dissolution in 1792 and then enlisted in the national Legion of the Moselle, was "discharged as a foreigner" from the latter unit in February 1795. He did not serve again in the French army until the creation of new Swiss auxiliary corps in 1798.[3] The *contrôles de troupe* offer further examples of individuals whom officers or military commissioners discharged after the ratification of the Constitution of 1795 specifically because they were foreign.[4]

At the same time, French authorities treated deserters from foreign armies who arrived in France as prisoners of war, rather than celebrating them as symbols of the Revolution's universal appeal in the way they had earlier in the revolutionary decade. In many cases these deserters enjoyed hospitable treatment, and by the autumn of 1794 the government had begun allowing many prisoners to return to their countries of origin.[5] Still, it was telling that, even as the large-scale war against France's enemies continued and the demand for soldiers remained constant, the government issued orders for local officials to round up foreign deserters in their jurisdictions and employ them on farms or in public works projects in the interior of France, with no consideration of the possibility of enlisting them in the French army as they had done in prior years.[6]

Contributions of Foreign Soldiers to Post-Thermidor France

Despite the rigid exclusion of foreigners from the army during most of the years of the Directory's rule, many of those who did serve played particularly important roles. Some, such as a deserter from the Prussian army named Gosselapzlibiz who helped identify enemy spies who had infiltrated French ranks, assisted with intelligence.[7] On a broader scale, foreign soldiers tended to be among the most seasoned troops in their units. This trend stemmed largely from the increasing difficulty foreigners had faced in enlisting since the prohibitions against their enrollment came into effect starting in 1791. As a result of these laws, most of the foreign troops who were still serving after the Terror had first enrolled considerably earlier, which meant that they had greater military experience than many of their French comrades. The difference often amounted to much more than a few extra years of service. For instance, fewer than a dozen of the approximately three thousand soldiers present under the Directory in the 123rd Demi-Brigade, which had inherited one battalion of the former German Regiment of Salm-Salm when the government amalgamated the line army and volunteer battalions, were foreign. Of this group, however, the majority had served in the French army since the 1770s. They stood out from the rest of the personnel in their unit, most of whom had begun their military careers only when they enlisted in volunteer battalions in 1792 or later.[8] The situation was similar in the 177th Demi-Brigade, which comprised part of the former German Regiment of Royal-Deux-Ponts. In that unit, the average number of years for which the 102 officers present in November 1794 had served in the French army was 10.5. In contrast, the mean length of service in France for the demi-brigade's fourteen officers of foreign origin, almost all of whom had entered the French army by enlisting in the Royal-Deux-Ponts Regiment under the Old Regime, was nearly twice as long, 19.4 years.[9] Meanwhile, many of the non-commissioned officers in the 105th Demi-Brigade, which had inherited part of the former German Regiment of Alsace, were of German origin even though the bulk of the corps's personnel were French natives. These foreigners likely occupied higher ranks because they were among the most experienced men in the unit.[10] The same trend held true for demi-brigades that had inherited former Irish regiments.[11] The skills that such foreign officers and soldiers offered to the army were particularly important by the middle of the revolutionary decade, when France's military personnel as a whole, as a result of emigration, desertion, and the effects of war, had become on average decidedly younger and less professional than it was under the Old Regime.[12]

Expeditions against Britain and Ireland

In addition to the years of experience that foreigners brought to the army, many also offered special expertise that was particularly valuable during the Directory's expeditions to remote territories. These began with a series of attempts during the second half of the 1790s to invade Britain and Ireland, islands the French had attempted and failed to conquer time and again since the late seventeenth century.[13] From the beginning of preparations for the first such campaign, which culminated in an ill-fated expedition to the Irish harbor of Bantry Bay in December 1796, military planners in Paris floated the idea of recruiting foreigners for overseas operations, despite the tenets of the Constitution of 1795. In August 1796 an officer in a cavalry regiment named Beaupré suggested the creation of a corps of troops fluent in English for deployment in the invasion of British territory. He proposed acquiring most of the recruits for the unit from among French natives who had lived in Britain, but also envisioned enlisting former members of the Irish Brigades and American citizens living in France.[14]

Beaupré's proposal never bore fruit, but the regiments that the Directory authorized General Lazare Hoche to raise for the invasion of Ireland in November 1796, which became collectively known as the "Foreign Brigade," were open to foreign enlistees.[15] In the event, the Foreign Brigade did not succeed in enrolling many volunteers of any nationality, prompting French commanders responsible for the Ireland invasion to attempt to enlist about two thousand foreigners of diverse national origins in the campaign. Most of them were deserters from enemy armies who were being detained in French prisoner of war depots.[16] On November 22 these men began marching to Dunkirk for embarkation aboard transports that would land them in the British Isles.[17] Ultimately, however, military planners abandoned their efforts to enroll these foreigners in response to complaints from native French soldiers who were also preparing for the campaign and who refused to fight "for the defense of the Republic alongside enemy deserters who were rejected from their own ranks, and by the constitution itself."[18]

The invocation of the constitution as the basis for refusing to serve alongside foreigners during preparations for the Ireland campaign was driven home by a French soldier named Batteincourt, who reportedly encouraged his comrades to disobey their commanding officers by imploring them to aver "that they do not want to serve with foreigners. This declaration, which is supported by article 200-something of the constitution, cannot get you into trouble." He added that they could confirm that what he said was true by requesting a copy of the new constitution from local municipal authorities.[19] In all likelihood, Batteincourt and other French troops seized upon the illegality of enlisting foreigners not out of principle but simply as a pretense for escaping participation in an unpopular overseas expedition. Still, this episode pointed to the potency of the Constitution of 1795 for preventing French commanders from following through with the types of illegal foreign recruitment initiatives that flew in the face of official policy, but which had been easier to pursue before the period of the Directory.

Although respect for the constitution prevailed to exclude foreigners from the French expeditionary force that sailed for Ireland in 1796, foreign manpower nonetheless remained a key part of the equation for the campaign.[20] French military planners pinned the invasion's success on the anticipation that large swaths of the Irish population would flock to the standards of the approximately 15,000 regular French troops whom they deployed to Ireland, who arrived off the Irish coast at Bantry Bay on December 21. Their Irish allies gave them much encouragement in forming such plans; in 1795 Theobald Wolfe Tone, a leader of the United Irishmen organization of Irish revolutionaries and an exile from Ireland since the spring of that year, confidently promised that 500,000 Irish insurgents (a wildly optimistic number given that Ireland's total population amounted only to around 4.5 million at the time) would take up arms against the British as soon as French soldiers set foot in Ireland.[21] He also suggested that the French press Irish rebels to take an oath "to be loyal to France as well as to Ireland."[22] Tone was not the first to propose such an idea; since the early days of the Revolution in France some Irish political dissidents, inspired by events in Paris and hopeful that revolution might spread to their own homeland, had sworn to be "true to the French."[23] The reliance of the French expeditionary force on the contributions of these insurgents, who would not enroll directly in the French army but whom the French nonetheless expected to express particular fidelity to the French state, represented the first major example of the Directory's attempts to sidestep the constitution by enlisting foreign manpower in its military campaigns without formally accepting foreigners into the army.

Even if the residents of Ireland were as eager as Tone claimed to swear loyalty to France, they never received the chance to do so during the invasion of 1796. Although the British navy proved largely ineffective in preventing the French invasion fleet from reaching Ireland, extraordinarily harsh weather conditions achieved what British warships did not by making it impossible to put French troops ashore. After several days lingering off the coast of Ireland in steadily deteriorating weather, those ships of the invasion fleet that had not been wrecked by storms began returning to Brest, their port of origin. Tone, who was aboard one of the frigates, lamented that England had not enjoyed such good fortune since the destruction of the Armada.[24]

The disappointing results of the Irish expedition of 1796 notwithstanding, the Directory retained its commitment to landing troops in the British Isles. An American, William Tate, played a central role in the next venture in this vein, the invasion of Wales that took place in February 1797. As chapter 3 noted, Tate had received a commission in the French army from the diplomat Michel-Ange-Bernard Mangourit earlier in the Revolution, when he raised what he called the American Revolutionary Legion for France in preparation for an abortive campaign against Spanish possessions in North America. After authorities in the United States foiled that endeavor and attempted to prosecute Tate and his followers for recruiting troops for a foreign power on American soil, he fled to France in 1795.[25] Once in Paris, despite never learning to speak the language, he remained eager to bear arms for the French Republic.[26] In the fall of 1795 he requested confirmation of the appointment as an officer in the French army that he had received in North America, but the government concluded that "given the article in the constitution" prohibiting the recruitment of foreigners, Tate was not eligible to serve.[27] This setback did not stop him the next year from soliciting the Directory's support for an invasion he hoped to lead of Bermuda, which he presented as an ideal base for harassing British trade and launching further attacks against British possessions in the New World. He also promised that the former officers of his American Revolutionary Legion would be eager to join him in the Bermuda expedition if only the French government would supply some troops, ships, and provisions.[28]

The government never entertained the Bermuda proposal, but instead selected Tate to lead an assault against the decidedly less sunny shores of western Britain. Reversing its earlier refusal to accept Tate into the army, the Directory appointed him *chef-de-brigade* of a unit known as the Black Legion, which was preparing for an attack against the port of Bristol. The objective of the campaign was to engender a *chouannerie,* or popular rebellion, in the English countryside, fueled by the ostensible grievances of British peasants and workers against their government.[29] To facilitate this goal—and, most likely, to rid France of some troublesome individuals— military commissioners filled the Black Legion, which had a strength of approximately one thousand men and derived its name from the dark tint of its uniforms, mostly with prisoners and convicts.[30] A majority of these soldiers were French, including one hundred former émigrés whom republican forces had captured during the botched Quiberon Bay invasion by British and émigré forces in the summer of 1795. The government also, however, appointed several Irish natives to accompany Tate as officers in the Black Legion. These included Barry St. Leger, a native of Limerick who had spent most of his life in the United States, and captains Tyrrell and Morrison, who were of Irish birth but had emigrated to France before the Revolution. Fluency in English determined the incorporation of these men into Tate's invasion force, as it had also probably inspired Tate's appointment to command the expedition, a reflection of the particular value of foreigners for campaigns against the British Isles.[31]

Although the Directory initially intended for Tate's Black Legion to sail for England at the same time that the Bantry Bay expedition departed for Ireland in December 1796, poor planning prevented Tate's force from being ready in time. When the fleet finally did set sail on February 16, 1797, it enjoyed predictably little success. Pushed off course by unfavorable currents, the invasion force missed its target of Bristol and landed instead at Fishguard, Wales. Lacking sufficient provisions and a clear objective, and finding none of the sympathy among the local population that the expedition's planners in Paris had promised, the tiny army surrendered to British forces on February 24, two days after wading ashore. Its capitulation brought to an end what has remained to the present day the last successful landing of hostile soldiers in Britain.[32] The British held Tate as a prisoner of war until exchanging him back to France in 1798, at which time the government granted him a retirement pension of 1,500 livres for his services. He never again held an active military post in France, but he remained in the country as a civilian until returning to the United States in 1809.[33]

Neither the signal failure of the Bantry Bay and Fishguard expeditions, nor the coup in Paris of 18 Fructidor Year IV (September 4, 1797), which threatened to renew political turmoil inside France, put an end to the Directory's designs for invading the British Isles. Several developments in

1797 reinvigorated hopes that such a campaign might yet prove successful. The treaty of Campo-Formio, which Bonaparte had dictated to the Austrians in October, restored peace on the Continent, leaving Britain as France's only major adversary and freeing 50,000 veteran soldiers of the Army of Italy for potential deployment in a cross-Channel invasion force.[34] At the same time, mutinies aboard British warships encouraged hopes among the French and their United Irishmen allies that Britain's naval superiority might be neutralized by the apparent revolutionary inclinations of its own rank-and-file. Finally, Bonaparte, who in the fall of 1797 left Italy to become commander of the Army of England, which was forming in northern France in preparation for an invasion of the British Isles, remained eager for a new military venture to justify the maintenance of a large army and to reinforce his political ambitions.[35]

As they had during the expeditions to Bantry Bay and Fishguard, foreigners played central roles in the campaigns that the French engineered against the British Isles in 1797 and 1798. The first of these invasion attempts relied entirely on foreign manpower in the form of 13,500 troops belonging to the Batavian Republic, a sister-republic of France that the French and Dutch revolutionaries had established in January 1795 after defeating the forces of the Stadtholder William V in the Netherlands. This force embarked aboard transports in July 1797 in preparation for a landing in Britain, and for six weeks waited vainly for favorable winds. Their failure to materialize led to the cancellation of the expedition, but a half year later, Batavian naval resources featured significantly in the grand cross-Channel invasion scheme Bonaparte drew up in February 1798.[36] He never carried the plan out, however, opting instead for an expedition to the eastern Mediterranean, which began the following May with most of the troops that had comprised the Army of England.

In Bonaparte's absence Charles Jennings Kilmaine, an Irish native and longtime veteran of the French army, became the new commander of what remained of the forces in northern France ostensibly still preparing for an invasion of the British Isles.[37] Derided by British newspapers as "Paddy Kilmaine," the general assured the French government that his Irish birth and renown among the Irish people constituted particularly valuable assets for French designs to conquer Ireland.[38] Describing himself as "the most likely General of the Republic to be successful" in the expedition, he promised that "by consulting the Irishmen who are in Paris, the Directory can satisfy itself that my name would suffice to rally round me in Ireland a very large number of the friends of Liberty and Independence, particularly in the provinces of Connacht and Leinster."[39]

Serving under Kilmaine was another prominent Irishman, Tone, who despite his foreign nationality had received an extraordinary commission in the French army from Carnot in July 1796.[40] Even while serving as an officer in France, however, Tone's transnational commitments were such that he managed to secure custom stationary emblazoned with the words "ERIN GO BRAH!" alongside the traditional "Liberté" and "Egalité" of official French letterhead.[41] In January 1798 he rose further to the rank of adjutant general and a few months later offered to join a French expedition to India, which he incorrectly presumed to be the target of the invasion fleet Bonaparte was preparing at Toulon.[42] The government declined, however, leaving Tone in northern France to serve as a liaison with insurgents in Ireland during ongoing preparations for a French invasion of the island.

Military planners also attempted, with little success, to enlist large numbers of foreigners for the rank and file of expeditions against Britain and Ireland in 1798 by enrolling Irish prisoners of war aboard warships. In July 1798 the minister of the navy, observing that "the animosity and hatred which exist between Irish patriots and the English have become particularly pronounced in depots where prisoners of war of the two nations are detained together," invited Tone to travel to the prisoner of war camps of Laon, Orléans, Fontainebleau, and Versailles in order to "identity Irish and other individuals who wish to serve the cause of liberty" by enlisting in the French navy, where they would enjoy "all the rights afforded to French seamen."[43] There is no evidence that significant numbers of Irish prisoners, most of whom had presumably been captured while serving in the British army and had no prior experience as sailors, entered French service in this way. Nonetheless, the suggestion that Tone might deploy Irish troops aboard French warships represented an innovative strategy for incorporating foreign manpower into French campaigns against the British Isles without violating the constitution, since the document prohibited the recruitment of foreigners for the army but did not mention the navy.

The first of the invasions of Britain and Ireland that the French had spent the spring and summer of 1798 planning finally launched in the late summer. In August, an invasion fleet of 1,099 soldiers under the command of General Jean-Joseph-Amable Humbert arrived off the northwest coast of Ireland at Killala and easily made its way ashore. The French intended for Humbert's expedition to serve as only the first wave of a series of landings; another force of 3,000 men based at Brest, commanded by General Jean Hardy with Tone serving under him, was to have sailed for Ireland at the same time, while a third invasion fleet was assembling at Dunkirk.[44] Poor weather and lack of cash, however, delayed the departure of both of these additional forces. Nonetheless, Humbert, with the aid of thousands of Irish rebels who had taken up arms since May 1798, when the United Irishmen began an uprising in Country Kildare that quickly spread to other parts of the island, enjoyed remarkable success on his own. He defeated British forces decisively on August 27 at what became known as the Castlebar Races, because of the haste with which the British militiamen reportedly fled the field. He then progressed steadily through northwestern Ireland with the goal of converging with rebel forces in the midlands and marching on Dublin.[45] Meanwhile, reinforcements finally set sail from France, with a small force commanded by James Napper Tandy, a United Irishman, embarking at Dunkirk on the same day as Humbert's victory at Castlebar, and the larger fleet that Hardy had assembled at Brest departing on September 16.

Unfortunately for the Irish rebels and their allies in France, the heady anticipation of late summer 1798, when victory over British forces in Ireland and the establishment of an Irish sister-republic seemed more probable than ever (indeed, Humbert did proclaim an Irish republic upon landing, which took the form of the short-lived Republic of Connacht) rapidly turned to disappointment.[46] Charles Cornwallis, the British general perhaps best known for his capitulation to French and American forces at Yorktown in 1781, delivered a crushing defeat to the main body of Irish insurgents at Granard in early September. Shortly thereafter, on September 8, Humbert and the small squadrons of Irish rebels who remained with his army surrendered to vastly superior British forces at the village of Ballinamuck. News of Humbert's defeat and the collapse of the Irish rebellion led Napper Tandy to return to France soon after arriving off the Irish coast, while British warships intercepted Hardy's invasion fleet en route to the island on October 12 and captured almost all of the 2,500 soldiers aboard.[47] These included Tone, who, despite protesting that he was a "French citizen and officer," was condemned to death the following month in Dublin as a rebel against the British Crown. (Tone slit his own throat before authorities could execute the sentence.[48]) An additional, small expeditionary force that had sailed for Ireland with about three hundred grenadiers, half of them from the Batavian Republic, also fell prey to the British navy on October 24.[49] This final defeat brought the Directory's efforts to invade Ireland, which had amounted to seven separate operations between May and October 1798 alone, to a definitive end.

Campaign in the Orient

After the disappointing outcomes of the campaigns against the British Isles, the government shifted its attention to the opposite flank of the European periphery, where Bonaparte launched his expedition to the Middle East in the late 1790s. Even more than the Irish campaigns, the Egyptian venture presented numerous opportunities for enlisting foreign soldiers, many of them natives of distant regions where French troops had never before traveled. The integration of these men into the French army, and the subsequent migration of some of them to France itself, attested to the role that military service continued to play during the closing years of the revolutionary decade in amalgamating peoples and cultures from disparate parts of the world.

The first major pool of foreign recruits to become available to Bonaparte's army as it traveled eastward toward Egypt was the population of Malta, which the French expeditionary force that departed from Toulon in May 1798 overran the following month. Upon conquering the island, Bonaparte dissolved the Maltese army and reorganized part of its personnel into the Maltese Legion, which entered into the service of France. This unit, which comprised 1,500 men who were natives mostly of Malta but who included some Italians as well, sailed with the rest of the French expeditionary force to Egypt and participated in the campaign there.[50] Four additional companies of Maltese soldiers who, because of sickness or old age, were unfit for the expedition to the Middle East served in the Maltese National Veterans corps, which Bonaparte levied to guard his conquests in Malta.[51] These companies remained in French service until the British captured Malta in 1800 and transported the remnants of the Maltese forces to France. Military authorities there dumped the Maltese natives into a recruiting depot in the town of Condrieu, near Lyon, where they nominally became part of the Maltese Legion, the rest of which was still serving in Egypt.[52]

The group of Maltese troops in the depot at Condrieu was small, amounting only to fifty-six men in April 1800. The officers overseeing it, however, hoped that it might become a rallying point for larger numbers of foreigners by taking in "all the Egyptian and Maltese soldiers" who might enter France as the campaign in the Middle East wound down.[53] In May 1801, even as the curtains were closing on the Egyptian campaign, one optimistic French general also suggested redeploying the Maltese soldiers in France to the Middle East to serve as guides and interpreters for the remnants of the French army there, because they "speak the Arabic language perfectly."[54] He perhaps oversold the ability of the Maltese troops to communicate with natives of Egypt; although Maltese was a Semitic language that originated during the Arabic colonization of Malta in the Middle Ages, it had been heavily influenced during the early-modern period by Sicilian and Italian, and by the early nineteenth century it bore little affinity with Egyptian Arabic.[55] On the other hand, at least one native of Malta and veteran of the Maltese Legion was appointed as an interpreter in Egypt for the French general Louis-Nicolas Davout, presumably because of his Arabic skills.[56] Whether or not all Maltese soldiers spoke Arabic equally well, the importance that French officers assigned to these troops because of the linguistic asset they perceived in them was clear.

The surrender by French forces in Egypt to the British at the end of the summer of 1801 ensured that the Maltese veterans in southern France never served in the Middle East. The depot at Condrieu, where Maltese and Egyptian veterans never numbered more than sixty, closed in September of the same year.[57] Although plans had circulated earlier for repatriating the Maltese troops to their native island, the French instead incorporated them into the Expeditionary Legion, a new unit assembling at Toulon for service in the French colonies.[58] Maltese troops remained in the legion at least until 1802. While the fates of the former members of the companies of Maltese veterans after that date are difficult to trace, it is likely that they comprised part of the group of approximately five hundred Maltese refugees who remained in France and to whom the French government continued to provide pensions until 1804.[59]

The thirst for recruits that had led Bonaparte to incorporate Maltese troops into his army remained pressing following his landing in Egypt on July 1, 1798. Soon after, the French formed a Company of Janissaries, composed of mounted troops and infantry who by all indications were natives of the Middle East.[60] Following the battle of the Pyramids on July 21, 1798, they organized another company of local soldiers from Ottoman prisoners of war and volunteers, whom they deployed as guides for French forces.[61]

Two years later, a larger corps of foreigners came into existence when General Jean-Baptiste Kléber, who became commander in chief of the Middle East campaign after Bonaparte returned to France in August 1799, formed the Greek Legion at the end of June 1800.[62] He did not explicitly restrict recruitment to Greeks, but its commander, Nicole Papas-Oglou, was a native of Greece who had served in the Ottoman navy until the battle of the Pyramids, when he switched to French service.[63] In a reflection of French commanders' eagerness to enlist foreigners from the eastern Mediterranean in the Egyptian campaign, one general, Jacques-Zacharie Destaing, celebrated Papas-Oglou for his "impressive reputation in the Orient, and especially in Greece; he can enroll a number of good recruits there, and yet more notably, at this moment the princes of parts of Albania and Morea are offering him 4,000 men."[64] Living up to such promises, the Greek Legion proved quite effective for recruiting natives of Greece and other parts of the eastern Mediterranean, who had been almost completely absent from the ranks of the French army prior to the Egyptian campaign. More than half of the unit's officers were born in Greece, and natives of Armenia and Italy accounted for substantial proportions of its roster as well.[65]

In July 1800 Kléber levied a second force, the Coptic Legion, in order to strengthen French relations with the Christian population of Egypt.[66]

Clothed in indigenous dress but furnished with accessories to identity them as soldiers of the French Republic, the men of this legion served primarily under the command of French officers, although almost all of the soldiers were natives of Egypt.[67] They were also armed with European weapons.[68]

In January 1802, after the remnants of the French forces in Egypt had withdrawn to France, officers dissolved both the Greek and Coptic legions and incorporated their personnel into a new unit that they called the Battalion of *Chasseurs* of the Orient.[69] Still, the demand for enlisting soldiers indigenous to the eastern Mediterranean remained strong enough in September 1802 for Bonaparte to augment the battalion's size from 375 to 1,000 men in order to accommodate "the many Greek, Coptic, Egyptian and Syrian individuals who have followed the French army" as it retreated from the Middle East.[70] Commanded by Papas-Oglou, the new battalion remained in service under the Napoleonic Empire until 1814, garrisoning various localities throughout the Mediterranean, from Toulon to Corfu.[71]

While the natives of Greece, Egypt, and other parts of the Mediterranean basin who served with the French in the Egyptian campaign did so voluntarily, the French also enrolled a significant number of recruits from sub-Saharan Africa whom they purchased from slave traders. On June 22, 1798, Bonaparte ordered General Louis Desaix to enlist two thousand slaves from Ethiopia, and Kléber acquired additional recruits from slave caravans in Egypt.[72] In some senses, enrolling slaves in the army was an illiberal act that flew in the face of French legislation outlawing slavery. From another perspective, however, the enlistment of slaves in the French army constituted the fulfillment of high-minded republican abolitionist goals by facilitating the manumission of such men.[73] Either way, the policy underlined the lengths to which French generals were willing to go to fill the ranks of the army in the Middle East with recruits who very likely had known almost nothing of France until Bonaparte's army arrived in Egypt in 1798.

Some of these former slaves, like the soldiers of the Greek and Coptic legions, eventually found their way to France itself during the retreat from Egypt, highlighting the amalgamation of peoples and cultures from very different parts of the world that the recruitment of foreign troops in the eastern Mediterranean facilitated. To be sure, only a small number of the Greeks, Egyptians, Syrians, and black soldiers who had served with the French in the Orient emigrated to French shores after the campaign, but there were enough of them that in 1803 eighty-three of the soldiers in the Twenty-First Demi-Brigade, which had returned from the east and was stationed at that time in Provins, in central France, were natives of Egypt, and one of "Barbary."[74] A squadron of "Mamelukes," composed initially of refugees from the Middle East who had followed French forces on their return to Europe, also served until 1814 as part of Napoleon's personal guard, where they functioned as potent symbols of the emperor's exotic, cosmopolitan ambitions.[75] Some of those Egyptian troops who emigrated to France were accompanied by their wives, and in certain cases these soldiers served actively in the French army until as late as 1819.[76] At least one of them even requested naturalization as a French citizen in 1810 on the basis of his military service for France.[77]

Canada Expedition

While the Egyptian campaign represented the most distant military venture that the Directory actually undertook, it was not the only operation on a foreign continent that French leaders seriously attempted at the time. In a sequel to the expeditions of George Rogers Clark and William Tate in 1793 and 1794, French authorities again plotted with sympathizers in the United States in 1796 in a scheme that they hoped would oust the British from Canada and turn the territory into a sister-republic of France with the assistance of militia from Vermont serving under the French flag.

The plan, which first came to the Directory's attention in the summer of 1796, was the brainchild of Ira Allen, a brother of Ethan Allen, the prominent military leader from the American Revolutionary War. Ira Allen, who had also served with distinction in the American Revolution and helped in 1777 to found the independent Republic of Vermont (which in 1791 joined the United States), was residing in Europe during the later 1790s. He hoped to invade Canada in August 1797 with an army of Vermont militiamen operating on behalf of France, aiming ultimately to establish an independent republic that he hoped to call United Columbia on the territory they would conquer. He had a personal interest in the scheme, which stood to pay rich financial dividends for his family if the British lost control of Canada. To entice French support, he promised that the expedition would weaken Britain and the Catholic Church, whose properties in Canada the French would confiscate. Allen anticipated an easy conquest not only due to the small size of British garrisons in Canada, but also because "the grand majority of the people is composed of Frenchmen" or their descendants who, he claimed, would naturally sympathize with the invaders. He promised that he could execute the project if the French government provided 20,000 livres in cash, a paltry sum for an operation with such substantial potential, in addition to arms and provisions of an equivalent value.[78]

For the most part Allen was unspecific about the extent to which the French government would play an explicit role in the campaign, probably intending to leave it up to the Directory to decide. He did, however, request some French officers to help command the army he hoped to raise from citizens of the United States. He asked as well for a commission for himself in the French army, which he believed would help him to attract recruits within Vermont.[79] In addition, he inquired about a French fleet to support the invasion, and he requested blank certificates of enrollment in the French army, which he presumably planned to distribute to the American soldiers he would recruit.[80] He also went so far as to sew a prototype of the flag he envisioned for United Columbia that symbolically embodied the cooperation between Americans and the French that he deemed central to the expedition. Bearing patches of red, white, and blue to represent the French Republic, the flag was partitioned through its center by a green stripe signifying "the people of Vermont invading the middle of Canada," according to Allen.[81] Allen did not receive the commission certificates he requested, nor did the colors of United Columbia ever fly. Nonetheless, these items underlined the premium he placed on forging official connections to the French army for himself and the American citizens he hoped to enlist in the campaign.

While the invasion plan Allen envisioned was ambitious and probably overly optimistic, the Directory took it seriously enough to furnish 20,000 muskets and twenty-four artillery pieces in July 1796.[82] In order to maintain secrecy, the French government did not send the weapons outright to North America but instead sold them to Allen at Ostende, Belgium, ostensibly for use by the Vermont state militia. With the assistance of Stephen Thorn, an acquaintance from Granville, New York, Allen loaded the munitions aboard a ship he had chartered called, ironically, the *Olive Branch.* The vessel put out to sea on November 11, 1797, somewhat behind the schedule Allen had originally laid out for the campaign.[83]

Like so many French overseas invasion schemes, however, this one fell prey to the British navy, which intercepted the *Olive Branch* only days after its departure. Allen languished for the next seven months in British jails, endeavoring to convince British authorities that the cargo aboard the ship had no connection to the intelligence reports they had received about a plot against Canada. Unsuccessful, he returned to France in May 1798 to seek support from the French government, whose intervention he hoped would convince British authorities to return the cargo to him. At the same time, he pressed French officials not to abandon the scheme for invading Canada. Allen enjoyed no sympathy from the Directory, however, which incarcerated him with no explanation. Although it released him after several months, he never succeeded either in renewing French interest in the Canada expedition or in securing the release of the *Olive Branch's* cargo from the British. In November 1800 he returned to the United States.[84]

His project ended in failure, but the willingness of French authorities to extend serious support to the campaign, even though it entailed enrolling foreigners in French military service, constituted the most quixotic example of the Directory's efforts to leverage foreign manpower for achieving its military and diplomatic goals.[85]

Sister-Republics and Foreign Troops

Political and military authorities planning expeditions to such distant locations as Ireland, Egypt and Canada were often able to skirt official policies prohibiting the recruitment of foreigners for the French army.[86] The government was less willing, however, to accept such practices closer to France. Nonetheless, the Directory found an expedient for working around the constitutional restrictions on foreign recruitment by partnering with the sister-republics that covered much of western Europe during the second half of the 1790s. Officially independent from France but operating in practice as client states, these countries provided the French government with a means of recruiting foreigners who served nominally under the flags of allied powers while participating in campaigns dictated by leaders in Paris.

The first friendly government on whose military resources the French drew extensively was the Batavian Republic, which had been subject to heavy French influence from the time of its establishment in early 1795.[87] Since developing the Netherlands as a buffer against threats from northern Europe remained central to France's strategic interests in the period, the relationship between the French and the Batavians centered around military affairs. It was also a relationship that the French dominated, with the two states concluding a mutual-defense treaty at The Hague on May 16, 1795, that placed most of the burden on the Batavians. French reciprocity amounted to pittances such as returning Dutch prisoners of war who were being held in France.[88] At the same time, as noted above, the French requisitioned Batavian troops and ships during the Irish expeditions, and the military of the Batavian Republic, like the country as a whole, remained subject to orders from French leaders until Napoleon dissolved the state and replaced it with the kingdom of Holland, ruled by his brother Louis Bonaparte, in 1806.

The Directory's reliance on sister-republics for sidestepping the restrictions of the Constitution of 1795 on foreign recruitment became yet more explicit in the case of the Polish legions it levied during the 1790s. In November 1795 three Polish patriots—Jan Henryk Dabrowski, Józef Wielhorski, and Józef Wyzkowski—presented separate proposals to the French government for forming legions from the population of Poland, which by that time no longer existed as an autonomous state.[89] They hoped that such units would serve as the kernel of a Polish army-in-exile that could eventually deliver Poland from foreign domination, while at the same time diminishing the forces of Poland's occupiers by enticing Poles who had enlisted in Austrian, Prussian, and Russian armies to desert and join the Polish legions of France.[90]

Although eager to capitalize on the military and diplomatic opportunities that these legions presented, the Directory hesitated to approve their formation as part of the French army because of the constitutional article prohibiting the recruitment of foreign soldiers. French leaders conceived an expedient around this obstacle in October 1796 when they addressed instructions to Bonaparte, commander of French forces in Italy, "to see whether it would be possible to determine the government of a state such as Milan, Modena, etc. to take" the Polish soldiers under its direction.[91] By January 1797 Bonaparte found a willing partner in the sister-republic of Lombardy, where the government agreed to raise a Polish legion under the command of Dabrowski, who was already present in Italy to oversee its formation.[92] According to the convention that established the legion, it was to serve officially under the Lombard flag, and Dabrowski ordered that its uniforms conform to those that Polish soldiers traditionally wore. Nonetheless, in a sign of the legion's cosmopolitan aspirations and its close association with France, the uniforms also bore the inscription "Free men are brothers," and the troops sported the tricolor French cockade as a symbol of France, "the nation that protects free men," in Dabrowski's words.[93]

In contrast to many of the legions that the French had levied during the first half of the revolutionary decade, the Polish corps enjoyed remarkable success in acquiring recruits. Tadeusz Kosciuszko, a Polish patriot and veteran of the American Revolution, attested that it had enlisted as many as 3,600 men by the spring of 1797.[94] While Dabrowski issued a spirited appeal to Poles throughout Europe to rally beneath the flags of his legion in Italy, however, in practice many of the enrollees came from French prisoner of war camps. The depot at Lille supplied 800 Polish soldiers alone.[95] Other volunteers for the legions were Poles who had previously served in the French army, such as the artilleryman Polwinsky, who had fled his native country for Turkey and then the United States prior to enlisting in a French volunteer battalion in 1792.[96]

Even if many of Dabrowski's recruits were not the deserters from enemy armies that he had promised when pitching the corps to the French government, he was successful enough in attracting volunteers that the French approved the formation of a second Polish legion under the direction of Charles Kniaziewicz in September 1799.[97] Both of these units served in campaigns in Italy, where they remained officially under the control of the Republic of Lombardy, and later the Cisalpine Republic, but in practice they received their orders from French generals.[98] French officials celebrated the legions' effectiveness in advancing France's diplomatic and military agenda, observing that "having Polish troops in the French army means maintaining in wartime an active desertion" from enemy armies, and suggesting that the French army retain the corps after the conclusion of the war in order to promote favorable Franco-Polish relations.[99] The British were also reportedly wary enough of the Polish legions to attempt to bribe their officers into deserting, apparently with little success.[100]

If the Polish legions constituted a signal success in some respects, however, they were not immune to the vexations that had troubled many other foreign units in French service since the beginning of the revolutionary era. For one, an effort to integrate French officers into the corps failed because of their "lack of language skills and willingness to serve in these units, where they were regarded as intruders."[101] Political intrigues within the Polish expatriate community also presented difficulties when a sous-lieutenant named Neyman initiated a concerted effort to denounce Dabrowski. In several memorandums and petitions that Neyman addressed to the French war ministry—underscoring the French government's actual control of the legions, their nominal association with sister-republics notwithstanding—he complained that Dabrowski had conspired with the Prussians and Austrians and was a traitor to the Polish national cause, and therefore to France as well.[102] French officials afforded little credence to these claims and allowed Dabrowski to remain in command of his legion. Still, Neyman's defamations highlighted the risk that the Polish corps posed for enveloping the French government in the political infighting of foreign refugee groups. At the same time, some of the Polish legionnaires themselves expressed dissatisfaction with the French contrivance of obliging them to serve under the flags of an Italian state that had no visible concern for the fate of Poland. They complained, according to a French general, that this arrangement distanced them from France, the nation in which they placed genuine hopes for the liberation of their native country and "a power whose interests they have always defended with consistency and courage."[103]

The winding down of hostilities in Italy and a lack of concerted French interest in reestablishing an independent Poland—an issue French diplomats did not even bother to raise at the peace conference of Lunéville in 1801, where Polish patriots had hoped their military service on behalf of France might pay dividends in the form of Polish autonomy—led to the demise of the Polish legions.[104] In February 1800 the two Polish legions merged into a single unit in the service of the Italic Republic, another

French sister-republic, and a second reorganization in December 1801 transformed that unit into demi-brigades.[105] In the interest of appeasing the Austrians, Prussians, and Russians, who were no longer at war with France, the French denied these demi-brigades the privilege of carrying the appellation "Polish."

If that policy constituted a rude expression of ingratitude on the part of France toward the former Polish legionnaires, however, the fate many of them subsequently suffered when the French dispatched two of the demi-brigades to help quell the revolt in the colony of Saint-Domingue was yet harsher.[106] Decimated by yellow fever and disillusioned by their role in suppressing a rebellion against an imperial power that seemed to share affinities with the Polish independence movement, many former Polish legionnaires deserted the French flag, some to enroll in the forces of the primarily black rebels. The Polish demi-brigades that sailed overseas all but disintegrated during the war in the Caribbean. Although some Poles eventually made their way back to France, enough remained in the New World that the Haitian constitution of 1805, which denied property rights to white men, granted an exception to former Polish and German soldiers who had abandoned the French army.[107]

Reviving Foreign Recruitment: The Swiss Demi-Brigades

Other groups of foreign troops met similarly ignominious ends during the first years of the nineteenth century in the Caribbean, where the French government dispatched them after they were no longer necessary in Europe. These included portions of the Swiss demi-brigades, which the Directory began levying in 1798 in what partially resembled an attempt to revive the Swiss regiments of the Old Regime. It also signaled a definitive break with the strategy of enlisting foreign troops under the flags of sister-republics.

Even after the French government abolished the Swiss regiments in 1792, a special relationship persisted between France and the Swiss cantons, driven in part by persistent French concern for Swiss soldiers. By August 1794 the French government began granting special dispensations to Swiss troops whom the French had captured from enemy armies by allowing them to return to Switzerland, a policy it codified by a decree of 10 Vendémiaire Year III (October 1, 1794).[108] In the words of one French official, the favor the French extended to Swiss soldiers during this period, like the Swiss regiments that France had maintained until 1792, advanced France's diplomatic and political interests by "making French generosity shine before the eyes of the small cantons" of Switzerland.[109]

By the spring of 1798, France's interests vis-à-vis the Swiss states had shifted considerably, however. A French invasion of Switzerland dissolved the Swiss Confederation, the loose alliance between the cantons that had existed since medieval times, and replaced it on March 28, 1798, with the Helvetic Republic.[110] With Switzerland under the control of a regime that owed its existence to the French, and transformed into a sister-republic closely allied with France, forging a stronger diplomatic relationship was no longer a major consideration in policies regarding the treatment of Swiss soldiers. Defending Switzerland from hostile armies seeking to cleave it from the French axis, however, remained a chief concern. As a result, the French war minister, Barthélemy-Louis-Joseph Schérer, called on the Directory in late October 1798 to order the Helvetic Republic to levy six demi-brigades for the purpose of assuring the defense of Switzerland against Austrian troops menacing its eastern borders. Schérer was ambiguous on the issue of whose flag the Swiss soldiers would officially serve under, but he made it clear enough in his communications with officials in Paris that the French government should retain control over the troops, which recruiters would place "at your disposition . . . to be employed at the locations you deem appropriate."[111]

The Directory acceded to the war minister's recommendations. On December 19, 1798, French diplomats at Lucerne signed a capitulation with representatives of the Helvetic Republic for the formation of the six demi-brigades, totaling 18,000 men, in order to augment the force of approximately 30,000 French troops already occupying Switzerland.[112] The terms of the capitulation recalled some of the key characteristics of the Swiss regiments of the Old Regime. Most notably, they guaranteed the Swiss soldiers immunity from French juridical authorities and provided the Swiss government generous financial compensation in exchange for its role in organizing the units. In addition, Louis Watteville, who had been colonel of the Swiss Regiment of Ernest until its troubled departure from France in 1792, commanded one of the new Swiss units.[113] Many of the other officers in the demi-brigades had also served in Swiss regiments in the French army prior to their dissolution earlier in the revolutionary decade.[114]

Despite these affinities with the Swiss units of the Old Regime, the demi-brigades that the Directory raised diverged from their predecessors in that the capitulation of 1798 clearly affirmed the French government's freedom to deploy the demi-brigades in any way it saw fit, regardless of the wishes of Swiss authorities. Although Swiss negotiators had initially sought a clause exempting the demi-brigades from deployment outside of Switzerland, the final agreement included no such provision. It instead subjected the Swiss corps to "act in concert with and as auxiliaries of French troops against the enemies that will be designated by the French government to the Helvetic government."[115] Yet even the capitulation did not specify whether the demi-brigades would serve under the French or Helvetic flags.

Nonetheless, in contrast to the units of foreign troops that the Directory had previously raised, the French government paid the Swiss demi-brigades directly, a policy that some contemporaries interpreted as a clear indication that the units comprised part of the French army itself. This stipulation prompted outrage inside France; the legislator Jean-Gérard Lacuée complained, for instance, that the Swiss demi-brigades were "composed, it is true, of [men who are] patriots, but who are nonetheless foreigners." He also complained that their presence on the French military payroll violated the constitution and threatened to "substitute foreigners for French citizens." Reviving rhetoric deployed against foreign regiments earlier in the Revolution, he added that the demi-brigades subjected France once again to the perils of maintaining in its army foreign troops, which "have always, in all times and countries, and especially in republics, shattered the glory of citizens and led to the reversal of liberty itself." French leaders could have avoided all of these difficulties, he concluded, if only they had ordered the Helvetic Republic to retain nominal possession of the demi-brigades.[116]

Opponents of the Swiss corps perhaps found some consolation in the problems that authorities in Switzerland and France experienced actually levying the units. From the beginning the Helvetic government had been unenthusiastic about raising the demi-brigades. Despite a French general's offer to use personal connections in Switzerland to promote recruitment, by December 1799 the corps had enlisted only about three thousand men, one-sixth of their nominal strength.[117] The difficulty acquiring recruits from among a population with a long tradition of military service for France stemmed in large part from the French government's failure to supply adequate food, provisions, and pay to the demi-brigades; as an inspector of one of the Swiss units wrote, it was shocking that they were able to attract any enlistees at all given that "the soldiers are naked and the men who arrive in the corps find nothing of what the French government is supposed to furnish to them."[118] The French had also not honored promises of extending enlistment bonuses to men who enrolled in the units.[119] But perhaps most damaging to the recruitment effort were memories of the experiences of veterans from the Swiss regiments that the French had expelled in 1792, to whom France still owed overdue pension payments in some cases as late as 1805.[120]

Rather than addressing these problems, the French war ministry resorted to the expedient of bringing the demi-brigades up to strength by incorporating into them two battalions of infantry that had formerly comprised part of the army of the Helvetic Republic.[121] Even this move failed to guarantee sufficient troops, however, and in January 1800 French generals reduced the six Swiss demi-brigades to three.[122] Rather than defending Switzerland, detachments from these units subsequently found themselves fighting in the Caribbean colonies of Guadeloupe and Saint-Domingue, where they fared no better than the Polish legionnaires who fought in the New World around the same time.[123] In 1805 Napoleon reorganized the remnants of the Swiss demi-brigades into the First Swiss Regiment, which comprised part of the assemblage of allied units of the Empire that the next chapter discusses.[124]

Foreign Recruitment under the Late Directory and Consulate

The Directory's commitment to the constitutional principle prohibiting the recruitment of foreign troops, which was already waning when the French government assumed responsibility for paying the Swiss demi-brigades in 1798, evaporated entirely by the final months of the regime's existence. The military crisis of 1799 prompted the government to abandon article 287 of the constitution, paving the way for the establishment of a number of explicitly foreign units. In April, the Directory integrated several regiments and demi-brigades from the Cisalpine Republic, a sister-republic in northern Italy that had been overrun by Austrian and Russian forces, into the French army. This Italian contingent grew larger in September with the creation of the Italic Legion, which recruited both on territory in Italy that the French occupied and in foreign states. The Italic Legion and other corps from Italy remained part of the French army until Bonaparte's victory at Marengo in June 1800, which facilitated the restoration of the Cisalpine Republic and the transfer of France's Italian corps into its service, where they fought alongside French troops.[125]

The pace of foreign recruitment quickened after Bonaparte's Brumaire coup in November 1799, which replaced the Directory with the Consulate. Beginning in early 1801, the government created several companies and battalions in which it intended to enlist foreign deserters of various nationalities for service under French officers.[126] At the same time, larger numbers of foreigners served in the Caribbean with the Expeditionary Legion. Despite having no official prerogative for recruiting foreigners, and notwithstanding the order from the ministry of the colonies in 1800 prohibiting noncitizens from enrolling for service in the colonies because of "their status as foreigners," this corps enlisted an array of men who were not French natives.[127] The personal stories of many of these troops attested to the French government's various experiments with foreign soldiers since the beginning of the Revolution. Fréderic Rieger, a native of Berlin who had served previously in the Germanic Legion, became an officer in the Expeditionary Legion. So, too, did Jacques O'Conor, a veteran of the former Irish Regiment of Walsh who later took part in the expedition against Ireland in 1796, and a native of Malta named Joseph Gery who had entered French service after Bonaparte overran that island. Auguste Lachaise, the creole born in New Orleans who (as chapter 3 noted) had been an officer in George Rogers Clark's Independent Revolutionary Legion of the Mississippi in 1793, also went on to command a brigade in the Expeditionary Legion.[128]

While the Expeditionary Legion and the other foreign units that existed during the era of the Consulate exemplified the French state's willingness to accept foreigners back into the army, most of these corps, which were small in size and which officials relegated in many cases to service in the colonies, were of little political significance for French rulers.[129] Of greater importance in heralding new practices of military service and nationality was the corps known as the Legion of the Franks of the North, which was created in 1799. Ironically, although this legion ended up enlisting many foreigners, the considerations that prompted its creation had the quite opposite design of reinforcing the integration into French society of men who had acquired French citizenship only recently, when the French Republic annexed the territories in which they lived.

The use of the army as a tool for enhancing France's relationship with the populations of recently acquired territories was neither a new idea in the era of the Directory and Consulate, nor one unique to the Rhineland, where the Legion of the Franks of the North was raised. As chapter 1 noted, French officials under the Old Regime had advocated the formation of special regiments for binding the nobility of provinces on France's periphery more tightly to the French Crown. In addition, since the beginning of the revolutionary war, even before conquered territories had formally become part of France, French authorities had attempted to enlist residents living under French occupation not only for the purpose of acquiring soldiers, but also in the hope that military service would inculcate republican virtues among local populations. It was with this goal in mind that General Custine had attempted, with the support of the local Jacobin club, to raise a corps of troops in Mainz during the winter of 1792–93, after he occupied the German electorate.[130] Later, French generals levied troops in 1794 and 1795 from among the communities of the Palatinate that France annexed in March 1793.[131] Beyond France's eastern frontier, a number of units of the Belgian military became part of the French army when French forces overran Belgium earlier in the revolutionary war, and in November 1798 the French government decreed that residents of Belgium, which it formally annexed in October 1795, "will be considered French citizens, and as such admitted to serve" in the French army.[132] The annexation of Piedmont also prompted French assimilation of military units that formerly served the Sardinian sovereigns of that territory, as well as the creation of demi-brigades for enlisting Piedmontese residents.[133]

In practice, recruiting from among the populations of territories that French armies had recently conquered, even after their inhabitants had formally received French citizenship, often proved problematic. In some cases the threat of enlistment in the French army, which was rarely as voluntary as French leaders pretended, prompted young men to flee across the border, back into the arms of the foreign sovereigns from whom French troops had supposedly liberated them.[134] Further difficulties stemmed from the uncertain juridical status of the inhabitants of regions that had only recently come under French control. The annexation of Geneva in 1798, for instance, engendered ambiguity regarding whether its residents should be subject to the same military policies as those of other Swiss principalities, which had remained independent of France. The French government ultimately decreed that, since upon Geneva's annexation its inhabitants had been "declared French-born," Genevans were eligible neither for the special dispensations granted to other Swiss prisoners of war, nor for service in the Swiss demi-brigades that the Directors had levied in 1798.[135]

The uncertainties for the military that the territorial expansion of France created during the revolutionary decade, however, did not prevent private citizens and French officials from pursuing the establishment of the unit that became known as the Legion of the Franks of the North in the hope that it would cement the loyalty to France of the Republic's newest citizens in the Rhineland. Shortly after the French annexation on January 23, 1798, of conquered territory on the left bank of the Rhine, Johann Kaspar Schorp, a native of Coblenz and self-styled "homme de lettres" who had entered France at the beginning of the Revolution and lived there for eight years, wrote to the Directory in Paris proposing the formation of a unit that he called the Legion of the Four Departments. The departments that inspired its moniker were those of Mont-Tonnerre, the Roër, the Sarre, and the Rhin-et-Moselle, all nascent jurisdictions established by the annexation of January 1798.[136] The war ministry, however, rejected Schorp's plan in October 1798 on the grounds that it would not be possible to incorporate the legion into the French army as it existed at the time.[137] This unfavorable response prompted Schorp to express disappointment at his inability to be of service to France by raising troops in his native German principality, which he deemed in the wake of French conquest "my regenerated *patrie*."[138]

The lack of interest from Paris notwithstanding, Schorp found support from the local administration of the Mont-Tonnerre department. Officials there elaborated on his vision in May 1799 by proposing the establishment of what they labeled the Cisrhenian Legion, which they intended to recruit inhabitants of the Rhineland departments. To promote the integration of these men into the Republic, the corps would be commanded in part by officers native to prerevolutionary France, with the remainder hailing from the population of the annexed territory. The administrators further envisioned the legion as the only unit of the French army in which natives of the Rhineland could legally serve.[139]

Unlike Schorp's petition, the Mont-Tonnerre directory's endorsement of a special legion for the French Rhineland gained the favorable attention of officials in Paris, who on September 8, 1799, authorized "the levy of a legion, under the name of the Legion of the Franks of the North, composed of the inhabitants of the land between the Meuse and Rhine and the Rhine and Moselle."[140] They placed the legion under the command of Rudolf Eickemeyer, a native of Mainz who had served in the army of the elector of that principality until switching to the French camp in 1793.

In theory the new legion constituted the only unit of the army in which French Rhinelanders could enroll (in practice its officers did not fully enforce this stipulation), and Eickemeyer appealed to fellow French citizens in the Rhineland to enlist in the corps by stressing its role in reinforcing their newfound association with France.[141] French officials echoed Eickemeyer's sentiments, with the justice minister, Charles-Joseph-Mathieu Lambrechts, reassuring the administrators of Mont-Tonnerre that it was by encouraging the population of the Rhineland departments to enlist that "you will speed the arrival of the moment in which the Republic . . . will finally be able to count its adoptive children as unambiguous members of its traditional family, and see in them nothing but Frenchmen."[142] Similarly, a civil commissioner promised that Rhinelanders would translate the zeal they had exhibited for military service under the Old Regime, and their bitterness toward the former political authorities of the region, into eagerness for bearing arms for France, forming "a legion of avengers" in which they "will follow their ancestors in careers of glory."[143]

Such promises notwithstanding, acquiring enlistees for the Legion of the Franks of the North proved more difficult than the corps's organizers had hoped. As of March 1800 only twenty men were present in the unit's recruitment depot at Aix-la-Chapelle, a hopelessly small fraction of the ten thousand troops it intended to enlist. In response, Eickemeyer devised a new strategy for acquiring volunteers that broadened the legion's base of recruitment to include not just the four Rhineland departments, but also Belgium and groups of Germans and Hungarians whom other French military recruiters had refused to enlist because of their nationalities.[144] Independently of Eickemeyer, the war ministry authorized the legion to enroll volunteers from any department of France, not just those of recent annexation.[145] As a result of these policies, the legion became a space for amalgamating men who were French citizens by birth with those who had recently acquired citizenship via French acquisition of the territory where they lived, as well as foreigners from across central Europe.

The personnel of the legion proved diverse indeed. Of fifty-one officers whose places of birth were recorded on a roster from early 1801, forty-three had been born within France's prerevolutionary borders, three in German territory beyond the left bank of the Rhine, two in Switzerland, and one each in Moldavia, Coromandel, India, and the Aegean island of Naxos.[146] The non-commissioned troops in the unit were of similarly heterogeneous national origins, representing not only France but also foreign territories as diverse as Germany, Russia, Hungary, Saxony, and Poland.[147]

The proportion of foreigners within the legion increased further in December 1799, when it gained a new battalion for recruiting Irish soldiers. Many of the officers responsible for this Irish battalion were natives of Ireland and former members of the United Irishmen, and some had served in the Irish expeditions the French pursued between 1796 and 1798.[148] Although these men could no longer be useful in French plans for invading the British Isles, they promised French authorities that they would be of particular value in fighting on the Continent against British troops because of "their familiarity with the English language and English customs, and above all because Irishmen comprise a large part of the British army." The implication was that Irish soldiers in British service would prove less willing to fight against French forces that included other Irishmen.[149]

If the national origins and linguistic talents of men in the Irish battalion represented a potential asset on the battlefield, however, the variety of languages that the troops of the Legion of the Franks of the North spoke contributed to the slew of difficulties that befell the unit. One of its commanders lost his post because he could not communicate with the German speakers serving under him, and few of the officers of the Irish battalion were conversant in German.[150] Also problematic was the legion's lack of discipline and provisions, as well as the government's habit of discarding into the corps unruly French officers who had proven problematic elsewhere in the army.[151] The attitudes of some of the Irish recruits, who characterized France as an ally but recognized only Ireland as their *patrie*, undoubtedly did not help morale within the legion.[152] And if the legion's supporters had envisioned it as a tool for encouraging the inhabitants of recently annexed territories to turn a sympathetic eye toward the government in Paris, the disorders it caused among civilians had quite the opposite effect, at least in Mainz, where according to one French general "the Legion of the Franks of the North is viewed with horror by all the inhabitants . . . I would need a volume to enumerate all of the complaints lodged against a number of the individuals composing it."[153]

Such ill repute, combined with the legion's failure even by Eickemeyer's admission ever to enlist more than 4,000 men, of whom 1,500 deserted shortly after enrolling, excluded it from combat.[154] It served instead as a policing unit on the Dutch frontier, where it assisted in the collection of customs duties and anti-smuggling operations. In April of 1801 the French washed their hands of the unit by transferring it to the service of the Batavian Republic, and a decree of June 21, 1801, dissolved it entirely.[155] Most of the 1,620 troops present in the legion at the time of its suppression, of whom 218 were foreigners, transferred to other units of the French army.[156] Some of its officers were less fortunate, however; Eickemeyer faced an investigation for allegedly mishandling the unit's finances, and the war ministry dispatched several of his subordinates to unhappy posts in the colonies.[157]

Foreigners and Military Conscription

While the Legion of the Franks of the North ultimately did little to help assimilate frontier territories into the Republic, new opportunities for leveraging military service to advance the government's political agenda emerged with the adoption on September 5, 1798, of the Jourdan Law, which institutionalized military conscription in France. Although the legislation chiefly targeted French natives, it had significant consequences both for soldiers who lacked French citizenship and for residents of recently annexed territories whom the state wished to mold into French citizens.

In practice if not in word, conscription had existed in France well before 1798. Under the Old Regime, males had been subject to obligatory service in the *milice royale,* a branch of the military that Louis XIV introduced in 1688 to supplement the line army.[158] During the Revolution, starting in 1792, authorities responsible for filling the ranks of the "volunteer" battalions resorted in some cases to compulsory means of enlisting recruits.[159] By February 1793, when the National Convention declared all unmarried or widower men between the ages of eighteen and forty in a permanent state of requisition for the army, universal male conscription had become an institution.[160] Yet the Jourdan Law, which provided the government with unprecedented power to force men to serve in the army, gave a new impetus to conscription in France. It represented a novel means of deploying military service as a tool for shaping into French citizens those groups whom the state sought to include in the republican national community, and isolating those it did not.

In the case of populations that had only recently acquired French citizenship as a result of territorial expansion, conscription offered republican officials a means of conferring special favor, as well as of gauging loyalty to France. Despite French officials' high hopes for acquiring large numbers of recruits in the Rhineland departments, whose occupants were reputedly particularly receptive to military service, the Jourdan Law did not come into effect in those territories until July 1802.[161] Similarly, the treaty that annexed Geneva to France in 1798 included a special provision excusing the city's residents from participation in the conscription lottery for five years.[162] Even in the Basque region of the Pyrenees frontier, which had long been under French control but whose population was perceived from Paris as somewhat less French due to its heterodox language and culture, officials attempted to offer special privileges to conscripts because of the belief that they could not successfully amalgamate these men into the regular army.[163]

Such exemptions did not prevent local administrators shortly after the institutionalization of conscription elsewhere in France from appealing to their constituents to enlist in the French army voluntarily. Those in the Ruhr department, for instance, encouraged local citizens to volunteer in order to avoid the ignominy of finding themselves among "the last who want to take part in the glory of the great nation" of France.[164] French citizens in the Rhineland also received strict warnings against enlisting in the armies of foreign states, an act punishable by the confiscation not only of the property of the soldiers serving abroad, but of their parents' as well.[165] Such approbations aside, the special treatment that the central government extended to geographically peripheral populations through the conscription regime underlined the utility of military service for easing newly annexed territories into France. It also highlighted the government's wariness toward subjecting men who had only recently become French citizens (and who, in the case of Rhineland recruits, were likely to have to fight against enemy troops who spoke the same language and hailed from the same region) to the same terms of service as French natives.[166]

For similar reasons, the government deemed individuals who lacked French citizenship ineligible for conscription. As early as May 1795, in keeping with the draft constitutional provision limiting service to French citizens, a decree exempted foreigners residing in France from the forms of compulsory military service in effect at that time.[167] Three years later, the text of the Jourdan Law, which declared that "every Frenchman is a soldier" and that in time of war "all Frenchmen are called" to France's defense, left little ambiguity regarding the legislation's applicability to foreigners.[168] Such exclusions, though often welcomed by foreigners with little interest in forcibly serving in the army, were nonetheless subject to contestation.

In response to the effort by a draftee named Jean Wendeling Mühlhauser from Bergzabern, a Palatine village that France had annexed, to claim exemption from service on the basis of not being a French citizen, one local prefect wrote, "I think that, even if seven years of residency are necessary for a foreigner or former noble to exercise the rights of French citizenship, such should not be the case for the defense of the *patrie;* to be included in military conscription it suffices to establish residency in France." The war ministry overruled the official, however, citing article 287 of the constitution to conclude that Mühlhauser, because he had not yet become a naturalized citizen, was ineligible for obligatory enlistment.[169] Elsewhere, some residents of annexed frontier regions temporarily crossed the border to renounce their French citizenship in order to avoid conscription, even though they continued to reside on French territory.[170]

Regardless of foreigners' own attitudes toward conscription, the fact that French authorities took pains to ensure that only men who were French citizens—and, in the case of newly annexed jurisdictions, had been French for at least a few years—were eligible for compulsory induction into the army highlighted the role that military service assumed in delineating the boundaries of the national community and distinguishing Frenchmen from foreigners. During the era of the Consulate, acquiring manpower for the army remained a paramount concern, to the extent that Bonaparte insisted, while drafting the Civil Code in 1801, on expansive definitions of French nationality that would make as many men as possible eligible for conscription.[171] Yet because military service, whether one perceived it as a privilege or an obligation, had become strictly contingent on nationality, foreigners remained exempt from compulsory enlistment for the same political reasons that had led the government to purge them from the army earlier in the revolutionary period.

FOR FOREIGN TROOPS IN THE FRENCH ARMY, the era of the Directory and the Consulate was a relatively unremarkable one, despite the dramatic overseas expeditions that constituted much of France's military activities at the time. Compared to the earlier part of the revolutionary decade and to the Napoleonic Empire, the number of foreigners who retained active posts in the French army during the late 1790s and early 1800s was minimal. Meanwhile, foreigners who bore arms on behalf of France by serving under the flags of sister-republics were of little political or ideological concern for French officials, who had ushered responsibility for these troops into the hands of allied governments precisely because they wished to resolve the complications of foreign recruitment.

Yet the period of the Directory and Consulate illuminated the relationship between military service and nationality that had emerged out of the Revolution in sharper perspective than ever. By adopting and enforcing strict policies prohibiting the recruitment of foreigners for the army during much of this time, French officials affirmed military service as the privilege and duty of French citizens alone to an extent of which their predecessors had only dreamed. At the same time, by deploying the army as a tool for bolstering the integration of new citizens into France, the government made military enlistment not just contingent upon French nationality, but actually a constitutive element of French citizenship. Just as foreigners could not serve because they were not French, men who had only recently received citizenship, and who were effectively in the process of becoming French, received special consideration within the military regime as a means of promoting that process.

On the surface, the reintroduction of foreign units to the French army beginning in 1799 implied a return to the policies that had been in place before the Terror, when France had last maintained foreign legions and regiments. Yet by relegating foreigners mostly to peculiar corps that policed the interior of France or were dispatched to fight the Republic's brutal overseas wars, as well as by drawing stark distinctions between foreigners and French citizens when applying laws on conscription, the state in the late eighteenth and early nineteenth century continued to exclude noncitizens from full participation in France's military and political institutions. As the next chapter shows, this situation changed little under the Napoleonic Empire, when the state revived large-scale foreign recruitment yet remained suspicious of foreign troops regardless of their political loyalties.

REVOLUTIONARY CONTINUITIES

NAPOLEON'S FOREIGN TROOPS

MOST STUDIES OF FOREIGNERS in revolutionary France do not extend into the period of the First Empire. The few that do tend to portray Napoleon's treatment of foreigners as part and parcel of his broader objectives of securing the state against internal and external threats on the one hand, and, on the other, rolling back the more radical policies of the revolutionary decade in order to reconstruct France's fractured society. To bolster state power, Napoleon encouraged legislation on nationality and citizenship that expanded the number of men whom the state could count as French, and who were therefore eligible for conscription.[1] He also maintained an extensive police system that placed foreigners in France under closer surveillance than ever.[2] And he revived several of the key policies toward foreigners that had prevailed under the Old Regime by reintroducing the *droit d'aubaine,* restoring definitions of nationality as a personal relationship between the ruler and the ruled (rather than between the more abstract entity of the "nation" and the citizen) and expanding the prerogative of the executive power to treat foreigners as it saw fit on a case-by-case basis.[3]

These changes suggest that Napoleon's treatment of foreigners, as a general group, constituted a sharp break with the practices of the revolutionary decade. Yet in several important respects, his policies on foreign soldiers in particular highlighted the extent to which the Empire, far from resurrecting all of the practices of the Old Regime, preserved many of the nationalist orthodoxies of the revolutionary decade. First, although Napoleon officially restored foreign regiments to the army, he consigned most of the foreign corps of the Empire to second-class status. With the exception of exotic troops from far-off regions, such as the Egyptian Mamelukes who served in the Imperial Guard, foreign troops under Napoleon functioned chiefly as reserves of manpower, not tools for enhancing the political or diplomatic prestige of the state as they had under the absolute monarchy. The lengths to which Napoleonic officials went to ensure that the personnel of the foreign regiments remained subordinate to French officers recalled revolutionary practices and sharpened yet further the role of military service in delineating nationals from foreigners.

Second, the closing years of the Empire witnessed the abolition of most of the foreign corps of the imperial army in response to doubts over their political loyalty, a decision that closely mirrored the nationalization of the foreign regiments during the Revolution. Napoleon, however, went even further than his predecessors by not only prohibiting further recruitment of most groups of foreigners, but also rounding up and disarming thousands of those already serving in his army, even at a moment when he needed military manpower and expertise more than ever.

Finally, Napoleon expanded upon the practices that the Directory had introduced of pressing foreigners into French service by enlisting them nominally under the flags of allied states, as well as calling on the populations of territories that France had recently annexed to furnish recruits for the imperial armies under special conditions. Such policies represented another inheritance from the revolutionary decade that was informed not only by the pragmatic needs of the state, but also the continuing development of service in the army as a tool for advancing the political and diplomatic interests of the regime and helping to define the national community.

Foreigners from Annexed Territories

Like the multinational Napoleonic Empire, Napoleon's armies counted among their ranks troops from an immensely diverse range of territories who spoke a variety of languages and wore a multitude of uniforms. The majority of the soldiers and officers serving Napoleon who had not been born in France, however, were in fact French subjects (which title the regime officially revived in 1806 to replace "citizen," the egalitarian term of the revolutionary decade).[4] As the Empire expanded to unprecedented geographical extremes, annexing territories from Catalonia to Italy to the Balkans and transforming them into French departments, vast numbers of formerly foreign peoples gained French nationality. Many of them, whether voluntarily or not, also became French soldiers, helping alongside the rest of the imperial population to sustain Napoleon's incessant demand for troops.

Many residents of peripheral territories during the Napoleonic era, like their predecessors in the French Rhineland under the Directory whose experiences chapter 5 detailed, served in special units that the government levied to help integrate these frontier populations into the Empire. In the northern and central portions of the Italian peninsula, which France formally annexed between 1805 and 1808, collaboration with local elites lay at the core of Napoleon's strategy for assimilating Italians into the Empire.[5] Military service featured centrally in this endeavor, which included the recruitment of honor guards that called upon the sons of Italian aristo-crats to serve.[6] The French also hoped they could "civilize" Italians living in mountain villages, where imperial influence was weakest, through con-scription into the army.[7] Such aspirations inspired the formation in 1810 of a special unit, the Regiment of the Mediterranean, for enlisting inhabi-tants of the Alpine departments who attempted to dodge the conscription lottery.[8] Imperial administrators also levied a variety of other units at the local level across the Italian departments for service in the regular imperial army, reinforcing the integration of their inhabitants into the Empire.[9] Even in his native Corsica, which had belonged to France since well before the Revolution, Napoleon established special battalions in which only Cor-sicans could serve and which aimed, in the words of one French official, "to do honor to the Corsican nation" at the same time that they reinforced French influence on the island.[10]

The German departments of the Empire similarly furnished their share of recruits to corps with strong local ties. In addition to the Rhineland jurisdictions that the Directory had incorporated into France, Napoleon annexed additional territory in northern Germany in 1810 to create the departments of Ems Supérieur, Bouches du Weser, Bouches de l'Elbe, and La Lippe.[11] The following year he issued orders to form four new combat regiments from among the populations of these jurisdictions, as well as companies of veterans charged with garrisoning local cities.[12]

In the same region, the annexation to France in 1810 of the kingdom of Holland, which until that time had existed as an independent state ruled by Napoleon's brother, Louis Bonaparte, facilitated the integration into the imperial army of the approximately 27,000 troops that had comprised the Dutch military.[13] Even after Holland's incorporation into the Empire, however, Napoleon placed a premium on preserving the former Dutch regiments as units in which only natives of the Dutch departments could serve. This policy represented another example of the deployment of mil-itary service as a political tool even in a region that had been solidly under French influence for more than a decade prior to annexation. Napoleon ordered the war minister to permit Dutch natives to serve as officers within the units.[14] He also expressly mandated the rejection of foreigners from the corps, taking extra care to ensure that French nationality was a prerequisite for service in these newest additions to the imperial army, even though the bulk of their personnel had only very recently become French subjects.[15]

Farther east, Napoleonic officials were eager to exploit the military talents they attributed to the inhabitants of the Illyrian provinces, the parts of modern Croatia and Slovenia that became part of the French Empire.[16] Although subject to poor discipline, the "horde of Tartars" residing on the eastern periphery of Napoleon's dominions enjoyed a reputation as "a bellicose population whose inconstancy and indiscipline may be kept in check by just and severe laws," as well as a group particularly amenable to military service, according to one official.[17] To capitalize on this reserve of skilled soldiers, Napoleon levied six regular regiments in the Illyrian departments, in addition to a special unit that performed policing duties on the Turkish frontier.[18] He raised a Croat hussar regiment as well in 1813.[19] Meanwhile, on the extreme frontiers of the Empire, the French levied several corps of local peoples, including an Albanian regiment and the Battalion of the Seven Islands, which they assigned to the defense of the Ionian islands.[20]

Not all recruits from France's "new" departments served in local units of this type. Many thousands also enlisted in regular regiments or battalions of the line army that recruited troops from throughout the Empire, largely through conscription.[21] In 1813 alone the state called up 22,930 men from departments of recent annexation for induction into the line army, accounting for about 6.8 percent of the total conscription class of that year.[22] Thus, while the Napoleonic regime continued the practice that the Directory had introduced of offering peripheral populations special opportunities for service in units with local identities, it also amalgamated tens of thousands of the residents of recently nationalized territory into the rest of the army, where they served alongside natives of prerevolutionary France.

Allied Forces

Client states beyond the Empire's borders also helped to ensure a constant supply of soldiers for Napoleon's military campaigns. During the Napoleonic period, the proportion of allied forces among the total troops at the Empire's disposal ranged from 8 to 22.3 percent, depending upon the year. The contributions of allied governments grew especially important during the heaviest periods of military campaigning, underlining the importance of foreign manpower to French military success.[23] In addition, although the French at first tended to deploy the forces of allied states in their territories of origin for second-line duties such as providing garrisons, the exhaustion of the imperial army's own units, combined with the ever-increasing scale of Napoleon's campaigns, resulted in steady augmentations of the representation of allied forces among those participating in offensive campaigns on the Empire's frontiers. In 1805 allied troops constituted 15.3 percent of the Grande armée, a figure that grew by 1809 to 28.3 percent. Yet the full weight of the contributions of client states to Napoleon's campaigns did not become evident until 1812, when a staggering 47.5 percent of the soldiers with whom Napoleon invaded Russia served under the flags of foreign states allied to France.[24] As noted below, these forces became a liability when French defeats prompted many client states to defect from the Napoleonic axis during the final years of the Empire, but their centrality to imperial military operations for most of the period was nonetheless clear.

The German states, which remained nominally independent of France apart from those in the Rhineland and northern Germany that the French annexed, provided the bulk of the allied forces upon which Napoleon relied. In the final days of the Consulate, the electorate of Hanover, which was under French occupation, raised a legion for French service, and German principalities in Westphalia supplied a regiment to Napoleon in 1806.[25] The Confederation of the Rhine also raised a number of troops, which it pressed into Napoleon's service, after its establishment in 1806 as a protectorate of the French Empire. Similarly, the Rhineland duchy of Berg, which was ruled by Napoleon's marshal Jérôme Murat and later by his nephew Napoléon-Louis Bonaparte, furnished a cavalry regiment that served as part of the Napoleonic Imperial Guard.[26]

The Empire also drew heavily on allied governments in Switzerland to bolster its armies. The Swiss cantons, which Bonaparte's Act of Mediation had reestablished in 1803, following the dissolution of the Helvetic Republic, were bound by an agreement of September 27 of that year to supply France with four regiments totaling 16,000 troops.[27] These units, which the cantons began raising only in 1805, inherited the remnants of the Swiss demi-brigades that the Helvetic Republic had levied for France in 1798.[28] Like the Swiss regiments of the Old Regime, those that served the Empire were subject to a capitulation that guaranteed them certain privileges, including exemption from deployment overseas (and thus from the onerous fate that had befallen some of their predecessors in the Swiss demi-brigades that served in the Caribbean under the Consulate), freedom of religion for their personnel, and autonomy from French legal jurisdiction.[29] In contrast to their predecessors of the prerevolutionary era, however, Napoleon's Swiss regiments did not enjoy exemptions from having to fight against other Swiss troops, as indeed they found themselves doing during the rebellion against Napoleonic rule in Spain, where Swiss soldiers fought for France's enemies.[30]

Also unlike the Old Regime monarchy, Napoleon enjoyed no more success recruiting troops for the Swiss regiments than the Directory had experienced after levying the Swiss demi-brigades several years earlier. Swiss officers blamed the dearth of volunteers on the insufficient enlistment bonuses the French government offered and a lack of recruiters with connections to influential local figures in Switzerland.[31] Napoleon, however, placed fault in the hands of the Swiss governments. In late 1806 he

warned that he would interpret their continued failure to produce accept-
able numbers of recruits as a sign of "poor disposition on the part of the
cantons."[32] Such attempts at intimidation produced few results, however.
Despite the enrollment of Swiss prisoners of war to augment the ranks of
the Swiss regiments, difficulties meeting their recruitment quotas persisted until at least 1810.[33]

The chronic problems that the Swiss regiments faced under the Empire
had a predictably deleterious effect on the tradition of Franco-Swiss military cooperation that stretched back centuries. A new capitulation for the
Swiss regiments that the French signed with the cantons on March 8, 1812,
imposed harsh terms on the Swiss states, requiring them to replace deserters from the units at their own expense and to call up additional troops
to serve France upon demand. It also prohibited them from entering into
agreements to furnish troops to any power besides France, a practice in
which they had traditionally engaged for hundreds of years.[34] Although
Swiss soldiers continued to fight on behalf of France until the final days of
the Empire and beyond, with around 90,000 serving under Napoleon in
total, the terms of their service were never again comparable to those that
had governed the Swiss regiments of the Old Regime. Nor did the Swiss
units of the nineteenth century enjoy the privileges or prestige that had
distinguished their predecessors.[35]

Black Troops

While troops from client states in Switzerland and Germany supplied a
majority of the allied units that served in Napoleon's campaigns, the kingdom of Naples provided one of the most significant corps from a political
and symbolic perspective in the form of the Royal African Regiment. This
unit, composed mostly of men of African descent who had emigrated from
France's Caribbean colonies to the metropole, was the indirect successor
to the Legion of the Americans that had served in the French revolutionary army. The paths that led its black soldiers to Europe varied; many had
served in French forces in colonial territories before being deported by
French authorities seeking to disarm the population there; some had fled
the colonies voluntarily to escape British conquest and the reintroduction
of slavery that they feared would follow; some were servants who had
followed white planters to Europe; others were "collaborators" who had
worked with the French in the colonies and sought to escape reprisals from
other blacks when French forces retreated during slave uprisings; and still
others were soldiers who had served in French units in the Caribbean until
the British captured them and transported them to France. In total, 1,950
men, women, and children whom contemporary documents categorized

as "colored" emigrated to France between 1791 and 1803, providing a pool of recruits for the Royal African Regiment.[36]

The regiment traced its direct lineage to 1798, the year in which the French government began forming some of the black refugees in France into companies of laborers and employing them in works projects in the interior of the country.[37] Serving under the command of whites and far removed from any combat role, these companies had more in common with penal corps than with the units in which blacks had served in France and the Caribbean earlier in the Revolution. Their situation changed little after the government raised a new unit for black refugees, the Battalion of African Marksmen, in January 1803 that was ostensibly part of the regular army.[38] Indeed, even the corps's title was tantamount to an epithet, since the adjective "African" recalled the servile and uncivilized origins that contemporaries attributed to black soldiers—who, in many cases, were not even natives of Africa, but rather of the New World.[39] The government abandoned the term in May 1803 when it reorganized the Battalion of African Marksmen, along with other companies of black soldiers in existence at the time, into a new corps called the Battalion of Black Pioneers. This unit assumed an active combat role in French campaigns in Italy.[40]

The Black Pioneers battalion belonged to the imperial army until August 1806, when Napoleon transferred it to the service of the kingdom of Naples, a client state on whose throne he had installed his brother, Joseph Bonaparte, earlier that year.[41] Although nominally part of the Neapolitan military after this date, the corps, which Neapolitan leaders rechristened the Royal African Regiment, continued to maintain recruitment depots throughout France.[42] It drew most of its personnel from among groups of refugees from the New World, but at least some natives of Africa were present as well.[43] Ultimately, however, recruits for the regiment proved to be in short supply, even after the police ministry performed a census in 1807 of all blacks residing within the Empire for the purpose of assisting in the unit's recruitment.[44]

If French officials were eager to fill the ranks of the Royal African Regiment, however, it was not because they shared the emancipatory sentiments of their predecessors from the revolutionary era, when abolitionists and blacks themselves had used military service to reinforce blacks' claims to French citizenship. On the contrary, racial prejudice plagued the unit throughout its history. In contrast to the Legion of the Americans, the Legion of Equality and other units that existed during the revolutionary decade in which blacks, in theory and sometimes in practice, enjoyed the same access to promotion as whites, the commanding officers of the Battalion of Black Pioneers and the Royal African Regiment were mostly white.[45] This racial hierarchy within the unit represented a microcosm of the new society that the French state sought to construct in the colonies during this period, when it reintroduced slavery and deemed the submission of blacks to whites vital to the restoration of order in the postrevolutionary Caribbean.[46] Some blacks did hold commissions in the regiment as officers or sub-officers, but the whites serving alongside them sought their removal on the pretense that they lacked the education necessary to maintain regimental records properly.[47] In a similar vein, the French general François Muller demanded the retirement of the black officers in the unit, complaining that "the mixing of white and black officers . . . in a single corps poses serious problems."[48] More prejudicial still was the attitude of the military governor of Brest, who suggested in 1807 that the Royal African Regiment should serve only as a dumping ground for blacks who had managed to enlist in other units of the imperial army, since "one can desire nothing other than to see France purged of these races of color."[49]

In the event, blacks became a minority in the Royal African Regiment beginning in December 1810, when Joachim Murat, who had replaced Joseph Bonaparte as king of Naples upon the former's accession to the throne of Spain in 1808, reorganized the corps as a regular line regiment of the Neapolitan army and permitted the enlistment of white Neapolitans and foreigners.[50] He subsequently dispatched the regiment to serve with the Grande armée, where Napoleon's final campaigns decimated its ranks. The unit officially ceased to exist in early 1814.[51] Its legacy proved ephemeral, to the point that even relatively recent scholarship has questioned the unit's very existence.[52]

Black soldiers and officers serving in other units of the imperial army fared little better than those in the Royal African Regiment. A group of nine black officers who had commanded troops in the colonies before authorities there deported them to France received commissions in the Expeditionary Legion, which military authorities later rescinded. This broken promise proceeded despite the proclamations of certain of the officers of their "zeal for the *patrie*" and affirmations of the great personal sacrifices they had endured "in order to make themselves useful to the Republic" while fighting in the Caribbean.[53] Similarly, in 1815 French commissioners turned away black troops seeking to enroll in a colonial regiment composed mostly of Spanish and Portuguese troops, ostensibly because they were not natives of Iberia, but more probably because of their race.[54]

To be sure, in some cases black and mulatto troops were able to enlist without issue in various units of the army. As chapter 5 noted, for example, Auguste Lachaise, a native of Louisiana who was of mixed African and European ancestry, served as an officer in the Expeditionary Legion, and Jean Malouin, a mulatto from Saint-Domingue who had apparently fled to Cuba during the Revolution, enrolled around 1804 as a regular soldier in the Fifth Light Infantry Regiment, where most other soldiers were white.[55] Moyse Soubrette, who began his military career in 1785 in a militia unit in Martinique and served continuously through at least 1806, was also able to accede to an officer's rank despite being black, as was Etienne Noël Delor, a native of Saint-Domingue who rose through the ranks to become a sous-lieutenant in the Mameluke Company of the Imperial Guard.[56] These men, however, were exceptions at a time when Napoleon's rolling back of the revolutionaries' liberation of blacks and reintroduction of slavery to the French colonies meant that the service of black troops in the army, and the principles of racial equality and commitment to France that it demonstrated, no longer converged with the agenda of the state.

The marginalization of black troops in the Napoleonic army notwithstanding, advocates of emancipation continued to seize on the military service of blacks to reinforce arguments for racial equality. In a treatise published in 1808 that highlighted the cultural and intellectual contributions of people of African descent to France, the abbé Henri Grégoire enumerated the services of blacks in the French army during the 1790s, when "incorporated among French troops, they shared their dangers and glories."[57] To drive home the importance of blacks' military contributions, Grégoire cited a sixteenth-century Portuguese historian who claimed that soldiers of African descent were preferable even to elite Swiss troops, suggesting surreptitiously that they might be a replacement for the once-hallowed Swiss regiments that the French regimes of Grégoire's day had proven chronically unable to resurrect.[58] Yet it was telling that Grégoire did not mention the corps of black troops serving the kingdom of Naples at the time he was writing his treatise, implying that the prejudices to which the Battalion of Black Pioneers and the Royal African Regiment had been subject undercut the conceptual link between military service and racial equality that he sought to develop. Unfortunately, advocates of emancipation under the Napoleonic Empire could look only to France's past, not its present, to find examples of blacks whose participation in the army had reinforced their integration as full citizens of French society.

Foreign Regiments and Legions

In addition to the units imperial officials levied in France's newest departments and the troops that client states supplied, Napoleon raised an array of foreign regiments, battalions, and legions to enroll foreigners directly into the imperial army. Although these corps recalled the foreign regiments of the Old Regime in some superficial respects, they never enjoyed the political and military significance, prestige, or autonomy of their pre-revolutionary predecessors. They instead exemplified the novel contingencies that characterized foreign recruitment in the era of the Empire, illuminating the permanent reconfigurations of military service, as well as the French national community, that had emerged out of the revolutionary era.

FIRST, SECOND, AND FOURTH FOREIGN REGIMENTS

The first foreign regiments to officially gain titles as such under the Empire appeared in 1805, when Napoleon levied the regiments of La Tour d'Auvergne and Isembourg. These units, which military administrators later rechristened the First and Second Foreign Regiments, respectively, recruited troops along France's eastern frontier.[59] As the first corps to exist in France since 1792 for the express purpose of enlisting foreigners for the line army, these foreign regiments recalled those of the Old Regime to a certain extent, but they differed in several important respects. For one, instead of enjoying special privileges, they were subject to the same regulations, discipline, internal organization, pay, and dress code as other units of the imperial army. They also did not restrict their recruitment activities, either in principle or in practice, to any single group of foreigners, but instead received authorization to enlist men of any nationality so long as they were not French.[60] As a result, the officers of the units represented an agglomeration of different countries; a large proportion came from the German states and Austria, but many officers from Italy, Ireland, Spain, and Poland were present as well.[61] Former French émigrés also enlisted as officers.[62] Meanwhile, the rank-and-file of the foreign regiments was yet more diverse, with the Isembourg Regiment counting thirteen different nationalities (including a sizable number of French natives, the prohibition against recruiting French subjects for the foreign regiments notwithstanding) among its soldiers in 1813.[63] Both of these regiments remained in service until 1815.[64]

The successful formation of the first two foreign regiments in 1805 encouraged the creation of a third, the Regiment of Prussia (later the Fourth Foreign Regiment), in November 1806.[65] Germans accounted for the bulk of its personnel, but a handful of its officers were natives of Poland, Sweden, and Britain.[66] By the later years of the Empire, many French officers were serving in the regiment as well, despite explicit orders from the war ministry in 1807 that the corps was not to enroll any French subjects.[67] Its soldiers, like those of the First and Second Foreign Regiments, represented a diverse array of nationalities, including a number of French subjects from territories in Germany that France had annexed.[68] In November 1813, in the midst of Napoleon's rush to disarm foreign soldiers, he dissolved the Fourth Foreign Regiment and incorporated its personnel into other corps or detained them as prisoners of war.[69]

IRISH LEGION

In addition to the three regiments that appeared in 1805 and 1806, a fourth foreign corps existed in the form of the Irish Legion, which later became known as the Irish Regiment and finally the Third Foreign Regiment.[70] The French levied the corps on August 31, 1803, in anticipation of invading the British Isles. The government's high hopes that the Irish Legion would prove vital to a campaign in Britain or Ireland were such that the corps's existence remained a secret within the war ministry until the end of 1803. Unlike Napoleon's other foreign regiments, which recruited soldiers of all nationalities, the Irish Legion officially enlisted only Irish natives or their sons, and received special permission to recruit Irishmen already serving in other units of the army.[71]

Despite the enthusiasm with which French military authorities created the Irish legion, difficulties and intrigues plagued it for much of its history. Although volunteers for the officer posts in the unit were readily available, many were underqualified at best. A number of them had fought as insurgents in Ireland during the rebellion of 1798, and a handful had served in the Irish battalion that comprised part of the Legion of the Franks of the North several years earlier. For the most part, however, few of the officers in the legion had serious military experience or ambitions to serve for a long period in Napoleon's army.[72] Most were simply political refugees from Ireland who hoped the unit would prove to be a stepping-stone for returning to their native island and advancing non-military careers.[73] In addition, while many of the Irish officers expressed a strong desire to fight against the British and serve the cause of Irish independence, several were reluctant to swear the requisite oath of loyalty to the Empire and Napoleon that the law required of soldiers in the imperial armies.[74] One, a captain named Markey, went so far as to declare "that if an Angel were to descend from the heavens, and that Angel were not Irish, [I] would take no orders from him."[75]

Political infighting between the Irish officers of the unit added to the problems it faced, prompting French authorities to appoint an Italian, Antoine Petrezzoli, as its commander. This native of Parma had little success, however, in either stemming rivalries between officers or raising the corps's morale, which plummeted when it became clear by 1805 that no invasion of Ireland was materializing and the unit suffered a monotonous existence garrisoning the Breton village of Morlaix.[76] A sous-lieutenant summarized these sentiments when he complained in a letter of resignation from the corps in September 1805, "In the time I have spent with the Legion, I have been mortified over the organization which renders it incapable of serving either the French government or the people of Ireland."[77]

Morale deteriorated further when the war ministry began enrolling prisoners of war of various nationalities as soldiers in the legion, which had not acquired enough volunteers of Irish origin to fill its ranks.[78] The new enlistees included not only Irish natives but also prisoners from Scotland and England, many of whom apparently enrolled under the false pretense of being from Ireland or the United States.[79] The presence of English subjects proved particularly objectionable for Irish nationalists in the legion and prompted the war minister in 1810 to order the removal of all of its Scottish and English troops.[80] Meanwhile, about 1,200 prisoners from central Europe, most of them Poles captured while serving in the Prussian army, joined the legion in 1806.[81]

After these enrollments had augmented its ranks, the Irish corps left western France in late 1806 to serve in the rear of the Grande armée in Germany. Some of the unit's officers, who had grown weary of the tedium of garrison duty, welcomed this change, but it prompted the resignation of several others who objected to continuing to serve a cause that had no connection to the liberation of Ireland. As one lieutenant wrote:

> When I received from Your Excellence a commission in the Irish Legion, that Corps seemed to be particularly destined to serve against the English, and I only took up arms to contribute to the crushing of that tyrant of my country. Unfortunately, events have postponed that expedition . . . Now that it is the intention of His Majesty the Emperor to employ the Irish Corps in the continental war, I request that Your Excellence grant me permission to retire from a service that is foreign to me, and to permit me to reside in Paris where I will resume my first occupation, that of working for the liberation of Ireland.[82]

By 1812 so many Irish officers had resigned from the Irish corps or requested transfer to other units that only half of those who remained were of Irish descent. Among the rest, sixty-four percent were French, thirty percent German, one was from Poland and another from Austria.[83] After sending detachments to fight in the Low Countries and Spain, the Irish Regiment suffered heavy losses in 1813 while serving in Napoleon's campaign in eastern Europe.[84] It was probably only due to the patronage of the war minister, Henri-Jacques-Guillaume Clarke, duc de Feltre, who descended from an Irish Jacobite family that had fled to France under the Old Regime and who demonstrated a special attachment to the Irish unit, that military commissioners did not dissolve the legion altogether in the wake of the 1813 campaign. Instead, it existed until September 1815, when Louis XVIII finally abolished it.[85]

IBERIAN LEGIONS AND REGIMENTS

While the decline of the Irish Legion brought the centuries-long tradition of Irish military service in France to an unceremonious conclusion, the Napoleonic army made up for the loss by enlisting large numbers of men from the Iberian peninsula, a region that had traditionally supplied very few recruits to France. The most prominent corps in which these men served was the Portuguese Legion, which originated from the remnants of the Portuguese forces that Napoleon integrated into the imperial army after his subordinate, Jean-Ardoche Junot, overran Portugal in 1807. In his instructions on reorganizing the newly conquered territory (which the French occupied but never annexed), Napoleon instructed Junot to march between 5,000 and 6,000 veteran Portuguese troops to France and order them to swear loyalty to the Empire and emperor.[86] Napoleon intended for these troops to serve the dual purpose of contributing manpower to the French army while also allowing French authorities in Portugal to "get rid of a lot of men" who might otherwise violently resist French rule.[87] In this way, the admission of a Portuguese contingent into the imperial army not only introduced a new nationality to its ranks, but also reflected a novel strategy on the part of Napoleon for recruiting foreign troops as a means of helping to pacify regions that had recently come under French control.[88]

In May 1808, Napoleon formed the Portuguese Legion from six of the Portuguese regiments, which totaled 3,600 soldiers, that Junot had dispatched to France.[89] He also attempted to deploy recruiters to Portugal to acquire additional volunteers for the unit. The uncertain political and military situation there, however, rendered recruitment difficult and prompted French authorities instead to augment the ranks of the legion with Spanish-speaking Germans who had fought in the Peninsular War, as well as Spanish prisoners of war.[90] The legion served in several of the major campaigns of the Grande armée in central and eastern Europe until February 8, 1813, when Napoleon, bitterly disillusioned by the nationalist uprisings in the Iberian peninsula, informed the war minister that "I no longer want to recruit the Portuguese; I want none of these troops," and dissolved the legion. French authorities briefly reorganized its personnel into a new unit called the Portuguese Regiment, but soon afterward they disarmed the men and rounded them up as prisoners of war as part of the purges of foreigners from the imperial army that occurred in late 1813.[91]

Napoleon's dual interests in obtaining manpower for his armies and mitigating the ability of foreign peoples to resist his rule also led to the recruitment for the first time in French history of large contingents of Spanish troops. Evoking the Second Treaty of San Ildefonso of 1796, by which Spain and France had established a defensive alliance, French diplomats in 1806 demanded 14,000 troops from the Spanish crown. They sought these soldiers to augment French forces in central Europe, as well as to reduce the military resources at the disposal of the Spanish government, whose loyalties to the French Empire were in doubt.[92] Once under French control, these Spanish troops first formed a unit known as the Corps of the Romana. After many of that corps's personnel mutinied and deserted to the British camp, however, French officials dissolved it in 1808, disarmed the troops who remained and sorted them into prisoner of war depots in France.[93]

Still hungry for soldiers, Napoleon was unwilling to leave Spanish manpower untapped. In February 1809 he formed a new Spanish corps, composed largely of Spanish prisoners from the camps in France, that he named the Regiment of Joseph-Napoléon, in honor of his brother, whom he had made king of Spain in 1808. Although Napoleon initially planned for this unit to serve as part of the allied army of Spain, the Joseph-Napoléon Regiment instead joined the Grande armée in central Europe, at the behest of officers who feared that massive desertion would ensue if the Spanish soldiers returned to Iberia.[94]

This assignment disillusioned the Spaniards in the corps, many of whom had exhibited little enthusiasm for serving the French in the first place. As a report from the war ministry warned, the soldiers feared being "expatriated in an irrevocable manner." It continued, "If they believe that the new regiment will remain in the service of France, like the Regiment of Prussia, the Irish Legion and others, they will have an extreme repugnance" to serve.[95] From a practical perspective, it is likely that the Spanish soldiers' objections to fighting outside of Spain stemmed more from their desire to return as quickly as possible to their native country, where they could be closer to their homes and operate among a population that spoke their language, than from a principled preference to fight for the client state established under Joseph Bonaparte rather than for the Empire itself. In any case, the regiment's nominal association with the king of Spain notwithstanding, the corps served only in central and eastern Europe until Napoleon dissolved it in 1813.[96]

POLISH TROOPS

Like the Spanish troops, many of the Poles who served in the armies of the Napoleonic Empire were wary of fighting far from home for a cause that rarely seemed to be their own. Nonetheless, one contemporary estimated in 1810 that there were between 15,000 and 20,000 Polish troops in French service at the time.[97] Many of these men were scattered across the various foreign units of the imperial army, but two explicitly Polish units existed as well. Known as the First and Second Legions of the Vistula, they were levied by Napoleon in 1807 and 1809, respectively. They comprised part of the remnants of the Polish corps that had served under the Directory and Consulate.[98] In addition, several other Polish regiments and companies entered French service under the Empire, some as part of the elite troops of Napoleon's Imperial Guard and others after the client state of the Duchy of Warsaw could no longer retain them within its own forces.[99]

Other Foreign Corps

In addition to the foreign regiments and legions, a number of other assorted foreign units served under the Empire. These included the First, Second, and Third Foreign Battalions, which the French levied between 1802 and 1809.[100] Napoleon's officers also recruited foreigners for the Regiment of White Pioneers, a unit he raised in February 1806 to perform duties in the interior of France. In 1810 Napoleon dissolved this regiment, most of whose personnel were unarmed, to create five new companies of Foreign Pioneer Volunteers. He intended these units to recruit Austrian prisoners of war, but in practice they enlisted men of a wide range of nationalities, including French subjects, whose enrollment the war ministry sanctioned in March 1806.[101] Other noncombat units of foreigners appeared in February 1811, when Napoleon raised thirty-eight battalions of Spanish prisoners of war for the construction of fortifications and public-works projects.[102] A small number of Spaniards also enlisted in a pioneer company that military commissioners created in 1811 for receiving soldiers from the Regiment of Joseph-Napoléon whom they deemed unfit for combat duty.[103] Finally, an array of "veteran" companies existed for recruiting soldiers of various foreign nationalities who had retired from active military duty but who could still be useful to the Empire by serving in garrisons or performing other light duties.[104] Napoleon's interest in keeping these foreigners in the service of the Empire even when they were no longer physically fit to fight in his campaigns underlined the importance he assigned to foreign troops as a vital supplement to the demographic resources of France.

Policies on Foreign Troops under the Empire

The array of foreign regiments, legions, battalions, and independent companies in the service of the Empire made clear the readiness with which the Napoleonic regime, in contrast to the governments that had ruled France during most of the 1790s, accepted foreigners into the army. To interpret the Napoleonic period in this regard as a return to the practices of the Old Regime, however, would be to overlook the important differences that distinguished Napoleonic practices from those of the prerevolutionary era with regard to recruitment, military organization, and the integration of foreign troops into French society. While the Old Regime monarchy had extended a litany of special privileges to foreign soldiers and officers, incorporated them into the core of the French army, and treated them in many respects no differently from French natives, the Napoleonic state rarely recognized foreign troops as anything more than a stock of manpower for a regime engaged in near-constant warfare.

One of the signal distinctions between the foreign troops of Napoleonic France and those of the Old Regime was the way the French recruited them. The recruitment patterns of the prerevolutionary period, as chapter 1 noted, had already largely broken down by the eve of the Revolution. The dearth of foreign enlistment in France during most of the revolutionary decade, however, combined with the diplomatic and political reconfiguration of Europe that resulted from the revolutionary wars, meant that traditional strategies for enrolling foreign volunteers in French service had grown almost completely ineffective by the time Napoleon acceded to power. A handful of foreign volunteers still traveled to France to enlist of their own accord, while others, such as the German Karl Schehl, who declared that he "owed his existence to the French Revolution," enthusiastically enrolled alongside French troops occupying their native territories.[105] The number of foreigners whom imperial forces acquired by these means, however, came nowhere close to matching the thousands of foreign soldiers and officers who had volunteered for French republican armies during the Revolution.[106] The other major paths by which foreign recruits had traditionally come to France had also ceased to function by the early nineteenth century. Irish officers no longer covertly traveled to Ireland to enlist local men, who in any case had considerably less incentive to join Continental armies after the British government's passage of the Catholic Relief bills starting in 1778 relaxed the repression of Catholics in Ireland.[107] In addition, French annexation of parts of Germany, combined with Napoleon's consolidation of the remaining German states into the Confederation of the Rhine, dispensed with the petty German princes who might otherwise have been willing to establish recruitment conventions with the French, as they had in earlier decades. And in Switzerland, as this chapter already noted, where the reciprocity of the Old Regime capitulations was a thing of the past, recruitment for the Empire proceeded only with the aid of substantial French coercion.

In a few instances, French recruiters still attempted, as they had prior to the Revolution, to run recruitment operations across the Empire's border, with or without the consent of local foreign governments.[108] Such efforts bore increasingly little fruit, however, as opposition to Napoleon's regime mounted. As the colonel of the First Foreign Regiment lamented in 1807, "no longer having possessions in Germany, and with the German princes themselves arming everyone in their states," imperial authorities found recruits from across the border to be in short supply.[109] The colonel of the Second Foreign Regiment similarly pointed to anti-French sentiment among the German population as a severe hindrance for French recruiters when he reported in 1813 that enlistments of volunteers from Germany had become "almost null" because "the officers who were recruiting on the other side of the Rhine have been obliged to return as a result of popular riots" against the French.[110] If recruiters for the foreign regiments were wary of braving hostile civilians, however, they were not averse to attempting to steal recruits from one another "through violence or trickery," a practice that contributed to disorganization and poor morale within the foreign contingent of the army.[111]

Given the variety of obstacles that impeded the recruitment of soldiers abroad, Napoleonic officials increasingly took recourse to the expedient of filling the ranks of foreign units with troops they had captured from enemy armies. Prisoners of war were in abundant supply, and in at least some cases they willingly enlisted in the Empire's service as an alternative to languishing in prisoner camps. The enrollment of English and Scottish prisoners in the Irish Legion has been noted above, and groups of Austrian prisoners began enlisting in the First Foreign Regiment at least as early as 1806.[112] In November 1809 the war ministry expanded on this practice by authorizing each of the four foreign regiments to dispatch recruiters to Strasbourg "for the purpose of enrolling as many foreigners as they can from the columns of Austrian prisoners of war who pass by."[113] In some cases recruiters enlisted foreigners under detention in France even if they had not served previously in enemy armies; thus authorities impressed Pierre Vonzaiser, a native of Austria whom they arrested for lacking personal identity documents, into service in the Second Foreign Regiment in 1812 because of his "age of eighteen years and strong constitution."[114] The French navy, for its part, enrolled sailors captured from enemy fleets.[115] Although in some instances the French officers responsible for enlisting prisoners claimed to be pleased with the soldiers they acquired in this manner, the recruits themselves tended to express a predictable eagerness to return home rather than serve in the imperial army.[116]

Despite the wariness of many foreign recruits toward enlisting in imperial armies, evidence shows that some of those who served the Empire later retired in France with pensions comparable to those received by French veterans.[117] In contrast to the Old Regime, however, French officials under Napoleon rarely looked approvingly upon this practice. In several cases, authorities preferred forcing foreign men whom they no longer considered physically fit for service to remain in the army instead of permitting them to retire in France.[118] By 1813, the war ministry systematically denied pensions to foreigners from states with which France was at war, with the objective of preventing them from using retirement from the imperial army as a pretext for returning to their countries of origin and reenlisting in enemy forces.[119] Without a doubt, such practices reflected Napoleonic officials' concern with keeping as many soldiers at their own disposal, and out of the hands of their adversaries, as possible. As the discussion below of the treatment of many foreign soldiers and officers in the final days of the Napoleonic regime indicates, however, the reluctance to allow foreign veterans of the imperial army to remain in the Empire after they had ceased to serve as soldiers also reflected the unwillingness of the state to accept such men permanently into the French population. This trend diverged sharply from the practices of the Old Regime and revealed the extent to which Napoleon shared the revolutionaries' reluctance to integrate foreigners into the national community, regardless of their fidelity to the state.

Napoleonic authorities also echoed the sentiments of the revolutionary decade, and broke with those of the Old Regime, by expressing little esteem for the foreign corps in general. Imperial commanders almost never celebrated the foreign units as symbols of the state's prestige or diplomatic clout. Apart from the "Mamelukes" of the Imperial Guard, which helped to exoticize the regime and served as reminders of Bonaparte's glorious victories in the Middle East, most foreign units were dismissed by Napoleonic officials as marginal components of the army that could be useful only when subject to strict supervision by French natives. For this reason, several of the colonels of the four foreign line regiments were French. Imperial officials also ordered that "all the officers and half of the non-commissioned officers" in the three foreign battalions should be French natives, even though the same regulations prohibited the recruitment of French subjects as ordinary soldiers for those units.[120] While a few foreign officers managed to enlist in the battalions, the vast majority of the men in command were indeed French.[121] This arrangement would have pleased critics of the foreign regiments during the Revolution, who, as chapter 2 noted, advocated for the amalgamation of French citizens into the foreign corps in order to ensure that the foreigners were subject to proper supervision.[122]

The trend of placing French officers at the heads of foreign corps reflected doubts over the loyalty and enthusiasm of the foreign troops. One inspector of the First Foreign Battalion wrote in 1808 that the troops displayed a "good attitude," but concluded nonetheless that, since the unit was composed of foreigners, "a national spirit [*esprit national*] cannot exist in this corps."[123] This lack of faith in the imperial loyalty of foreign soldiers stemmed not only from the presumption that foreigners could not experience patriotic feelings to the same extent as French natives, but also from the amalgamation of men of so many different nationalities within the foreign units, which seemed to hinder their development as effective soldiers. General Charles-Antoine Morand lamented that because the Second Foreign Battalion was "composed of deserters from all the nations, severe surveillance and discipline are the only means of maintaining order and subordination" in the unit.[124] Even during the Hundred Days, as Napoleonic officials scrambled to reorganize the army, they turned away foreigners of certain nationalities because officers feared that enlisting them alongside foreigners from other countries "would be detrimental to the organization of the corps."[125] Such concerns were not without merit. Foreigners themselves sometimes objected vociferously to serving in foreign units alongside men of different national origins.[126]

National Diversity and Its Discontents in the Napoleonic Army

While the extraordinary diversity of nationalities present within the foreign regiments created a problem for imperial military officials, it also reflected another important distinction between the foreign corps of the Old Regime and those of Napoleon's armies. During most of the eighteenth century, the French army had drawn the bulk of its foreign recruits from a handful of particular groups, particularly the Swiss, Germans, and Irish. Small contingents of troops from more distant locations, such as the black cavaliers of the Volontaires de Saxe Regiment of the Old Regime and the Maltese, Greek, and Egyptian troops who served in the Middle East campaign, occasionally enlisted as well, but for the most part they were extraordinary cases. By the time of the Empire, however, large numbers of men from nearly every corner of Europe were serving under Napoleon's standards. These included the troops of the Portuguese, Spanish, and Polish regiments and legions, in addition to many Russians and even Greeks.[127] Turks and Hungarians were present in appreciable numbers as well.[128] This diversity stemmed in large part from the expansiveness of the Napoleonic wars, when campaigns to the peripheries of the Continent became common and the French army's need for soldiers was greater than ever. Yet the multiplicity of nationalities that became the norm in Napoleon's foreign regiments also meant that the army under the First Empire functioned as a social institution able to amalgamate men of diverse national, linguistic, and cultural origins on a scale that exceeded that of its Old Regime predecessor.

This national heterogeneity posed practical problems for commanding foreign troops, especially because of differences of language. Like the Old Regime monarchs, and in contrast to the Jacobin revolutionaries, Napoleon expressed little concern with linguistic diversity among his subjects or soldiers. He reportedly declared that Alsatian troops were free to "speak German as long as they wield their swords in French."[129] Within the foreign regiments, however, the task of ensuring that men of different nationalities could communicate with one another and with their imperial superiors represented a persistent challenge that Napoleonic officials never fully resolved. For the most part, their strategy for mitigating the problem of linguistic heterogeneity centered on assigning multilingual officers, usually of French origin, to command the foreign corps. Thus a sous-lieutenant named Joseph became adjutant major in the Second Foreign Battalion in 1808 because he "can explain the drill in German, French and Italian, a valuable thing for a unit where there are men from all the nations, and many Germans in particular."[130] A French soldier named Chesnard received a similar recommendation for the position of adjutant major in the First Foreign Regiment in 1809 because he had served previously in Germany and spoke German fluently. One of his colleagues became a sous-lieutenant in the same regiment because he had "completed his studies in Strasbourg, where he learned at the same time to speak and write with ease in German."[131]

While the appointment of multilingual officers to the foreign corps undoubtedly helped to overcome language barriers to an extent, they hardly eradicated them. A reviewer of the Second Foreign Battalion reported in 1805 that although "there exists in this corps several educated and distinguished [French] officers, many do not know at all how to speak the language" of the foreigners they commanded.[132] Several years later, a French general warned the war ministry that the First Foreign Battalion was in desperate need of officers who understood German, since they represented "the only means of determining the spirit of these troops and of commanding them."[133] Meanwhile, among the fifty-five Irish officers in the Irish Legion, only forty-five could read and write in French, and doubtless fewer spoke the languages of the Poles and other prisoners of war from central Europe who enrolled in the unit.[134] The limited polyglot talents among these officers were perhaps to their advantage, however, since under the Napoleonic regime foreigners who spoke too many languages could be subject to suspicion. This was the case for a captain in the Regiment of Prussia named Kalkhauser, whose comrades denounced him as a spy for the British because, although he claimed to have been a Habsburg aristocrat and formerly served the Austrian monarchy, "he speaks all the languages and no one is sure of his origins." The war ministry relieved him of his post because of doubts over his true background.[135]

The Army as Repatriation Service

If the Napoleonic regime was eager to purge the army of men such as Kalkhauser whose loyalties to the Empire it deemed uncertain, it also faced the challenge of reintegrating into the army soldiers of both French and foreign origin who had served in France previously, but had left during the Revolution and returned under the Empire. The reasons for which these men had departed France varied; some were émigrés who had fled abroad for political reasons, others were simple deserters from the French army, and a significant number had enrolled in foreign armies after enemy forces captured them. Whatever the particulars of their experiences, their integration into the Napoleonic army became a priority of the state not only because of their usefulness as veteran soldiers, but also as a component of the project of national reconciliation that the Napoleonic regime pursued as it sought permanent closure to the upheavals of the revolutionary decade.

The number of foreign soldiers who had left France during the Revolution and returned under the Empire was relatively small, but those who did so included many skilled veterans. One, Henri Dillon, had been an officer in the Irish regiment of his name until 1791, when he allegedly attempted to embezzle the unit's funds following the National Assembly's order to nationalize the regiment. He then left France and entered British service. He returned to France around 1806, when he claimed to be a devoted subject of Napoleon and, despite his birth in London, affirmed "the pride that I have taken in being French."[136] Once back in France he sought a post in the Irish Legion, although he ultimately declined the commission of captain that the war ministry offered to him because he desired a higher rank.[137] The dissolution of the British army's foreign regiments, which enrolled some foreign soldiers who had served in France under the Old Regime or during the first years of the Revolution and then emigrated, also occasioned the return to France of many foreign troops.[138]

Most foreigners who reentered France to reenlist in the army enrolled in foreign units. These corps served as well, however, as a destination for repatriated officers of French origin, who frequently received appointments to command the foreign corps. Indeed, as one French general wrote, one of the most useful qualities of the foreign regiments was their ability to enroll former French émigrés who, "upon returning to a country where they found neither family nor fortune, had no other resource than that of military service."[139] Meanwhile, although policies generally prohibited French natives from enrolling in the foreign corps as ordinary soldiers (a policy from which French soldiers who had served previously in foreign units were sometimes exempt), these troops received a battalion of their own.[140] In 1802, at the same time that the Consular government created the corps later known as the First and Second Foreign Battalions for enrolling foreign deserters, it levied a unit, which came to be known generally as the Battalion of Repatriated Frenchmen, for the purpose of recruiting these men.[141] The corps functioned as a point of collection for French subjects who had deserted from the French army or whom enemy forces had captured and repatriated to France. It also enrolled French natives who managed to enlist as soldiers in the foreign regiments and subsequently had to leave those units because of their nationality.[142] The personnel of the unit, which military authorities conceived as a kind of penal corps for reintegrating French soldiers whose backgrounds and political loyalties were in many cases dubious, suffered a reputation as the "rubbish and shame of the army . . . incorrigible drunks, thieves, murderers." Nonetheless, the Battalion of Repatriated Frenchmen remained in service until 1814.[143]

In a reflection of the complexities that conditioned military service in an era of shifting borders and unstable definitions of nationality, the Battalion of Repatriated Frenchmen also sought to recruit enemy prisoners of war who, although they had never served in the French army or resided on French territory, were natives of lands that the French had annexed. In this way, these men, as one French general put it, "found themselves repatriated Frenchmen ['se trouvoient français rentrés'] via the reunion of their countries to the French empire."[144] The complex histories of its recruits aside, the Battalion of Repatriated Frenchmen highlighted the role of the army in reshaping into Napoleonic subjects men whose experiences abroad rendered them unready for service in the regular army, but whose birth in France prevented them from serving in the foreign regiments.

While the Battalion of Repatriated Frenchmen served as a symbol of Napoleon's willingness to accept back into the army and society even those soldiers who had returned to France after deserting and, in many cases, bearing arms against the French state, policies on French natives who willingly remained in the service of the enemy were decidedly harsher. A law of April 6, 1809, collectively condemned to death all French subjects who, at any time since September 1804, had enrolled in the forces of powers that were at war with France.[145] In another example of the complexities that resulted from the frequent territorial annexations of the period, the lists of soldiers whom officials proscribed under the terms of the decree included men who were natives of regions that had not been French at the time of their births and who had left prior to French annexation, but whom the Napoleonic regime nonetheless considered French subjects because their places of birth had become part of the Empire.[146] Napoleon granted an amnesty on April 20, 1810, that allowed French subjects serving foreign powers to return to France without punishment, but few men did so.[147] Still, the effort reflected not only the state's interest in augmenting the ranks of its armies, but also the importance of military service as a component of the Napoleonic project for reconstructing French society and integrating back into its ranks those who had rejected France at earlier dates.

Disarming Foreigners

Despite the Napoleonic regime's eagerness during most of its tenure to accept back into the French army soldiers of both French and foreign origin who had served abroad, by the closing years of the Empire the hospitality it extended to foreign troops began evaporating, as Napoleon expressed increasingly little faith in their loyalty to him. This shift culminated in orders from Napoleon in November 1813 to disarm most of the foreigners serving in the army and transfer them to the interior of France. Motivated by military setbacks that cast doubt over the survival of the regime, this decision echoed the initiative the revolutionaries had undertaken two decades earlier when they nationalized or disbanded the foreign regiments they had inherited from the Old Regime, and subsequently decreed the arrest, in theory if not in practice, of most foreigners serving in the army during the Terror. Napoleon, however, went further than his predecessors by not only prohibiting his forces from enlisting any additional foreigners, but also following through quite fully with a policy that resulted in the incarceration of most of the foreign soldiers who had served in his armies over the course of more than a decade.

The disastrous campaign in Russia in 1812, which preceded Napoleon's defeat at Leipzig in October 1813, precipitated the defection of many of the client states that had provided troops to Napoleon's armies, both as part of allied contingents and in the foreign regiments, battalions, and legions of the imperial army itself. Under these circumstances, several high-ranking foreign officers serving the French deserted to the enemy, calling the loyalty of foreign troops as a whole into question.[148] Napoleon summarized the situation plainly when he declared on November 15, 1813, that "we are in a moment where we should not count on any foreigner. That can be nothing but extremely dangerous."[149] Ten days later, an imperial decree consolidated all of the foreign units in French service into three new corps in which only Irish, Polish, Swiss, and Italian troops—all representatives of national groups that retained favorable views toward France—could serve, along with French conscripts who would join the new units to bring them up to strength.[150] Foreign soldiers of all other origins present on soil under French control, including those troops serving in the forces of allied states, received orders to surrender their combat weapons and became prisoners of war in the interior of France.[151] There, French authorities organized most of the foreign veterans into pioneer corps, where they allowed them to wield only pickaxes.[152] Although the decree of November 1813 exempted troops of nationalities deemed friendly to the regime, by early 1814 French officials began disarming certain of these soldiers as well in response to doubts over their loyalty.[153]

The reactions of some foreign troops to these policies mirrored the sentiments of the foreign soldiers and officers during the Revolution who had professed loyalty to France despite the suspicions to which they found themselves subject. One German officer sharply protested the orders that he and his comrades had received to surrender their weapons and reportedly "wailed to find himself considered an enemy of France."[154] Meanwhile, the concentration of foreign troops within pioneer units in the interior of France posed problems for civil authorities, who complained that they were "dangerous to the public peace."[155] Yet Napoleonic officials steadfastly enforced the November 1813 decree on foreign troops until Napoleon's first abdication in April 1814.

Without a doubt, the harsh treatment of foreign soldiers and officers during the final months of Napoleon's first reign resulted in large part from pragmatic concerns regarding the loyalty of these men to the regime at a moment when many foreigners were defecting. The decision to disarm most of the soldiers after the government deemed them unfit, because of their nationalities, for service on the frontier also reflected the army's desperate need for weapons after the campaigns of 1812 and 1813 had starved it of munitions.[156] Yet the fact that Napoleon so emphatically and collectively disarmed foreigners, many of whom had served in imperial armies for a number of years without exhibiting signs of disloyalty to the regime, and made them prisoners of war revealed the survival into the Napoleonic period of the political apprehensions toward foreign troops that had emerged during the Revolution. Like the foreign regiments of the Old Regime, which the revolutionaries dissolved because of anxieties that in many cases had little connection to the foreign troops' actual behavior, the foreign corps of the Empire met a demise that stemmed from a politically determined fear of allowing foreigners to continue to bear arms on behalf of the state, regardless of their actions or professions of loyalty. Napoleon thus finished where the revolutionaries had begun, categorically purging the army of foreigners for the simple reason that their place of birth excluded them from membership in the national community.

The First Restoration and the Hundred Days

As a result of Napoleon's purging of virtually all foreigners from the combat units of his army, the Bourbons found only a minuscule contingent of foreign troops still serving within the regular forces that they inherited upon their first restoration to the throne in April 1814. They issued orders for some of these foreign veterans, specifically those of Polish, Austrian, Dutch, and Belgian origin, to report to specific cities in France in order to rejoin the forces of their nominal sovereigns. The remainder of the troops from the foreign regiments that had served Napoleon amounted to 452 officers and 841 non-commissioned officers and soldiers on active duty in December 1814, well short of the approximately 13,000 troops who were supposed to fill the three foreign regiments that still existed on the eve of Napoleon's first abdication.[157]

Bourbon officials essentially ignored these troops and undertook few real changes to the treatment of foreign soldiers in France during the brief period of the First Restoration. Although they did not abolish the foreign regiments Napoleon had created, they excluded them from plans for the reorganization of the army in December 1814, despite the professions by many foreign officers and soldiers of loyalty to the new regime.[158] The Bourbons used the foreign regiments at this time primarily as a dumping ground for French natives who, after having become prisoners of war in enemy states, returned to France upon the cessation of hostilities.[159]

The Bourbons also created a new foreign regiment of Spanish and Portuguese troops in December 1814 for service in the colonies. This corps constituted an expedient for putting to use Iberians who had served formerly in the Portuguese Legion and the Regiment of Joseph-Napoléon and whom the governments of Spain and Portugal had proscribed because of their services in Napoleon's army, preventing them from returning to their countries of origin.[160] At the same time, Louis XVIII ordered his Belgian soldiers, whose native territory France had ceded upon the collapse of the Empire, to count themselves as foreigners and transfer to foreign regiments.[161] Meanwhile, the foreigners whom Napoleon had disarmed and enrolled in pioneer units in the interior of France received orders to return to their countries of origin. This was a clear indication that the Restoration monarchy had no intention of allowing foreign troops, even the ones Napoleon had deemed disloyal to his regime, to stake claims to French nationality or retire in France, as Old Regime monarchs had done.[162] The only group of foreign soldiers who received favorable treatment after Napoleon's abdication were those in the Swiss regiments. These remained in active service, and in July 1814 the Bourbons took the further step of reviving the Company of the Hundred Swiss, which had not existed since its dissolution early in the Revolution.[163]

These changes did not last long, as Napoleon's return from Elba in the spring of 1815 occasioned yet another reorganization of the foreign contingent of the army. By this time Napoleon, eager for any and all soldiers he could levy as his enemies prepared to march against him once again, exhibited none of the wariness toward the recruitment of foreigners that had characterized the final years of his first reign. Although the Swiss cantons' entry into the new coalition against Napoleon prompted his dissolution of the Swiss regiments shortly after he arrived back in Paris, on April 11, 1815, he levied five new foreign regiments.[164] He also retained the colonial regiment of Spanish and Portuguese troops that the Bourbons had created, reorganizing it as the Sixth Foreign Regiment.[165]

In a sign of Napoleon's awareness of the problems of morale, language, and organization that had impacted the foreign corps that served him previously, he ordered each of the new foreign regiments to enlist troops of a specific nationality, rather than amalgamating foreigners of diverse origins.[166] In addition, he authorized the former Irish Legion to readopt its appellation of "Irish," which it had officially lost during the First Restoration, as well as to wear green uniforms again in place of the blue ones that the Bourbons had imposed on the unit.[167] This generosity toward the Irish soldiers flowed despite the resignation of some of the officers of the former legion on the grounds that they could not serve Napoleon again in good faith. Their betrayal was tempered, however, by other Irish troops who promised after Napoleon's return from Elba that "we Irish patriots will never go to the enemy's camp, to fight against France, our adopted country."[168]

The Irish were not the only group of foreign troops whose loyalties to Napoleon during the Hundred Days proved inconsistent. Some prominent foreign officers, such as the Italian general Pierre-Marie-Barthélemy Férino, readily swore fidelity to the new regime.[169] But others remained committed to the Bourbons, a fact that prompted a half-dozen officers in one of the foreign regiments in late March 1815 to request reappointment to a different unit because "it is impossible for us to live in good harmony with those who have demonstrated a manner of thinking too much in opposition to the government of His Majesty the Emperor."[170] Similarly, a group of 130 foreign soldiers deserted their corps in April 1815 on the grounds that "our officers decided to cast their lots with the King. Nearly all of us have always defended the cause of the Emperor . . . although foreigners (but French by the length of our service) we have attempted . . . to rejoin the battle standards that have led us many times to glory."[171]

Sorting out disputes such as these between supporters and dissidents of the new regime was of secondary importance during the Hundred Days, when Napoleon's greatest military priority was raising as many troops as possible. Toward this end, he appealed enthusiastically to his former soldiers residing beyond France's borders, including those in regions that had been part of the French Empire but returned to the jurisdictions of foreign powers at the time of the First Restoration, to rally once again under his flags.[172] Napoleon's hope that many foreigners would rejoin his cause was such that, when preparing a broadside for distribution along the frontiers of France encouraging troops to enlist, he ordered the printing of up to 15,000 copies in German, 5,000 in Italian, and 4,000 in Flemish, as well as 6,000 in French.[173]

The recruitment of foreigners during the Hundred Days was successful enough for Napoleon to levy two additional foreign regiments in May 1815, bringing the total number of foreign corps in service at the time to eight.[174] Even foreigners who had never before served the emperor responded to his call to cross the border into France and join his army in 1815.[175] Spanish refugees willing to fight for Napoleon, especially officers, were also in ready supply, inspiring Napoleonic officials in the weeks before Waterloo to dispatch recruiters to the Spanish frontier. They hoped in this manner not only to acquire more troops, but also to foment political dissent against Napoleon's enemies in Spain by using the Spanish recruits to "establish and maintain communications with the disaffected peoples of Catalonia, the Bay of Biscay and Aragon."[176]

Ultimately, few of the foreign units that Napoleon levied during the Hundred Days were fit to march for his final campaign. The only foreigners to see action during that time were the Swiss troops of the Second Foreign Regiment, which was decimated during fighting near Wavre that occurred as Napoleon's shattered army retreated following its defeat at the battle of Waterloo on June 18, 1815.[177] Napoleon's abdication four days later brought the period of the Hundred Days to a close, and with it the last concerted effort to rebuild the foreign contingent of the French army.[178]

IN MOST ACCOUNTS, the period between 1789 and 1815 in French history was one of constant breaks: moderate, liberal revolution gave way to the Jacobin Terror, which was followed by the Thermidorian Reaction and later the rise to power of Napoleon, who dismantled the republican institutions his predecessors had painstakingly constructed. With the exception of warfare, few continuities wove these disparate phases of the revolutionary era together. Yet diverse as they were, the various regimes that ruled France during these years shared a common set of political priorities that guided their policies on foreign troops and represented a departure only from the Old Regime.

Like his predecessors in the revolutionary decade, Napoleon found himself constrained by pragmatic realities when forming policies on foreign troops. His decision at the beginning of his reign to reintroduce large-scale foreign recruitment to the army, and to raise a new assortment of foreign units, constituted practical steps toward achieving his ambitious military goals. His ultimate treatment of foreign troops, however, was a signal reflection of the political thinking that had emerged out of the revolutionary decade, when military service had become firmly enveloped within the contours of nationality and citizenship. Napoleon kept most of his foreign recruits out of the regular army, and he eventually rounded them up as prisoners of war amid the explosion of xenophobic paranoia that marked the closing years of the Empire. Military exigency ensured foreigners' invitation to serve Napoleon once again during the Hundred Days, but even then they played no appreciable role in his final campaign.

The opposite was true of Jews, who, as the next chapter shows, contributed significantly to the Napoleonic military, as they had to the revolutionary armies as well. In this regard, too, Napoleon followed closely in the footsteps of the revolutionaries, leveraging military service to integrate Jews into the national community while at the same time—and for the same political reasons—marginalizing or excluding foreigners.

SEVEN

JEWS, SOLDIERING, AND CITIZENSHIP IN REVOLUTIONARY AND NAPOLEONIC FRANCE

ALFRED DREYFUS, who with little doubt stands as the most famous Jewish military officer in French history, has been the subject of vast quantities of scholarship.[1] In contrast, the name of Dreyfus's predecessor Anselme Nordon, who in September 1792 became the first Jew to serve as an officer in the professional French army, remains almost completely unknown. The numerous other Jews who commanded French troops during the era of the French Revolution are subject to similar obscurity; indeed, one leading synthesis of modern Franco-Jewish history, skipping over the pioneering experiences of these men, implies that it was not until several decades after the turn of the nineteenth century that Jews first served as military officers in France.[2]

The same lack of meaningful scholarly attention affects the common soldiers of Jewish origin who fought in revolutionary and Napoleonic armies, despite their having numbered in the thousands and included representatives of all of France's disparate Jewish communities. Remarkably, there exists but one systematic study of Jewish soldiers in the French revolutionary army, an essay published by Zosa Szajkowski in 1957 that, although rich in empirical data, restricts its focus primarily to the first years of the Revolution and includes little consideration of the political and ideological implications of Jewish soldiering.[3]

Yet the military service of Jews, which this chapter illuminates by revisiting many of Szajkowski's sources as well as investigating archival material absent from his work, played a vital role in two major respects in shaping the Jewish experience in France during the century separating Nordon's enlistment in 1792 from Dreyfus's denunciation in 1894. First, it constituted one of the earliest and most powerful means by which the Revolution initiated the transformation of France's Jews into citizens not just in principle but also in practice. Prefiguring the army's role during the nineteenth century in molding "peasants into Frenchmen," both French leaders and Jews themselves embraced military service as a tool for forging citizens out of individuals whom the regime had treated prior to 1789 as members of a foreign nation.[4]

This trend is particularly notable given the little short-term significance that traditional historiography has attributed to the revolutionaries' "emancipation" of the Jews. As Ronald Schechter pointedly observed, for instance, the tangible implications of the famous emancipation decree of September 27, 1791, were limited, since the law modified the legal status of only the minuscule minority of Jews wealthy enough to qualify for active citizenship.[5] More broadly, historians have typically portrayed Jewish integration into French society as a gradual process that did not gain momentum until the nineteenth century, when capitalism presented new professional opportunities for Jews and when lingering symbols of their inequality, such as the *more judaico* oath, which persisted until 1846, gradually disappeared.[6]

It is true that full integration did not occur overnight, and that accession to the army did not on its own eradicate the marginalization of France's Jews. Yet the enrollment of Jews in the army in substantial numbers represented a juncture at which the Revolution, if not the emancipation decree itself, did exert a real and immediate influence on the disparate Jewish communities spread across France. Moreover, because of the close conceptual relationship that emerged during the revolutionary era between soldiering and citizenship, military service provided Jews with a particularly powerful basis on which to construct rhetorical claims for full integration into French society. Viewed from this perspective, the participation of Jews within the nation-building project of revolutionary France, a topic often absent from scholarship on French nationality and nationalism, gains sharper focus.

Equally significant was the role of service in the army in generating a paradigm of Franco-Jewish citizenship that became central to Jewish life in France during the nineteenth and twentieth centuries. The Jewish officers and soldiers of the revolutionary and Napoleonic armies, who devoted themselves to the service of the nation and relegated Judaism to nothing more than a personal religious commitment, represented in a very real sense the first examples of what the historian Pierre Birnbaum has labeled "State Jews."[7] At a time when many of their communities retained much of the autonomy that the revolutionary reforms had only theoretically abolished, Jewish troops contributed to the construction of new forms of identity for Jews in France oriented around a close relationship with and faith in the French state. They helped to forge a path that prominent Jewish figures such as Léon Blum and Marc Bloch later followed, and which the Dreyfus Affair and Vichy put to the ultimate test.

For all of these reasons, Jewish soldiers in the revolutionary and Napoleonic armies were key in setting an example that contrasted sharply with the experiences of foreign troops during the same period. As the preceding chapters have shown, the French revolutionaries, and Napoleon after them, were eager to purge the army of men whom they did not deem French citizens as part of their effort to reconfigure the armed forces into a national institution that embodied the sort of state and society they hoped to forge. At the same time, however, French leaders actively wielded the army as a tool for integrating Jews into the national community once they extended citizenship to them at the beginning of the Revolution.

Jewish troops, who in many cases spoke Yiddish, rarely associated with Christians, and benefited from no historical precedent for gaining civil rights in France through military service, were less obviously French in many senses than foreigners who had served in the army for decades under the Old Regime. Yet within the political and military landscape of the revolutionary era, these factors proved much less important than whether or not the government wished to include Jews in the national community, and by extension allow them to serve in the army. And in a context where the treatment of France's comparatively small Jewish communities was of outsize importance to revolutionary and Napoleonic leaders, who seized upon the Jews' "regeneration" as a symbol of the new regime's emancipatory promise and power, integrating Jews into the army became a particularly strong priority.[8]

The lingering prejudices that Jewish soldiers confronted from some quarters even after they began enlisting in the army highlighted the practical challenge of fully implementing the policies that French leaders envisioned. Ultimately, however, the success of Jews in gaining access to military institutions that the state had nationalized, and in using service in the army to reinforce their newfound status as French citizens, cast in stark relief the theoretical exclusion of foreigners and other minority groups from the armed forces due to the fact that the state did not consider them French nationals.

Debating Jewish Soldiering

Unlike their counterparts in the Holy Roman Empire, where Joseph II invited Jewish subjects to enlist in the army beginning in 1768, French Jews under the Old Regime monarchy rarely bore arms or came into close contact with military institutions.[9] Residing in autonomous communities, they paid a special tax to avoid conscription into the unpopular *milice* and the burden of billeting royal troops.[10] Nonetheless, Jewish soldiering under the Old Regime was not unheard of, if the case of André Simon Moïse may be taken as evidence. As chapter 1 noted, Moïse converted to Catholicism in March 1689 at the age of thirty-two, when he was baptized in the town of Longwy. His act of baptism, however, which described him as "Of the Jewish nation [*Juif de nation*], native of Metz, soldier in the regiment of Champagne," indicated that he had perhaps enlisted in the line army even prior to conversion.[11] The role that military service might have played in inspiring or necessitating his baptism is difficult to ascertain, and the relative infrequency of conversions of French Jews under the Old Regime suggests that Moïse's was an extraordinary case.[12] Nonetheless, his experience makes clear that soldiers of Jewish origin existed in France prior to the Revolution.[13]

Despite the precedent that such men set, opponents of Jewish emancipation at the outset of the Revolution demonstrated little willingness to accept Jews into the army, arguing that the religious tenets of Judaism rendered its followers unfit to bear arms. The cleric and deputy Jean-Sifrein Maury declared before the National Assembly in December 1789 that Jews were unfit for French citizenship not only because they offered few contributions to the French economy and cultural life, but also because "even when they have the patriotism and bravery to rally beneath our battle standards, they will be of little use. I do not know of a single general in the world who would want to command an army of Jews on the day of the Sabbath." The bishop of Nancy, Henri de la Fare, seconded Maury's criticisms, asserting that Jews were ineligible for French citizenship because Jewish law prohibited participation in the army, among other professions.[14]

Advocates of Jewish emancipation, citing the presence of Jews in National Guard companies since the beginning of the Revolution, challenged the factual basis of such claims. The assembly of the Commune of Paris, for example, heard a presentation on January 28, 1790, the day the national government granted active citizenship to Sephardic Jews, pointing to the patriotic zeal among Jews which, "since the advent of the Revolution, has transformed their souls and covered them in patriotic fervor, making out of them brave and tireless soldiers entirely devoted to the wellbeing and prosperity of the nation."[15] Similarly, the abbé Henri Grégoire, who had emerged as one of the strongest supporters of Jews in 1788 with his *Essai sur la régénération physique, morale et politique des Juifs,* responded in the National Assembly a year later to opposition to Jewish emancipation by reiterating the ability of Jews to fulfill the functions demanded of French citizens, including army service.[16] Grégoire condemned the exclusion of Jews from the National Guard of Nancy, the jurisdiction he represented as a deputy in the Assembly, lamenting that his community had "not wanted as soldiers of the *patrie* men whom the inhabitants of Paris and Bordeaux, more righteous than us, raised to the rank of captain."[17] He added that Jewish soldiers benefited from dispensations exempting them from religious obligations while serving in the army, and he emphasized the substantial military contributions that Jews had offered to other European states:

It should come as no surprise if I want to make a Jew into a soldier. The Jews of Paris and Bordeaux have entered eagerly into the National Guard, several of them attaining the rank of captain. Do not believe that they are required to refuse service on the day of the Sabbath. In the Talmud and the writings of Maimonides, the most preeminent of their philosophers, one finds two passages that formally permit it, and the Jewish writers of Berlin have enthusiastically cited these articles to reassure the consciences of their brothers, 3,000 of whom have enrolled in the armies of the Holy Roman Emperor. . . . This [Jewish] nation, which has supplied a skilled general to Portugal, a commodore to England, which distinguished itself during the last century at the sieges of Bude and Prague, which served brilliantly during the attack against Port Mahon, is it unworthy of marching beneath French battle standards?[18]

As the latter part of this chapter notes, it was not until Napoleon's convocation of the Grand Sanhedrin in 1807 that the rabbis of France formally invoked the maxim of *dina d'malkhuta dina* to exempt their followers from religious obligations that conflicted with military service.[19] Nonetheless, as Grégoire pointed out, Jews from the earliest days of the Revolution had proven themselves perfectly able and willing to serve in the army. Some Jewish national guards, such as those of Saint-Esprit who feature below, did request and receive permission to hire substitutes to perform their quotidian duties on the Sabbath, an endeavor that constituted one of the earliest manifestations of the effort by French Jews to integrate into French society without abandoning the practices distinctive to their communities.[20] Despite the claims of opponents of Jewish emancipation, however, there is no evidence that Jews refused to enlist in the army on the basis of Jewish law, or that religious observances prevented them from serving to the satisfaction of their commanders.

Beyond endeavoring to dispel claims that Jews were ineligible for military service, and by extension for the obligations of French citizenship, supporters of Jewish emancipation presented Jewish enlistment in the army as evidence that Jews already fulfilled the roles of citizens, even before they had formally received citizenship rights. Representatives of the Commune of Paris declared before the National Assembly in early 1790 that "the patriotic enthusiasm that [the Jews] have exhibited has preemptively incorporated them into the French nation because, like all other citizens, they have accepted and continue to accept the duties of service in the National Guard."[21] A Christian member of the National Guard of Nancy similarly made the case that military service by Jews facilitated their integration into French society, cleansing them in the process of the vices that he believed to be at the root of their resentment by many of their neighbors.[22] Jews themselves, despite the little voice they enjoyed in the debates on their political fate, advanced the argument early in the Revolution that their service in the National Guard should at the very least entitle them to the abolition of the special taxes the state levied against them.[23]

Jews Become Citizen-Soldiers

The association of Jewish soldiering with citizenship during the first years of the Revolution, combined with other arguments in favor of Jewish emancipation, led to the extension of citizenship to France's Sephardic Jewish communities on January 28, 1790. On September 27, 1791, the National Assembly expanded this decision by declaring the emancipation of all Jews in France. Yet such momentous change in the policy of the French government toward France's Jews did not on its own extinguish opposition to Jewish military service. On the contrary, heated debates continued for several years on the question of Jewish enlistment in French armies. These contestations, which were similar to those of the same period concerning foreigners in the army but notably different in that they ended with the acceptance of Jewish soldiers rather than their exclusion, revealed larger tensions within French society regarding the willingness of contemporaries to support Jewish citizenship in practice and not merely in theory.

Some of these frictions stemmed from marked anti-Jewish prejudice that lingered despite the official incorporation of Jews into the French nation. The municipal council of Metz reported in its deliberations of February 21, 1792, for example, several months after the emancipation decree, that a majority of the citizens of the town refused to serve in the National Guard alongside Jewish volunteers because of "the real danger of frequent interactions and daily, personal contacts with Jews, a majority of whom suffer from a hereditary illness that spreads easily and is perpetuated by their way of life, to which they cling despite decrees ordering the dissolution of their community." Local authorities subsequently voted to refuse Jews admission to the National Guard, a decision the town did not revoke until the summer of 1793.[24]

In other cases, unwillingness on the part of Christian authorities to grant Jewish soldiers the same flexibility they afforded to other French volunteers complicated the ability of Jews to enlist. Although local politicians allowed Jews in the community of Saint-Esprit to join the National Guard after the emancipation of the Sephardim in January 1790, they denied them the right to hire substitutes to perform their military duties on days when religious observances prevented them from bearing arms, according to a complaint to the national government. The Jewish volunteers also reported that Christians forced them to participate in Catholic ceremonies. The affair was resolved only through the intervention of the Constitutional Committee in Paris, which reminded the leaders of the municipality that Jews enjoyed the same prerogative as Christian national guards to provide substitutes in order to avoid performing duties that conflicted with their religious beliefs. Highlighting the symbolic significance it attached to France's Jews, the Committee also warned that the unfair treatment of Jewish soldiers threatened both the social harmony of the nation and France's image in the eyes of foreign supporters.[25]

Members of the Jewish community of Avignon and Comtat Venaissin, where sympathizers with the French Revolution formed a National Guard corps even before the Constituent Assembly's annexation of the papal territory to France in September 1791, also faced prejudice when enlisting in the army. Although Avignonese Jews were present in the National Guard beginning in 1790, they suffered vilification by a local publisher who produced a satirical pamphlet ridiculing an officer in the local militia for being of reputed Jewish origin.[26] At the same time, municipal authorities in Avignon accused Jews of shirking their military duties under the pretext of religious laws, prompting a Jewish deputation to declare that the Jews of the city were patriotic citizens eager to serve, and to present a number of men for immediate enlistment. Nonetheless, it was not until the intensification of the foreign war that Jews began entering in large numbers into the National Guard of Avignon and the Comtat, and that they acceded to the officer ranks there.[27]

For several years after the emancipation decree, anti-Jewish sentiment also entered into legal disputes involving soldiers in ways that divulged lingering unease among some Christians about accepting Jews as full members of the French nation. In one example, Moïse Brunsvik, a Jewish native of Alsace who had lived in Paris since the mid-1780s, faced an interrogation by the revolutionary committee of the section of Réunion, where he resided, in May 1793. Brunsvik was charged with having hurled obscenities at the Christian captain of the National Guard company in which he served, as well as threatening him with violence, because he was upset about orders for the corps to deploy to the Vendée, which he felt imposed an unfair burden on poor local families. Although Brunsvik's religion played no direct role in the incident, his interrogators dwelt on it, demanding to know to which Jewish community he belonged (*"de quel judé il est"*) and why witnesses had spotted him prior to his confrontation with the captain conversing with other Jews in a language, presumably Yiddish, that they could not understand.[28]

Similarly, Anselme Isräel, another Jew of Alsatian birth who resided in Paris during the Revolution and served in the Germanic Legion, answered charges in November 1792 that he had participated in the looting of a storage facility. Claude Emmanuel, who interrogated Isräel, made a point of demanding to know whether the defendant was an acquaintance of Jews in Paris who had been found in possession of luxury goods around the time of the theft. Israël answered that he was not and that he suspected that authorities had erroneously executed the arrest order against him due to a confusion over names. The court eventually acquitted him.[29] Nonetheless, the preoccupation on the part of the interrogators of Brunsvik and Israël with their religion suggests a tendency among French authorities for some time after the emancipation decree to view Jewish soldiers as particularly suspect, even in military and legal contexts where Judaism did not distinguish them from Christian troops in any tangible way.

As the Revolution progressed, however, the marginalization of Jews within the National Guard and the army gradually dissipated. In a trend consistent with the experiences of Brunsvik and Isräel, Marat singled out Louis Benjamin Calmer as a Jew while denouncing the personnel of his National Guard battalion in March 1791.[30] Yet three years later, when Calmer faced the revolutionary tribunal on charges of having served as a royalist spy, the court made no mention of his Jewish heritage, although the public prosecutor did take note of his Dutch birth while preparing the case.[31] That Calmer suffered marginalization as a foreigner but not as a Jew suggests that French authorities had ceased to view Jews as a suspect group by the spring of 1794, when the revolutionary tribunal condemned him to death.

The case of Jacob Péreire, another Jewish soldier executed during the Terror, was similar to Calmer's in that Péreire, though charged with having ties to France's enemies abroad, was never identified during his trial as a Jew. A tobacco merchant and member of the Parisian National Guard, Péreire also served briefly as a civil commissioner overseeing the French army in Belgium, where he helped to restore order in the wake of Dumouriez's defection in April 1793.[32] Later that year, Péreire came under suspicion for association with the radical Hébertiste movement, but the prosecutor never distinguished him from the other suspects for being Jewish. In addition, Péreire enjoyed the support during his trial of fellow soldiers in the artillery company in which he served, who on December 5, 1793, addressed a petition to the municipal authorities of the section of Bonconseil attesting "the sadness caused to them by the detention of citizen Péreire, one of their comrades, whose actions have always appeared to be those of a good republican."[33] The eagerness of Péreire's comrades, who were almost certainly mostly of Christian descent, to come to his defense highlighted the role military service played in reinforcing his integration into French society.[34] Péreire himself, meanwhile, cited his military service with his neighbors at length as he pleaded for release from prison: he wrote in a letter to the authorities that he had fought enthusiastically with his National Guard company on the revolutionary *journées* of August 10, 1792, and May 31, 1793, and claimed to have received a bullet wound while serving alongside "my true Jacobin brothers."[35] Although such arguments attested to the role that service in the National Guard played from Péreire's own perspective in facilitating his incorporation into the fraternity of French Jacobins, they did not spare him from condemnation and execution by the revolutionary tribunal in the spring of 1794.[36]

It was not simply by bringing Jews such as Péreire into closer contact with Christians that military service reinforced Jewish integration into French society and facilitated the transformation of Jews into citizens. Because the French revolutionaries redefined the image of the soldier and bound service in the army, both conceptually and legally, to patriotism and citizenship, Jews who bore arms could stake claim to particular honors and privileges unavailable to most other members of their communities. For one, as soldiers, they belonged to a group held in hallowed esteem by supporters of the Revolution, who replaced the negative Old Regime connotations of soldiering with a new image of the soldier as a patriot, citizen and defender of revolutionary ideals.[37] In addition, the National Assembly legally linked military service to citizenship beginning in 1790, when it granted active citizenship to all men with sixteen years of service in the army, making them eligible to vote and hold political office even if they were otherwise too poor to exercise those rights. Jews who enlisted in the army during the first years of the Revolution, of course, would have had to wait a long time before they could benefit from this privilege, which became largely obsolete after the elimination of voting-eligibility requirements in August 1792. Nonetheless, the mere fact that service in the revolutionary army offered Jews a path toward full political participation within the state was significant at a time when a majority of them, like the French population as a whole, fell far short of meeting the financial requirements for active citizenship. It remained important after Thermidor, when the Constitution of 1795 guaranteed full citizenship to all men who had participated in at least one military campaign since the founding of the Republic.[38] Military service on its own could not eradicate distinctions between Jewish and Christian citizens of France, but it did function as a vital tool for reaffirming Jews' full membership in the nation in ways in which few other activities could.[39]

While only men were eligible for the citizenship rights associated with military service, the military experiences of Jewish soldiers affected their families as well. The revolutionary redefinition of soldiering did not merely entail the state's recognition of an unprecedented responsibility for men serving in the armies; the parents, wives, children, and other relatives of Jewish men who enlisted shared in their military experiences in ways that ensured that service by Jews reverberated throughout the Jewish communities of France.[40] Gabriel Bloch, a great-grandfather of the historian Marc Bloch and a volunteer on the front against the Prussians in 1793, kept his family in Alsace abreast of his activities as a soldier via the letters he sent home emphasizing the difficulty and danger of his mission, but also affirming his religious faith and his desire for an end to the war.[41] Other families were not so fortunate. The parents of Israel Nattan, a native of Metz and a volunteer in the Fifth Battalion of *chasseurs francs,* wrote to the war ministry in 1794 requesting information on the whereabouts of their son, from whom they had not heard in some time. They received the unhappy response that Nattan had disappeared near Tournai in May 1794 and was presumed killed or captured.[42] Cases such as these underline the way in which the enlistment of Jewish men in the French army affected Jewish communities as a whole, reinforcing the awareness of all Jews of their relationship with the state and their newfound role in the destiny of the French nation.

The volunteer battalions of the National Guard, which were organized locally and generally exercised relaxed policies of admission and discipline, served as the exclusive point of entry for Jews into the army during the initial years of the Revolution. By the time of revolutionary France's first existential military crisis in the late summer of 1792, however, Jews began enlisting in the ranks of the line army as well. This trend was particularly remarkable because the soldiers who chose to enroll in these units were more likely to view the army as a career and serve for long periods of time.[43]

The rise of men such as Anselme Nordon to officer ranks outside the National Guard thus reflected significant progress in integrating Jews into institutions of the state to which they had had almost no access only a few years earlier. Born in Metz in 1756 to a Jewish family, Nordon later moved to Paris and served from 1789 to 1792 in a National Guard battalion as a sergeant and second lieutenant. He also claimed later in his life to have been a member of the Regiment of Swiss Guards when it defended the Tuileries Palace on the revolutionary *journée* of August 10, 1792, but this assertion is dubious.[44] What is certain is that on September 4, 1792, Nordon enlisted as a first lieutenant in the Germanic Legion, becoming the first Jew to attain an officer rank outside of the volunteer battalions.[45] He rose to the rank of captain before revolutionary authorities dissolved the legion in the spring of 1793, in which year he passed to the Fourteenth Light Infantry Regiment, retaining his officer's commission. He received a certificate of discharge in 1796 for wounds he suffered in the Vendée, but after recovering he reenlisted, retiring definitively only after losing a leg at the battle of Landshut in June 1800. In all, Nordon served in the army for a total of nearly twelve years and received the considerable pension of 1,278 livres upon his retirement.[46]

Salomon Lévy, a native of Lay-Saint-Christophe in the Meurthe-et-Moselle department, also engaged in a long military career that demonstrated the ability of Jews to succeed in the professional army. Lévy first enlisted on September 23, 1792, days after the founding of the Republic, when he joined the 76th Regiment of the line army as a common soldier. He became a corporal in 1793, *fourrier* in 1795, sergeant in 1802, second lieutenant in 1810, and finally a captain in 1813, the same year in which he was inducted into the Légion d'honneur. Wounded three times during his career, he served in a number of major campaigns of the Revolution and the Empire.[47]

While soldiers such as Nordon and Lévy took advantage of a new military culture rooted in merit rather than social status to ascend the ranks and become officers, other Jews pursued formal military training in order to advance their careers.[48] Samson Marx Berr, a member of a prominent Jewish family from Strasbourg, served at the beginning of the war as a volunteer in a dragoon unit in the Army of the Rhine. Later, however, he entered the École de Mars, an academy established by the National Convention in 1794 at Neuilly-sur-Seine for the military education of patriotic young men. He cited his military training at the École, where he claimed to have "much improved my competence for the cavalry," in 1796 when seeking promotion to the rank of second lieutenant in the Fifth Dragoon Regiment. His request received the support of the colonel of the regiment and several representatives in the National Convention.[49] The access of Jews such as Berr to formal institutions of military instruction reflected not only the more liberal social policies of revolutionary France but also a degree of integration of Jews into French institutional life that had been unimaginable for most members of France's Jewish communities prior to 1789, and which anticipated the careers of prominent nineteenth-century "State Jews."

Jewish soldiers such as Berr, Lévy, and Nordon did not represent outliers within their communities. Although the absence during the Revolution of administrative institutions that collected data on Jews makes it impossible to know precisely how many served in the army during the revolutionary decade, the available evidence indicates that their numbers were substantial. While advocating for Jewish emancipation in 1790, one contemporary claimed that more than 100 of the 500 Jews residing in Paris had enrolled in the National Guard.[50] In Saint-Esprit, which counted about 1,000 Jewish residents, there were enough Jewish national guards for local authorities to attempt to create two exclusively Jewish companies in order to segregate Jews from Christians in November 1790.[51] Between July 1792 and November 1793, 69 Jews from Carpentras and Avignon, which had a Jewish population of about 2,500, enlisted in volunteer battalions or line regiments, while 51 Jews served in just one battalion from the Haut-Rhin department.[52] It is clear from numbers such as these that service by Jews in the revolutionary armies was not an exceptional phenomenon that involved only a handful of the 40,000 Jewish residents of France; it was an activity in which a large number of Jewish men engaged beginning in the first years of the Revolution.

Nor was enrollment in the army restricted to certain Jewish communities. The wealthier and more assimilated Sephardim were the first to take up arms, presenting an example that Grégoire and other advocates of emancipation cited frequently during the debates on Jewish citizenship early in the Revolution. Many of the Ashkenazim of the eastern departments later followed the lead of their southwestern coreligionists, however, as did the Jews of the Comtat and Avignon. To be sure, not all Jews enlisted with equal enthusiasm; well into the Napoleonic period, as the latter part of this chapter shows, the Ashkenazim lagged behind their counterparts in furnishing recruits. Nor were the experiences of Jewish soldiers from different communities uniform. Many of the Ashkenazim, whose social and cultural integration into French society was much more halting than that of Sephardic Jews and who tended to adhere more strictly to traditional religious tenets, exhibited greater wariness toward military duties incompatible with their religious values.[53] And by no means did Jewish enlistment in the army lead to the instant dissipation of the many cultural, social, and economic characteristics that distinguished France's various Jewish communities from one another.

Nonetheless, as a phenomenon common to the Jewish communities scattered across France, service in French revolutionary armies represented a vital early step toward the evolution of a more cohesive French Jewry. In an era when the various Jewish populations of France did not at all share a unified identity or agenda and would not emerge as a single collectivity until after the Napoleonic reforms of the nineteenth century, service in the army was an activity that Jews from throughout France shared.[54] Even as most Ashkenazim remained eager to retain the autonomous status of their communities and showed little interest in participating in French political life—a trend that frustrated Sephardic leaders who hoped their coreligionists in eastern France would follow in their footsteps by embracing their newfound status as French citizens—many Ashkenazic Jews did at least enlist in the military.[55] Indeed, several of the earliest Jewish officers, such as Nordon, Lévy, and Berr, hailed from Ashkenazic communities. In this sense the military service of Jews contributed to the integration of those diverse communities not only into the French nation but also among one another, promoting the emergence of a single French Jewry with common aspirations and behaviors.

The Army and Jewish Civilians

In addition to bearing arms for France, Jews affirmed their incorporation into French society by rendering services to the army in other ways, particularly those that drew on the unique resources of France's Jewish communities. While these activities did not fall explicitly under the category of soldiering, Jews portrayed them as vital services to the nation, and received acclamations from French authorities that reinforced this perspective. In this way, the military presented opportunities even for Jews who could not bear arms themselves to offer special contributions to the nation into which they had only recently received official incorporation, thereby reaffirming their newfound status as French citizens.

Among the most fascinating examples of Jews who contributed to the war effort without enrolling in the army was that of Joseph Godchaux. An engraver, Godchaux was recruited by the mayor of Thionville, a town in northeastern France threatened by enemy armies, shortly after the declaration of war against Austria in April 1792 to gather intelligence on enemy troops. Godchaux accepted the mission, in his words, "for the honor of the *patrie*." Leveraging their relationships with Jews living across the border, Godchaux and a companion named Abraham Lazare were able to travel between France and the enemy headquarters at Coblenz to compile information on troop formations and supply depots, which they relayed back to French commanders. By August 1792, however, the French general Georges Félix de Wimpffen had grown suspicious that Godchaux was a double-agent, prompting the latter to respond with a formal denunciation of Wimpffen for military misconduct. The affair petered out in the wake of the French victory the following month at Valmy, which relieved the threat against Thionville and eliminated the need for Godchaux's reconnaissance trips across the border; nonetheless, Godchaux, in the memoir he wrote to defend himself against charges of serving the émigrés, justified his intelligence activities for the French army as a vital patriotic duty toward "such an honest nation, which gave even to the Hebrew people the same equality and liberty as to the other citizens."[56]

Godchaux was not alone in taking advantage of his membership in a Jewish community that spanned European borders to support the French war effort. The young Jew Jacob Mayer Lyon, who resided in Paris but spoke both French and German, deployed his linguistic talents toward the same end. Born in 1777, Lyon was too young to bear arms during the first campaigns of the Revolution, but he served during that time as a German-language interpreter in a military hospital attached to the Army of the Ardennes.[57] Bilingual personnel such as Lyon played critical roles in an army that, given the linguistic diversity of France's population during the eighteenth century and the recruitment of foreign volunteers and deserters, counted among its troops many soldiers from germanophone territories who spoke French imperfectly or not at all.

Finally, Jews who could not serve the army directly supported the war effort by participating in the funding drives known as *dons patriotiques* that communities throughout France organized for the defense of the Republic. The Jews of Metz, despite the controversy that erupted in that city regarding Jewish service in the National Guard early in the Revolution, volunteered funds for the purchase of weapons and supplies for soldiers. They also donated their labor for the construction of fortifications and offered a religious service "in thanksgiving for the success of the armies of the Republic in Savoy."[58] Similarly, at least fifty-four Jews in Avignon contributed *dons patriotiques* for the arming and equipping of volunteer battalions, a remarkable number given that the size of the Jewish community of the jurisdiction in 1789 was only about 350 individuals, some of whom left during the first years of the Revolution, and that only heads of households were likely to make donations.[59] Jewish communities elsewhere emulated these activities, reaffirming Jews' membership as equals within the French nation by making financial sacrifices alongside Christian civilians to bolster republican armies.[60]

Napoleon's Jewish Troops

While there is little evidence to support claims by some historians that Bonaparte sought to levy a "Jewish legion" during his campaign in the Middle East in the late 1790s, the close relationship between Jews and the army persisted throughout the Napoleonic period.[61] Napoleon marshaled the institution of conscription, which provided the state with an unprecedented capacity not only to recruit soldiers but also to promote the social and political integration of marginal communities via the tool of military service, as a central element of the reform program for the French Empire's Jewish communities that he launched in 1806. The sixth of the twelve questions that Napoleon posed in that year to the Assembly of Notables, a body of Jewish elites whom he convened to address unsettled issues regarding the relationship between France's Jews and the state, concerned the willingness of Jews to accept conscription and defend the *patrie*. This inquiry reportedly elicited enthusiastic cries of *"jusqu'à la mort!"* from the assembly, an unsurprising response given the important role military service had assumed in forging a close relationship between Jews and the state since the time of the Revolution.[62]

The Grand Sanhedrin, a group of Jewish leaders whom Napoleon assembled in 1807 to confirm the decisions of the Assembly of Notables and to extend to them the weight of Jewish law, similarly affirmed Jews' commitment to military service. Among the duties that the sanhedrins recognized as the formal responsibilities of rabbis was to reinforce among their followers, "in all circumstances, obedience toward the law, particularly that relating to the defense of the *patrie.*" They also elaborated upon the maxim of *dina d'malkhuta dina* as they promised "to make Jews consider military service a sacred duty, and to declare to them that, during the time they are engaged in military service, the law exempts them from religious observances that are incompatible" with bearing arms.[63] To be sure, the relationship between Napoleon and the Jews was more complex in practice than the acquiescent pronouncements of the Assembly of Notables and the Grand Sanhedrin implied. Jews successfully maneuvered to retain their own agency and the freedom to formulate policies on issues such as military service on their own terms, without bending subserviently to Napoleon's will.[64] Nonetheless, the pronouncements of the Jewish assemblies satisfied Napoleon's objective of developing a clear definition of the role of the Jewish soldier in France. At the same time, they promoted service in the army as not only a civil but also a religious obligation for French Jews.

Without a doubt, Napoleon's interest in encouraging Jews to serve in the army reflected, in part, his broader drive to put as many men under arms as possible and to root out resistance to conscription, a chronic problem for French authorities.[65] Because the 71,000 Jewish inhabitants of the Napoleonic Empire never represented more than one quarter of one percent of its total population, however, they did not constitute a very important source of manpower for the imperial armies. Indeed, as Schechter has argued, it was only because of Jews' symbolic utility in helping to legitimize the Bonapartist regime that Napoleon took such a strong interest in the tiny Jewish communities in the first place.[66] The evidence thus suggests that the centrality of military service to the Jewish reform program that Napoleon launched in 1806 did not stem primarily from the hope that Jews would provide crucial contributions to the war effort. Instead, it resulted from Napoleon's recognition of soldiering as a tool for reinforcing Jews' integration into the French national community, expanding on a practice that dated to the first years of the Revolution.

In an era when large numbers of draftees in France as a whole refused to cooperate with conscription or deserted the army shortly after induction, the willingness of many Jews to accept the burdens of military service extended well beyond the formal promises of Jewish elites in the

Assembly of Notables and the Grand Sanhedrin. Data compiled both by the Jewish consistories, which Napoleon set up to administer the Jewish communities in the Empire, and by French authorities indicates that Jews served in substantial numbers, in certain cases even surpassing the rate of enlistment for Christians. In all, slightly more than two million men were conscripted into the French army between the institutionalization of conscription in 1798 and the final Napoleonic levy in 1813.[67] Averaging around 139,000 soldiers each year, these troops comprised approximately 0.51 percent of the French population annually.[68] In contrast, the Jews of the department of Vaucluse, who totaled 647 around 1810, contributed 50 conscripts to the French army between 1798 and 1811, which amounted to 0.57 percent of their community annually.[69] Yet more remarkably, 24 of the 230 Jews in Nice were conscripted in the decade following the *loi Jourdan*, averaging 1.04 percent of the population each year.[70]

Rates of Jewish enlistment were lower elsewhere, particularly among the Ashkenazic communities of eastern France. The 60 Jewish families of the Rhône department furnished only 10 soldiers by 1810, or 0.3 percent annually; the 80 Jewish households in the Vosges, where the Jewish population totaled 374 individuals in 1808, had provided 12 conscripts by that year (0.32 percent); the 48 Jewish families of Wissembourg supplied 7 recruits by 1810 (0.26 percent).[71]

In part, these lower numbers are attributable, first, to the fact that these examples do not cover the final years of the Empire, when conscription rates were highest; and, second, to the relative poverty of the Ashkenazic communities and the poor health their members suffered as a result. In Wissembourg, for example, only one of sixteen Jews requisitioned for service in 1808 was deemed physically qualified to bear arms.[72] More important, however, these statistics also reflected the tendency of Ashkenazic Jews during the nineteenth century to remain less enthusiastic to serve in the army than their coreligionists elsewhere in France. From the time conscription was instituted in the 1790s until as late as the twentieth century, many Jews in Alsace and Lorraine practiced rituals that they hoped would spare them from drawing unlucky numbers in the draft lottery.[73] In other cases, Alsatian Jews may have sought to emigrate from France to escape conscription.[74] This reluctance to serve did not escape the notice of French authorities in the eastern departments. The prefect of the Bas-Rhin wrote in 1806 of the Jews in his jurisdiction, for instance, that "the great majority of that sect constantly seeks to elude the laws and particularly those *regarding conscription.*"[75] To be sure, many Ashkenazic Jews, like their coreligionists elsewhere in France, did cooperate with the Napoleonic conscription, and Alsatian Jewish leaders encouraged their followers to bear arms as a mark of patriotism.[76] Nonetheless, it is clear that the Jews of eastern France were much slower than their counterparts elsewhere in the country to embrace military service.

Such antipathy toward conscription among some of France's Jews, combined with the central importance of military service to Napoleon's Jewish reform program, led French authorities to implement special policies for maximizing the number of Jews who served in the army. For one, they forbade Jews during most of the Napoleonic period to purchase replacements in order to escape conscription, a common practice among better-off Christian families. It was not until 1812 that the state permitted Jews to hire substitutes, and even then the replacements had to be Jewish as well.[77] Jewish religious leaders were also denied the benefits of the imperial decree of March 7, 1806, which exempted Christian clergy from conscription but which the government, despite the protests of the Central Consistory, refused to apply to Jews.[78] While such policies, which reinforced the separateness of Jews by treating them differently from other French citizens and imposed hardships on Jewish communities, risked proving counterproductive to the goal of better integrating Jews into French society, they elicited few qualms from French authorities bent on using the army to mold Jews into citizens.[79]

At the same time, many Jews themselves, echoing rhetoric that had first emerged during the revolutionary debates on Jewish emancipation, seized on the contributions of their communities to Napoleon's armies to affirm their equality and integration. The Jews of the Seine department, for example, requested exemption from the "Infamous Decree" of March 17, 1808, which subjected Jews to harsh anti-usury surveillance, by pointing to the presence of a number of their children in the Légion d'honneur and the armies of the Empire. The Jews of Wissembourg argued for the same privilege in 1810 when they asserted that the fathers of their community "took it as a personal duty to present their sons to the conscription lottery; that those who have been called to serve have faithfully obeyed; that the Jewish community does not count a single refractory conscript."[80]

Even Jews beyond France's borders associated military service during the Napoleonic era with affirmations of equality and escape from persecution. A young Jew from Amsterdam named L. S. Boas declared that he had "always regarded a military career as the most glorious and the one to which he was most naturally inclined," but regretted that "previously, because of the state of oppression in which the Jews in Holland found themselves, he could not have expected to be able to obtain the necessary skills." Boas received the opportunity to bear arms in June 1809 when Louis Bonaparte, Napoleon's brother and king of Holland from 1806 until 1810, established the "Korps Israelieten," in which Boas served as a captain. Composed exclusively of Jews, this unit of the Dutch army represented the first force of its kind in modern Europe.[81] The corps dissolved in 1810, but Boas was able to continue his military career in the French army following Napoleon's annexation of Holland in the same year. In 1811 the French war minister, praising Boas for having "undertaken great efforts to eliminate among the Jews the prejudice that they maintain toward military service," awarded him an appointment as a second lieutenant in the 127th Infantry Regiment.[82] Even if the war minister clung to the stereotype of Jews as unwilling to bear arms, such was clearly not the case for Boas.

The Army and the Forging of Franco-Jewish Identity

The story of Boas, like those of the many other Jews who served as soldiers and officers in the armies of revolutionary and Napoleonic France, bears witness to the central importance of military service to the emancipation and integration of Jews into the French national community born during the Revolution. As the experience of Dreyfus made clear, Jewish contributions to the French military did not come close to eradicating anti-Jewish sentiment in France, which would indeed flourish and take on horrifying new forms in the late nineteenth and twentieth centuries. Nor did they facilitate complete integration. They did, however, constitute one of the earliest and most powerful opportunities by which Jews demonstrated their patriotic devotion to the state, engendering an enduring relationship that played a vital role in defining the modern Jewish experience in the country. Men such as Péreire, who took up arms alongside his Jacobin neighbors to defend republican ideals to which he was firmly committed, and Nordon, who ceased to fight for the First Republic only after he could no longer walk, were among the very first representatives of their communities to display the qualities that, many decades later, bound Jewish civil servants, generals, and lawmakers so tightly to the Third Republic.

The accession of Jews to the army during the revolutionary era was thus not merely one product of a historical watershed that elevated France's Jews from the marginality and poverty they had generally known during the eighteenth century into the figures of political, intellectual, and economic prominence that many French Jews became during the nineteenth century. Rather, Jewish soldiers in the revolutionary and Napoleonic armies became, via the transformative agency of military service, some of the earliest pioneers of that shift. It was in the tradition they established that Léopold Sée, who received his military education at the elite Saint-Cyr academy and served as an officer under three French regimes during the nineteenth century, became the first Jewish general in France in 1870.[83] It was in their image that Dreyfus appealed for justice by emphasizing his patriotic devotion as "a soldier who has always loyally and faithfully served his *patrie*, who has sacrificed to it everything, prestige and fortune."[84] And it was with reference to them that Marc Bloch, a veteran of two world wars, declared in the era of Vichy that should anyone question whether he was a true French citizen, he would respond that "my great-grandfather was a soldier in 1793; that my father, in 1870, fought at Strasbourg. . . and when my turn came, I did my utmost to defend France as best I could."[85] The tragic irony, as Bloch's own experience during the Second World War attested, was that the French state ultimately failed to protect the Jews who, from the time of modern France's first great foreign war in the eighteenth century to its last in the twentieth, risked their lives as an expression of commitment to it.

THE JEWISH CITIZEN-SOLDIERS of the revolutionary era demonstrated the centrality of military service in defining the contours of the national community. In contrast to foreigners, whom the state endeavored to exclude from the army precisely because it did not consider them members of the French nation, and unlike blacks, whose opportunities and prestige within the army shifted along with policies on emancipation and slavery, Jews successfully seized upon military service, beginning in some cases even before the emancipation decrees, as a way of reinforcing their inclusion in the nascent French nation-state. To be sure, some Jewish communities contributed many more soldiers to the army than others. It is also true that the halting and gradual acceptance of Jews as soldiers reflected the difficulty of forging new institutions that fully embodied the political tenets of the nation-state the revolutionaries envisioned.

Still, both the mere opportunity of Jews to serve as soldiers and officers, and the fact that thousands of them did so throughout nearly all units of the French army, powerfully demonstrated the tremendous extent to which access to the army in the revolutionary era was not only contingent upon citizenship, but also helped to constitute it. Once the revolutionaries decided to count Jews as citizens, they eagerly included them within the army and the nation, in total contrast to men who were not French natives.

CONCLUSION

FOREIGN SOLDIERS AND THE
REVOLUTIONARY LEGACY

RESTORED TO THE THRONE ONCE AGAIN in the wake of Napoleon's second abdication, Louis XVIII (or *Louis deux fois neuf,* as his critics in France mocked him) wasted little time in doing away with the foreign regiments that Napoleon had raised during the Hundred Days. Although some of the foreign troops quickly swore fidelity to the Bourbons after Waterloo, a royal ordinance of September 6, 1815, dissolved all of the foreign corps in France and reorganized them into a new unit called the Royal Foreign Legion.[1] Foreign soldiers and officers who did not receive appointments in the new legion, which was too small to accommodate all of the foreign troops in France at the time, received orders to return to their countries of origin.[2] This mandate created particular problems for Spanish and Portuguese officers whose native states still proscribed them (in some cases along with their wives, who had accompanied them to France) because they had served Napoleon. It was only by obtaining *lettres de naturalité* from the Bourbons that most of these officers were able to resolve their difficulties by remaining in France permanently.[3]

In addition to forming the Royal Foreign Legion, Louis XVIII resurrected the Hundred Swiss Company once again, although its official title, *Compagnie des gardes à pied ordinaires du corps du roi,* did not mention its foreign nationality.[4] Meanwhile, his government reached an agreement with the Swiss cantons to raise six new regiments for French service via a capitulation of June 1, 1816.[5] The convention permitted some of the Swiss corps to enlist a limited number of non-Swiss foreigners as well, and affirmed the reestablishment, "as before 1789," of the Swiss troops' freedom of religion and immunity from French justice.[6]

Yet if the reintroduction of Swiss regiments during the first years of the Second Restoration recalled the traditions of the Old Regime, the subsequent treatment of foreign soldiers by Louis XVIII and his successors pointed to the lasting influence of the revolutionaries' reformulation of policies on military service and citizenship. The Swiss corps remained in service only until 1830, and the Royal Foreign Legion retained its title as a foreign unit for less than a year. In June 1816 it was renamed the Legion of Hohenlohe, after its commander, the prince of Hohenlohe-

Waldenburg-Bartenstein, and in 1821 it became the Regiment of Hohen-lohe. Ten years later, by which time few foreigners remained in the corps, royal officials reorganized it as a regular line regiment of the army.[7]

In the same year, king Louis Philippe raised a new foreign corps, the French Foreign Legion, which remains in existence today. Foreigners continued to serve in that unit under the French flag throughout the nineteenth and twentieth centuries, and the Foreign Legion later developed into one of the hallmarks of modern French military identity, as chapter 3 noted. The Foreign Legion of 1831, however, which the monarchy permitted to serve only beyond the borders of metropolitan France and which was plagued during its early years by poor discipline and ill repute, bore few similarities to the prestigious foreign regiments of the Old Regime.[8]

By abolishing foreign regiments and replacing them with a short-lived foreign legion that they soon nationalized, then creating another foreign legion that they relegated to colonial service, Napoleon's successors trod with remarkable precision on the path the revolutionaries had forged several decades prior. The early years of the Revolution had also witnessed the nationalization and dissolution of the foreign regiments, followed by a brief experiment with foreign legions whose disbandment set the stage for the Constitution of 1795 to close the door firmly on foreign recruitment. In their policies on foreign troops, at least, the postrevolutionary monarchs closely emulated the republican regime of the 1790s, whose antithesis the Bourbons purported to represent.

Yet neither the Restoration kings, nor the various regimes that succeeded them from the mid-nineteenth century up to the present, proved capable of bringing the project of nationalization that the revolutionaries undertook in 1789 to total fulfillment. For nearly two centuries, France has continued to rely on the Foreign Legion as a matter of pragmatic military necessity. Like its predecessors in the armies of Old Regime, revolutionary, and Napoleonic France, the Foreign Legion is characterized by a great deal of racial and cultural diversity. And like the elite Swiss regiments of Louis XVI, the foreign legions the revolutionaries raised in the early 1790s to spearhead offensives into enemy territory, and the foreign expeditionary troops who sailed to Haiti, Ireland, and Egypt later in the revolutionary decade, the modern Foreign Legion performs a critical military function for France. It is frequently among the first units the French government deploys to volatile regions of the world, including most recently in French military interventions in Africa, since the casualties it suffers pose fewer political risks to officials than the deaths of regular French soldiers.[9] In this way, it functions as an expedient for achieving the French state's military goals while minimizing the government's political liability.

YET IF THE MODERN FOREIGN LEGION continues to provide an opportunity for noncitizens to enroll in the French army, its status as a peculiar corps, which has spent most of its history waging war on colonial frontiers where generals and politicians deemed foreigners more expendable than French nationals, reflects the endurance in modern France of political principles that bind military service to nationality and citizenship, while favoring the exclusion of individuals who are not French by birth, culture, race, or language from full participation in the national community. To be sure, the political visions and understandings of national sovereignty that the various regimes of France have embraced since the 1790s have varied widely. Still, the inseparability of French citizenship from military service in the regular army, and a vision of the armed forces as a microcosm of society, have remained key tenets for all of these governments. For the revolutionaries, these values meant systematically purging the army of foreigners at the same time that the state aggressively endorsed the enlistment of Jews, residents of peripheral territories, and other groups whom they had only recently deemed a part of the national community. Later, Napoleon distanced foreign troops from the center of the army and subjected them to oversight by native French officers, reflecting the hierarchical imperial state and society he sought to forge. After the revolutionary era came to a close, the constitutional monarchs of the Restoration had little need to maintain foreign corps at all in an era when kings' ability to rule had come to rest upon the political will of their subjects, rather than the prestige and diplomatic clout that foreign regiments helped to assure under the Old Regime.

Yet if the modern French state in theory constitutes a polity in which political principles alone form the basis for national unity, the history of noncitizen soldiers helps to explain why, in practice, France today remains rife with tensions emanating from differences of race, religion, culture, and language. At the outset of the Revolution, France's leaders proclaimed a new society that included all men (French women, of course, would wait until the twentieth century to gain citizenship rights) who endorsed "the natural, unalienable, and sacred rights of man," to quote from the Declaration of the Rights of Man and Citizen of 1789, which remains a founding document of the present-day French polity. Yet in reality, as this book has shown, the revolutionaries only welcomed men whom they considered fully French, on the basis of place of birth, language, culture, or race, to comprise one of the largest of the new state's institutions, the army. If noncitizens continued to serve under certain circumstances, it was because the state desperately needed them for pragmatic reasons, not because French leaders at any point during the revolutionary era departed from the exclusionary vision of the army that had emerged at the outset of the Revolution. It took longer for the French to reject all foreigners from inclusion within the nation, and for the state to begin leveraging the army to reinforce the citizenship rights of marginal groups, like Jews and, at times, people of color, whom it wanted to integrate more firmly within the national community. The goal of eliminating foreigners from the army at all stages of the Revolution, however, followed by Napoleon's deep ambivalence about foreign troops, belied the xenophobic anxieties embedded within the very core of the political and ideological foundations of modern France.

PLACES OF BIRTH FOR TROOPS IN FOREIGN REGIMENTS

The following tables indicate the places of birth of soldiers from various foreign regiments during select periods of time, as recorded in randomly selected entries from the *contrôles de troupe*. *SHD* denotes the Service historique de la Défense, Vincennes, France.

Regiment of Lee (Irish)
1710–1737 (SHD 1Yc 406)

Alsace	1	0.97%
Brabant	2	1.94%
England	9	8.74%
France ("fils d'Irlandois")	4	3.88%
Holland	1	0.97%
Ireland	82	79.61%
Liège	1	0.97%
Scotland	3	2.91%
Total Result	*103*	*100.00%*

Regiment of Clare (incorporated into the Regiment of Berwick in 1775) (Irish)
1690–1722 (SHD 1Yc 256)

England	11	14.29%
France	2	2.60%
Ireland	56	72.73%
Scotland	8	10.39%
Total Result	*77*	*100.00%*

Regiment of Berwick (incorporated the Regiment of Clare in 1775) (Irish)
1770–1786 (SHD 1Yc 140)

Brabant	7	6.93%
England	3	2.97%
Flanders	7	6.93%

France	3	2.97%
Germany	20	19.80%
Holland	11	10.89%
Ireland	7	6.93%
Italy	3	2.97%
Liège	15	14.85%
Luxembourg	1	0.99%
Savoy	10	9.90%
Scotland	1	0.99%
Spain	1	0.99%
Switzerland	12	11.88%
Total Result	*101*	*100.00%*

Regiment of Dillon (Irish)
1770–1785 (SHD 1Yc 305)

Alsace	15	4.36%
Angers	1	0.29%
Austria	1	0.29%
Brabant	118	34.30%
England	7	2.03%
France	25	7.27%
Germany	56	16.28%
Holland	10	2.91%
Ireland	30	8.72%
Italy	6	1.74%
Liège	43	12.50%
Luxembourg	9	2.62%
Savoy	4	1.16%
Scotland	5	1.45%
Spain	4	1.16%
Sweden	1	0.29%
Switzerland	7	2.03%
United States	2	0.58%
Total Result	*344*	*100.00%*

Regiment of Alsace (German)
1730–1741 (SHD 1Yc 12)

Bohemia	2	11.98%
Denmark	1	0.60%
France	100	59.88%
Germany	57	34.13%

Luxembourg	3	17.96%
Switzerland	4	2.40%
Total Result	*167*	*100.00%*

1760–1775 (SHD 1Yc 15)

Alsace	58	31.69%
Austria	1	0.55%
Bohemia	4	2.19%
Brabant	2	1.09%
France	14	7.65%
Germany	96	52.46%
Italy	1	0.55%
Liège	1	0.55%
Poland	1	0.55%
Scotland	1	0.55%
Spain	1	0.55%
Switzerland	3	1.64%
Total Result	*183*	*100.00%*

Regiment of La Marck (German)
1712–1728 (SHD 1Yc 445)

Alsace	8	7.77%
Bohemia	8	7.77%
Brabant	8	7.77%
Denmark	1	0.97%
France	3	2.91%
Germany	56	54.37%
Holland	4	3.88%
Hungary	1	0.97%
Liège	9	8.74%
Luxembourg	2	1.94%
Switzerland	3	2.91%
Total Result	*103*	*100.00%*

Regiment of Nassau-Saarbrück (German)
1745–1747 (SHD 1Yc 586)

Alsace	27	18.75%
Austria	2	1.39%
Bohemia	4	2.78%
France	14	9.72%

Germany	84	58.33%
Hungary	4	2.78%
Lorraine	1	0.69%
Saltzbourg	1	0.69%
Spain	1	0.69%
Switzerland	5	3.47%
Unknown	1	0.69%
Total Result	*144*	*100.00%*

1770–1786 (SHD 1Yc 585)

Alsace	65	39.16%
Brabant	1	0.60%
Flanders	1	0.60%
France	35	21.08%
Germany	60	36.14%
Holland	2	1.20%
Luxembourg	1	0.60%
Switzerland	1	0.60%
Total Result	*166*	*100.00%*

Regiment of Royal-Suédois (German)
1717–1741 (SHD 1Yc 833)

Alsace	14	16.47%
Bohemia	2	2.35%
Brabant	2	2.35%
Denmark	1	1.18%
Flanders	1	1.18%
France	7	8.24%
Germany	48	56.47%
Italy	1	1.18%
Luxembourg	3	3.53%
Poland	1	1.18%
Sweden	1	1.18%
Switzerland	4	4.71%
Total Result	*85*	*100.00%*

1770–1786 (SHD 1Yc 900)

Alsace	140	31.39%
Austria	8	1.79%
Bohemia	4	0.90%
Born in regiment	6	1.35%
Brabant	11	2.47%
Flanders	1	0.22%

France	46	10.31%
Germany	212	47.53%
Ireland	1	0.22%
Liège	4	0.90%
Luxembourg	2	0.45%
Piedmont	1	0.22%
Poland	2	0.45%
Savoy	1	0.22%
Sweden	1	0.22%
Switzerland	6	1.35%
Total Result	*446*	*100.00%*

THE FOREIGN REGIMENTS IN 1789

The tables below list the foreign infantry regiments (and the Company of the Hundred Swiss) that existed in 1789 and their dates of creation. Since most of the regiments were named after their colonels, their titles changed over the course of the Old Regime period. The names below represent those by which the units were known during the Revolution.

The tables omit foreign cavalry regiments, since none of them contained significant concentrations of foreigners on the eve of the Revolution. The two Italian regiments of Royal-Italien and Royal-Corse, which disbanded in 1788, are also omitted.

Swiss

Name	Created
Hundred Swiss	1481
Swiss Guards	1616
Watteville (Ernest)	1672
Salis-Samade	1672
Sonnenberg	1672
Castella	1672
Vigier	1673
Châteauvieux	1677
Diesbach	1689
Courten	1690
Salis-Grison	1734
Steiner	1752
Reinach	1758

German

Name	Created
Alsace	1654
Salm-Salm	1670
La Marck	1680
Royal-Suédois	1690
Royal-Hesse-Darmstadt	1709
Nassau	1745

Bouillon	1757
Royal-Deux-Ponts (Zweibrücken)	1757

Liégeois

Name	Created
Royal-Liégeois	1787

Irish

Name	Created
Dillon	1690
Berwick	1690
Walsh	1698

NOTES ON ARCHIVAL SOURCES

This non-exhaustive annotated bibliography of archival sources provides a sketch of the unpublished materials of greatest interest to scholars researching foreign or minority troops in the revolutionary-era French army.

Contrôles de troupe. Housed in series Yc at the Service historique de la défense (SHD) in Vincennes, these rosters record the name, birthplace, and other basic biographical data for virtually every individual who served in the French line army as an ordinary soldier or non-commissioned officer between the early eighteenth century and the "Amalgam" of the mid-1790s. (*Contrôles* for commissioned officers exist in a separate series at Vincennes, but are less significant because other files, such as personnel dossiers, generally provide more detailed information on officers.) In general, the series covers all of the foreign regiments apart from Royal-Liégeois, which did not exist long enough to produce a *contrôle*. The *contrôles* for certain foreign regiments during particular years are missing, especially for the Swiss corps during the Revolution, apparently because some of the Swiss *contrôles* from the 1790s were returned to Switzerland or lost by Swiss officers at the time of the regiments' disbandment. (On this phenomenon, see SHD Xg 36, item 7, and the letter of October 22, 1795, SHD Xg 37.) Yet the *contrôles* that have survived in France suffice for illustrating the major trends of foreign recruitment.

In general, the *contrôles* present an excellent source for quantifying the contributions of foreigners to the French army, tracing the changing proportions of foreigners to natives within the foreign regiments as the eighteenth century progressed and locating anecdotes about the experiences of particular foreign soldiers, on whom administrators occasionally recorded special notes in the margins of the *contrôles*. Some *contrôles* also indicate the confessional affiliation of each soldier, making the documents a vital source on topics related to the religion of foreign troops.

The physical descriptions of soldiers that all of the *contrôles* provide also help to identify soldiers of color within the ranks. In many cases, these descriptions are too ambiguous to identify "black" soldiers definitively, but measured against other data that the *contrôles* provide, such as place of birth and rank (many black troops served as *tambours*), the information illuminates the role that troops of color played in the French metropole under the Old Regime and during the Revolution.

André Corvisier, *Les contrôles des troupes de l'Ancien Régime*, 4 vols. (Vincennes: Service historique de l'armée de Terre, 1968), remains the essential reference on the *contrôles de troupe.*

SHD sub-series Xb and Xg. These collections contain, among other miscellaneous documents, troop reviews and inspection reports for all of the foreign regiments, as well as the demi-brigades into which the foreign regiments were later incorporated during the Old Regime and the early Revolution. (The Xg files deal with the Swiss regiments, while Xb contains records for other regiments.) Although officers sometimes falsified data in the inspection reports, their summaries of the national origins of soldiers in the foreign regiments, as well as changes in desertion rates from year to year, are excellent sources. In addition, boxes in these series offer a wide range of rich sources of other types, most of them not produced in a systematic way and some of them quite unexpected, such as reports on the languages spoken by foreign troops, assorted (though usually incomplete) correspondence files regarding particular regiments, copies of the *capitulations* that the French government contracted with foreign sovereigns to recruit their subjects, and *historiques de corps* describing the history of certain regiments. Most of the documents in these boxes, which probably originated from the administrative files that the foreign regiments left behind at the time of their dissolution or departure from France during the Revolution, are from the revolutionary period, but some documents date to much earlier in the eighteenth century.

SHD sub-series Xk. This sub-series houses documents relating to "special troops," including the foreign legions and free companies formed during the revolutionary decade, among other types of non-standard army corps. Similar in content to SHD Xb and SHD Xg, this series includes an array of rich sources of various types, ranging from copies of laws on foreign corps to enlistment rosters to eccentric proposals received by the French war ministry for levying special units of foreigners.

SHD sub-series Xh. This sub-series covers foreign regiments, battalions, and legions, as well as corps of black troops and certain other special units, that Napoleon levied during the First Empire period. Like the documents in sub-series Xk, those in this one are highly miscellaneous in nature, but copies of laws, reports on corps from government officials, rosters of soldiers and officers, and various other types of sources available in these boxes are among the most useful for studying foreign and minority troops under Napoleon.

Personnel dossiers. These files on individual generals and officers, housed in SHD series Yd and Ye, provide an efficient and effective means of researching the careers and personal lives of foreign and minority soldiers. Virtually all personnel dossiers contain registers noting troops' birthplaces and career histories, and many include additional documents of interest, such as marriage certificates and petitions to the war ministry regarding pensions, promotions, or persecution during the Terror. A finding aid for the Yd series titled "Officiers généraux de l'armée de terre et des services (Ancien Régime—2010)," maintained by the archive staff at Vincennes, notes which files correspond to foreign generals, affording researchers a particularly time-efficient means of locating material on foreigners.

Mémoires et reconnaissances. Originating primarily from the Old Regime and often of anonymous authorship, these sources, which form SHD sub-series 1M, include a number of studies and treatises, as well as occasional maps and images, on foreign troops in the army, among a variety of other topics. Most were apparently produced by officers or officials in the war ministry with an eye toward influencing military policy.

Colonial troops. SHD sub-series Xi, which covers colonial troops and expeditions, is particularly useful for research on foreign corps that were administered by the Marine, the ministry responsible for overseas jurisdictions under the Old Regime.

Reports on the army to the Committee of Public Safety. A decree of 1 Thermidor Year II (July 19, 1794) ordered the collection of information on the composition of each unit in the army. In addition to listing the birthplaces of officers, thereby helping to identify foreigners, the resulting reports, stored under the AF/II sub-series at the Archives nationales–Paris (AN), provide invaluable information about the linguistic skills and political sentiments of foreign personnel, as government officials evaluated them.

Comité militaire papers. Housed in AN sub-series D/XV, the correspondence, petitions, and other miscellaneous documents produced by or for the Comité militaire (later reorganized as the Comité de la guerre) are an invaluable source for the treatment of foreign corps during the first several years of the Revolution, including the period of the dissolution of the Swiss regiments in 1792.

Papers of deputies on mission. Assorted documents of diverse provenance in the AN D/§1 sub-series, formed from the materials of deputies on mission with the armies and in the provinces during the Revolution, are particularly useful for studying the ways in which laws and decrees from Paris on foreign and minority troops were applied in the field.

Ministre des cultes papers. This constitutes the most comprehensive set of sources regarding Jewish troops under Napoleon. Housed in AN sub-series F/19, it includes requests from Jews for dispensation from military service, statistics on Jewish conscripts, and petitions for exemption from the terms of Napoleon's "Infamous Decree" of 1808, which many Jewish communities sought to escape by citing their contributions to the army.

Police files. The extensive files in the AN F/7 sub-series, which deal mostly with police activities involving individuals, are an excellent source of information on foreign officers and soldiers who were subject to surveillance or charged with crimes during the Revolution and under the First Empire.

Revolutionary Tribunal files. The trial records and pieces of evidence in the AN W series provide rich information on foreign and Jewish troops who appeared before the Revolutionary Tribunal in Paris.

NOTES

Abbreviations

AD BR   Archives départementales du Bas-Rhin, Strasbourg, France

AN   Archives nationales, Paris, France

AP   *Archives parlementaires de 1787 à 1860. Recueil complet des débats législatifs & politiques des Chambres françaises, première série (1787–1799)*, ed. M. J. Mavidal and M. E. Laurent, 82 vols. (Paris: Paul Dupont, 1879–1913)

ARTFL   Project for American and French Research on the Treasury of the French Language digital archive

BHVP   Bibliothèque historique de la ville de Paris, Paris, France

BnF   Bibliothèque nationale de France, Paris, France

SC   Society of the Cincinnati Library and Archives, Washington, D.C.

SHD   Service historique de la Défense, Vincennes, France

Introduction

1. SHD 7Yd 13, "Etat des Services de M. Lynch"; Hayes, *Biographical Dictionary*, 158.

2. Hayes, *Biographical Dictionary*, 158.

3. SHD 7Yd 13, letter of 18 Prairial Year VI.

4. Six, *Généraux*, 70; Corvisier, *L'armée française*, 2:734–35.

5. Bell, *First Total War*, 187; Dry, *Soldats ambassadeurs*, 1:377; Corvisier, *L'armée française*, 1:273–74; Fieffé, *Histoire des troupes étrangères*, 1:280–81.

6. Furet and Ozouf, *Dictionnaire critique*, 801–3, 868–69.

7. *AP* 12:521–23. All translations are my own except where noted.

8. Sahlins, *Unnaturally French*, 1–16.

9. The word *étranger* referred variously during the Revolution to people who were foreigners to a particular locality, juridically foreign to the French nation, or simply deemed enemies of the nation. I use "foreign" and "foreigner" as a shorthand to describe individuals who were not born in France or whom contemporaries considered for other reasons to be less than fully French; during the Revolution, however, the meaning of the word *étranger* was far more fluid than this expedient conveys. See Wells, *Law and Citizenship*; Weil, *How to Be French*, 14; and Heuer, *Family and the Nation*, 10–11.

10. Forrest, *Conscripts and Deserters*, esp. 21–26.

11. Lynn, *Bayonets of the Republic*, 50–51.

NOTES TO PAGES 4–8

12. Scott, *Response of the Royal Army*, 109–18.

13. Fieffé's *Histoire des troupes étrangères* is the only major work on foreigners in general in the French armies of the Old Regime, Revolution, and Empire. Studies of Swiss troops include Watteville, *Régiment de Watteville;* Haas, *Régiment suisse;* and Czouz-Tornare, *Vaudois et Confédérés.* For Irish troops, see O'Callaghan, *History of the Irish Brigades;* Hayes, *Irish Swordsmen;* Gallaher, *Napoleon's Irish Legion;* and Genet-Rouffiac and Murphy, *Franco-Irish Military Connections.* For foreign generals, though not officers and soldiers of lower ranks, Six's *Dictionnaire biographique* and *Généraux* are useful sources, especially for the list of all generals of foreign birth who served France during the revolutionary era, which appears in the former work, and the chapter on foreign generals in the latter.

14. Bertaud's *Révolution armée* included a short section on foreign legions and free companies in the revolutionary army. Corvisier's *L'armée française* also incorporated material on foreigners in the army, but his work dealt only with the Old Regime. Other important texts on the political, social, and ideological significance of soldiering in the revolutionary era, none of which mentions foreign troops more than in passing, include Lynn, *Bayonets of the Republic;* Hippler, *Soldats et citoyens;* Edelstein, "Le militaire-citoyen"; Crépin et al., *Civils, citoyens-soldats et militaires;* Scott, *Response of the Royal Army;* and Forrest, *Conscripts and Deserters.*

15. Weil, *How to Be French;* Sahlins, *Unnaturally French;* Brubaker, *Citizenship and Nationhood;* Borgetto, "Être français sous la Révolution"; Vanel, *Évolution historique;* and Waldinger et al., *French Revolution.* Generalized studies of foreigners in revolutionary France include Mathiez, *Révolution et les étrangers;* Rapport, *Nationality and Citizenship;* and Wahnich, *L'impossible citoyen.*

16. Brubaker, *Citizenship and Nationhood,* 35. To be sure, many scholars have hesitated to identify revolutionary France as a prototypal nation-state. Some authors, such as Anderson (*Imagined Communities*), have emphasized the importance of revolutions in the New World, rather than Europe, in laying the foundations of the modern nation-state. Others, including Belissa ("De l'ordre d'Ancien Régime à l'ordre international"), have argued that France essentially functioned as a nation-state well before 1789. Yet portrayals of revolutionary France as a nation-state are central to other scholarship. For another important example beside Brubaker's, see Sewell, "French Revolution."

17. Chassin, *Elections,* 4:78, 347.

18. Mathiez, *Révolution et les étrangers.*

19. Wahnich, *L'impossible citoyen.*

20. Furet, *Interpreting the French Revolution,* esp. 80–131; Arendt, *Origins;* Edelstein, *Terror of Natural Right.*

21. Rapport, *Nationality and Citizenship,* 15.

22. The classic expression of such interpretations is Brubaker, *Citizenship and Nationhood.*

23. This is particularly true of scholarship on foreigners in revolutionary France. Both Rapport (*Nationality and Citizenship*) and Wahnich (*L'impossible étranger*) relied nearly exclusively on the official political discourses of French legislators, as the *Archives parlementaires* recorded them, for sources. Among works seeking to

investigate how such theory played out in practice, the most important is Heuer, *Family and the Nation.*

24. Rigg, *Hitler's Jewish Soldiers.*

25. Frank, *Unfriendly Fire.*

26. While there is no shortage of literature on the "guest-worker question" in different societies, a few notable examples include Haruo Shimada, *Japan's "Guest Workers": Issues and Public Policies* (Tokyo: University of Tokyo Press, 1994); David Griffith, *American Guestworkers: Jamaicans and Mexicans in the U.S. Labor Market* (Philadelphia: Pennsylvania State University Press, 2006); and Rita Chin, *The Guest Worker Question in Postwar Germany* (Cambridge: Cambridge University Press, 2007).

27. Bien, "Manufacturing Nobles"; Smith, *Nobility Reimagined.* On the effects of the rethinking of merit and nobility on the French revolutionary army, see also Blaufarb, *French Army.* In other contexts, the official abolition of feudal privilege early in the Revolution exerted limited influence in practice, as Jones pointed out in *Peasantry,* 85.

28. Bell, *Cult of the Nation;* Caron, *La nation,* esp. 42–48; Brubaker, *Citizenship and Nationhood,* esp. 35–49.

29. Weber, *Peasants into Frenchmen,* 292–302.

30. *AP* 73:425.

31. Brun, "Les unités étrangères," paragraphs 11–12.

32. Nelson, "'Black Horror.'"

33. Fogarty, *Race and War in France;* Richardot, *100.000 morts;* Stovall, "Color Line behind the Lines"; Jodi Rudoren, "Service to Israel Tugs at Identity of Arab Citizens," *New York Times,* July 13, 2012; Peled, *Question of Loyalty;* Krebs, *Fighting for Rights.*

ONE. The Army before the Nation

1. Heuer, *Family and the Nation,* 3.

2. Weil, *How to Be French,* 12; Boizet, *Lettres de Naturalité.*

3. Sahlins, *Unnaturally French,* 248.

4. Fieffé, *Histoire des troupes étrangères,* 1:3–4.

5. Following contemporaries, I use the term "national" to designate units of the French army that the Crown did not consider foreign. While this usage can have some anachronistic implications, it is less ambiguous for modern readers than the alternative label, "French," which could suggest that non-"French" units did not comprise part of the French army. On foreigners in national regiments, see Scott, *Response of the Royal Army,* 13. National regiments with the greatest number of foreigners in 1716 included those of Tournaisis, Nice, Royal-Roussillon, and Béthune-cavalerie (Corvisier, *L'armée française,* appendix to vol. 1).

6. Stradling, *Spanish Monarchy;* Murphy, *Irish Brigades;* Czouz-Tornare, *Vaudois et Confédérés,* 7; Guillaume, *Histoire des Gardes Wallones.*

7. Corvisier, *L'armée française,* 1:728, 734–35; Six, *Généraux,* 70–79.

8. Rapport, *Nationality and Citizenship,* 49.

9. Fieffé, *Histoire des troupes étrangères,* 1:393–420.

10. Royal ordinances of March 17, 1788, dissolved the two Italian regiments, Royal-Italien and Royal-Corse, and reorganized them into light-infantry battalions that the monarchy authorized to recruit only French subjects, although it permitted Italians who were already serving to remain in the light-infantry battalions. See "Ordonnance du Roi, Portant réforme du régiment Royal-Italien," BnF RES F 1121 (4); and "Ordonnance du Roi, Portant réforme du régiment Royal-Corse," BnF RES F 1120 (11). Royal-Corse, although nominally associated with Corsica, retained its designation as a foreign regiment until its dissolution in 1788, despite Corsica's annexation to France in 1769.

11. Zurlauben, *Histoire militaire des Suisses.*

12. Hubert-Brierre, *Cent-Suisses,* 15.

13. Fieffé, *Histoire des troupes étrangères,* 1:135–42, 393–406.

14. Haas, *Régiment suisse,* 1.

15. Ibid.; Czouz-Tornare, *Vaudois et Confédérés,* 16–17.

16. Czouz-Tornare, *Vaudois et Confédérésm,* 25–26, 33, 34.

17. Fieffé, *Histoire des troupes étrangères,* 179–80.

18. The regiment that in 1789 carried the title Royal-Suédeois was created in 1690, but was named after its various colonels until 1742, when the Crown rechristened it Royal-Suédeois at the request of the Swedish monarchy (Fieffé, *Histoire des troupes étrangères,* 1:411; SHD Xb 92). A minority of its officers (14 of 41 listed on a register dated February 6, 1754, in SHD Xb 96, for instance) were natives of Sweden, but virtually none of its enlisted men was Swedish: of 438 men who enrolled in the regiment between 1741 and 1749, for example, only one, a native of Bergen, hailed from territory under Swedish control (SHD 1Yc 901).

19. Dufraisse, "Populations," 107.

20. Ibid., 108–9.

21. Fieffé, *Histoire des troupes étrangères,* 1:35, 169; Michel, *Écossais en France,* 1–56.

22. Micheline Kerney Walsh, "The Wild Goose Tradition," in *Irishmen in War,* 180–82; Canny, *Making Ireland British.*

23. Fieffé, *Histoire des troupes étrangères,* 176.

24. Charles Petrie, "Ireland in Spanish and French Strategy, 1558–1815," in *Irishmen in War,* 198.

25. Although there is some debate regarding the precise number of Irish troops who fled to France between 1690 and 1692, most scholars agree on 19,000 as an approximate figure. See Nathalie Genet-Rouffiac, "Les Jacobites à Paris et à Saint-Germain-en-Laye," in Corp, *L'autre exil,* 109; MacGeoghan, *Histoire de l'Irlande,* 2:748.

26. *Résumé de l'historique du 88e régiment d'infanterie;* Genet-Rouffiac, *Grand Exil,* 413.

27. One example was Robert Anderson, whose daring escape from the Irish Brigades (as he reported it) was detailed in *Gentleman's Magazine* 28:242.

28. Corvisier, *L'armée française,* 1:271–72.

29. Hayes, *Ireland and Irishmen,* 255.

30. Hayes, *Irish Swordsmen of France*, 11; Fieffé, *Histoire des troupes étrangères*, 1:333–34.

31. Fieffé, *Histoire des troupes étrangères*, 1:183.

32. Of 197 troops surveyed from Royal-Corse's *contrôle* for the years 1787–89, 153 were natives of Corsica, 39 of Germany, and 23 of Alsace.

33. Fieffé, *Histoire des troupes étrangères*, 2:182–86, 276–77; Corvisier, *L'armée française*, 1:273.

34. Convention of October 18, 1787, SHD Xb 105; BnF F 4771 (12).

35. Fieffé, *Histoire des troupes étrangères*, 144; BnF F 23626 377.

36. Boissau, "La levée de Bercheny-hussards," 1.

37. Fieffé, *Histoire des troupes étrangères*, 1:278–79.

38. Corvisier, *L'armée française*, 1:269–70.

39. Rodosto is a historical name for present-day Tekirdag (Boissau, "La levée de Bercheny-hussards," 2, 4, 10, 24).

40. Fieffé, *Histoire des troupes étrangères*, 1:279.

41. The fourth edition of the *Dictionnaire de l'Académie française*, published in 1762, defined *nègre* as a word that "ne se met point ici comme un nom de Nation, mais seulement parce qu'il entre dans cette façon de parler. *Traiter quelqu'un comme un nègre*, pour dire, Traiter quelqu'un comme un esclave." Jean-François Féraud's *Dictionaire [sic] critique de la langue française*, from 1787 to 1788, however, applied the term simply to the inhabitants of the coast of Africa, although it emphasized in particular those who were transported to European colonies as slaves. Thus *nègre* in Old Regime France was an ambiguous word that, although associated with the African slave trade, implied no precise geographic origin or racial lineage (ARTFL, "Dictionnaires d'autrefois," accessed January 11, 2012, http://artflx.uchicago.edu/cgi-bin/dicos/pubdico1look.pl?strippedhw=négre).

42. Corvisier, *L'armée française*, 1:273–74; Fieffé, *Histoire des troupes étrangères*, 1:280–81; SHD 3Yc 278.

43. SHD 1Yc 446.

44. SHD 1Yc 158.

45. Ibid.

46. SHD 1Yc 304; SHD 1Yc 446.

47. Boulle, "Les gens de couleur," 160; Gainot, *Officiers de couleur*, 45; Peabody, *"There Are No Slaves in France,"* 4.

48. Thus the French empire integrated populations from across the world in ways that paralleled the cosmopolitan British empire of the same period, which historians have studied in greater detail; for example, see Linda Colley, *The Ordeal of Elizabeth Marsh: A Woman in World History* (New York: Pantheon, 2007), and David Hancock, *Citizens of the World* (Cambridge: Cambridge University Press, 1995).

49. SHD 1Yc 259.

50. Ó Hannracháin, "Irish Brigade at Lafelt," 9.

51. SHD 1Yc 305.

52. Donavan, "Germans in Louisbourg."

53. SHD Xg 28; Fieffé, *Histoire des troupes étrangères*, 1:268; BnF 4 LG6 425; BnF F 23624.

54. Some but not all of these Protestants converted to Catholicism. See Havard and Vidal, *Histoire de l'Amérique française*, 89; Moogk, *La Nouvelle France*, 60–61; SHD Xi 66.

55. Donavan, "Germans in Louisbourg."

56. *Letters of Brunswick and Hessian Officers*, 43.

57. Bragelongne, *Journal*.

58. Bodinier, *Dictionnaire*, 7–8; SHD Xi 67.

59. Selig, "German Soldier in America."

60. SHD Xb 12.

61. Chartrand, *French Army*, 13, 47.

62. SHD Xb 99; SHD 7Yd 35; Hayes, *Irish Swordsmen of France*, 176–77.

63. SHD Xb 86.

64. SHD Xi 67; AN MAR G 229, item 89.

65. Vergé-Franceschi, *La Marine française*, 395–96; Genet-Rouffiac, *Grand Exil*, 207.

66. AN D/XVI/14, item 68.

67. Vergé-Franceschi, *La Marine française*, 402.

68. Maurice de Saxe, "Considérations politiques et militaires sur les Régiments étrangers," SHD 1M 1722; Haas, *Régiment suisse*, 33. Various other authors of treatises in SHD 1M 1722 repeated this "three-men-as-one" argument in favor of foreign recruitment, but Saxe appears to have been the first to advance it. It remained prevalent into the Revolution; see *AP* 23:59.

69. Dupâquier, "French Population in the 17th and 18th Centuries," 154.

70. Quoted in Corvisier, *L'armée française*, 1:259.

71. "Considérations politiques et militaires sur les Régiments étrangers," date unknown (but probably 1780, according to a penciled note in the margin) (SHD 1M 1722).

72. Memorandum of July 1740, SHD Xb 96.

73. Untitled treatise of April 8, 1773, SHD 1M 1771.

74. BnF F 23627 (378).

75. Haas, *Régiment suisse*, 1.

76. SHD 1M 1722; Chartrand, *Louis XV's Army*, 17, 19.

77. SHD 1M 1722.

78. Ibid.

79. SHD 1M 1770; Merrill, *Germans of Louisiana*, 20–24.

80. Hippler, *Soldats et citoyens*, 58; Machiavelli, *The Prince*, 47–52; Rousseau, *Considérations*; Rousseau, *Projet*.

81. Guibert, *Essai général de tactique*, 76.

82. Servan, *Soldat citoyen*.

83. Lanier, *Général Joseph Servan*.

84. Servan, *Soldat citoyen*, 278–79, 484; Bertaud, *Révolution armée*, 59–60; Blaufarb, *French Army*, 68–70.

85. Van Kley, *Religious Origins*, 11–12; Sahlins, "Fictions," 86. During the Seven

Years' War, Frederick II of Prussia circulated billets within Germany presenting the conflict as an attack on Protestantism by Catholic powers (Corvisier, *L'armée française*, 1:266).

86. Corvisier, *L'armée française*, 1:262–63. For an example of the guarantee of freedom of religion to foreign troops, see article 45 of the capitulation for Swiss regiments of September 3, 1764, in SHD Xg 1, which mandated that "Les protestants qui pourront se trouver parmi les dittes Troupes, aurons le libre exercice de leur Religion, comme ils l'ont toujour eu jusqu'a présent." See also the capitulation signed on May 27, 1763, between the duc de Choiseul, minister of war, and General Nicolas Luckner, which promised, "Comme M. de Lukener n'est point neé dans le Royaume de France la liberté de conscience ne peut luy être refusée" (SHD 2Yd 255).

87. The author of "Considérations politiques et militaires sur les Régiments étrangers" (SHD 1M 1722), which was probably produced circa 1780, argued that one of the most efficacious means of enticing Greeks to enlist in French service was to promise them freedom of religion.

88. Protestant veterans did, however, receive higher pensions in lieu of admission to the Invalides (Corvisier, *L'armée française*, 1:262–63).

89. Watteville, *Régiment de Watteville*, 10. Guibert wrote in a memorandum of February 1, 1789, that the Crown should take advantage of the upcoming renewal of capitulations for the Swiss regiments to grant them both Catholic and Protestant ministers (SHD 1M 1790).

90. An ordinance of January 17, 1710, lifted the ban on entry to the Invalides for wounded Swiss troops (Réthoré, *Gardes Suisses à Argenteuil*). One of the first acts of the Legislative Assembly was the abolition, on September 21, 1791, of the *Ordre du Mérite militaire* and the declaration that all officers were eligible for the *Ordre de Saint-Louis* regardless of religion. The *Ordre du Mérite militaire* reappeared during the Bourbon Restoration, but only for a brief period (Watteville, *Régiment de Watteville*, 44–45; Steenackers, *Histoire des ordres de chevalarie*, 275–77).

91. The academy was founded at Colmar in Alsace (Roverea, *Mémoires*, 7, 10).

92. Girard, *Histoire abrégée*, 28.

93. Pierre-Louis Coudray, "'Irlandois de nation': Irish Soldiers in Angers as an Illustration of Franco-Irish Relationships in the Seventeenth and Eighteenth Centuries," in Genet-Rouffiac and Murphy, *Franco-Irish Military Connections*, 94–108: 103.

94. Réthoré, *Gardes Suisses à Argenteuil*, 21.

95. AN D/XV/2, dossier 7, item 64.

96. Corvisier, *L'armée française*, 1:560.

97. SHD 1Yc 446.

98. Of ninety-three men surveyed who served in the unit between 1763 and 1765, Protestants comprised 26.9 percent (SHD 8Yc 19).

99. SHD Xb 76.

100. Czouz-Tornare, *Vaudois et Confédérés*, 20.

101. None of the *contrôles* that survive for the Irish regiments record soldiers' religion, a fact which suggests that most were Catholic.

102. Irish refugees initially suffered cold receptions in France; the Parlement of Brittany went so far as to expel them from the province, on pain of being hanged

and quartered. Over time, however, French Catholics, who came to sympathize with the religious plight of Irish refugees, began to view them more favorably (Hayes, *Ireland and Irishmen*, 1–2, 252).

103. Hayes, *Irish Swordsmen of France*, 11–12.

104. Quoted in Gallaher, *Napoleon's Irish Legion*, 123–24.

105. Corvisier, *L'armée française*, 1:562.

106. Quoted in Corvisier, *L'armée française*, 1:562. The *contrôle* for the Volontaires de Saxe Regiment (SHD 3Yc 278) did not indicate the religion of its personnel. On the Muslim cavalry unit that served Napoleon, see Fieffé, *Histoire des troupes étrangères*, 2:140.

107. Fieffé, *Histoire des troupes étrangères*, 2:140.

108. Corvisier, *L'armée française*, 1:294–95.

109. Departmental archives of Meurthe-et-Moselle E supplément?7[1], cited in Job, *Inventaire*, 15–16.

110. Bell, *Cult of the Nation*, 171–72; Brunot, *Histoire de la langue française*; Cohen, "Courtly French."

111. An official interpreter, with the title "Exempt François," served within the Company of the Hundred Swiss beginning in 1626. This practice extended to other foreign regiments as well (*Discours sommaire;* Malaguti, *Historique,* 92; BnF F 4727).

112. Bois, "Maurice de Saxe," paragraph 22.

113. In 1779, when Ogilvy addressed papers to the war ministry related to his pension, he had to hire a translator (SHD 4Yd 2379).

114. An ordinance of January 1763 (the exact date is unclear), which forbade recruiters for the foreign regiments to enroll French subjects, excepted those who spoke foreign languages (SHD 1M 1722).

115. *Ordonnance du Roy sur l'exercice de l'infanterie.*

116. By September 1755, a major in the Swiss Guards regiment named Settiers had published a German translation. A corporal-major in the Regiment of Royal-Italien submitted an Italian translation around the same time, while an unnamed officer in the Irish Regiment of Clare had completed a translation into English by the end of the year, providing commands largely identical to those used in the British army at the time. All of these translations are available in SHD Xg 1. For comparisons between the English translations and the commands used in British service, see the military instructions published in Cavan, *New System of Military Discipline.*

117. The original text of these criticisms reads: "Ce mot your parvins aussi esté employé indifferement pour exprimer *le la vostre vos,* et cependant un [sic] trouver quelquefois *the* pour rendre *le* et la" ("Observations sur l'Imprimé de la Traduction angloise," SHD Xg 1).

118. "Observations sur la traduction des Commandemens pour es Regs. Allemands," SHD Xg 1.

119. Memorandum dated 1755 and the letter of September, 2, 1755, SHD Xg 1.

120. O'Callaghan, *History of the Irish Brigades*, 161–62.

121. Memorandum of April 1, 1789, SHD 1M 1722.

122. Haas, *Régiment suisse au service de France*, 4.

123. Capitulation for the Reinach Regiment, SHD Xg 37; Haas, *Régiment suisse au service de France*, 12.

124. Haas, *Régiment suisse au service de France*, 4.

125. Brierre, *Cent-Suisses*, 73–74.

126. To cite the text of one oath: "Vous jurerés de servir fidellement et en tout honneur Sa Majesté très Chrêstinne le Roy de France, de procurer en tous ses avantages, de tourner de tout vôtre pouvoir ce qui pourroit être prejudiciable à sa Justerete, et de vous opposer à tous ceux qui seroient contre nôtre dis Roy; nous nous reservons néanmoins en cecy nos souverains seigneurs et Peres des Cantons et leurs alliés; en sorte qu'il nous sera loisible, conformément à nôtre Capitulation de retournée en nôtre Païs touttes foict et quant il plaira à notre souveraine de nous rappeller" (letter of June 2, 1759, SHD Xg 1). See also Lynn, *Giant of the Grand Siècle*, 367; Corvisier, *L'armée française*, 1:360; and Scott, *Response of the Royal Army*, 27.

127. Corvisier, *L'armée française*, 1:262–63.

128. Letter of December 7, 1712, SHD Xg 31.

129. AD BR C/537.

130. Letter of September 14, 1770, SHD Xg 17.

131. Coudray, "'Irlandois de nation,'" 100.

132. Zwilling, *Discours sommaire*, 5.

133. See "Memoire contenant les faits qui Etablissent le privilege qu'ont les officiers Suisses" and "Memoire du 8 Octobre 1728," AN O/1/3679.

134. Corvisier, *L'Armée française*, 260.

135. Réthoré, *Gardes Suisses à Argenteuil*, 6.

136. Haas, *Régiment suisse au service de France*, 33–34.

137. Memorandum of 1713, quoted in Corvisier, *L'armée française*, 1:260; memorandum of April 1, 1789, SHD 1M 1722.

138. Rapport, *Nationality and Citizenship*, 38–42.

139. Corvisier, *L'armée française*, 119–20; Scott, *Response of the Royal Army*, 42–44.

140. Quoted in Lynn, *Bayonets of the Republic*, 62–63. This translation is Lynn's.

141. Colin Jones, "The Military Revolution and the Professionalization of the French Army Under the Ancien Régime," in Rogers, *Military Revolution Debate*, 161–64.

142. Corvisier, *L'armée française*, 1:543; Corvisier, *Contrôles de troupe*.

143. SHD 1Yc 140; SHD 3Yc 278. Mozambique, of course, was a colony of Portugal, explaining why the author of the *contrôle* counted it as part of that country; nonetheless, this example highlights the ambiguities inherent in working with the *contrôles*.

144. SHD 1Yc 158.

145. SHD Xg 36, item 7; letter of October 30, 1795, SHD Xg 37.

146. SHD 1Yc 304

147. SHD 1Yc 305.

148. SHD 1Yd 447; "Memoire concernant Les Recrües des Regiments Irlandais,"

SHD 1M 1771; ordinance of March 13, 1783, SHD Xb 76; "Instruction particulière concernant le travail des recrües des régimens allemands," AN MAR G 174.

149. SHD 1Yc 446.

150. Because most of the *contrôles* for the Swiss regiments have disappeared, the troop reviews in the Xg sub-series at SHD are the only major source of data on their composition at the time of the Revolution. These documents do not record the exact locality of each recruit's place of birth, but they provide general national categorizations for the corps as a whole. A review for the Castella Regiment from September 14, 1789, in SHD Xg 31 shows that of 975 men present, 679 were Swiss, 274 were foreigners of other nationalities, and 22 were French subjects. Statistics for the Salis-Samade and Sonnenberg regiments were similar: 734 of 971 and 742 of 978 of their personnel were Swiss in 1789 (SHD Xg 30; SHD Xg 32).

151. Quoted in Corvisier, *L'armée française*, 1:274.

152. Memorandum of January 1763, SHD 1M 1722.

153. Quoted in Hayes, *Irish Swordsmen of France*, 11–12.

154. Ordinance of 1763, SHD 1M 1722.

155. Herlaut, *Colonel Bouchotte*, 1:2; Chuquet, *Prince jacobin*, 259; "Les débuts du ministre de la guerre Bouchotte," 71.

156. September 17, 1879, SHD Xb 101.

157. Corvisier, *L'armée française*, 1:261.

158. Letter of September 29, 1747, SHD Xb 12.

159. "Mémoire pour obtenir une retraite," SHD Xb 86; letter of November 19, 1773, SHD 1M 1771.

160. Memorandum of 1742, SHD 1M 1722; "Mémoire Sur les Recrües de l'Infanterie Allemande et Irlandoise," SHD 1M 1722.

161. According to one anonymous observer, the French would need to dispatch about fifty noncommissioned officers to Germany each year, along with one captain and two lieutenants, in order to acquire between 1,100 and 1,200 men (SHD 1M 1771).

162. SHD Xb 101; SHD Xb 104.

163. "Réponse à l'Extrait du Plan du Recrutement," SHD 1M 1722.

164. SHD 1M 1722.

165. SHD 1M 1722; June 25, 1775, SHD Xb 101; November 1, 1758, SHD 1M 1771; October 15, 1777, SHD 1M 1771.

166. "Mémoire Sur les Recrües de l'Infanterie Allemande et Irlandoise," SHD 1M 1722.

167. "Projet de Levée de Milice Etrangére," SHD 1M 1770.

168. Hubert-Brierre, *Cent-Suisses*, 72.

169. Sahlins, "Fictions of a Catholic France," 88.

170. Hayes, *Irish Swordsmen of France*, 293; BnF F 23628 (45); Corvisier, *L'armée française*, 1:270; AN MAR G 229, item 86.

171. *Mémoire pour Michel de Reilly*. A handwritten note in the margin of the Bibliothèque nationale de France's copy of this pamphlet (BnF 4 FM 32713) indicates that Reilly won his case.

172. Memorandum of July 24, 1752, SHD 1M 1722. See also the Count of Clare's memorandum of 1757, SHD 1M 1722.

173. Hayes, *Irish Swordsmen of France*, 119.

174. Quoted in Haas, *Régiment suisse*, 4–5; Réthoré, *Gardes Suisses à Argenteuil;* Genet-Rouffiac, *Grand Exil*, 305. Examples of foreign officers of various nationalities who married French women under the Old Regime included Dominique Sheldon (see his personnel dossier, SHD 3Yd 1317); Joseph Miaczynski (see SHD 4Yd 3875); and the comte de Berchény (see Boissau, "La levée de Bercheny-hussards," 21). Théobald Dillon, meanwhile, took a French woman as a common-law wife and had several children with her, although they never married (Hayes, *Irish Swordsmen of France*, 33).

175. Girard, *Histoire abrégée des officiers suisses*, 28.

176. Hayes, *Irish Swordsmen of France*, 225, 249–52.

177. "Etat de M.M. Les Officiers reformés," SHD Xb 102.

178. Scott, *Response of the Royal Army*, 6; reports on officers' semester leaves in SHD Xb 94, SHD Xb 95, and SHD Xb 104.

179. Hayes, *Irish Swordsmen of France*, 11–12.

180. Rapport, *Nationality and Citizenship*, 35; Scott, *Response of the Royal Army*, 148; Forrest, "Citizenship and Military Service," 160–61. See also France, *Mercenaries and Paid Men*, esp. 1–13, 43–60.

181. Corvisier, *L'Armée française*, 1:163.

182. Scott, *Response of the Royal Army*, 7.

183. Rogers, *Military Revolution Debate*, esp. 149–67; Parrott, "Strategy and Tactics"; Lynn, "Recalculating French Army Growth"; Jeremy Black, *Military Revolution?*.

184. Corvisier, *Dictionnaire d'art et d'histoire militaires*, 571.

185. While one late-fifteenth-century source described *mercenaires* as "foreigners who serve in an army for money," a review of the excellent ARTFL database shows that dictionaries from the seventeenth and eighteenth centuries defined a *mercenaire* as anyone who performed work in exchange for money, often but not necessarily with the connotation of selfishness or opportunism on the part of the worker. None of the dictionary definitions mentioned soldiers or the military in particular until the publication of the fifth edition of the *Dictionnaire de l'Académie française* in 1798 ("Mercenaire," Centre national de ressources textuelles et lexicales, http://www.cnrtl.fr/etymologie/mercenaire, accessed September 23, 2014; ARTFL, "Dictionnaires d'autrefois," http://artflx.uchicago.edu/cgi-bin /dicos/pubdico1look.pl?strippedhw=mercenaire, accessed November 30, 2011). The evolution of the word "mercenary" in English largely paralleled that of its French cognate. Within the first years of the Revolution denunciations of foreign troops as *mercenaires* abounded; for example, see Marat, *Oeuvres politiques*, 3:1710–11; *Crimes du 10 août*; AP 54:287.

186. Sahlins, *Unnaturally French*.

TWO. Nationalizing the Army

1. Furet, *Interpreting the French Revolution*.

2. Mathiez, *Révolution et les étrangers*, 2.

3. Furet, *Interpreting the French Revolution*, esp. 81–131; Cobban, *Social In-*

terpretation; Jones, "Bourgeois Revolution Revivified"; Maza, *Myth of the French Bourgeoisie.*

4. Mathiez, *Révolution et les étrangers,* 138–40; Rapport, *Nationality and Citizenship,* 135.

5. Wahnich, *L'impossible citoyen,* 11–13.

6. Rapport, *Nationality and Citizenship,* 10.

7. *Elections,* 4:78.

8. Ibid., 3:195.

9. Ibid., 4:347.

10. Alain-Jacques Czouz-Tornare, "Les formations suisses, substituts aux gardes nationales dans les capitales provinciales en 1789–1790," in Bianchi and Dupuy, *La Garde nationale,* 223–48: 224.

11. Ibid.

12. Scott, *Response of the Royal Army,* 51.

13. See chapter 1.

14. Rapport, *Nationality and Citizenship,* 91; "Mouvements de Troupes qui ont eu lieu dans la Génerálité de Paris," AN BB/30/161.

15. Deschard, *L'Armée et la Révolution,* 174.

16. Rapport, *Nationality and Citizenship,* 91; Scott, *Response of the Royal Army,* 58; "Rapport fait au Comité de Recherches des Représentans de la commune," AN BB/30/161.

17. "Rélation de la prise de la Bastille."

18. After surviving the attack on the Bastille and his subsequent capture, Flue returned to the Salis-Samade Regiment, where in 1791 he was promoted to captain (SHD Xg 30, item 23).

19. *AP* 8:209; Wright, *Napoleon and Europe,* 72.

20. Duveyrier and Bailly, *Procès-verbal,* 3:147, 299.

21. *AP* 15:404.

22. Aulard, *Société des Jacobins,* 1:86–90.

23. Ibid., 2:619.

24. Marat, *Oeuvres politiques,* 1:651; 3:1627, 1774; 6:3716; 7:3994, 3996.

25. *AP* 54:287.

26. Mathiez, *Victoire en l'an II,* 37.

27. Deschard, *L'Armée et la Révolution,* 175–77.

28. Czouz-Tornare, *Vaudois et Confédérés,* 54, 58.

29. Ibid., 41.

30. Mathiez, *Victoire en l'an II,* 37.

31. *Le Salve des troupes étrangeres campees au Champ de Mars, Adressé aux Parisiens* (n.p., 1789), 3, 8.

32. Review of September 15, 1789, SHD Xg 34.

33. Scott, *Response of the Royal Army,* 61.

34. Review of August 9, 1789, SHD Xg 32.

35. Desertions in the Diesbach Regiment between 1784 and 1788 averaged thirty-five per year. See the reviews of 1785, 1786, 1787, and 1788 in SHD XG 34.

Salis-Samade lost only ten men to desertion in the year preceding the attack on the Bastille, according to a review dated September 20, 1789, SHD Xg 30.

36. Scott, *Response of the Royal Army*, 61.

37. Ibid., 61–62.

38. Scott, *Response of the Royal Army*, 74–75.

39. Czouz-Tornare, "Les formations suisses," 224–26.

40. Poisson, *L'Armée et la Garde nationale*; Dupuy, *La Garde nationale*.

41. Czouz-Tornare, "Les formations suisses," 226.

42. Scott, *Response of the Royal Army*, 67.

43. Czouz-Tornare, "Les formations suisses," 227.

44. Scott, *Response of the Royal Army*, 91–95; Fieffé, *Histoire des troupes étrangères*, 1:357–59; *AP* 19:616–44.

45. *AP* 18:511.

46. Marat, *Oeuvres politiques*, 5:3168. While reports in the summer of 1789 affirmed that members of the Châteauvieux Regiment, like those belonging to some of the other of the foreign units in Paris, had vowed not to attack the people of the city, it is unclear on what evidence Marat based the claims that the Châteauvieux troops had been the first to express support for the Revolution, or that they explicitly swore not to shed the blood of civilians. It is likely that he invented these details to bolster criticism of the units that suppressed the Nancy mutiny (Czouz-Tornare, *Vaudois et confédérés*, 54).

47. *AP* 30:678–79; 31:444.

48. *AP* 36:350–51; 34:560.

49. *AP* 36:364.

50. *AP* 36:715–16.

51. Ibid., 716–17.

52. Ibid., 721.

53. Although the Châteauvieux soldiers who were condemned to the galleys numbered forty-one at the time of their judgment, only forty survived when they were released (*AP* 41:387–91).

54. *AP* 41:409; Pétion, *Réponse de M. Pétion*; AN D/XV/3, dossier 23.

55. *Adresse au département de Paris par des volontaires*.

56. *Adresse aux François*.

57. Roberts, *Jacques-Louis David*, 282–83; Aulard, *Société des Jacobins*, 3:459.

58. Initial reports on the troubles in Belfort implicated the Lauzun hussar regiment as well as Royal-Liégeois, but later documents indicated that the Lauzun troops were not involved: *AP* 20:106, 136–40, 340, 346–50, 415–16; reports of October 21 and October 29, 1790, AN F/9/45; *Lettre au Roi, Et exposé de la conduite de MM.; Détail du projet de contre-révolution*.

59. *AP* 20:138.

60. Marat, *Oeuvres politiques*, 3:1710–11.

61. Ibid., 5:3119–20.

62. *AP* 28:471–72.

63. Fieffé, *Histoire des troupes étrangères*, 1:371.

64. Von Fersen, *Comte de Fersen,* v–lxxvii.

65. These included four German infantry regiments (Royal-Hesse-Darmstadt, Bouillon, Deux-Ponts, and Nassau) and two Swiss ones (Castella and Reinach), as well as ten detachments from various cavalry units, including elements of Royal-Allemand and Esterhazy (Bouillé, *Mémoires,* 188, 219).

66. Ibid., 232.

67. Scott, *Response of the Royal Army,* 103.

68. Based on the emigration figures for the twelve German, Irish, and Liégeois infantry regiments and for twelve French regiments selected at random in *État des officiers généraux.* The list included no information on emigration in the Swiss regiments.

69. *Contrôle* for officers of the émigré army, SHD Xu 1. A majority of the foreign officers came from the regiments of Alsace, Salm-Salm, Royal-Hesse-Darmstadt, and Walsh. I counted as foreign not only officers who had served in foreign regiments prior to enlisting in the émigré army, but also those officers whose military service history the émigré records did not document but who had foreign names; thus the actual number of foreign officers serving with the émigrés was likely smaller than the estimate here.

70. *Quellen zur Geschichte des Rheinlandes,* 2:188; *AP* 43:345.

71. Marat, *Oeuvres politiques,* 7:4079; *AP* 44:83; 52:494.

72. Many of the officers from the Saxe Regiment remained with the émigrés (*AP* 44:112, 135).

73. Ibid., 234–46.

74. The National Convention approved their incorporation into another hussar regiment (*AP* 64:710–12).

75. The British Irish Brigade suffered great difficulty acquiring recruits and was decimated during service in the colonies. British authorities disbanded it after a few years. As late as 1810, however, a Dillon Regiment, composed in part of French émigrés (not all of them of Irish descent) who had left France early in the Revolution, remained in British service. Even while serving the British king, it seems that these men continued to consider themselves French, affirming that they were "Sujets de Sa Majesté Très Chretienne [of France] . . . au service de Sa Majesté Britannique." Some of the officers of the British Irish Brigade eventually returned to France and reenlisted during the Restoration period (Hayes, *Ireland and Irishmen,* 81–86, 152–56; SHD 8Yd 2249; letter of December 16, 1814, SHD Xu 15; AN F/7/6369, dossier 7533).

76. Like all the Swiss corps, the Ernest Regiment took the name of its colonel, who until May 1792 remained officially Béat-Rodolphe, baron d'Ernest. Because the baron d'Ernest was ill from the beginning of the Revolution and unable to command the regiment personally, however, the acting commander was Louis de Watteville, whose name was adopted by some contemporaries to refer to the unit even before he formally became its colonel in May 1792 (Scott, *Response of the Royal Army,* 139–42; Watteville, *Régiment de Watteville;* Fieffé, *Histoire des troupes étrangères,* 2:398).

77. *AP* 34:459–60, 494–95, 674–75, and 676–78; dossier 7, AN D/XV/6; Scott, *Response of the Royal Army,* 139–42.

78. Letter of October 19, 1791, AN D/XV/6.

79. *AP* 34:674–75.

80. Watteville, *Régiment de Watteville*, 24–29; Haas, *Régiment suisse*, 18–20; *Lettre de M. Pujet-Barbentane*; Roverea, *Mémoires*, 81–83; Scott, *Response of the Royal Army*, 142; Rapport, *Nationality and Citizenship*, 151. Scott erroneously identified the February 1792 incident as having occurred in Marseille, not Aix, an oversight that Rapport repeated.

81. *AP* 40:431–32.

82. Watteville, *Régiment de Watteville*, 34–35.

83. Haas, *Régiment suisse*, 20.

84. *AP* 9:38.

85. "Mémoire anonime qui Prouve la nécessité de Conserver les Troupes Suisses, économie qui peut en résulter," SHD 1M 1722. See also Guibert's "Mémoire concernant les Régimens Suisses," SHD 1M 1790.

86. *AP* 10:517.

87. Ibid., 12:699–700.

88. Ibid., 12:521–23, 595–612.

89. Ibid., 12:615–20.

90. Ibid., 12:557–58.

91. Ibid., 11:626–27.

92. Ibid., 15:403–06.

93. Ibid., 11:741.

94. Ibid., 16:469–70.

95. Ibid., 16:470, 17:74–77.

96. See chapter 3.

97. *AP* 18:142, 31:424–25.

98. Ibid., 23:728.

99. Ibid., 23:57–70, 728–30, 755.

100. The law mandated that the regiments adopt numerical designations instead of the names of their colonels (*Règlement Sur la Formation, les Appointements & la Solde de l'Infanterie*). Swiss regiments retained their traditional names. *Règlement Sur les Appointemens & Solde des Régimens Suisses & Grisons*.

101. *AP* 28:212.

102. SHD Xb 67.

103. *AP* 28:472; *Patriote français* 712 (July 22, 1791). Reprinted in *Le patriote français* (Frankfurt am Main: Keip Verlag, 1989). The reprint has no page numbers.

104. Review of October 1, 1788, and September 21, 1789, SHD Xb 102.

105. *AP* 28:472.

106. SHD 14Yc 141.

107. *AP* 57:120–25, 40:521–22. See also the comments of Nicolas Boucher, AN D/§1/16.

108. AN AF/II/371, dossier 3002, item 14; roster of 2 Messidor Year VI, SHD Xi 20.

109. *Décret portant déclaration de guerre sanctionné*, 2.

110. Schreiber, *Französische Ausweisungspolitik*, 110.

111. Aulard, *Société des Jacobins*, 3:559–60.

112. *AP* 47:394–97.

113. *AP* 49:33.

114. Mathiez, *Révolution et les étrangers*, 63.

115. Letters of April 27, 1792, SHD B2 104.

116. *AP* 49:93–94.

117. *AP* 48:357. The proclamation did, however, provoke the publication and distribution in France of a propaganda pamphlet titled "Réponse des Soldats Autrichiens & Prussiens à la soi-disante déclaration du Peuple François" (AN D/XV/2, dossier 7, item 58).

118. *AP* 47:396, 49:36. Once the August 2 decree was translated into German, its dissemination along the border increased, thanks in part to Flemish peasants who reportedly inserted copies into the bread they sold to the Austrian army (Chuquet, *Légion germanique*, 4). On Oberlin's career see also David A. Bell, "Nation-Building and Cultural Particularism in Eighteenth-Century France: The Case of Alsace," *Eighteenth Century Studies* 21 (Summer 1988): 472–90.

119. AN D/XV/6, dossier 98, item 1. For an example of an expatriated French soldier attempting to return to France under the terms of the August 1792 decrees, see the letter to the war minister from Theodore Joseph Oudart, AN D/XL/28.

120. Dufraisse, "Les populations de la rive gauche," 123; *Détail de l'Armée du Général Luckner.*

121. Marat, *Oeuvres politiques*, 8:4945.

122. *AP* 54:52.

123. Scott, *Response of the Royal Army*, 109–18.

124. *AP* 44:47, 246–47.

125. *AP* 44:349, 585–86.

126. *AP* 55:151.

127. Quoted in Wahnich, *L'impossible citoyen*, 252–53. On the decree of 7 Prairial Year II, see pages 237–79 of Wahnich's work; on French revolutionary constructions of the British as "the enemy of mankind," see pages 281–310.

128. AN D/§1/16, dossier 14.

129. Weil, *How to Be French*, 13–14.

130. AN AF/II/55, dossier 400, item 28. See also AN AF/II/55, dossier 400, item 31.

131. Dillon, *Observations historiques;* Hayes, *Ireland and Irishmen*, 78. On Louis XIV's naturalization of Irish troops, see chapter 1, page <x-ref>.

132. Hayes, *Ireland and Irishmen*, 79.

133. Hesse to the mayor of Orléans, July 3, 1793, SHD 3Yd 1294.

134. Chuquet, *Prince jacobin*, 44, 51. See also Hesse's letters of June 16, 1791, and August 4, 1793, SHD 3Yd 1294.

135. AN F/7/4689, plaquette 4, item 102, page 15. On Eustace's background, including his service in the Continental Army (where he apparently had a close relationship with Baron Friedrich Wilhelm von Steuben) and the path that brought him to France during the Revolution, see Tozzi, "Between Two Republics"; SC Mss L1971.1.42 M; and SC Mss L2010F60 1792 M.

136. Letter of 11 Floréal Year II, SHD Xg 24.

137. *AP* 10:558.

138. *AP* 15:406.

139. Lecointre, *Discours.*

140. A draft law submitted to the Assembly by the Military Committee on February 1, 1790, included the provision that "Après trente ans de service dans l'armée, un militaire français ou *devenu Français* ... jouira de la plénitude des droits du citoyen actif" (emphasis added). Another proposed law drafted by Wimpffen in the same month granted active citizenship to "tout militaire français ou *devenu Français*" (emphasis added) after twenty-five years of service. A third proposed decree from August 3, 1792, however, lacked any language alluding to naturalized foreigners and extended active citizenship only to "tout Français" who had served for a fixed period of time. Ultimately, these nuances become a null issue, since the sweeping away of voting-eligibility requirements after the collapse of the monarchy in August 1792 rendered laws linking active citizenship to military service obsolete (*AP* 11:412, 628; *AP* 47:421; Edelstein, "Le militaire-citoyen," 591).

141. *AP* 11:732, 742, 16:449–50.

142. *AP* 39:69.

143. *AP* 48:418–19.

144. Marat, *Oeuvres politiques,* 4:2429–30.

145. Ibid., 5:2961.

146. See, for example, the oath signed by fifty-five officers of the Regiment of Courten on July 22, 1791 (SHD Xg 33).

147. *AP* 16:95.

148. *AP* 19:67–68.

149. *AP* 30:646; Rapport, *Nationality and Citizenship,* 151.

150. *AP* 38:412–13.

151. Brissot, *Rapport fait au nom de la Commission,* 2.

152. *AP* 37:705.

153. Ibid., 42:468, 544.

154. Ibid., 44:190–91. Private citizens reacted to this incident more harshly; see Tremblay, *Grand détail.*

155. *AP* 46:507. Swiss soldiers enlist in the *gendarmerie,* as indicated by the appearance of a delegation of Swiss gendarmes before the Assembly in March 1793 (ibid., 61:24).

156. Ibid., 46:575.

157. Ibid., 46:575–76; Marat, *Oeuvres politiques,* 8:5038.

158. *AP* 46:576.

159. Ibid., 47:167–68, 478–82.

160. Rapport, *Nationality and Citizenship,* 154; *AP* 48:2.

161. *AP* 47:640, 48:14.

162. Ibid., 48:417–18.

163. Brissot, *Rapport fait au nom de la Commission,* 2.

164. AN D/XV/4, dossier 40, item 7.

165. Mortimer-Ternaux, *Histoire de la Terreur,* 3:406–8.

166. Charavay, *Correspondance générale*, 1:68. Armand Louis de Gontaut-Biron, who abandoned his title of duc de Lauzun during the Revolution, was the same officer who had raised an eponymous legion composed largely of foreign troops for the French army during the American Revolution. See chapter 1.

167. *AP* 48:418–19.

168. *Crimes du 10 août*, 3.

169. The bonuses and pensions for retired Swiss soldiers varied by rank and length of service, but examples are available in SHD Xg 22.

170. *AP* 48:417–18.

171. See article 9 of the decree (ibid).

172. *AP* 50:82.

173. Ibid., 53:89–90, 97–98, 460.

174. "Apperçu des moïens compatibles avec la Constitution Démocratique de la France, qui pourraient être emploïeés pour attirer les Suisses au Service de la République" (SHD Xg 25).

175. Czouz-Tornare, *Vaudois et confédérés*, 249–50.

176. Letter of January 26, 1793, SHD Xg 25.

177. Czouz-Tornare, *Vaudois et confédérés*, 249.

178. Letters of 26 Prairial Year II and 14 Brumaire Year III, SHD Xg 24; letter of 29 Fructidor Year II, SHD Xg 21.

179. *AP* 60:231; letter of 24 Floréal Year III, SHD Xg 23; SHD Xg 25; *Code général français*, 21:113.

180. Letter of April 1, 1793, SHD Xg 25.

181. See the case of Michel Martin, who had served as a volunteer in the Sixth Battalion of the Bas-Rhin but secured his replacement on October 12, 1792, by a veteran of the Swiss Regiment of Vigier named Timptoff (AD BR 1 L 1412). On the sometimes involuntary nature of recruitment for the volunteer battalions, see Forrest, *Conscripts and Deserters*, 25; and Lynn, *Bayonets of the Republic*, 44.

182. SHD 14Yc 94.

183. SHD Xg 23; SHD Xg 92, dossier "Joost."

184. Dumay, *Historique du 66e régiment*, 16.

185. Letter of March 22, 1793, SHD Xg 25.

186. AN D/XV/1, dossier 1b, item 15.

187. "Infanterie Légère: Moyen proposé d'y incorporer les Suisses licenciés," SHD Xg 25.

188. Pension reports of 25 Thermidor Year II, 1 Germinal (no year specified), 18 Thermidor Year III, and 22 Thermidor Year III, all in SHD Xg 23.

189. SHD Xg 92, dossier "Kalbermatten." For other examples of Swiss troops serving enemy armies after their regiments left France, see AN D/XL/28, item 23; AN D/XV/1, item 97b; AN D/§1/16, dossier 8; Rapport, *Nationality and Citizenship*, 156; La Rochejaquelein, *Mémoires*.

THREE. Foreign Legions from the Old Regime to the Terror

1. Edith Piaf sang of the French Foreign Legion in "Mon légionnaire" and "Le Fanion de la Légion." Porky the Pig served as a legionnaire in the 1936 Looney Tunes

short *Little Beau Porky,* and another Looney Tunes character enlisted in the Legion in episode 19 of the *Bugs Bunny Show,* which first aired in 1952.

2. Works that briefly mention the legions include Mathiez, *Révolution et les étrangers,* 58–69; Bertaud, *Révolution armée,* 85–88; Rapport, *Nationality and Citizenship,* 158–64; and Gainot, *Officiers de couleur,* 22–32.

3. Jean Nicot's *Thresor de la langue francoyse* in 1606 defined *légion* only as a body of soldiers of a fixed size. By 1694, the inaugural edition of the *Dictionnaire de l'Académie française* gave two definitions, the first referring to ancient Roman legions and the second having a figurative meaning of "Un trop grand nombre." The fourth edition of the same dictionary, which appeared in 1762, retained these two senses while adding a third: "Le nom de *Légion* a été donné autrefois en France à certains Corps d'Infanterie" (ARTFL, "Dictionnaires d'autrefois," accessed December 11, 2011, http://artfl-project.uchicago.edu/node/17).

4. Bertaud, *Révolution armée,* 85–86.

5. Saxe, *Mémoires,* 374–79.

6. Bertaud, *Révolution armée,* 86. See also the anonymous memorandum of 1755, SHD 1M 1707; and "Essai de Tactique: Projet d'une Ordonnance à La Macédonniene," SHD 1M 1713.

7. Manuscript attributed to Rostaing, SHD 1M 1707.

8. Guibert's *Essai général de tactique* and Servan's *Soldat-citoyen* are the best-known examples, but a wealth of unpublished reformist treatises abounds in SHD series 1M. See also Pichichero, "Le Soldat Sensible"; Pichichero's forthcoming book, *The Military Enlightenment in France: 1701–1789;* and Osman, *Citizen Soldiers.*

9. Manuscript attributed to Rostaing, SHD 1M 1707.

10. Anonymous memorandum, SHD 1M 1770.

11. "Considérations politiques et militaires sur les Régiment étrangers," SHD 1M 1722.

12. "Etat des étrangers servant dans les Légions," SHD 1M 1722.

13. Bertaud, *Révolution armée,* 86; Guibert, *Essai general,* 49.

14. Anonymous treatise, SHD 1M 1707.

15. Bertaud, *Révolution armée,* 86.

16. Gainot, *Officiers de couleur,* 24. As Gainot noted, a Légion de Luxembourg was created in 1780 despite the dissolution of the legions four years earlier.

17. Gainot, *Officiers de couleur,* 25.

18. *AP* 38:613.

19. Belissa, *Fraternité universelle,* 254.

20. *AP* 10:607–08.

21. Gainot, *Officiers de couleur,* 25.

22. *AP* 37:625–26.

23. Ibid., 38:614.

24. French citizens could enlist in the legions as well under the terms of the proposal of February 1792 (ibid., 613–14).

25. Ibid., 614.

26. *AP* 39:69.

27. Bertaud, *Révolution armée,* 91–99.

28. *AP* 42:253–54.

29. Ibid., 42:256.

30. Ibid., 42:333–40, 359–60, 382–84, 473–75.

31. Ibid., 44:234–36; Bertaud, *Révolution armée*, 86.

32. Ibid., 44:235–36

33. Ibid., 44:236.

34. Croix, *Traité de la petite guerre*.

35. *AP* 42:222.

36. Ibid., 256.

37. Ibid., 334.

38. Ibid., 44:234–36.

39. Rosters dated May 3, 1793, and August 30, 1793, SHD Xk 7.

40. AN D/XV/6, dossier 55, item 2.

41. "Plan Proposé par Monsieur Le Maréchal de Luckner Commandant En chef L'armée du Rhin, pour la formation des six Légions que l'assemblée Nationale se propose de décreter incessamment," SHD Xk 45.

42. AN D/XV/6, dossier 55, item 1.

43. AN D/XV/6, dossier 55, item 4.

44. Gainot, *Officiers de couleur*, 32.

45. *AP* 36:229; Mathiez, *Révolution et les étrangers*, 64; Borgnet, *Révolution liégeoise*, 2:173–74.

46. Mathiez, *Révolution et les étrangers*, 64.

47. Ibid., 64–65.

48. *AP* 46:246.

49. Ibid., 47:147–52.

50. Mathiez, *Révolution et les étrangers*, 65; AN AF/II/398, dossier 3241.

51. Fieffé, *Histoire des troupes étrangères*, 2:20; AN AF/II/400, dossier 3257.

52. *AP* 59:614, 64:54.

53. Scott, *Response of the Royal Army*, 194–95.

54. AN AF/II/400, dossier 3257; AN AF/II/398, dossier 3241.

55. Letter of September 12, 1793, and roster dated 4 Frimaire Year II, SHD Xk 46.

56. Letter signed by the commissioner Bourdon, SHD Xk 46.

57. Letters of October 15, 1792, and October 26, 1792, SHD Xh 3.

58. Fieffé, *Histoire des troupes étrangères*, 11; letter of January 20, 1793, AN D/§2/4–5.

59. Letters of July 24, 1792, and September 24, 1792, AN D/XV/1, dossier 3.

60. Letter of May 24, 1793, AN AF/II/55.

61. Folliet, *Volontaires de la Savoie*, 2.

62. Ibid., 3; Bussigny, *Réponse de la Légion franche allobroge*.

63. *AP* 47:291, 376–77, 557–59.

64. Folliet, *Volontaires de la Savoie*, 8–9, 17; SHD 16Yc 695. Fieffé (*Histoire des troupes étrangères*, 2:26) wrote that most of the troops in the legion were from the former French province of Dauphiné, but I have uncovered no evidence for this claim.

65. Folliet, *Volontaires de la Savoie*, 5–6; letters of 25 Fructidor Year V and 5 Pluviôse Year VII, SHD 7Yd 96.

66. Letter of November 9, 1792, SHD Xk 10.

67. Folliet, *Volontaires de la Savoie*, 5; letter of 13 Vendémiaire Year VI, SHD 7Yd 96; AN AF/II/399, dossier 3250; letter of November 9, 1792, SHD Xk 10.

68. Folliet, *Volontaires de la Savoie*, 10.

69. *Réponse de la Légion franche allobroge.*

70. AN AF/II/281, dossier 2344, item 7.

71. *Réponse de la Légion franche allobroge*; Mathiez, *Révolution et les étrangers*, 66.

72. Borrel, *Histoire de la Révolution en Tarentaise*, 124–26; Folliet, *Volontaires de la Savoie*, 11–12.

73. Letter of 8 Thermidor Year IV, SHD 7Yd 96; *AP* 57:507.

74. Folliet, *Volontaires de la Savoie*, 51.

75. Ibid., 26–57, 59–60.

76. *AP* 48:357.

77. *AP* 49:41.

78. Arthur Chuquet, *Légion germanique*, 16–18; Mathiez, *Révolution et les étrangers*, 66–67.

79. *AP* 49:249–50, 349–50; Chuquet, *Légion germanique*, 278–79; SHD Xk 3.

80. AN AF/II/16, dossier 113, item 5.

81. Mathiez, *Révolution et les étrangers*, 67; Saiffert, *Faits justificatifs*, 2.

82. AN AF/II/16, dossier 113, items 16 and 17.

83. Memorandum of 21 Vendémiaire Year III, SHD Xk 3; Bertaud, *Révolution armée*, 20; Lynn, *Bayonets of the Republic*, 64–65.

84. Chuquet, *Légion germanique*, 13, 61, 289, 301, 311, 333.

85. Ibid., vi, 27–65; SHD 16Yc 699; Roger Dufraisse, "Les populations de la rive gauche," 121.

86. Chuquet, *Légion germanique*, vii.

87. Ibid., 62.

88. Ibid., 68.

89. Ibid., 96–97.

90. *AP* 60:634.

91. Chuquet, *Légion germanique*, 104–5.

92. Marat, *Oeuvres politiques*, 10:6656–67.

93. Ibid., 9:6072–73, 6252–54, 10:6568–69.

94. AN AF/II/16, dossier 113, item 12; *AP* 64:65–66.

95. Letter of September 6, 1793, SHD Xk 3.

96. *AP* 66:83–84.

97. Saiffert, *Faits justificatifs*, 3; AN AF/II/16, dossier 113, item 15, page 6; Quency, *Additions*, 1–2; Dambach and Heyden, *Exposé succinct*, 3; SHD Xk 3.

98. Memorandum on the Germanic Legion dated 21 Vendémiaire Year III, SHD Xk 3.

99. Dambach and Heyden, *Exposé succinct*, 1; AN AF/II/16, dossier 13, item 5.

100. Chuquet, *Légion germanique*, 37, 337.

101. Letter of 22 Prairial Year III, SHD Xk 3.

102. Letters of October 1, 1793, and 30 Thermidor Year II, SHD Xk 3.

103. Chuquet, *Légion germanique*, 128–30, 137–63, 167–68, 172, 189–210. On German corps see also *AP* 49:357, 53:21–22.

104. Marcel Dorigny, "Brissot et Miranda en 1792, ou comment révolutionner l'Amérique espagnole?" in Dorigny and Rossignol, *La France et les Amériques*, 98, 102–3.

105. Turner, "Origin of Genet's Projected Attack," 654; Vaughan, *Citizen Genêt Affair;* Ammon, *Genêt Mission.* This translation is Turner's.

106. Turner, "Origin of Genet's Projected Attack," 658.

107. Ibid., 665.

108. "Documents on the Relations of France to Louisiana," 511–15; roster of 4 Fructidor Year VIII, SHD Xi 72.

109. SC MSS L1984.1.10.

110. SHD 8Yd 721.

111. Jones, *Last Invasion,* 275–77.

112. Ahlstrom, "Captain and Chef de Brigade," 186.

113. Ibid., 185.

114. Alderson, *This Bright Era.*

115. Murdoch, "Correspondence of French Consuls," 74–75.

116. Ahlstrom, "Captain and Chef de Brigade," 187; Memorandum on Tate's legion, 9 Vendémiaire Year IV, SHD 17Yd 12.

117. Ahlstrom, "Captain and Chef de Brigade," 187.

118. SHD 17Yd 12.

119. Treatise of 9 Vendémiaire Year IV, SHD 17Yd 12.

120. Ibid.

121. Murdoch, "Correspondence of French Consuls," 76.

122. SHD 17Yd 12.

123. Ibid.

124. Memorandum of 9 Vendémiaire Year IV, SHD 17Yd 12; Murdoch, "Correspondence of French Consuls," 76.

125. Memorandum of 9 Vendémiaire Year IV, SHD 17Yd 12.

126. Turner, "Origin of Genet's Projected Attack," 667, 671; "Documents on the Relations of France to Louisiana," 514.

127. SHD 8Yd 721; Ahlstrom, "Captain and Chef de Brigade," 187.

128. Rapport, *Nationality and Citizenship,* 19.

129. Gainot, *Officiers de couleur,* 12–17.

130. Dorigny, "Brissot et Miranda," 99.

131. *AP* 57:2.

132. Proclamation of April 19, 1793, AN D/XXV/9; Lacroix, *Mémoires,* 161.

133. *Dictionnaire de la conversation,* 8:261

134. Dubois, *Colony of Citizens,* 193–98.

135. Popkin, *You Are All Free,* 212.

136. Marley, *Wars of the Americas,* 1:537.

137. *AP* 64:710–11.

138. Quoted in Gainot, *Officiers de couleur,* 56.

139. *AP* 49:598.

140. Letters of July 18, 1793, and August 30, 1793, AN D/XXV/23.

141. See chapter 1.

142. Boulle, "Les gens de couleur à Paris," 1:165–66; Raguet, "Du Pionniers Noirs"; rosters of 30 Vendémiaire Year III, 26 Brumaire Year III, and 13 Frimaire Year III, SHD Xi 71.

143. Gainot, *Officiers de couleur,* 34–35.

144. *AP* 49:429.

145. Gainot, *Officiers de couleur,* 39.

146. Ibid., 40.

147. Ibid., 40–41; Spurr, *Life and Writings,* 264; Reiss, *Black Count.*

148. Gainot, *Officiers de couleur,* 49–51.

149. Ibid.

150. Ibid., 59.

151. *AP* 64:710–11.

152. Tyler Stovall, "Love, Labor, and Race: Colonial Men and White Women in France during the Great War," in Stovall and van den Abbeele, *French Civilization and Its Discontents,* 297–321; Fogarty, *Race and War.*

153. The Légion des Montagnes should not be confused with the unrelated Légion de la Montagne that French patriots formed in Marseille later in 1793. See *AP* 58:10–11; Charavay, *Correspondance générale de Carnot,* 1:352, 255; decree of January 29, 1793, SHD Xk 11; Bertaud, *Révolution armée,* 88; Guilhaumou, *Marseille républicaine,* 221–23.

154. "Situation de La Ville de Bruxelles et des Lieux circonvoisins, depuis l'entrée des français," AN D/§2/4–5, dossier 5.

155. *Pétition présentée par le citoyen Mayer;* memorandum on the Légion de la Propagande, SHD Xk 45.

156. SHD Xk 45; Mathiez, *Révolution et les étrangers,* 68; Erdman, *Commerce des Lumières.*

157. Bertaud, *Révolution armée,* 87.

158. Bussigny, *Réponse de la Légion franche allobroge.*

159. AN D/§2/4–5, dossier 18, items 1 and 2; AN D/XV/1, dossier 1a, item 45.

160. Roster of March 28, 1793, and letter of August 26, 1793, SHD Xk 9.

161. Forrest, *Conscripts and Deserters,* 21–22.

162. Blanning, *French Revolutionary Wars,* 95; Bély, *History of France,* 81. Ascertaining the number of foreign legionnaires within this group is difficult because few *contrôles de troupe* for the foreign legions levied during the first half of the 1790s exist at SHD; further, most of those that are available, such as the one for the Germanic Legion (SHD 16Yc 699), contain no actual enlistment records. It is certain, however, that only six foreign legions (the Allobroge Legion included) ever served in Europe and that the total theoretical strength of each one averaged no more than around two thousand men. Since several of the foreign legions never came close to reaching this theoretical total, and some of the men they enrolled were French citizens, it is unlikely that the total number of foreign legionnaires ever exceeded ten thousand.

163. *AP* 52:80.

164. *AP* 64:65–66.

165. A significant minority of the officers in Kellermann's Legion had served previously in France's foreign regiments, and a few others were foreigners who had never before served in France, but the surviving evidence does not indicate that a majority of the legion's personnel comprised foreigners (SHD Xk 9).

166. *AP* 65:66.

167. Belissa, *Fraternité universelle*, 254.

168. *AP* 68:507, 78:455, 702.

169. *Collection générale des décrets*, 10:81–82.

170. *AP* 80:526.

FOUR. The Limits of Pragmatism

1. Blanning, *French Revolutionary Wars*, 119–20; Bertaud, *Révolution armée*, 113–26; Forrest, *Conscripts and Deserters*, 26; Scott, *Response of the Royal Army*, 110; Lynn, *Bayonets of the Republic*, 67–73; Blaufarb, *French Army*, 88–89.

2. Higonnet, "Terror, Trauma," 122.

3. Weil, *How to Be French*, 13–15, 19.

4. Valynseele et al., *Dictionnaire des Maréchaux*, 274–75; Horstmann, *Generallieutenant Johann Nicolaus von Luckner*, 15–75; and Luckner, *Dernier corsaire*, 121–24.

5. Luckner, *Dernier corsaire*, 123.

6. Valynseele, *Dictionnaire des Maréchaux*, 274.

7. Letter of June 20, 1763, and capitulation of May 27, 1763, SHD 2Yd 255.

8. Luckner, *Dernier corsaire*, 123; Valynseele, *Dictionnaire des Maréchaux*, 274.

9. *AP* 36:336; Valynseele, *Dictionnaire des Maréchaux*, 274.

10. Hennet, *Etat Militaire*, 5–6.

11. Marat, *Oeuvres politiques*, 8:4784. The deputy Hérault noted in July 1792 that "la manière dont M. Luckner s'exprime en français a pu me faire perdre quelques-unes de ses expressions" (BHVP 967201).

12. Valynseele, *Dictionnaire des Maréchaux*, 274.

13. Ibid.

14. Letter of August 29, 1792, SHD B2 108.

15. Hennet, *Etat Militaire*, 6–9; Six, *Dictionnaire biographique*; SHD 3Yd 1271.

16. Fieffé, *Histoire des troupes étrangères*, 2:87; Hayes, *Ireland and Irishmen*, 142.

17. *AP* 15:405.

18. AN D/XV/6, dossier 80, item 3.

19. SHD 14Yc 137.

20. SHD 14Yc 114.

21. Lynn, *Bayonets of the Republic*, 50–51; Bertaud, *Révolution armée*, 65; Jean-Paul Bertaud, "Enquête sur les volontaires de 1792," 154–55.

22. AN D/XL/28, items 169, 174 and 175; roster of May 3, 1793, SHD Xk 7.

23. Forrest, *Conscripts and Deserters*, 25; Bertaud, "Enqûete sur les volontaires de 1792," 156–59.

24. AN D/XV/3, dossier 23.

25. AN D/§1/16, dossier 14.

26. Scott, *Response of the Royal Army*, 166–67.

27. Ibid., 184.

28. SHD 16Yc 377; SHD 16Yc 372; SHD 16Yc 877; SHD 16Yc 379; SHD 16Yc 837; SHD 16yc 348; SHD 16Yc 403; SHD 16Yc 387.

29. SHD 16 Yc 442.

30. SHD 16Yc 377; SHD 16Yc 442

31. *AP* 76:131.

32. Ibid., 72:131, 271, 688–90.

33. Bell, *Cult of the Nation*, 171–95.

34. *La Grillade, ou Les Suisses aux enfers.*

35. For a similar text, see "La Mère Duchesne à Lyon, ou Conversation très-vérdique entre la Mère Duchesne, un soldat suisse, la Mère Capillon, et un volontaire des frontières appelé La Peur," reprinted in Balleydier, *Histoire politique et militaire*, 3:xvii–xxvi.

36. Roster of 2 Messidor Year VI, SHD Xi 20; AN AF/II/372 3012; AN AF/II/371 3002.

37. AN AF/II/371, dossier 3001; AN AF/II/372, dossier 3012.

38. Under the Old Regime and into the first years of the Revolution, the foreign regiments received templates of administrative documents in their native languages to facilitate administrative tasks, but this ceased to be the case after the abolition of the foreign corps early in the Revolution. For examples of these templates, see the reviews of the Regiment of Salm-Salm, SHD Xb 76.

39. Hayes, *Irish Swordsmen of France*, 6; Hayes, *Biographical Dictionary*, 68; "Notice de Services" for Théobald Dillon, June 27, 1886, SHD 4Yd 3816.

40. Hayes, *Irish Swordsmen of France*, 14–15, 22–23.

41. *Rélation du mouvement exécuté les 28 et 29 avril.*

42. Hayes, *Irish Swordsmen of France*, 23–28; SHD 4Yd 381; Moore, *Journal*, 135; *Rélation de l'assassinat de M. Théobald Dillon*, 7.

43. Marat, *Oeuvres politiques*, 7:3968–70.

44. Hayes, *Irish Swordsmen of France*, 30, 33; decree of May 8, 1792, SHD 4Yd 3816; *Pétition de M. Arthur Dillon.*

45. Marat, *Oeuvres politiques*, 7:3968–70, 3982–83; AN D/XL/28, document 119.

46. *Rélation de l'assassinat de M. Théobald Dillon*, 7.

47. Hayes, *Irish Swordsmen of France*, 29.

48. Marat, *Oeuvres politiques*, 8:4945.

49. Michaud, *Biographie universelle*, 21:494–95; Hayes, *Irish Swordsmen of France*, 133.

50. Quoted in Hayes, *Ireland and Irishmen*, 143. This translation is Hayes's.

51. Ibid., 145–46; Alger, *Englishmen in the French Revolution*, 176–77. The translation of Marat's statement, which is quoted in both Hayes and Alger, is Alger's.

52. Marat, *Oeuvres politiques*, 9:5687. Marat himself appeared eager to keep knowledge of his foreign birth under wraps. The singular reference to his national origins within his revolutionary publications, which did not specify his place of

birth, was a brief acknowledgment that he had "passed his childhood" in Neuchâtel (*Oeuvres politiques,* 9:5790).

53. Jarrousse, *Auvergnats malgré eux,* vi.

54. Mathiez, *Révolution et les étrangers,* 122; Weil, *How to Be French,* 16.

55. Parra-Pérez, *Miranda,* 222; *Réimpression de l'ancien Moniteur, depuis la réunion des États-Généraux jusqu'au Consulat,* 15:773.

56. Quoted in Mathiez, *Révolution et les étrangers,* 127.

57. Chuquet, *Légion germanique,* 117.

58. *AP* 70:109; Mathiez, *Révolution et les étrangers,* 138–40.

59. *AP* 70:183.

60. Ibid., 183–84.

61. Ibid., 70:452–53, 73:462–63.

62. Mathiez, *Révolution et les étrangers,* 140–41, 161; Rapport, *Nationality and Citizenship,* 197–99.

63. Chuquet, *Prince jacobin,* 257.

64. Ibid.

65. *AP* 80:526; Chuquet, *Légion germanique,* 117.

66. Jarrousse, *Auvergnats malgré eux,* 178; decree of 4 Frimaire Year II, AN AF/II/230; "Resultat des Observations d'un Citoyen français sur les moyens d'avoir une Marine républicaine," AN D/XVI/1.

67. Rapport, *Nationality and Citizenship,* 214.

68. Decree of 6 Ventôse Year II, AN AF/II/230, dossier 1984.

69. Decree of 29 Messidor Year II, AN AF/II/230, dossier 1984.

70. AN AF/II/230, dossier 1984, items 15 and 40.

71. Quoted in Hayes, *Irish Swordsmen of France,* 188–90. This translation is Hayes's.

72. Chuquet, *Prince Jacobin,* 257; Hayes, *Irish Swordsmen of France,* 187–91.

73. Hayes, *Irish Swordsmen of France,* 176.

74. Ibid.; Chuquet, *Hondschoote,* 93–94.

75. *Correspondance générale de Carnot,* 2:328.

76. Chuquet, *Prince Jacobin,* 257.

77. Report to the Committee of Public Safety, 17 Frimaire Year III, SHD 3Yd 1317.

78. Hayes, *Irish Swordsmen of France,* 98; pamphlet by O'Moran, August 17, 1793, SHD 7Yd 2.

79. Pamphlet by O'Moran, August 17, 1793, SHD 7Yd 2.

80. AN D/XV/6, dossier 120, item 1.

81. AN W/355.

82. Quoted in Hayes, *Irish Swordsmen of France,* 104. This translation is Hayes's.

83. Letter of 2 Brumaire Year II, SHD 20Yd 102; Alger, *Englishmen in the French Revolution,* 177.

84. 4 Thermidor Year II, AN W/429; Alger, *Englishmen in the French Revolution,* 177.

85. Hayes, *Irish Swordsmen of France,* 113–21; SHD 3Yd 1271.

86. Charges against Dillon included corresponding with an enemy general and

publicly condemning the arrest of the king on August 10, 1792 (Hayes, *Irish Swordsmen of France*, 126–29, 134, 145–46, 153–63; Alger, *Englishmen in the French Revolution*, 171–74; AN W/345; AN C/235, dossier 205, item 19; *AP* 48:415).

87. Quoted in Hayes, *Irish Swordsmen of France*, 167. This translation is Hayes's.

88. *Copie de la lettre du maréchal Luckner.*

89. AN D/XV/4, dossier 41, item 1.

90. AN D/XV/1, dossier 1b, item 22; BHVP 967201.

91. *Lettre de M. Luckner;* Scott, *Response of the Royal Army,* 91, 98–100; Lynn, *Bayonets of the Republic,* 119–62; Martin, "Journaux d'armées."

92. The six agitators reportedly targeted Lafayette's army as well (letter of June 26, 1792, SHD 2Yd 255).

93. AN D/XV/3, dossier 22; BHVP 600745.

94. Marat, *Oeuvres politiques,* 6:3301, 7:3920, 7:4134, 7:4145.

95. *Reproches faits au maréchal Luckner,* 5. The precise identity of Luckner's sons and other descendants is unclear. Besides those who reportedly served in the Danish army, one of Luckner's children may have been Ferdinand, Baron of Luckner, who was born in Holstein in 1762 and enlisted in the French army in the German Regiment of Royal-Deux-Ponts. He fought under Rochambeau during the American Revolutionary War but deserted on May 11, 1782, to become ambassador of the king of Denmark at the Hague (Bodinier, *Dictionnaire,* 318). On Luckner's descendants, see also the dossier devoted to this topic in SHD 2Yd 255.

96. 14 Nivôse Year II, AN W/307.

97. Valynseele, *Dictionnaire des Maréchaux,* 275; AN W/307.

98. Bois, *Dumouriez,* 223.

99. SHD 4Yd 3875.

100. AN AF/II/16, dossier 11, item 16; AN AF/III/151/B, dossier 710, items 116, 117, and 120.

101. Letter of October 21, 1792, SHD 4Yd 3875.

102. AN W/271; "Extrait de la Minute du Dépôt du Greffe du cy-devant Tribunal révolutionnaire," SHD 4Yd 3875.

103. Parra-Pérez, *Miranda,* xiii, lvi, 16–20. See also Galway, *Les généraux de la Révolution: Francisco de Miranda;* and Racine, *Francisco de Miranda,* 105–40.

104. While serving with the Army of the North, Miranda declined an appointment to command a French expedition in Saint-Domingue, a decision he attributed later in his life to his opposition to imperial enterprises. Some deputies also briefly nominated him as minister of the French navy, but he received little support (SHD 7Yd 3; Dorigny, "Brissot et Miranda en 1792," 92–105:99; letter of January 12, 1793, SHD 7Yd 3; Parra-Pérez, *Miranda,* 123).

105. Parra-Pérez, *Miranda,* 59–60, 219; letter of July 6, 1793, AN F/7/477447.

106. *AP* 62:673.

107. Dávila, *Archivo del General Miranda,* 8:213.

108. AN W/271, dossier 30.

109. Parra-Pérez, *Miranda,* 247–48.

110. Ibid., 252; Palmer, *Twelve Who Ruled,* 32.

111. Marat, *Oeuvres politiques,* 9:6388.

112. Parra-Pérez, *Miranda,* 257, 266, 267, 294.

113. "Relevé de services," SHD 7Yd 242.

114. Note of 9 Pluviôse Year III and letter of January 9, 1793, SHD 7Yd 242.

115. Letters of February 28, 1793, and 22 Frimaire Year III, SHD 72Yd 242.

116. Ibid.; AN W/272, dossier 41, item 8.

117. Letter of June 2 Year II [1793], SHD 7Yd 242; AN D/§2/4–5, dossier 9, item 21.

118. "Relevé de services," SHD 7Yd 242; AN W/272, dossier 41.

119. "Relevé de services," SHD 7Yd 242; letter of 22 Frimaire Year III, SHD 72Yd 242.

120. See chapter 2.

121. Quoted in Chuquet, *Prince jacobin,* 258.

122. Ibid.

123. Ibid.

124. Ibid., 259, 261.

125. Ibid., 263–65; AN W/307, dossier 386, item 1.

126. AN W/307, dossier 386, item 6.

127. Chuquet, *Prince jacobin,* 265–66.

128. Mathiez, *Révolution et les étrangers,* 182–83.

129. Ibid., 183–85; Rapport, *Nationality and Citizenship,* 258.

130. Kilmaine commanded about two thousand national guards and "gilded youth" in defense of the Convention during the revolt of 1 Prairial Year III (May 20, 1795). He was reintegrated into the army on June 13, 1795 (SHD 7Yd 35; Hayes, *Irish Swordsmen of France,* 192–93; Six, *Dictionnaire biographique,* 2:7; Gendron, *La jeunesse doree,* 230).

131. Letter of 23 Germinal Year III, SHD 7Yd 230.

132. "Etat des Services de M. Lynch," SHD 7Yd 13.

133. Report to the Committee of Public Safety, 17 Frimaire Year III, SHD 3Yd 1317.

134. Letter of Pluviôse Year III (exact day unspecified), SHD 7Yd 242.

135. Chuquet, *Prince jacobin,* 267–72, 339.

136. Brown, "Politics, Professionalism," 138–41.

137. Letters of 27 Prairial Year III and 3 Ventôse Year IV, SHD 3Yd 1294.

138. Letter of 21 Vendémiaire Year III, SHD Xk 3.

139. Letter of 22 Prairial Year III, SHD Xk 3; Chuquet, *Légion germanique,* 200–201.

140. Some French deputies supported Eustace's request for French citizenship; see the letter from Lamarque, Laporte, and Bruat (no recipient specified), 27 August 1792, AN F/7/4689, plaquette 4, item 102. The National Assembly never acted on his petition, however. Eustace claimed (see his notes on a copy of the letter by Lamarque et al. in Dávila, *Archivo del General Miranda,* 7:419–20) that the Assembly did not grant him citizenship because it was too busy with other affairs during the tumultuous month of August 1792, but this position seems dubious given that the legislators did find time on August 26, 1792, to adopt a number of other prominent foreigners as French citizens (Weil, *How to Be French,* 14–15).

141. Letter of July 1, 1792, SHD 4Yd 3927.

142. Eustace to the war minister, August 5, 1792, SHD 4Yd 3927.

143. AN F/7/4689 item 102, plaquette 4, page 15; Marat, *Oeuvres politiques*, 8:5367–68.

144. Dávila, *Archivo del General Miranda*, 11:185–87.

145. AN F/7/4701, dossier 4; letter of 25 Nivôse Year III, SHD 7Yd 35.

146. Eustace, *Traité d'amitié*, 57.

147. Parra-Pérez, *Miranda*, 321–34, 369–80.

148. Miranda, *Opinion du général Miranda*, 12–13.

149. Edelstein, "Le militaire-citoyen," 591.

150. Miranda, *Opinion du général Miranda*, 12–13.

151. Rapport, *Nationality and Citizenship*, 218.

152. Mathiez, *Révolution et les étrangers*, 177, 182; Rapport, *Nationality and Citizenship*, 217–18; Wahnich, *L'impossible citoyen*, 11.

153. Furet, *Interpreting the French Revolution*, 62–63.

FIVE. Constitutionalism and Innovation

1. *Constitution de la République française*, 85–86.

2. Letter of 30 Thermidor Year II, SHD Xk 3; AN AF/II/205, dossier 1736, item 19; Chuquet, *Légion germanique*, 324.

3. SHD Xg 92, dossier "Joost."

4. Entries for Jean Ourea and François Manck, SHD Yc 442; and Leonard Pretorius, SHD 14Yc 141.

5. Jarrousse, *Auvergnats malgré eux*, 200.

6. Letters of 21 Floréal Year IV and 28 Nivôse Year V, AD BR 1 L 1414. Most studies of prisoners of war in the interior of France after Thermidor approach the topic from regional perspectives, but useful examples include Jarrousse, *Auvergnats malgré eux*; Duverger, *Déserteurs et prisonniers*; and Henwood, "Les prisonniers de guerre anglais."

7. AN AF/II/230, dossier 1986, item 58.

8. SHD 17Yc 126; Bertaud, *Révolution armée*, 96; Fieffé, *Histoire des troupes étrangères*, 2:406–20.

9. Roster of 27 Brumaire Year III, SHD Xb 218.

10. Register of officers of the 105th Demi-Brigade, 24 Prairial Year III, SHD Xb 212.

11. Roster of 4 Thermidor Year II, SHD Xb 217.

12. Scott, *Response of the Royal Army*, 183–84.

13. Hayes, *Ireland and Irishmen*, 5–6, 18; Bragelongne, *Journal de la navigation d'une escadre française*; Desbrière, *Projets et tentatives de débarquement*, 1:13–53; Hayes, *Irish Swordsmen of France*, 145–46; AN AF/III/186b, dossiers 857 and 858.

14. AN AF/III/186b, dossier 859, item 22.

15. Fieffé, *Histoire des troupes étrangères*, 2:34. According to Fieffé, the *Brigade étrangère*, which included the regiments of Lee, O'Meara, Ferdut, and La Châtre, was so-called not because authorities intended for it to recruit many foreigners, but because its officers were of Irish origin. On this point Fieffé seems to be incorrect; the government initially ordered the *Brigade étrangère* to recruit "sur le territoire

ennemi," and even as the Directory moved to abolish the regiments of the *Brigade* in February 1799, objections arose that France should preserve them because "il était nécessaire de conserver quelques cadres de corps propres à recevoir les Étrangers." In the event, however, the corps was not very successful in recruiting any troops, either of French or foreign origin; according to a report of 18 Pluviôse Year VII, the theoretical strength of the infantry regiments comprising the brigade was 8,288 men, yet only 648 troops were present. Of the troops who enrolled, only a small minority of officers were foreign, according to rosters in SHD Xh 17; and of the 255 soldiers for whom entries exist in the only surviving *contrôle de troupe* for the *Brigade* (SHD 23Yc 213, for the Regiment of Ferdut), only three had been born outside France: one in Spain, one in Switzerland, and one near Liège. The *Brigade étrangère* finally disbanded on 3 Ventôse Year VII. On its history and efforts to recruit foreigners, see SHD Xh 17.

16. Jones, *Last Invasion*, 21; E. H. Jones, *Invasion That Failed*, 94.

17. SHD B11 1; "Etat des officiers á proposer pour la composition d'un Bataillon," AN AF/III/186b.

18. Letter of 8 Brumaire Year V, SHD B11 1.

19. AN AF/III/186b, dossier 860, item 105. Batteincourt and his comrades were also upset by rumors that French émigrés would take part in the campaign. French authorities did indeed take steps to recruit such men, issuing a printed appeal to émigrés who resided in Britain and had become disillusioned with the British government to enlist in what they called the "Armée Independante," for operations on British territory (AN AF/III/186b, dossier 860, items 95 and 110).

20. Although the government never recruited foreigners wholesale for the Bantry Bay expedition of 1796, there is evidence that some Irish exiles participated on an individual basis; for example, see Jacques O'Conor, discussed later in this chapter.

21. Memorandum of August 10, 1795, SHD 17Yd 14; Freeman, *Ireland*, 120; Connell, *Population of Ireland*, 25; Elliott, *Partners in Revolution*.

22. AN AF/III/186b, unnumbered dossier, item 21.

23. Hayes, *Ireland and Irishmen*, 8.

24. Pakenham, *Year of Liberty*, 17–19.

25. Ahlstrom, "Captain and Chef de Brigade," 188.

26. AN AF/III/186/B; Jones, *Last Invasion*, 53, 57.

27. Vendémiaire Year IV (exact date unspecified), SHD 17Yd 12.

28. Jones, *Last Invasion*, 54; AN AF/III/186/B, dossier 658, item 32, and dossier 859, items 62, 63, 70 and 83; AN AF/III/147, dossier 254, item 694.

29. Jones, *Last Invasion*, 20–21, 61; *Authentic Copies of the Instructions Given by General Hoche to Colonel Tate, Previous to His Landing on the Coast of South Wales, in the Beginning of 1797* (London, 1798).

30. Jones, *Last Invasion*, 62.

31. Ibid., 55, 60–61.

32. Ibid., 68, 115.

33. Ahlstrom, "Captain and Chef de Brigade," 191.

34. Pakenham, *Year of Liberty*, 29.

35. Ibid.; N. A. M. Rodger, *The Command of the Ocean* (New York: Norton, 2004), 441, 445–47, 448–51, 452.

36. Pakenham, *Year of Liberty,* 29, 31.

37. AN AF/III/149, dossier 700, item 9; Hayes, *Irish Swordsmen of France,* 212; SHD 7Yd 35.

38. "Memoir of General Kilmaine, Commandant of Lombardy and General of the Armée d'Angleterre," *Dublin University Magazine* 47 (1856): 464–74, 473.

39. Quoted in Hayes, *Irish Swordsmen of France,* 215. This translation is Hayes's.

40. SHD 17Yd 14.

41. Hayes, *Irish Swordsmen of France,* 296–97.

42. Letter of 7 Prairial Year VI, SHD 17Yd 14.

43. Letter of 13 Messidor Year VI, SHD 17Yd 14.

44. Pakenham, *Year of Liberty,* 298.

45. Ibid., 309–11, 325.

46. Maxwell, *History of the Irish Rebellion,* 225.

47. Pakenham, 322, 325–26, 331–33, 338.

48. Letter of 19 Brumaire Year VII, SHD 17Yd 14.

49. Desbrières, *Projets et tentatives de débarquement,* 149, 212–13; AN AF/III/149, dossier 701, item 82; AN AF/III/149, dossier 702, item 150.

50. Fieffé, *Histoire des troupes étrangères,* 2:47, 82; SHD 20Yc 1.

51. SHD Xl 33.

52. Guido to the war minister (undated letter), SHD Xl 33.

53. Letter of 1 Floréal Year VIII, SHD Xl 33.

54. Letter of 26 Floréal Year IX, SHD Xl 33.

55. Brincat, "Languages in Malta."

56. Entry for Alexandre Chantre, SHD 20Yc 1.

57. Report of 15 Fructidor Year IX, SHD Xl 33.

58. Fieffé, *Histoire des troupes étrangères,* 2:47.

59. Roster of 26 Germinal Year X, SHD Xi 72; "Note sur les réfugiés maltais résultant des documents existant dans les Bureaux de l'Intendance Militaire de la 17eme Division," SHD Xl 33.

60. "Compagnie de Jannissaires: Contrôlle des officiers, sous officiers et Jannissaires qui Composent laditte Compagnie," SHD Xl 33.

61. Fieffé, *Histoire des troupes étrangères,* 2:48.

62. Ibid.; order of June 28, 1800, establishing the Légion grecque, SHD Xl 33.

63. Ibid.; Fieffé, *Histoire des troupes étrangères,* 2:48.

64. Letter of 12 Frimaire Year X, SHD Xl 33.

65. Roster of 9 Pluviôse Year IX, SHD Xl 33.

66. Fieffé, *Histoire des troupes étrangères,* 2:48.

67. Decree of July 7, 1800, SHD Xl 33; roster of 9 Vendémiaire Year X, SHD Xl 33.

68. Fieffé, *Histoire des troupes étrangères,* 2:49.

69. Ibid.

70. Anonymous letter to Napoleon (Fructidor Year X, exact date unspecified), SHD Xl 33.

71. Fieffé, *Histoire des troupes étrangères,* 2:49.

72. Gainot, *Officiers de couleur,* 148; Fieffé, *Histoire des troupes étrangères,* 2:49.

73. Gainot, *Officiers de couleur,* 148.

74. Roster of 12 Ventôse Year XI, SHD Xl 33.

75. Fieffé, *Histoire des troupes étrangères,* 51–52; Brun, "Les unités étrangères," paragraph 33.

76. Letters of March 16, 1811, and October 17, 1819, SHD Xl 33.

77. Letter of November 11, 1817, SHD Xl 33.

78. AN AF/III/186b, dossier 858, item 33; AN AF/III/186b, dossier 859, item 41; J. Graffagnino, "'Twenty Thousand Muskets!!!,'" 419; Ojala, "Ira Allen and the French Directory, 1796."

79. Allen and his collaborators envisioned three hundred French officers disembarking at Portsmouth, New Hampshire, for travel to Vermont (letter of September 10, 1797, SHD Xi 77; AN AF/III/186b, dossier 859, item 53).

80. AN AF/III/186b, dossier 859, item 56; Graffagnino, "'Twenty Thousand Muskets!!!,'" 410–17.

81. AN AF/III/186b, dossier 859, item 42.

82. AN AF/III/186b, dossier 859, item 56; letters of July 11, 1796, and October 5, 1796, SHD Xi 77.

83. Graffagnino, "'Twenty Thousand Muskets!!!,'" 421.

84. Ibid., 421–27.

85. Allen was not the last American to solicit French support for a campaign against British Canada. In 1807 an American prisoner of war named John Haig, whom the French apparently captured at sea, vainly sought permission to present Napoleon with a plan for the capture of Quebec (report of November 6, 1807, SHD Yj 19).

86. Rapport, *Nationality and Citizenship,* 276.

87. Jourdan, *La République batave;* Schama, *Patriots and Liberators,* 178–409, esp. 196–207; Leeb, *Ideological Origins,* 258–69.

88. Decree of 11 Prairial Year III, AN AF/II/231; letter of 20 Prairial Year III, AN D/§3/66, dossier 639.

89. Rapport, *Nationality and Citizenship,* 275.

90. Fieffé, *Histoire des troupes étrangères,* 2:40–41.

91. Letter of October 28, 1797, quoted in ibid., 2:41.

92. Rapport, *Nationality and Citizenship,* 277.

93. Fieffé, *Histoire des troupes étrangères,* 2:43; Dabrowski's instructions on the Polish legion, 16 Nivôse Year V, SHD Xl 3.

94. Tadeusz Kosciuszko, note on the history of the Polish legions, 6 Brumaire Year VIII, SHD Xl 3.

95. Fieffé, *Histoire des troupes étrangères,* 2:43–44; report of 2 Thermidor Year V and letter of 14 Prairial Year V, SHD B11 1.

96. Undated letter from Polwinsky to the war minister, SHD Xl 3.

97. Rapport, *Nationality and Citizenship,* 278.

98. Kosciuszko, note on the history of the Polish legions, 6 Brumaire Year VIII, SHD Xl 3.

99. Memorandums of 28 Fructidor Year IX and 14 Vendémiaire Year X, SHD Xl 3.

100. Aulard, *Paris sous le Consulat,* 2:31–32.

101. Memorandum of 28 Fructidor Year IX, SHD Xl 3. Some French natives remained in the legions despite these complaints, prompting the government to include a provision in the decree of 8 Ventôse Year VIII (SHD X 3) regarding the reorganization of the Polish legion in existence at that time that required all soldiers and officers of French origin serving in the unit to transfer to the French army, while Polish personnel would continue to serve under the Italic Republic.

102. Letters of 16 Germinal Year VI, 18 Messidor Year VII, 1 Brumaire Year VII, and 8 Thermidor Year VII, SHD 16Yd 85.

103. Letter of 16 Pluviôse Year X, SHD 16Yd 85.

104. Pachonski and Wilson, *Poland's Caribbean Tragedy,* 3.

105. Decrees of 21 Pluviôse Year VIII and 8 Ventôse Year VIII, SHD Xl 3; Fieffé, *Histoire des troupes étrangères,* 45–47; Pachonski and Wilson, *Poland's Caribbean Tragedy,* 4.

106. Fieffé, *Histoire des troupes étrangères,* 2:110; SHD Xi 27.

107. Pachonski and Wilson, *Poland's Caribbean Tragedy,* 5, 264–66, 295.

108. AN AF/II/231, dossier 1995, items 57, 59, 60, 62, and 63; AN AF/III/230, dossier 1986, item 53.

109. AN AF/II/231, dossier 1995, item 62.

110. Dame, *History of Switzerland,* 2:288, 290; Favez, *Nouvelle Histoire de la Suisse,* 497–500.

111. AN AF/III/149, dossier 702, item 96.

112. "Convention Spéciale," 29 Frimaire Year VII, SHD Xg 1; Fieffé, *Histoire des troupes étrangères,* 2:36–37; AN AF/III/150a, dossier 703, item 58.

113. Roster of 20 Messidor Year XI, SHD Xg 44; Fieffé, *Histoire des troupes étrangères,* 2:38.

114. Roster of 24 Fructidor Year X, SHD Xg 40.

115. "Convention Spéciale," SHD Xg 1; AN AF/III/150a, dossier 703, item 27.

116. Fieffé, *Histoire des troupes étrangères,* 2:66; *Le Courier de l'Empire: Journal historique, politique et litteraire* 196 (August 18, 1799), 781–82.

117. AN AF/III/150a, dossier 703, items 25 and 27; AN AF/III/152a, dossier 713, item 4; letter to the French Directory (December 26, 1799), SHD Xg 1.

118. Letter of 28 Prairial Year X, SHD Xg 40; report of 4 Pluviôse Year VIII, SHD Xg 1; review of Messidor Year XI (exact date unspecified), SHD Xg 44.

119. Letter of 27 Brumaire Year IX, SHD Xg 1.

120. SHD Xg 1.

121. Ibid.

122. Fieffé, *Histoire des troupes étrangères,* 2:38.

123. Ibid.; SHD Xg 42; SHD Xi 82.

124. Fieffé, *Histoire des troupes étrangères,* 2:38; report of 18 Prairial Year XIII, SHD Xg 40; report of May 7, 1817, SHD Xg 44.

125. Fieffé, *Histoire des troupes étrangères,* 2:32; Rapport, *Nationality and Citizenship,* 278.

126. Fieffé, *Histoire des troupes étrangères,* 2:53–54; SHD B5 1; SHD B5 2.

127. Letter of 21 Frimaire Year IX, SHD Xi 72.

128. Roster of 4 Fructidor Year VIII, SHD Xi 72; "Documents on the Relations of France to Louisiana," 511–15.

129. Fieffé, *Histoire des troupes étrangères*, 2:54.

130. *Quellen zur Geschichte des Rheinlandes*, 3:190; Schreiber, *Französische Ausweisungspolitik*, 109; AN AF/II/204bis, dossier 1725, item 41.

131. Chuquet, *Guerres de la Révolution*, 201; Sagnac, *Rhin français*, 97.

132. Fieffé, *Histoire des troupes étrangères*, 2:10–15; decree of 17 Brumaire Year VII, SHD Xh 1a; Dubois, *L'invention de la Belgique*, 116; *Belgique française*, ed. Hasquin.

133. Fieffé, *Histoire des troupes étrangères*, 2:27, 30–31.

134. Dufraisse, "Les populations de la rive gauche," 124.

135. AN AF/II/230, dossier 1985, item 37; memorandum of 28 Fructidor Year VI and letters of 18 Thermidor Year VII and 4 Fructidor Year VII, SHD Xg 1.

136. *Quellen zur Geschichte des Rheinlandes*, 4:1094; Dufraisse, "Les populations de la rive gauche," 126–27.

137. Letter of October 25, 1798, in *Quellen zur Geschichte des Rheinlandes*, 4:1094.

138. *Quellen zur Geschichte des Rheinlandes*, 4:1094.

139. Dufraisse, "Les populations de la rive gauche," 127; Rowe, *From Reich to State*, 163.

140. Ibid.; Grisot and Coulombon, *Légion étrangère*, 524–28.

141. Dufraisse, "Les populations de la rive gauche," 127; address of March 19, 1800, in *Quellen zur Geschichte des Rheinlandes*, 4:1260.

142. Letter of June 3, 1799, in *Quellen zur Geschichte des Rheinlandes*, 4:1092–93.

143. Letter of June 17, 1799, in *Quellen zur Geschichte des Rheinlandes*, 4:1092–93.

144. Dufraisse, "Les populations de la rive gauche," 127–28; Eickemeyer to the war minister (15 Pluviôse Year IX), SHD Xk 21.

145. Letter of 26 Brumaire Year VIII, SHD Xk 21.

146. Dufraisse, "Les populations de la rive gauche," 130. According to Dufraisse, this roster existed in SHD Xk 21, but I was unable to locate it there after an exhaustive search in March 2011.

147. Roster of 8 Messidor Year VIII, SHD Xk 21.

148. "Liste des Irlandais Réfugiés destinés à la formation d'un Bataillon," 25 Pluviôse Year VIII, SHD Xk 21.

149. Letter of 28 Fructidor Year VIII, SHD Xk 21.

150. Letters of 9 Pluviôse Year IX and 2 Germinal Year IX and roster of 8 Nivôse Year VIII, SHD Xk 21.

151. Rowe, *Reich to State*, 164; *Quellen zur Geschichte des Rheinlandes*, 4:1261.

152. Letter of 22 Thermidor Year VIII, SHD Xk 21.

153. Letter of 17 Ventôse Year IX and report of 3 Prairial Year IX, SHD Xk 21.

154. Dufraisse, "Les populations de la rive gauche,"129; Rowe, *Reich to State*, 164.

155. Dufraisse, "Les populations de la rive gauche," 129; decree of 7 Messidor Year IX, SHD Xk 21.

156. Dufraisse, "Les populations de la rive gauche," 131; decree of 7 Messidor Year IX, SHD Xk 21.

157. Eickemeyer was acquitted, but never again served in the army (Rowe, *Reich to State*, 165).

158. Forrest, *Conscripts and Deserters*, 9–11.

159. Ibid., 21–26.

160. Lynn, *Bayonets of the Republic*, 44.

161. Dufraisse, "Les populations de la rive gauche," 125.

162. Sylvain Sick, "Les nouveaux Français et l'armée dans les départements du Léman et du Mont-Blanc," in Crépin et al., *Civils, citoyens-soldats et militaires*, 78–86, 78.

163. "Notte sur la Composition des deux Bons. de Chasseurs Basques," undated letter signed Harriet ainé, decree of 9 Pluviôse Year IX and reports of 1 Prairial Year IX and 11 Prairial Year IX, SHD Xk 11.

164. *Quellen zur Geschichte des Rheinlandes*, 4:940.

165. Ibid., 4:1092.

166. Dufraisse, "Les populations de la rive gauche," 125–26; Sick, "Les nouveaux Français et l'armée," 79.

167. AN AF/II/15, dossier 108, item 130.

168. *Collection complète des lois*, 10:343.

169. Letters of 1 Messidor Year VII and 18 Messidor Year VII, AN F/9/288.

170. Letters of September 9, 1806, and September 25, 1806, AN F/9/288.

171. Advocates of a more restrictive definition of nationality prevailed over Napoleon (Weil, *How to Be French*, 22–25, 29).

SIX. Revolutionary Continuities

1. Weil, *How to Be French*, 22–31.

2. Rapport, *Nationality and Citizenship*, 321.

3. Ibid., 317, 319.

4. Ibid., 317.

5. Brun, "Les unités étrangères," note 11.

6. Broers, *Napoleonic Empire*, 237; Fieffé, *Histoire des troupes étrangères*, 2:115–17.

7. Broers, *Napoleonic Empire*, 223.

8. Fieffé, *Histoire des troupes étrangères*, 2:118.

9. Ibid., 2:115–20.

10. Decree of 17 Thermidor Year XIII and letter of 5 Thermidor Year X, SHD Xk 4.

11. Brun, "Les unités étrangères," note 11.

12. Fieffé, *Histoire des troupes étrangères*, 2:169–70.

13. Fieffé, *Histoire des troupes étrangères*, 2:173–77; decree of August 10, 1810, SHD Xl 13; Brun, "Les unités étrangères," note 11.

14. Fieffé, *Histoire des troupes étrangères*, 2:179.

15. Letter of November 21, 1810, SHD Xl 13.

16. Brun, "Les unités étrangères," note 11.

17. Fieffé, *Histoire des troupes étrangères*, 2:157.

18. Ibid., 2:156.

19. Ibid., 2:166.

20. Ibid., 2:152–55.

21. Ibid., 2:189–93.

22. Fieffé, *Histoire des troupes étrangères*, 2:189–93; *Guide des tribunaux militaires*, 2:692.

23. Brun, "Les unités étrangères," paragraph 6.

24. Ibid., paragraphs 11–12.

25. Fieffé, *Histoire des troupes étrangères*, 2:130–32; Terence Wise and Guido Rosignoli, *Flags of the Napoleonic Wars*, 3 vols. (Oxford: Bosprey, 1984), 3:10.

26. Fieffé, *Histoire des troupes étrangères*, 2:168–72.

27. Dame, *History of Switzerland*, 2:294; Fieffé, *Histoire des troupes étrangères*, 2:120; Roucaud, "La capitulation générale de 1803."

28. Fieffé, *Histoire des troupes étrangères*, 2:38, 126; "Projet de capitulation" (28 Prairial Year XI), SHD Xg 1.

29. Fieffé, *Histoire des troupes étrangères*, 2:120–26.

30. Brun, "Les unités étrangères," paragraph 22.

31. Letter of February 9, 1806, SHD Xl 13.

32. Memorandum of December 15, 1806, SHD Xl 13; "Circulaire aux Cantons Confédéres Confidentielle," SHD Xl 13.

33. Report of December 31, 1809, and "Rapport A Sa Majesté l'Empereur et Roi Du 8 Août an 1810," in SHD Xg 13.

34. Fieffé, *Histoire des troupes étrangères*, 2:125–26.

35. Roucaud, "La capitulation générale de 1803," paragraph 18.

36. Raguet, "Du Pionniers Noirs," 14–15; Gainot, *Officiers de couleur*, 166; rosters of 26 Brumaire Year III and 30 Vendémiaire Year III, SHD Xi 71; report of 11 Messidor Year XI, SHD Xi 72; roster of December 1808 (exact date not specified), SHD Yj 19.

37. Report of Fructidor Year XI (exact date not specified), SHD Xh 3; Raguet, "Du Pionniers Noirs," 18; Gainot, *Officiers de couleur*, 166–67; Fieffé, *Histoire des troupes étrangères*, 2:54.

38. Gainot, *Officiers de couleur*, 177.

39. Ibid.

40. Decree of 21 Floréal Year XI, SHD Xh 5a; Gainot, *Officiers de couleur*, 179–80, 200–201.

41. Fieffé, *Histoire des troupes étrangères*, 2:54; Raguet, "Du Pionniers Noirs," 67.

42. Note of October 2, 1807, SHD Xh 3; Gainot, *Officiers de couleur*, 210–11.

43. Letter of February 5, 1808, SHD Xh 3; Fieffé, *Histoire des troupes étrangères*, 2:54.

44. Note of October 2, 1807, SHD Xh 3; Gainot, *Officiers de couleur*, 211–12.

45. Raguet, "Du Pionniers Noirs," 98.

46. Gainot, *Officiers de couleur*, 180.

47. Letter of 13 Floréal Year XIII, SHD Xh 3.

48. Review of 30 Fructidor Year XIII, SHD Xh 3.

49. Letter of July 24, 1807, SHD Xh 3.

50. Raguet, "Du Pionniers Noirs," 84.

51. Ibid., 108.

52. Bourgogne, *Mémoires*, 404; Raguet, "Du Pionniers noirs," 2.

53. Report of 11 Messidor Year XI, SHD Xi 72.

54. Letters of May 23, 1815, and June 8, 1815, and "6e. Régiment Etranger. Etat des hommes nègres, en Subsistance audit Régiment, Venus du 4e. Régiment Etranger, pour Indication de leurs Services," SHD Xi 68.

55. Roster of 4 Fructidor Year VIII for the Légion expéditionnaire, SHD Xi 72; "Etat des Services de Messieurs les Officiers, S. Officiers & Soldats dudit Corps," SHD Xi 28.

56. Inspection report of 21 Vendémiaire Year XIII and roster of officers in the *Bataillon des français rentrés* of March 28, 1806, SHD Xk 37; entry for Delor, SHD 20Yc 4bis.

57. Grégoire, *De la littérature des nègres*, 93–95, 100.

58. Ibid., 92–93.

59. Fieffé, *Histoire des troupes étrangères*, 2:183.

60. Decree of 10 Brumaire Year IV, SHD Xh 7.

61. Decree of March 9, 1806, SHD Xh 6.

62. See the case of Louis-Claude Lavergne de Tressan, SHD Xh 11.

63. "Etat de Situation Sommaire des dits Bataillons à l'Epoque du 1er Novembre 1813," SHD Xh 13a; SHD 23Yc 189.

64. SHD Xh 10a; SHD Xh 13a.

65. Fieffé, *Histoire des troupes étrangères*, 2:186; "Notice pour servir à l'historique du Corps," SHD Xh 18a.

66. SHD Xh 18a.

67. Memorandum of October 30, 1807, and roster of December 19, 1811, SHD Xh 18a.

68. SHD 23Yc 209.

69. Decree of November 25, 1813, SHD Xh 18a.

70. Fieffé, *Histoire des troupes étrangères*, 2:184–85; Gallaher, *Napoleon's Irish Legion*, 96, 202; decree of April 13, 1809, SHD Xh 6; Nicholas Dunne-Lynch, "The Irish Legion of Napoleon, 1803–15," in Genet-Rouffiac and Murphy, *Franco-Irish Military Connections*, 189–218.

71. Decree of 13 Floréal Year XI, SHD Xh 6.

72. "Liste des Irlandais Réfugiés destinés à la formation d'un Bataillon," 25 Pluviôse Year VIII, SHD Xk 21; "Tableau des officiers proposés par l'adjudant commandant MacSheehy pour des emplois," SHD Xh 14; Fieffé, *Histoire des troupes étrangères*, 2:186.

73. Gallaher, *Napoleon's Irish Legion*, 35, 55; "Tableau des officiers proposés par l'adjudant commandant MacSheehy pour des emplois," SHD Xh 14.

74. Report from the war minister, Year XII (exact date unspecified), and report of 4 Messidor Year XIII, SHD Xh 14; Gallaher, *Napoleon's Irish Legion*, 42–44.

75. Quoted in ibid., 83. The translation is Gallaher's.

76. Ibid., 47–48.

77. Quoted in ibid., 73. The translation is Gallaher's.

78. Letter of November 8, 1809, SHD Xh 6.

79. SHD 23Yc 202.

80. Letter of August 1810 (exact date unspecified), SHD Xh 6; Gallaher, *Napoleon's Irish Legion,* 159–60; SHD 23Yc 202.

81. Gallaher, *Napoleon's Irish Legion,* 79.

82. Quoted in ibid., 80. The translation is Gallaher's.

83. Ibid., 174–75.

84. SHD Xh 14; Gallaher, *Napoleon's Irish Legion.*

85. Gallaher, *Napoleon's Irish Legion,* 84–85, 216.

86. *Correspondance de Napoléon 1er,* 16:157; Boppe, *Légion portugaise,* 4–5.

87. Quoted in Molière, *Expéditions françaises,* 393.

88. Boppe, *Légion portugaise,* 9.

89. "Procès Verbal d'Organisation de la Légion Portugaise," SHD Xh 6.

90. Boppe, *Légion portugaise,* 45–46, 51–52, 80–81, 90.

91. Ibid., 323, 327.

92. Boppe, *Espagnols,* 4, 7–8.

93. Boppe, *Espagnols,* 77–79; Fieffé, *Histoire des troupes étrangères,* 2:144.

94. Boppe, *Espagnols,* 103–04.

95. Ibid., 91.

96. Ibid., 166.

97. Bronikowski, "Notte sur les Troupes polonaises au Service de Sa Majesté," February 13, 1810, SHD Xh 6.

98. Fieffé, *Histoire des troupes étrangères,* 2:134–35.

99. Ibid., 2:135–40

100. Ibid., 2:187.

101. Memorandum of March 16, 1806, AN F/9/745; report of August 21, 1809, review of October 9, 1810, and roster of October 19, 1803, SHD Xh 4; SHD 23Yc 284.

102. Fieffé, *Histoire des troupes étrangères,* 2:147, 188.

103. Ibid., 2:146–47.

104. Fieffé, *Histoire des troupes étrangères,* 2:147; SHD Xn 23.

105. Quoted in Hippler, "Les soldats allemands."

106. Dossier for Charles d'Ehrenfelt, SHD Xh 5c; letters of January 24, 1810, and February 20, 1810, SHD Xh 12; SHD Xh 18a.

107. Stanbridge, *Toleration and State Institutions,* 191.

108. See the rosters of October 1, 1808, and January 1, 1809, SHD Xh 18a.

109. Letter of February 15, 1807, SHD Xh 8.

110. Letter of April 18, 1813, SHD Xh 13a.

111. Report of February 10, 1813, SHD Xh 13a.

112. Letters of March 31, 1806, and June 24, 1806, SHD Xh 8.

113. Undated note on recruitment, SHD Xh 6.

114. Letter of December 31, 1812, SHD Xh 13a.

115. AN F/7/6369, dossier 7527.

116. Letter of March 31, 1806, SHD Xh 8; letters of January 10, 1808, and March 16, 1808, SHD Xh 1a.

117. Report of November 10, 1813, SHD Xh 6.

118. Letter of 13 Messidor Year XIII and inspection of Thermidor Year XIII, SHD Xh 2a.

119. Report of November 10, 1813, SHD Xh 6.

120. Decrees of 7 Pluviôse Year IX and 2 Thermidor Year X, SHD Xh 2a.

121. Roster of 18 Floréal Year IX, SHD Xh 2a; letter of 17 Ventôse Year XI, SHD Xh 2a.

122. *AP* 11:626–27, 15:403–06.

123. Inspection report of 29 February 1808, SHD Xh 1a.

124. Inspection report of 30 Thermidor Year XIII, SHD Xh 2a.

125. Letter of April 29, 1815, SHD Xi 68.

126. Letter of June 23, 1813, SHD Xh 13a.

127. Note of October 7, 1808, SHD Xh 6.

128. Inspection of 30 Thermidor Year XIII, SHD Xh 2a.

129. Maugué, *Particularisme alsacien*, 146.

130. Letter of March 4, 1808, SHD Xh 5d.

131. Letters of July 10, 1809, and August 17, 1809, SHD Xh 9; "Tableau des officiers nommés Provisoirement pour faire Partie du Premier Bataillon franc allemand," SHD B5 2.

132. Inspection report of 30 Thermidor Year XIII, SHD Xh 2a.

133. Letter of March 31, 1809, SHD Xh 1a.

134. Gallaher, *Napoleon's Irish Legion*, 55.

135. Letters of September 27, 1807, and February 5, 1808, and report of October 19, 1808, SHD Xh 18a.

136. AN F/7/6503, dossier 818.

137. Gallaher, *Napoleon's Irish Legion*, 65–66.

138. AN F/7/6369, dossier 7533.

139. Letter of September 21, 1812, SHD Xh 7.

140. Decree of September 1, 1810, SHD Xk 45.

141. Decree of 2 Germinal Year X, SHD Xk 37.

142. Letters of February 8, 1806, June 6, 1809, June 16, 1810, and August 27, 1814, and report to the war minister of May 15, 1811, SHD Xk 37.

143. Letter of December 17, 1813, SHD Xh 6.

144. Letter of May 12, 1806, SHD Xk 37.

145. *Bullétin des lois* (Paris: Imprimerie impériale, 1809), 131.

146. Roster of October 1810, SHD Xp 1b; letter of May 14, 1817, SHD Xl 13.

147. *Table générale*, 1:6; AN F/7/6410, dossier 8154.

148. Letter of December 26, 1813, SHD Xh 7.

149. *Correspondance de Napoléon 1er*, 26:427, 466 466; letter of November 15, 1813, SHD Xh 7.

150. AN AF/IV/829, dossier 6653, item 11.

151. Brun, "Les unités étrangères," paragraph 41; Fieffé, *Histoire des troupes étrangères*, 2:169; AN AF/IV/829, dossier 6653, item 11.

152. Decree of November 25, 1813, SHD Xh 4SHD Xh 6; AN AF/IV/829, dossier 6653, item 11.

153. Brun, "Les unités étrangères," paragraph 43; letter to the war minister, January 3, 1814, SHD Xh 7.

154. Report of March 10, 1814, SHD Xh 6.

155. Letter of January 1814, SHD Xh 7.

156. Boppe, *Légion portugaise*, 327; *Carnet de la Sabretache* 49 (Jan. 1897): 4–19; AN AF/IV/829, dossier 6653, items 11, 13 and 14.

157. Fieffé, *Histoire des troupes étrangères*, 2:359–60; reports of January 13, 1813, and December 1814 (exact date unspecified), SHD Xh 6.

158. Fieffé, *Histoire des troupes étrangères*, 2:363; Boppe, *Légion Portugaise*, 334; Gallaher, *Napoleon's Irish Legion*, 200.

159. Letter of January 17, 1815, SHD Xh 7.

160. Fieffé, *Histoire des troupes étrangères*, 2:364; Boppe, *Espagnols*, 167–69; Boppe, *Légion Portugaise*, 358.

161. Letter of April 14, 1815, SHD Xh 7.

162. Fieffé, *Histoire des troupes étrangères*, 2:360.

163. Ibid.; Brun, "Les unités étrangères," paragraph 49.

164. Fieffé, *Histoire des troupes étrangères*, 2:364; *Nouvelle Histoire de la Suisse et des Suisses*, ed. Favez 499; Roucaud, "La capitulation générale de 1803," paragraph 19; decree of April 11, 1815, SHD Xh 7.

165. Decree of April 15, 1815, SHD Xi 68; roster of enrollees (July 1, 1815–July 31, 1815), SHD Xi 68; Boppe, *Légion portugaise*, 376.

166. Decree of April 11, 1815, SHD Xh 7; Boppe, *Légion portugaise*, 370.

167. Gallaher, *Napoleon's Irish Legion*, 211, 212.

168. Quoted in ibid., 209.

169. SHD 7Yd 224.

170. Letter of March 24, 1815, SHD Xh 13a.

171. Letter of April 21, 1815, SHD Xh 10a.

172. Letter of April 10, 1815, SHD Xh 7.

173. "Aux braves militaires qui ont vaincu sous les Aigles francaises," SHD Xh 7.

174. Fieffé, *Histoire des troupes étrangères*, 2:366–68.

175. Dossier "Keller," SHD Xg 92.

176. Letters of May 13, 1815; May 31, 1815; and June 3, 1815, SHD Xi 68.

177. Smith, *Napoleon's Regiments*, 218.

178. Fieffé, *Histoire des troupes étrangères*, 2:368–69; Gallaher, *Napoleon's Irish Legion*, 212.

SEVEN. Jews, Soldiering, and Citizenship in
Revolutionary and Napoleonic France

1. To cite a few important works: Bredin, *L'Affaire*; Forth, *Dreyfus Affair*; Burns, *Dreyfus: A Family Affair*.

2. Hyman, *Jews of Modern France*, 94.

3. Zosa Szajkowski, "French Jews in the Armed Forces during the Revolution of 1789," *Proceedings of the American Academy for Jewish Research* 26 (1957): 139–60. This article was later reprinted, unedited, in Szajkowski, *Jews and the French Revolutions*, 554–75.

4. Weber, *Peasants into Frenchmen*, esp. 292–302.

5. Schechter, *Obstinate Hebrews*, 151–53.

6. Benbassa, *Histoire des Juifs,* 133–38, 149–76; Hyman, *Jews of Modern France,* 33–35.

7. Birnbaum, *Mythe politique,* 30–48; Birnbaum, *Fous de la République,* 8.

8. On the symbolic significance of Jewish regeneration, see Schechter, *Obstinate Hebrews.*

9. Pietri, *Napoléon et les Israélites,* 17.

10. Corvisier, *L'Armée française,* 1:294.

11. Archives départmentales de Meurthe-et-Moselle, E supplement 971.

12. Job, "Note additive aux baptêmes de Juifs."

13. Corvisier, *L'Armée française,* 1:294–95.

14. *AP* 10:760.

15. *Discours prononcé le 28 janvier 1790,* 4.

16. Grégoire, *Essai sur la régénération; AP* 10:766–75; Sepinwall, *Abbé Grégoire,* 56–77.

17. *AP* 10:765.

18. Ibid., 10:772.

19. Hyman, *Jews of Modern France,* 41–44.

20. Ibid., 54; Benbassa, *Histoire des Juifs de France,* 149–54, 193–95; and Schechter, *Obstinate Hebrews,* 179.

21. *Adresse de l'Assemblée des Représentans de la Commune de Paris.*

22. *Apologie de l'opinion de M. Ranxin.*

23. Pietri, *Napoléon et les Israélites,* 22–23.

24. Quoted in H. Tribout de Morembert, "Les juifs de Metz et de Lorraine (1791–1795)," in Blumenkranz and Soboul, *Juifs et la Révolution française,* 93–94.

25. Letter of June 1790 (exact date unspecified), AN D/IV/6, dossier 93.

26. *Ran Tan Plan,* 12–13.

27. René Moulinas, "Les juifs d'Avignon et du Comtat et la Révolution française," in Blumenkranz and Soboul, *Juifs et la Révolution française,* 166–67.

28. Brunsvik answered that he was "de la judé d'Israel" (AN F/7/4620, dossier 2).

29. AN W/246.

30. Marat printed a letter in his *Orateur du Peuple* in March 1791 denouncing several members of Calmer's battalion for suspected royalist activities. The anonymous author of the letter singled out "le Juif Calmer" but did not mention the religions of any of the other soldiers (Marat, *Oeuvres politiques,* 4:2495).

31. AN F/7/4631, dossier 4; AN W/351, dossier 717. Calmer was a son of Liefman Calmer, who despite being Jewish purchased a noble office in France in 1774 (Loeb, "Un Baron juif français").

32. Kahn, *Juifs de Paris,* 235–47; Szajkowski, *Jews and the French Revolutions,* 458–59.

33. AN F/7/4774⁶⁷, dossier "Pereyra."

34. The available documents do not specify the names of the artillerymen who petitioned the Bonconseil section on Péreire's behalf, but because only about one hundred Jews served in the National Guard of Paris during the Revolution and were spread throughout different units, it is very unlikely that all of the men in Péreire's

company, which would have numbered around seventy-five soldiers, were Jews (*Discours prononcé le 28 janvier 1790*, 6).

35. Letter of 9 Ventôse Year II, AN F/7/4774[67].

36. AN W/339, dossier 617; Mathiez, *Conspiration*, 7–8.

37. Lynn, *Bayonets of the Republic*, 43–66; Bertaud, *Révolution armée*, 56–71; Osman, *Citizen Soldiers and the Key to the Bastille*.

38. Bertaud, *Révolution armée*, 63; Edelstein, "Le militaire-citoyen."

39. Bertaud, *Révolution armée*, 56–71; Lynn, *Bayonets of the Republic*, 43–66; Hippler, *Soldats et citoyens*, esp. 78.

40. Bertaud, *Révolution armée*, 20; Lynn, *Bayonets of the Republic*, 64–65. On soldiers' families see also Jennifer Heuer's forthcoming book, tentatively titled *The Soldier's Reward: Love and War in the Age of Napoleon*.

41. Fink, *Marc Bloch*, 1.

42. Letter of 26 Thermidor Year II, SHD Xk 7.

43. Scott, *Response of the Royal Army*, 183–84; Bertaud, *Révolution armée*, 65.

44. In a letter of October 24, 1824, addressed to King Charles X of France, Nordon claimed that he had served with the Swiss Guards Regiment and was wounded while fighting at the Tuileries Palace on August 10, 1792. He added that he survived the infamous massacre of Swiss soldiers that followed the assault only by fleeing to the residence of the Spanish ambassador. Since complete troop rosters for the Swiss Guards from the time of the Revolution no longer exist, it is difficult to corroborate Nordon's claim; however, the story seems doubtful, since Nordon failed to provide any specific information regarding his service in the Swiss Guards Regiment, such as his date of entry, rank or the name of the company in which he served. In addition, references to the Swiss Guards on official documents recording Nordon's services in the French army are curiously blotted out, further suggesting that he was unable to substantiate this claim. Nordon likely invented the story after the Bourbon Restoration in order to seek the king's favor, since the purpose of his letter was to request appointment to the Légion d'honneur. The letter and two documents with redacted references to the Swiss Guards are in SHD 2Yf 215.

45. Grégoire and other contemporaries mentioned the presence of Jews as officers in volunteer battalions before September 1792, a fact confirmed by the service of Nordon himself as a sergeant and second lieutenant in the Parisian National Guard prior to transferring to the Légion germanique. The historians Chuquet and Szajkowski, however, affirmed that Nordon was the first Jewish officer to serve in the French line army, an institution that remained distinct from and more professional than the National Guard during the first several years of the Revolution (Chuquet, *Légion germanique*, vii; Szajkowski, "French Jews in the Armed Forces," 146).

46. Chuquet, *Légion germanique*, vii, 42, 244; SHD 2Ye 3057; SHD 2Yf 215, dossier "Nordon"; SHD Xk 3; SHD 2Yf 215.

47. SHD 2Ye 2545, dossier "Salomon Lévy"; AN LH/1630/9.

48. Blaufarb, *French Army*.

49. AN AF/III/145/A, dossier 683, item 128.

50. *Discours prononcé le 28 janvier 1790*, 6.

51. The departmental directory annulled the segregation attempt in Saint-

Esprit (Szajkowski, "French Jews in the Armed Forces," 141; Hyman, *Jews of Modern France,* 33; Schechter, *Obstinate Hebrews,* 19).

52. René Moulinas, *Juifs du pape en France: les communautés d'Avignon et du Comtat Venaissin aux 17e et 18e siècles* (Paris: Belles Lettres, 1981), 441; Szajkowski, "French Jews in the Armed Forces," 146.

53. Ibid., 142–43.

54. Malino, *Sephardic Jews of Bordeaux,* 1–64, esp. 40–64; Schwarzfuchs, *Du Juif à l'israélite,* 19–37, 117–56.

55. Malino, *Sephardic Jews of Bordeaux,* 53, 57.

56. Quoted in Szajkowski, "French Jews in the Armed Forces," 145. The translation is Szajkowski's. See also Szajkowski, "French Jews in the Armed Forces," 145; AN AF/II/281, dossier 2347; and SHD 3Yd 1303.

57. AN F/7/4748, dossier 2.

58. Tribout de Morembert, "Les juifs de Metz et de Lorraine," 94–95.

59. Moulinas, "Les juifs d'Avignon et du Comtat," in Blumenkranz and Soboul, *Juifs et la Révolution,* 167; Moulinas, *Juifs du pape,* 59, 441; Szajkowski, *Jews and the French Revolutions,* 464.

60. Szajkowski, "French Jews in the Armed Forces," 149.

61. According to Pietri (*Napoléon et les Israélites,* 39–40), Napoleon was inspired by an Irish officer serving in his army named Thomas Corbet to raise a "legion" of Middle Eastern Jews during his campaign in the Levant in 1799. Napoleon reportedly intended the corps to win the sympathy of local Jewish communities for French troops, as well as to support the establishment of a Jewish state in the region which he envisioned as a counterweight to Ottoman influence. The only unambiguous reference to this proposal, however, was a brief report in the *Moniteur* of 3 Prairial Year VII which described a proclamation purportedly issued by Napoleon in the Middle East regarding a Jewish legion but did not include a copy of the proclamation itself, which historians have never located. In the absence of more thorough documentation, Pietri's claims on the Jewish legion appear exaggerated, and in any case there is no evidence of the French having ever pursued serious measures for levying the corps. See also Schechter, *Obstinate Hebrews,* 201.

62. Pietri, *Napoléon et les Israélites,* 14.

63. Dufau, *Collection des constitutions,* 1:303–04.

64. Charles Touati, "Le Grand Sanhédrin de 1807 et le droit rabbinique," in Blumenkranz and Soboul, *Grand Sanhédrin de Napoléon,* 47; Schechter, *Obstinate Hebrews,* 194–235, esp. 209–10, 215–20.

65. Forrest, *Conscripts and Deserters.*

66. Pietri, *Napoléon et les Israélites,* 35–36; Schechter, *Obstinate Hebrews,* 194–235, esp. 198–200.

67. As Forrest noted (*Conscripts and Deserters,* 20), Jacques Houdaille proposed a figure of 2,025,000 conscripts, while Roger Darquenne suggested 2,150,000. I averaged these numbers to arrive at the figure 2,087,500 conscripts over the period of fifteen years between 1798 and 1813, or 139,167 conscripts per year.

68. Scholars do not agree precisely on the total population of France during the revolutionary era, which in any case fluctuated significantly as territories were

annexed and ceded, and as wars and emigration took their toll. Colin Jones has suggested that France's population in 1789 amounted to 28.6 million individuals, a figure Jacques Dupâquier fixed closer to 26 million. Martyn Lyons advanced the calculation of 27.4 million for the year 1801. Averaging these numbers, one arrives at 27.3 million, the figure I have used as the basis for my calculations (Jones, *Great Nation,* 351; Dupâquier, "French Population," 155; Lyons, *France under the Directory,* 176).

69. "Réponses aux questions contenues dans une circulaire," AN F/19/11010.

70. H. J. de Dianoux, "Les juifs de Nice et la Révolution française," in Blumenkranz and Soboul, *Juifs et la Révolution,* 186.

71. "Tableau des Israélites du Département du Rhône" (October 4, 1810); report to the minister of the interior on the Vosges department (November 14, 1808); letter from Jews of Wissembourg to Napoleon (October 25, 1810), AN F/19/11010. The reports on the Rhône and Vosges departments, and the letter on Wissembourg, leave some ambiguities regarding the total size of the Jewish population of those communities and the date of their first contributions to the conscription; however, with the assumptions that each Jewish family averaged 4.7 individuals, a calculation based on the size of Jewish families in other departments, and that the first Jewish conscripts were called from each of these locations beginning with the institutionalization of the Jourdan law, one arrives at the figures cited.

72. AD BR 1R 60. See also Szajkowski, "French Jews in the Armed Forces," 144; and Freddy Raphael, "Les juifs d'Alsace et la conscription au dix-neuvième siècle," in *Juifs et la Révolution,* 133.

73. Raphael, "Les juifs d'Alsace," in *Juifs et la Révolution,* 121-24; Paula Hyman, *Emancipation of the Jews,* 69.

74. Caron, *Between France and Germany,* 21.

75. Quoted in ibid., 20. This translation is Caron's.

76. Hyman, *Emancipation of the Jews,* 70.

77. Raphael, "Les juifs d'Alsace," in Blumenkranz and Soboul, *Juifs et la Révolution,* 133, 137; Hyman, *Jews of Modern France,* 47.

78. *Correspondance du dépôt des lois,* 348; letters of October 8, 1812, and September 3, 1813, AN F/19/11052; letters of September 17, 1812, November 30, 1812, and August 11, 1813, AN F/19/11052.

79. Letter of June 27, 1812, AN F/19/11052.

80. Letters of March 28, 1808, and October 25, 1810, AN F/19/11010. It does not appear true that there were no refractory Jewish conscripts from Wissembourg; Isaac Meyer, one of sixteen Jewish recruits called up in 1808, failed to appear for induction, according to the register for Landau in AD BR 1R 60.

81. The first exclusively Jewish military unit in modern times was the Jewish militia in Dutch Suriname during the seventeenth and eighteenth centuries, but the Korps Israelieten was the first Jewish military force in the modern European metropole. On the militia in Suriname, see Ben-Ur, "Still Life," 54, 66; and Wolf, *American Jew,* 462.

82. Letter of February 28, 1811, and report of June 3, 1811, SHD Xl 13.

83. E. Rubin, without citing a source, presented Henri Rottembourg, who be-

came a brigadier general in the French army in 1811, as the first Jewish general in France; however, I have been unable to confirm that Rottembourg was born and remained a Jew. I have thus followed Birnbaum's judgment in affirming that Sée was France's first Jewish general. Born in Bergheim, Haut-Rhin, in 1822, Sée served as an officer with the Zouaves in Algeria and the Crimea before transferring to Napoleon III's Imperial Guard in 1858. He was wounded and captured by the Prussians near Metz in 1870 but returned in the same year to France, where the Government of National Defense appointed him a brigadier general. He continued his career under the Third Republic, reaching the rank of general of division before retiring in 1887. In addition to his military services, Sée was active as a representative of Paris to the Jewish Central Consistory (Rubin, *140 Jewish Marshals*, 100–103; Birnbaum, *L'affaire Dreyfus*, 33). Lévy Wolff, a Jew who enlisted in 1794 and became a general under Napoleon, was the first French general of Jewish descent, but he converted to Christianity prior to obtaining that rank (Szajkowski, "French Jews in the Armed Forces," 143).

84. Dreyfus, *Cinq années de ma vie*, 356.

85. Bloch, *L'Étrange défaite*, 35.

Conclusion

1. Letter of September 12, 1815.

2. Ordinance of September 6, 1815, SHD Xh 7.

3. Boppe, *Espagnols*, 169–70; Boppe, *Légion portugaise*, 337, 340, 358, 377; letter of July 23, 1815, SHD Xi 68; pamphlet of June 21, 1816, AN F/9/54.

4. Fieffé, *Histoire des troupes étrangères*, 2:374–75.

5. SHD Xg 27, dossier 1; Fieffé, *Histoire des troupes étrangères*, 2:375.

6. *Bibliothèque historique*, 2:45–68.

7. Fieffé, *Histoire des troupes étrangères*, 2:381–382; Grisot and Coulombon, *Légion étrangère*, 6.

8. Grisot and Coulombon, *Légion étrangère*, 6, 8.

9. Porch, *French Foreign Legion*. Harold Vormezeele, a Belgian who became a French citizen after serving in the Foreign Legion for eleven years, was the first French soldier killed in ground fighting in the recent conflict in Mali.

BIBLIOGRAPHY

Adresse au département de Paris par des volontaires de la seconde légion de la garde nationale Parisienne. Paris: Guilhemat, n.d.

Adresse aux François. Paris: Imprimerie Du Pont, 1792.

Adresse de l'Assemblée des Représentans de la Commune de Paris, à l'Assemblée Nationale, sur l'admission des Juifs à l'Etat Civil. Paris: Lottin, n.d.

Adresse des Anglois, des Écossois et des Irlandois, résidans et domiciliés à Paris, à la Convention nationale, et réponse du président. Troyes: Sainton, 1792.

Ahlstrom, John D. "Captain and Chef de Brigade William Tate: South Carolina Adventurer." *South Carolina Historical Magazine* 88 (Oct. 1987): 183–91.

A Jean Skei Eustace, Se disant Citoyen des États-Unis d'Amérique, & Général de Brigade des Armées Françoises. N.p., n.d.

Alderson, Robert J. *This Bright Era of Happy Revolutions: French Consul Michel-Ange-Bernard Mangourit and International Republicanism in Charleston, 1792–1794.* Charleston: University of South Carolina Press, 2008.

Alger, John G. *Englishmen in the French Revolution.* London: Dunstan's House, 1889.

Ammon, Harry. *The Genêt Mission.* New York: Norton, 1973.

Anderson, Benedict. *Imagined Communities: Reflections on the Origin and Spread of Nationalism.* London: Verso, 1991.

Apologie de l'opinion de M. Ranxin sur cette question: Les Juifs doivent-ils être admis dans la milice nationale? Par M. Valois, garde citoyen de la compagnie de Nicolas. N.p., n.d.

Appel aux Gardes Citoyens de la Ville de Nancy, sur la lettre anonyme à eux adressée. N.p., n.d.

Appel des étrangers dans nos colonies. Paris: Dessain Junior, 1763.

Arendt, Hannah. *The Origins of Totalitarianism.* New York: Harcourt, Brace & World, 1966.

Arielli, Nir, and Bruce Collins, eds. *Transnational Soldiers: Foreign Military Enlistment in the Modern Era.* London: Palgrave Macmillan, 2013.

Aulard, François Victor Alphonse. *Paris sous le Consulat: Recueil de documents pour l'histoire de l'esprit public à Paris.* Paris: Cerf, 1904.

———. *La Société des Jacobins: Recueil des documents pour l'histoire du Club des Jacobins de Paris.* Paris: Jouaust, 1889–97.

Au Roi. (Pour les Cent-Suisses, troublés dans leurs privilèges par le fermier des aides). N.p., 1641.

Autin, Jean. *Les frères Pereire: Le bonheur d'entreprendre.* Paris: Perrin, 1984.

Balleydier, Alphonse. *Histoire politique et militaire du peuple de Lyon pendant la Révolution française, 1789–1795.* Paris: Martinon, 1816.

Belissa, Marc. "De l'ordre d'Ancien Régime à l'ordre international: Approches de l'histoire des relations internationales." In *La Révolution à l'oeuvre, actes du colloque de janvier 2004,* edited by J. C. Martin, 217–27. Rennes: Presses universitaires de Rennes, 2004.

———. *Fraternité universelle et intérêt national (1713–1795): La cosmopolitique du droit des gens.* Paris: Éditions Kimé, 1998.

Bell, David A. *The Cult of the Nation in France.* Cambridge, Mass.: Harvard University Press, 2001.

———. *The First Total War: Napoleon's Europe and the Birth of Warfare as We Know It.* Boston: Houghton Mifflin, 2007.

Bély, Lucien. *The History of France.* Paris: Gisserot, 2001.

Benbassa, Esther. *Histoire des Juifs de France.* Paris: Seuil, 2000.

Benoit, Bruno. "Assassinat d'un soldat suisse à Lyon, le 19 juillet 1790." In *112e Congrès national des sociétés savantes: Autour des mentalités et des pratiques politiques sous la Révolution française,* 3:91–98. Paris: Éditions du CTHS, 1987.

Ben-Ur, Aviva. "Still Life: Sephardi, Ashkenazi, and West African Art and Form in Suriname's Jewish Cemeteries." *American Jewish History* 92 (Mar. 2004): 31–79.

Berges, Louis. *Valmy, le mythe de la République.* Toulouse: Privat, 2001.

Berlemont, D. "Le militaire est-il un modèle de citoyen? (septembre 1792 à juillet 1794)." Master's thesis, Université de Paris I, Paris, 1987.

Bertaud, Jean-Paul. "Enqûete sur les volontaires de 1792." *Annales historiques de la Révolution française* 272 (1988): 151–70.

———. *La Révolution armée: Les soldats citoyens et la Révolution française.* Paris: Robert Laffont, 1979.

———. *Valmy, la démocratie en armes.* Paris: Gallimard, 1973.

Bianchi, Serge, and Roger Dupuy, eds. *La Garde nationale entre nation et peuple en armes: Mythes et réalités, 1789–1871.* Rennes: Presses Universitaires de Rennes, 2006.

Bibliothèque historique, ou recueil de matériaux pour servir à l'histoire du temps. Paris: Hocquet, 1818.

Bien, David. "Manufacturing Nobles: The Chancelleries in France to 1789." *Journal of Modern History* 61 (Sept. 1989): 445–86.

Birnbaum, Pierre. *L'affaire Dreyfus: La République en péril.* Paris: Gallimard, 1994.

———. *Les fous de la République: Histoire politique des Juifs d'État, de Gambetta à Vichy.* N.p.: Fayard, 1992.

———. *Un mythe politique: La "République juive" de Léon Blum à Pierre Mendès France.* Paris: Fayard, 1988.

———. *Le peuple et les "gros": Histoire d'un mythe.* N.p.: Grasset, 1979.

Black, Jeremy. *A Military Revolution? Military Change and European Society, 1550–1800.* London: Saint Martin's, 1991.

Blaufarb, Rafe. *The French Army, 1750–1820: Careers, Talent, Merit.* Manchester: Manchester University Press, 2002.

Bloch, Marc. *L'Étrange défaite: Témoignage écrit en 1940.* Brussels: Albin Michel, 1957.

Blumenkranz, Bernhard. *Documents modernes sur les Juifs XVIe–XXe siècles. Tome I: Dépôts parisiens.* Toulouse: Edouard Privat, 1979.

———. *Les Juifs en France au XVIIIe siècle.* Paris: Commission française des archives juives, 1994.

Blumenkranz, Bernhard, and Albert Soboul, eds. *Le Grand Sanhédrin de Napoléon.* Paris: Edouard Privat, 1979.

———. *Les Juifs et la Révolution française: Problèmes et aspirations.* Toulouse: Edouard Privat, 1976.

Bodinier, Gilbert. *Dictionnaire des officiers de l'armée royale qui ont combattu aux Etats-Unis pendant la guerre d'Indépendance 1776–1783.* Versailles: Service historique de l'armée de Terre, 2005.

Bodmer, Walter. *L'immigration suisse dans le comté de Hanau-Lichtenberg au XVIIIe siècle.* Strasbourg: Heitz, 1930.

Bohorquez-Moran, Carmen Luisa. "Francisco de Miranda et le processus de constitution d'une identité américaine." PhD thesis, Université de la Sorbonne Nouvelle–Paris III, Paris, 1996.

Bois, Jean-Pierre. *Dumouriez: Héros et proscrit.* Paris: Perrin, 2005.

———. *Maurice de Saxe.* Paris: Fayard, 1992.

———. "Maurice de Saxe et Woldemar de Lowendal, deux maréchaux d'origine étrangère au service de Louis XV." *Revue historique des armées* 255 (2009): 3–14.

Boissau, Raymond. "La levée de Bercheny-hussards." *Revue historique des armées* 255 (2009): 15–21.

Boizet, Jacques. *Les Lettres de Naturalité sous l'Ancien Régime.* Paris: Maurice Lavergne, 1943.

Bons et braves Suisses, Ne donnez pas dans le panneau. Réponse à un écrit intitulé: Avis Aux Suisses, sur leur position envers le Roi de France. Paris: Desenne, 1791.

Boppe, Paul-Louis-Hippolyte. *Les Espagnols à la Grande-Armée.* Paris: Terena, 1986.

———. *La Légion portugaise, 1807–1813.* Paris: Berger-Levrault, 1897.

Borgetto, Michel. "Être français sous la Révolution." *Crises* 2 (1994): 75–86.

Borgnet, Adolphe, *Histoire de la Révolution liégeoise de 1789.* Liége: de Thier and Lovinfosse, 1865.

Borrel, Étienne Louis. *Histoire de la Révolution en Tarentaise et de la réunion de la Savoie à la France en 1792.* Moûtiers: Ducoz, 1901.

Bouillé, Marquis of. *Mémoires du marquis de Bouillé.* Paris: Badouin frères, 1823.

Boulle, Pierre H. "Les Gens de couleur à Paris à la veille de la Révolution." In *L'Image de la Révolution française: Congrès Mondial pour le Bicentenaire de la Révolution, Sorbonne, Paris 6–12 juillet 1989,* 1:159–68. Paris: Pergamon Press, 1989.

Bourgogne, Adrien. *Mémoires du sergent Bourgogne 1812–1813*. Paris: Hachett, 1978.

Bragelongne, Christophe Bernard de. *Journal de la navigation d'une escadre française*. Paris, 1772.

Bredin, Jean-Denis. *L'Affaire*. Paris: Presses Pocket, 1983.

Brincat, Joseph. "Languages in Malta and the Maltese Language." In *Malta: Roots of a Nation*, edited by K. Gambin, 213–24. Malta: Heritage Malta, 2004.

Brissot (de Warville), Jacques-Pierre. *Rapport et projet de décret concernant l'introduction dans la Ville de Genève, de 1600 Suisses des troupes de Berne et de Zurich*. Paris: Imprimerie nationale, 1792.

———. *Rapport fait au nom de la Commission extraordinaire, des Comités diplomatique et militaire, le 20 Août 1792, Sur le licenciement des Régimens Suisses au service de la France*. Paris: Imprimerie nationale, n.d.

Broers, Michael. *The Napoleonic Empire in Italy, 1796–1814*. London: Palgrave Macmillan, 2005.

Brown, Howard. *Ending the French Revolution: Violence, Justice, and Repression from the Terror to Napoleon*. Charlottesville: University of Virginia Press, 2006.

———. "Politics, Professionalism, and the Fate of Army Generals after Thermidor." *French Historical Studies* 19, no. 1 (1995): 133–152.

———. *War, Revolution and the Bureaucratic State: Politics and Army Administration in France, 1791–1799*. Oxford: Oxford University Press, 1995.

Brubaker, Rogers. *Citizenship and Nationhood in France and Germany*. Cambridge, Mass.: Harvard University Press, 1992.

Brun, Jean-François. "Les unités étrangères dans les armées napoléoniennes: Un élément de la stratégie globale du Grand Empire." *Revue historique des armées* 255 (2009): 22–49.

Brunot, Ferdinand. *Histoire de la langue française, des origines à 1900*. Paris: Armand Colin, 1905–38.

Burns, Michael. *Dreyfus: A Family Affair, 1789–1945*. New York: Harper Collins, 1991.

Camiscioli, Elisa. *Reproducing the French Race: Immigration, Intimacy, and Embodiment in the Early Twentieth Century*. Durham, N.C.: Duke University Press, 2009.

Canny, Nicholas. *Making Ireland British, 1580–1650*. Oxford: Oxford University Press, 2001.

Carnot, C. M. *Rapport sur la Garde du Roi, fait au nom du Comité militaire, par M. Carnot le Jeune, député du département du Pas-de-Calais*. Paris: Imprimerie nationale, 1792.

Caron, Jean-Claude. *La nation, l'État et la démocratie en France de 1789 à 1914*. Paris: Armand Colin, 1995.

Caron, Vicki. *Between France and Germany: The Jews of Alsace-Lorraine, 1871–1918*. Stanford, Calif.: Stanford University Press, 1988.

Cavan, Richard Lambart. *A New System of Military Discipline, Founded upon Principle*. Philadelphia: Aitken, 1776.

Charavay, Étienne, ed. *Correspondance générale de Carnot: Publiée avec des notes historiques et biographiques.* Paris: Imprimerie nationale, 1892.

Chartrand, René. *The French Army in the American War of Independence.* Oxford: Osprey, 1991.

——. *Louis XV's Army (3): Foreign Infantry.* Oxford: Osprey, 1997.

Chassin, Ch-L, ed. *Les Elections et les cahiers de Paris: Documents recueillis, mis en ordre et annotés.* Paris: Jouaust, 1889.

Chuquet, Arthur. *Les guerres de la Révolution: Hoche et la lutte pour l'Alsace (1793–1794).* Paris: Plon, 1893.

——. *Hondschoote.* Paris: Chailley, 1896.

——. *La Légion germanique.* Paris: Chapelot, 1904.

——. *Un prince jacobin: Charles de Hesse, ou Le général Marat.* Paris: Fontemoing, 1906.

Cloots, Anacharsis. *La République universelle ou Adresse aux tyrannicides.* Paris, 1792.

Cobban, Alfred. *The Social Interpretation of the French Revolution.* Cambridge: Cambridge University Press, 1964.

Code général français, Contenant les Lois et Actes du Gouvernment publiés depuis l'ouverture des Etats Généraux au 5 mai 1789, jusqu'au 8 juillet 1815. Paris: Menard et Desenne, 1825.

Cohen, Paul. "Courtly French, Learned Latin, and Peasant Patois: The Making of a National Language in Early Modern France." PhD thesis, Princeton University, 2000.

Cole, Juan. *Napoleon's Egypt: Invading the Middle East.* New York: Palgrave, 2007.

Colette, Jandot Danjou. *La Condition Civile de l'Étranger dans les trois derniers siècles de la Monarchie.* Paris: Siery, 1939.

Collection complète des lois, décrets, ordonnances, réglemens, avis du Conseil-d'état. Paris: Guyot, 1788–1892.

Collection générale des décrets rendus par la Convention nationale. Paris: Baudouin, n.d.

Correspondance du dépôt des lois, avec les fonctionnaires publics. Paris: Imprimerie du corps légal, 1806.

Conac, Gérard, and Jean-Pierre Machelon, eds. *La Constitution de l'an III: Boissy d'Anglas et la naissance du libéralisme constitutionnel.* Paris: Presses Universitaires de France, 1999.

Concordat entre le Saint-Siege et la Cour de France, Pour la restitution des Déserteurs des Troupes du Roi, qui se réfugient dans l'état d'Avignon & le Comtat Venaissin: Et concernant l'Engagement des Sujets desdits Etats, dans les Troupes de Sa Majesté. Paris: Imprimerie Royale, 1763.

Connell, K. H. *The Population of Ireland, 1750–1845.* Oxford: Oxford University Press, 1950.

Conner, Clifford D. *Arthur O'Connor: The Most Important Irish Revolutionary You May Never Have Heard Of.* Bloomington, Ind.: iUniverse, 2009.

Constitution de la République française, du 5 Fructidor, An III, acceptée par le peuple. Paris: Millet, 1795.

Copie de la lettre du maréchal Luckner au Roi, Au quartier général à Menin, le 18 Juin 1792, l'an 4e de la liberté. Le Mans: Pivron, 1792.

Corp, Edward T., ed. *L'autre exil: Les Jacobites en France au début du XVIIIe siècle.* Montpellier: Presses de Languedoc, 1992.

Correspondance de Napoléon 1er, publiée par ordre de l'empereur Napoléon III. Paris: Imprimerie impériale, 1858–60.

Corvisier, André. *L'Armée française de la fin du XVIIème siècle au ministère de Choiseul: Le soldat.* 2 vols. Paris: Presses universitaires de France, 1964.

———. *Les contrôles de troupe de l'ancien régime.* 4 vols. Vincennes: Service historique de la Défense, 1968.

———. *Dictionnaire d'art et d'histoire militaires.* Paris: Presses Universitaires de France, 1988.

Crépin, Annie, et al., ed. *Civils, citoyens-soldats et militaires dans l'Etat-nation (1789–1815).* Paris: Société des études robespierristes, 2006.

———. *La conscription en débat ou le triple apprentissage de la Nation, de la Citoyenneté, de la République (1789–1889).* Artois: Artois Presses Université, 1998.

Les crimes du 10 août dévoilés par les patriotes suisses. N.p., 1793.

Croix, Armand-François de la. *Taité de la petite guerre pour les compagnies franches.* Paris: Imprimeur du Roi, 1752.

Dambach, Frédéric, and Christian Friedrich Heyden. *Exposé succinct des faits qui doivent servir à la justification des Officiers et Soldats de la Légion Germanique, injustement arrêtés à Tours, le 4 mai dernier, et détenus en prison pendant trois mois.* Paris: H. J. Hansen, 1793.

Dame, William Frederick. *History of Switzerland. 3 vols.* Lewiston: Edwin Mellen, 2001.

Dávila, Vicente, ed. *Archivo del General Miranda.* Caracas: Parra Leon Hermanos, 1931.

"Les débuts du ministre de la guerre Bouchotte dans les Ardennes (1789–1790)." *Revue historique ardennaise* 12 (1905): 57–89.

Déclaration du Roi, Pour le renvoi des Cent-Suisses de la garde de Sa Majesté, Suisses des douze & des appartements, Suisses employés dans les châteaux, maisons, jardins & batiments de Sa Majesté, Suisses de portes & autres du canton de Schwitz, qui sont actuellement dans le Royaume. Paris: Imprimerie royale, 1765.

Déclaration du Roi, Qui ordonne que tous les Officiers, Gens de Guerre & Soldats étrangers qui auront servi pendant dix ans dans les Armées de SA MAJESTÉ, dont ils rapporteront des certificats en bonne forme, & qui viendront s'établir dans les Duchées de Lorraine & de Bar, seront reputés naturels François. Paris: Imprimerie royale, 1770.

Décret portant déclaration de guerre sanctionné. Lyon: P. Bernard, 1792.

Desbrière, Edouard. *Projets et tentatives de débarquement aux Iles Britanniques.* Paris: Chapelot, 1900.

Deschard, Bernard. *L'Armée et la Révolution: Du service du roi au service de la nation.* Paris: Éditions Desjonquères, 1989.

Détail de l'Armée du Général Luckner, de la prise de Porentruy, & de la désertion des Allemands. Marseille: Jouve, n.d.

Détail du projet de contre-révolution et du massacre commis à Bedfort, par le régiment de Royal-Liégeois et les hussards de Lauzun. Paris: Imprimerie patriotique, 1790.

Dictionnaire de la conversation et de la lecture. Paris: Béthune, 1833.

Dillon, Arthur. *Observations historiques sur l'origine, les services et l'état civile des officiers irlandais au service de la France, addressées à l'Assemblée Nationale.* Paris: Demonville, n.d.

Discours prononcé le 28 janvier 1790 par M. Godard. Paris, 1790.

Discours sommaire sur la création de la compagnie des cent gardes suisses ordinaires du Corps du Roy. Paris: Jacques Langlois, 1676.

"Documents on the Relations of France to Louisiana, 1792–1795." *American Historical Review* 3 (Apr. 1898): 490–516.

Dolman, Everett C. *The Warrior State: How Military Organization Structures Politics.* New York: Palgrave Macmillan, 2004.

Donavan, Ken. "Germans in Louisbourg, 1713–1758." *Huissier,* September 13, 2006.

Doppet, François-Amédée. *Mémoires politiques et militaires du général Doppet.* Paris: Badouin Frères, 1824.

Dorigny, Marcel, and Marie-Jeanne Rossignol, eds. *La France et les Amériques au temps de Jefferson et de Miranda.* Paris: Société des études robespierristes, 2001.

Dreyfus, Alfred. *Cinq années de ma vie: 1894–1899.* Paris: Charpentier, 1901.

Dry, A. *Soldats ambassadeurs sous le Directoire, an IV—an VIII.* Paris: Plon-Nourrit, 1906.

Dubois, Laurent. *A Colony of Citizens: Revolution and Slave Emancipation in the French Caribbean, 1787–1804.* Chapel Hill: University of North Carolina Press, 2004.

Dubois, Sébastien. *L'invention de la Belgique: Genèse d'un État-Nation, 1648–1830.* Brussels: Racine, 2005.

Dubost, Jean-François, and Peter Sahlins. *Et si on faisait payer les étrangers? Louis XIV, les immigrés et quelques autres.* Paris: Flammarion, 1999.

Dufau, P. A., J.-B. Duvergier, and J. Guadet, eds. *Collection des constitutions, chartes et lois fondamentales des peuples de l'Europe et des deux Amériques.* Paris: Chanson, 1821–25.

Dufraisse, Roger. "Les populations de la rive gauche du Rhin et le service militaire à la fin de l'Ancien Régime et à l'époque révolutionnaire." *Revue historique* 231 (1964): 103–40.

Dumay, Alfred-Hippolyte. *Historique du 66e régiment d'infanterie, 1672–1900.* Paris: Arrault, 1900.

Dupâquier, Jacques. French Population in the 17th and 18th Centuries. In *Essays in French Economic History,* edited by Rondo Cameron, 150–69. Homewood, Ill.: Richard D. Irwin, 1970.

Dupuy, Roger. *La Garde nationale, 1789–1872.* Paris: Gallimard, 2010.

Duverger, Michel. *Déserteurs et prisonniers de guerre des armées étrangères en Dordogne pendant la Révolution française (1793–1797).* N.p.: Périgueux, 1984.

Duveyrier, Honoré, and Jean Sylvain Bailly. *Procès-verbal des séances et délibérations de l'Assemblée générale des électeurs de Paris, Réunis à l'Hôtel de Ville le 14 Juillet 1789.* Paris: Baudouin, 1790.

Edelstein, Dan. *The Terror of Natural Right: Republicanism, the Cult of Nature, and the French Revolution.* Chicago: University of Chicago Press, 2009.

Edelstein, Melvin. "Le militaire-citoyen ou le droit de vote des militaires pendant la Révolution française." *Annales historiques de la Révolution française* 310 (1997): 585–600.

Eickemeyer, Rudolph. *Denkwürdigkeiten des Generals Eickemeyer.* Frankfurt am Main: Literarische Anstalt, 1845.

Elliott, Marianne. *Partners in Revolution: The United Irishmen and France.* New Haven, Conn.: Yale University Press, 1982.

Erdman, David V. *Commerce des Lumières: John Oswald and the British in Paris, 1790–1793.* Columbia: University of Missouri Press, 1986.

État des officiers généraux et de leurs aides de camp déserteurs ou émigrés. Paris: Imprimerie nationale, 1793.

Eustace, John Skey. *Letters on the Crimes of George III: Addressed to Citizen Denis; by An American Officer, in the Service of France: Part I & II.* Paris: Anjubault, Year II.

———. *Traité d'amitié de commerce et de navigation, entre Sa Majesté britannique et les Etats-Unis d'Amérique: Finalement ratifié par la législature américaine, suivi d'un projet fraternel, adressé aux Négocians français, pour effectuer la compensation des pertes occasionnées par les lois américaines, pendant leur commerce dans les Etats-Unis.* Paris: Desenne, Year 4.

Favez, Jean-Claude, et al., ed. *Nouvelle Histoire de la Suisse et des Suisses.* Lausanne: Payot Lausanne, 1986.

Fersen, Hans Axel von. *Le comte de Fersen et la cour de France: Extraits des papiers du grand maréchal de Suède, comte Jean Axel de Fersen.* Paris: Firmin-Didot, 1878.

Fieffé, Eugène. *Histoire des troupes étrangères au service de France.* 2 vols. Paris: Librarie Militaire, 1854.

Fink, Carole. *Marc Bloch: A Life in History.* Cambridge: Cambridge University Press, 1989.

Fitzsimmons, Michael P. "The National Assembly and the Invention of Citizenship." In *The French Revolution and the Meaning of Citizenship,* edited by R. Waldinger, P. Dawson and I. Woloch, 29–41. Westport, Conn.: Greenwood Press, 1993.

Fogarty, Richard. *Race and War in France: Colonial Subjects in the French Army, 1914–1918.* Baltimore: Johns Hopkins University Press, 2008.

Folliet, André. *Les volontaires de la Savoie, 1792–1799.* Paris: Librairie militaire, 1887.

Forrest, Alan. "Citizenship and Military Service." In *The French Revolution and the Meaning of Citizenship,* edited by R. Waldinger, P. Dawson, and I. Woloch, 153–65. Westport, Conn.: Greenwood Press, 1993.

———. *Conscripts and Deserters: The Army and French Society during the Revolution and Empire.* Oxford: Oxford University Press, 1989.

Forth, Christopher. *The Dreyfus Affair and the Crisis of French Manhood.* Baltimore: Johns Hopkins University Press, 2006.

France, John, ed. *Mercenaries and Paid Men: The Mercenary Identity in the Middle Ages.* Leiden: Brill, 2008.

Frank, Nathaniel. *Unfriendly Fire: How the Gay Ban Undermines the Military and Weakens America.* New York: Thomas Dunne Books, 2009.

Freeman, T. W. *Ireland: A General and Regional Geography.* London: Methuen, 1969.

Furet, François. *Interpreting the French Revolution.* Cambridge: Cambridge University Press, 1981.

Furet, François, and Mona Ozouf. *Dictionnaire critique de la Révolution française.* Paris: Flammarion, 1988.

Gainot, Bernard. *Les officiers de couleur dans les armées de la République et de l'Empire (1792–1815).* Paris: Éditions Karthala, 2007.

Gallaher, John. *Napoleon's Irish Legion.* Carbondale: Southern Illinois University Press, 1993.

Galway, Alphonse-Charles-Albert O'Kelly de. *Les généraux de la Révolution: Francisco de Miranda.* Paris: Honoré Champion, 1913.

Ganniers, Arthur de. "Un cas d'insubordination militaire: Dumouriez contre Luckner (Juillet 1792)." *Revue des Questions Historiques* 33 (1899): 498–559.

Ganter, Henri. *Histoire des régiments suisses à la solde de l'Angleterre, de Naples et de Rome.* Geneva: Eggimann, 1902.

Gendron, François. *La jeunesse doree: Episodes de la revolution française.* Quebec City: Presses universitaires du Québec.

Genet-Rouffiac, Nathalie. *Le Grand Exil: Les jacobites en France, 1688–1715.* Vincennes: Service historique de la Défense, 2007.

Genet-Rouffiac, Nathalie, and David Murphy, eds. *Franco-Irish Military Connections.* Dublin: Four Courts Press, 2009.

Gentleman's Magazine and Historical Chronicle. London: Urban, 1758.

Girard, François-Jean. *Histoire abrégée des officiers suisses qui se sont distingués aux services étrangers dans des grades supérieurs.* Fribourg, Switzerland: B. Louis Piller, 1781.

Gouttes, Gauthey des. *Les Suisses au Service de la France.* Paris: Jouve, 1917.

Graffagnino, J. Kevin. "'Twenty Thousand Muskets!!!': Ira Allen and the Olive Branch Affair, 1796–1800." *William and Mary Quarterly* 48 (Jul. 1991): 409–31.

Grégoire, Henri. *De la littérature des nègres.* Paris: Maradan, 1808.

———. *Essai sur la régénération physique, morale et politique des juifs.* Metz: Claude Lamort, 1788.

La Grillade, ou Les Suisses aux enfers, détail circonstancié de leur réception. Paris: Marchand de Nouveautés, 1792.

Grisot, Adolphe, and Ernest Auguste Ferdinand Coulombon. *La Légion étrangère de 1831 à 1887*. Paris: Berger-Levrault, 1888.

Guadet, Marguerite-Elie. *Rapport fait au nom de la Commission extraordinaire, sur la conférence de M. le Maréchal Luckner avec les Membres de cette Commission*. Paris: Imprimerie nationale, 1792.

Guédé, Alain. *Monsieur de Saint-George, le Nègre des Lumières*. Arles: Actes Sud, 1999.

Guibert, Count of. *Essai général de tactique*. Liége: Plomteux, 1773.

Guide des tribunaux militaires. Paris: Laguionie, 1838.

Guilhaumou, Jacques. *Marseille républicaine (1791–1793)*. Paris: Presses de Sciences Po, 1992.

Guillaume, Henri Louis Gustave. *Histoire des Gardes Wallones au service d'Espagne (1703–1822)*. Brussels: Montagne de Sion, 1858.

Haas, René. *Un régiment suisse au service de France: Bettens 1672–1792*. Pont l'Abbé: Kerentree, 1967.

Hampson, Norman. *La Marine de l'an II: Mobilisation de la flotte de l'océan*. Paris: CNRS, 1959.

Hansen, Joseph. *Quellen zur Geschichte des Rheinlandes im Zeitalter der Französischen Revolution, 1780–1801*. Bonn: Peter Hanstein, 1931–38.

Hasquin, Hervé, ed. *La Belgique française, 1792–1815*. Brussels: Crédit Communal, 1993.

Havard, Gilles, and Cécile Vidal. *Histoire de l'Amérique française*. Paris: Flammarion, 2003.

Hayes, Richard. *Biographical Dictionary of Irishmen in France*. Dublin: M. H. Gill & Son, 1949.

——. *Ireland and Irishmen in the French Revolution*. London: Ernest Benn, 1932.

——. "Irishmen in the Naval Services of Continental Europe." *Irish Sword* 1, no. 4 (1952–53): 304–15.

——. *Irish Swordsmen of France*. Dublin: M. H. Gill, 1934.

Hennessy, Maurice N. *The Wild Geese: The Irish Soldier in Exile*. New York: Devin-Adair, 1973.

Hennet, Léon. *État Militûete sur les vour l'année 1793*. Paris: Société de l'histoire de la Révolution française, 1903.

Henwood, Philippe. "Les prisonniers de guerre anglais en Bretagne au XVIIIème siècle." In *Colloque d'histoire maritime de Rochefort, 73–91*. Toulon: Service Historique de la Marine, 1987.

Herlaut, Auguste Philippe. *Le colonel Bouchotte: Ministre de la guerre en l'an II*. Paris: Poisson, 1946.

Herold, Christopher J. *Bonaparte in Egypt*. New York: Harper & Row, 1962.

Heuer, Jennifer. *The Family and the Nation: Gender and Citizenship in Revolutionary France, 1789–1830*. Ithaca, N.Y.: Cornell University Press, 2005.

Higonnet, Patrice. "Terror, Trauma, and the 'Young Marx' Explanation of Jacobin Politics." *Past and Present* 191 (2006): 121–64.

Hippler, Thomas. "Les soldats allemands dans l'armée napoléonienne d'après leurs autobiographies: micro-républicanisme et décivilisation." *Annales historiques de la Révolution française* 348 (Apr.–Jun. 2007): 117–30.

——. *Soldats et citoyens: Naissance du service militaire en France et en Prusse.* Paris: Presses Universitaires de France, 2006.

Horstmann, Theodor. *Generallieutenant Johann Nicolaus von Luckner und seine Husaren im Siebenjährigen Kriege.* Osnabrück: Biblio Verlag, 1997.

Hubert-Brierre, Jean. *Les Cent-Suisses garde rapprochée du Roy.* Paris: Mémoires d'Hommes, 2005.

Huntington, Samuel. *The Soldier and the State: The Theory and Politics of Civil-Military Relations.* Cambridge, Mass.: Harvard University Press, 1957.

Hyman, Paula. *The Emancipation of the Jews of Alsace: Acculturation and Tradition in the Nineteenth Century.* New Haven, Conn.: Yale University Press, 1991.

——. *The Jews of Modern France.* Berkeley: University of California Press, 1998.

Interrogatoire du général Westerman, Adjudant-général, commandant la Légion du Nord: Séance du Vendredi 19 Avril 1793, huit heuree du soir. Paris: Imprimerie nationale, 1793.

Irishmen in War: From the Crusades to 1798: Essays from the Irish Sword. Dublin: Irish Academic Press, 2006.

Isambert, François-André, ed. *Recueil général des anciennes lois françaises, depuis l'an 420 jusqu'à la Révolution de 1789.* Paris: Plon, 1821–33.

Iung, Théodore. *L'armée et la Revolution, 1789–1794: Dubois de Crancé.* Paris: Charpentier, 1884.

James, C. L. R. *The Black Jacobins: Toussaint L'Ouverture and the San Domingo Revolution.* New York: Dial, 1938.

Jarrousse, Frédéric. *Auvergnats malgré eux: Prisonniers et déserteurs étrangers dans le Puy-de-Dôme pendant la Révolution, 1794–1796.* Clermont-Ferrand: Institut d'Etudes du Massif Central, 1998.

Jaurès, Jean. *Histoire socialiste de la Révolution française.* Paris: Éditions sociales, 1969.

Job, Françoise. "Baptême de Juifs dans le duché de Lorraine au XVIIIème siècle." *Archives juives* 13 (1976): 44–48.

——. *Gustave Nordon (1877–1944).* Nancy: Presses Universitaires de Nancy, 1992.

——. *Inventaire de documents concernant les juifs conservés aux archives départmentales de Meurthe-et-Moselle.* Paris, 1998.

——. "Note additive aux baptêmes de Juifs dans le duché de Lorraine au XVIIIème siècle." *Archives juives* 14 (1977): 32–33.

Jones, Colin. "Bourgeois Revolution Revivified: 1789 and Social Change." In *Rewriting the French Revolution,* edited by Colin Lucas, 69–118. Oxford: Oxford University Press, 1991.

——. *The Great Nation: France from Louis XV to Napoleon.* London: Penguin, 2002.

Jones, E. H. Stuart. *An Invasion That Failed: The French Expedition to Ireland, 1796.* Oxford: Blackwell, 1950.

——. *The Last Invasion of Britain.* Cardiff: University of Wales Press, 1950.

Jones, Peter. *The Peasantry in the French Revolution.* Cambridge: Cambridge University Press, 1988.

Jourdan, Annie. *La République batave entre la France et l'Amérique: 1795–1806.* Rennes: Presses Universitaires de Rennes, 2008.

Kahn, Léon. *Les Juifs de Paris pendant la Révolution.* Paris, 1898.

Karamanoukian, Aram. "Les étrangers et le service militaire." PhD thesis, Université de Paris II, Paris, 1972.

Kennett, Lee. "John Skey Eustace and the French Revolution." *American Society Legion of Honor Magazine* 45 (1974): 29–43.

——. "Joshua Barney and the French Revolution." *American Society Legion of Honor Magazine* 44 (1973): 9–24.

Krebs, Ronald. *Fighting for Rights: Military Service and the Politics of Citizenship.* Ithaca, N.Y.: Cornell University Press, 2006.

Lacroix, Philippe. *Mémoires pour servir à l'histoire de la Révolution de Saint-Domingue.* Paris: Éditions Karthala, 1995.

La Jonquière, Clement-Etienne-Lucien de. *L'expédition d'Egypte (1798–1801).* Paris: Seuil, 1997.

Lanier, Jacques-François. *Le général Joseph Servan de Gerbey (Romans, 1741—Paris, 1808): Pour une armée au service de l'homme.* Valence: SRIG, 2001.

La Rochejaquelein, Marie-Louise-Victoire de. *Mémoires de Mme la marquise de La Rochejaquelein.* Paris: Badouin frères, 1823.

Lasseray, André. *Les Français sous les treize étoiles.* Paris: Désiré Janvier, 1935.

Latour-Chatillon de Zurlauben, Baron of. *Histoire militaire des Suisses au service de la France.* Paris: Desaint, 1751–53.

Lecointre, Laurent. *Discours prononcé à l'Assemblée Nationale, par Laurent Lecointre, Député du Département de Seine-&-Oise: Au sujet de la dénonciation faite contre lui par neuf Cent-suisses de la Garde du Roi, mis en état d'arrestation par la Municipalité de Béfort.* Paris: Imprimerie nationale, 1792.

Leeb, Leonard. *The Ideological Origins of the Batavian Revolution.* The Hague: Nijhoff, 1973.

Leff, Lisa Moses. *Sacred Bonds of Solidarity: The Rise of Jewish Internationalism in Nineteenth-Century France.* Stanford, Calif.: Stanford University Press, 2006.

Lémann, Joseph. *Napoléon et les juifs.* Avalon: Mercure, 1989.

Léonard, Émile. *L'Armée et ses problèmes au XVIIIe siècle.* Paris: Plon, 1958.

Letters of Brunswick and Hessian Officers during the American Revolution. Translated by William L. Stone. Albany: Joel Munsell's Sons, 1891.

Lettre au Roi, Et exposé de la conduite de MM. le comte de la Tour et de Grünstein, colonel et major du régiment Royal-Liégeois, sur les évènements qui ont eu lieu à Belfort, le 21 Octobre 1790. N.p., 1790.

Lettre de M. Luckner, maréchal de France, au roi. N.p., 1792.

Lettre de M. Pujet-Barbentane à M. Louis de Narbonne, sur l'événement arrivé à Aix et sur le départ du régiment d'Ernest de cette ville. N.p., 1792.

Lettres de sauvegardes, pour fair jouir les Fermes & Maisons appartenants à l'Hôtel-Dieu de Paris, de l'Exemption du Logement des Officiers & Soldats du Regiment des Gardes Suisses. Paris: Imprimerie royale, 1662.

Loeb, Isidore. "Un Baron juif français au XVIIIe siècle: Liefman Calmer." *Annuaire des archives israélites* 4 (1885–86): 25–36.

Lucas, Colin. "Nobles, Bourgeois and the Origins of the French Revolution." *Past and Present* 60 (Aug. 1973): 84–126.

Luckner, Félix von. *Le dernier corsaire (1914–1918).* Paris: La Loupe, 2007.

Luckner, Nicolas. *Lettre de M. Luckner, maréchal de France, au roi.* N.p., 1792.

Lynn, John. *Bayonets of the Republic: Motivation and Tactics in the Army of Revolutionary France, 1791–94.* Urbana: University of Chicago Press, 1984.

———. *Giant of the Grand Siècle: The French Army, 1610–1715.* Cambridge: Cambridge University Press, 1997.

———. "Recalculating French Army Growth during the Grand siècle, 1610–1715." *French Historical Studies* 18, no. 4 (1994): 881–906.

Lyons, Martyn. *France under the Directory.* London: Cambridge University Press, 1975.

MacGeoghan, James. *Histoire de l'Irlande ancienne et moderne.* Paris and Amsterdam: Antoine Boudet, 1758–63.

Machiavelli, Niccolò. *The Prince.* Translated by Luigi Ricci. London: Great Richards, 1903.

Malaguti. *Historique du 87e régiment d'infanterie de ligne, 1690–1892.* Paris: Imprimerie J. Moureau et Fils, 1892.

Malino, Frances. *A Jew in the French Revolution: The Life of Zalkind Hourwitz.* Oxford: Blackwell, 1996.

———. *The Sephardic Jews of Bordeaux: Assimilation and Emancipation in Revolutionary and Napoleonic France.* Tuscaloosa: University of Alabama Press, 1978.

Marat, Jean-Paul. *Oeuvres politiques 1789–1793.* Edited by Jacques de Cock and Charlotte Goëtz. 10 vols. Brussels: Pôle nord, 1995.

Marley, David. *Wars of the Americas: A Chronology of Armed Conflict in the Western Hemisphere.* Santa Barbara: ABC-CLIO, 2008.

Martin, Marc. "Journaux d'armées au temps de la Convention." *Annales historiques de la Révolution française* 44 (1972): 567–605.

Mathiez, Albert. *La conspiration de l'étranger.* Paris: Armand Colin, 1918.

———. *La Révolution et les étrangers: Cosmopolitisme et défense nationale.* Paris: Renaissance du Livre, 1918.

———. *La victoire en l'an II: Esquisses historiques sur la défense nationale.* Paris: F. Alcan, 1916.

Maugué, Pierre. *Le particularisme alsacien, 1918–1967.* Paris: Presses d'Europe, 1970.

Maxwell, W. H. *History of the Irish Rebellion in 1798.* London: Bell, 1894.

Maza, Sara. *The Myth of the French Bourgeoisie: An Essay on the Social Imaginary, 1750–1850.* Cambridge: Cambridge University Press, 2003.

May, Emmanuel. *Histoire militaire de la Suisse et celle des Suisses dans les différents services de l'Europe.* Paris: Heubach, 1788.

Méautis, Ariane. *Le Club helvétique de Paris (1790–1791) et la diffusion des idées révolutionnaires en Suisse.* Neuchâtel: La Baconnière, 1969.

Mémoire de la municipalité de Marseille, Sur les evènemens du 16 octobre 1791 & jours suivans, occasionnés par quelques Officiers Suisses du soixante-septième Régiment ci-devant Ernest. N.p.: Imprimerie Jean Mossy, n.d.

Mémoire pour Michel de Reilly, Ecuyer, Chevalier de l'Ordre Royal & Militaire de S. Louis, ancien Capitaine au Régiment de Bulkcley; & Demoiselle Amable de Butler, son Epouse, Intimés & Défendeurs. Paris: Chardon, 1763.

Merrill, Ellen. *Germans of Louisiana.* Gretna, La.: Pelican, 2005.

Michaud, Louis-Gabriel. *Biographie universelle ancienne et moderne.* Paris: Desplaces, 1843.

Michel, Francisque. *Les Écossais en France, les Français en Écosse.* London: Trübner, 1862.

Miller, Melanie Randolph. *Envoy to the terror: Gouverneur Morris & the French Revolution.* Dulles, Va.: Potomac Books, 2005.

Miranda, Francisco de. *Opinion du général Miranda sur la situation actuelle de la France, et sur les remèdes convenables à ses maux.* Paris, Year 3.

Molière, Michel. *Les expéditions françaises en Portugal de 1807 à 1811.* Paris: Publibook, 2002.

Monnier, Raymonde. *Citoyens et citoyenneté sous la Révolution française.* Paris: Société des études robespierristes, 2006.

Moogk, Peter. *La Nouvelle France: The Making of French Canada: A Cultural History.* East Lansing: Michigan University Press, 2000.

Moore, John. *Journal during a Residence in France, from the Beginning of August, to the Middle of December, 1792.* New York: Childs & Swain, 1793.

Mortier, Roland. *Anacharsis Cloots ou l'utopie foudroyée.* Paris: Stock, 1995.

Mortimer-Ternaux, Louis. *Histoire de la Terreur, 1792–1794: D'après des documents authentiques et inédits.* Paris: Lévy Frères, 1868.

Moulinas, René. *Les Juifs du pape en France: Les communautés d'Avignon et du Comtat Venaissin aux 17e et 18e siècles.* Paris: Commission française des archives juives, 1981.

Murdoch, Richard. "Correspondence of French Consuls in Charleston, South Carolina, 1793–1797." *South Carolina Historical Magazine* 74 (Jan. and Apr. 1973): 73–79.

Murphy, David. *The Irish Brigades, 1685–2006: A Gazeteer of Irish Military Service, Past and Present.* Dublin: Four Courts Press, 2007.

Nelson, Keith L. "The 'Black Horror on the Rhine': Race as a Factor in Post-World War I Diplomacy." *Journal of Modern History* 42 (Dec. 1970): 606–27.

Noiriel, Gérard. *Le Creuset français: Histoire de l'immigration, XIXe–XXe siècle.* Paris: Seuil, 1988.

Observations pour le citoyen Baruch Cerf-Berr, régisseur des achats des subsistances militaires, à l'armée du Rhin; En réponse au général Custines. N.p., 1793.

O'Callaghan, John C. *History of the Irish Brigades in the Service of France, from the Revolution in Great Britain and Ireland under James II, to the Revolution in France under Louis XVI.* Glasgow: Cameron & Ferguson, 1885.

O'Connell, Morgan John. *The Last Colonel of the Irish Brigade: Count O'Connell and Old Irish Life at Home and Abroad, 1745–1833.* London: Paul, 1892.

Ó Hannracháin, Eoghan. "The Irish Brigade at Lafelt 1747: Pyrrhic Victory and Aftermath." *Journal of the Cork Historical and Archaeological Society* 102 (1997): 1–22.

Ojala, Jeanne A. "Ira Allen and the French Directory, 1796: Plans for the Creation of the Republic of United Columbia." *William and Mary Quarterly* 36 (Jul. 1979): 436–48.

Opinion de M. Le Prince de Broglie, deputé de Colmar, Sur l'admission des Juifs à l'état civil. Paris: Imprimerie nationale, n.d.

Ordonnance du Roi, Portant création d'un Régiment d'Infanterie étrangère, sous le nom de Royal-Liégeois. Paris: Imprimerie royale, 1787.

Ordonnance du Roi, Portant réforme du régiment Royal-Corse, & reconstitution des deux bataillons qui composent ce régiment, en deux bataillons d'Infanterie légère, sous le nom, l'un de Chasseurs-Royaux-Corses, & l'autre, de Chasseurs-Corses. Paris: Imprimerie royale, 1788.

Ordonnance du Roi, Portant réforme du régiment Royal-Italien, & reconstitution des deux bataillons qui composent ce régiment, en deux bataillons d'Infanterie légère, sous le nom, l'un de Chasseurs-royaux de Provence, & l'autre, de Chasseurs-royaux du Dauphiné. Paris: Imprimerie royale, 1788.

Ordonnance du Roy, Portant deffenses aux Officiers du Regiment Royal Artillerie, d'enroller aucuns Soldats estrangers. Paris: Imprimerie royale, 1728.

Ordonnance du Roy, Pour l'entretenement du Regiment Suisse de Karrer au service de la Marine. Paris: Imprimerie royale, 1792.

Ordonnance du Roy sur l'exercice de l'infanterie, du 6 mai 1755. Paris: Faulcon, 1755.

Osman, Julia. *Citizen Soldiers and the Key to the Bastille.* London: Palgrave Macmillan, 2015.

Pachonski, Jan, and Reuel K. Wilson. *Poland's Caribbean Tragedy: A Study of Polish Legions in the Haitian War of Independence, 1802–1803.* Boulder, Co.: East European Monographs, 1986.

Palmer, R. R. *Twelve Who Ruled: The Year of the Terror in the French Revolution.* Princeton, N.J.: Princeton University Press, 1969.

Parkenham, Thomas. *The Year of Liberty: The History of the Great Irish Rebellion of 1798.* London: Panther, 1972.

Parra-Pérez, Carracciolo. *Miranda et la Révolution française.* Caracas: Banco del Caribe, 1989.

Parrott, David. "Strategy and Tactics in the Thirty Years' War: The 'Military Revolution.'" *Militärgeschichtliche Mitteilungen* 38, no. 2 (1985): 7–25.

Le patriote français: Journal libre, impartial et national: Par une Société de Citoyens, & dirigée par J. P. Brissot de Warville. Frankfurt am Main: Keip Verlag, 1989.

Pascal, Adrien. *Histoire de l'arme´e et de tous les re´giments, depuis les premiers temps de la monarchie franc¸aise jusqu'a nos jours.* Paris: Barbier, 1847–50.

Peabody, Sue. *"There Are No Slaves in France": The Political Culture of Race and Slavery in the Ancien Régime.* Oxford: Oxford University Press, 2002.

Peled, Alon. *A Question of Loyalty: Military Manpower Policy in Multiethnic States.* Ithaca, N.Y.: Cornell University Press, 1998.

Pétion, Jérôme. *Réponse de M. Pétion à M. Dupont au sujet de la fête célébrée à l'occasion de l'arrivée à Paris des Suisses de Châteauvieux.* Paris: J. R. Lottin, 1792.

Pétition de M. Arthur Dillon, à l'Assemblée nationale, prononcée dans la séance du soir du 1er mai 1792. Paris: Migneret, 1792.

Pétition présentée par le citoyen Mayer, capitaine dans la Légion du centre, à la Convention nationale, Le 6 november 1792 (Pour parvenir à la prompte formation d'un corps de 600 hommes, sous la dénomination de Légion de la Propagande). Paris: Imprimerie de la Société des Amis du Commerce, 1792.

Pichichero, Christy. "Le Soldat Sensible: Military Psychology and Social Egalitarianism in the Enlightenment French Army." *French Historical Studies* 31, no. 4 (2008): 553–80.

Pietri, François. *Napoléon et les Israélites.* Paris: Berger-Levrault, 1965.

Poisson, Charles. *L'Armée et la Garde nationale.* 4 vols. Paris: Durand, 1858–62.

——. *Les fournisseurs aux armées sous la Révolution française. Le Directoire des Achats (1792–1793): J. Bidermann, Cousin, Marx-Berr.* Paris: Margraff, 1932.

Popkin, Jeremy. *You Are All Free: The Haitian Revolution and the Abolition of Slavery.* Cambridge: Cambridge University Press, 2010.

Porch, Douglas. *The French Foreign Legion: A Complete History of the Legendary Fighting Force.* New York: Skyhorse, 2010.

Procès-verbal des séances et délibérations de l'Assemblée générale des électeurs de Paris, Réunis à l'Hôtel de Ville le 14 Juillet 1789. Paris: Baudouin, 1790.

Proclamation du Roi, Pour le licenciement de la Compagnie des Cent-Suisses de la Garde ordinaire de Sa Majesté. Paris: Imprimerie royale, 1792.

Proclamation du Roi, Sur un Décret de l'Assemblée Nationale, concernant les démarches qui ont été faites à Ruel & à Courbevoye, vers le corps des Gardes-Suisses. Paris: Imprimerie royale, 1790.

Quency, Louis Boisson de. *Additions aux faits justificatifs pour les chefs de la Légion germanique.* N.p., n.d.

Racine, Karen. *Francisco de Miranda, a Transatlantic Life in the Age of Revolution.* Charlottesville: University of Virginia Press, 2003.

Raguet, J. C. "Du Pionniers Noirs au Royal-Africain 1802–1813. Histoire d'une unité noire sous le Consulat et le 1er Empire." Master's thesis, Enseignement militaire supérieur de l'armée de terre, Paris, 1991.

Rambaud, Jacques. *Naples sous Joseph Bonaparte, 1806–1808.* Paris: Plon, 1911.

Ran Tan Plan, ou les loisirs d'un tambour de la milice citoyenne de Carpentras, étant de garde. N.p.: Imprimerie de La Liberté, 1790.

Règlement Sur la Formation, les Appointements & la Solde de l'Infanterie Allemande, Irlandoise & Liégeoise. Paris: Imprimerie Royale, 1791.

Règlement Sur les Appointemens & Solde des Régimens Suisses & Grisons. Paris: Imprimerie Royale, 1791.

Réimpression de l'ancien Moniteur, depuis la réunion des États-Généraux jusqu'au Consulat. Paris: René, 1860.

Reiss, Tom. *The Black Count: Glory, Revolution, Betrayal, and the Real Count of Monte Cristo*. Phoenix, Az.: Crown, 2012.

Rélation Curieuse, d'un Soldat Déserteur: Tres-utile & instructive à tous ceux qui font profession des Armes. Strasbourg: Louis François Rousselot, 1705.

Rélation de l'assassinat de M. Théobald Dillon, maréchal-de-camp, commis à Lille, le 29 avril 1792. Paris: Migneret, 1792.

"Rélation de la prise de la Bastille, le 14 juillet 1789, par un de ses défenseurs." *Revue historique, ou bibliothèque historique, contenant des mémoires et documens authentiques, inédits et originaux* 4 (1834): 284–98.

Rélation du mouvement exécuté les 28 et 29 avril par un détachement de la garnison de Lille. Paris: Migneret, 1792.

Réponse de la Légion franche allobroge aux ennemis de la République. Paris: Imprimerie des Directeurs du Cercle Social, 1793.

Réponses servant de justification des officiers, sous-officiers et soldats du premier bataillon du 92e régiment d'infanterie, ci-devant Walsh, sur les fausses inculpations faites à ce corps par une lettre d'un gendarme de Paris, écrite d'Epernay, le 8 septembre 1792, et insérée dans le Courrier Français, no. 258, du vendredi 14 septembre 1792, l'an 4e de la liberté. N.p., 1792.

Reproches faits au maréchal Luckner à la Convention nationale, avec la réponse à ces reproches. Paris: Imprimerie nationale, n.d.

Résumé de l'historique du 88e régiment d'infanterie. N.p.: T. H. Bouquet, 1899.

Réthoré, Edmond. *Les Gardes Suisses à Argenteuil et leur influence sociale*. N.p., 1952.

Réthoré, Louis Jean Baptiste. *Historique du 92e régiment d'infanterie*. Paris: Imprimerie Henri Charles-Lavauzelle, 1889.

Reuss, Radolphe. *La grande fuite de décembre 1793 et la situation politique et religieuse du Bas-Rhin de 1794 à 1799*. Strasbourg: Istra, 1924.

Richardot, Jean-Pierre. *100.000 morts oubliés: Les 47 jours et 47 nuits de la bataille de France, 10 mai-25 juin 1940*. Paris: Cherche midi, 2009.

Rigg, Bryan Mark. *Hitler's Jewish Soldiers: The Untold Story of Nazi Racial Laws and Men of Jewish Descent in the German Military*. Lawrence: University of Kansas Press, 2004.

Roberts, Warren. *Jacques-Louis David and Jean-Louis Prieur, Revolutionary Artists: The Public, the Populace and Images of the French Revolution*. Albany: State University of New York Press, 2000.

Robespierre, Maximilien. *Robespierre: Pages choisies*. Paris: Jean Schemit, 1908.

Rocaud, Michel. "La capitulation générale de 1803." *Revue historique des armées* 243 (2006): 108–11.

Rogers, Clifford, ed. *The Military Revolution Debate: Readings on the Military Transformation of Early Modern Europe*. Oxford: Westview Press, 1995.

Rojas, Aristide, ed. *Miranda dans la révolution française: Recueil de documents authentiques relatifs à l'histoire du général Francisco de Miranda, pendant son séjour en France de 1792 à 1798.* Paris: Imprimerie du gouvernement national, 1889.

Rousseau, Jean-Jacques. *Considérations sur le gouvernement de Pologne, et sur sa réformation projettée.* London, 1782.

———. *Projet de constitution pour la Corse.* N.p.: Calvi, 1763.

Roussel. *État militaire de France pour l'année 1780.* Paris: Onfroy, 1780.

Roverea, Félix de. *Mémoires de F. de Roverea, colonel d'un régiment de son nom, à la solde de Sa Majesté Britannique.* Berne: Charles Stämpfli, 1848.

Rowe, Michael. *From Reich to State: The Rhineland in the Revolutionary Age, 1780–1830.* Cambridge: Cambridge University Press, 2003.

Rubin, E. *140 Jewish Marshals, Generals and Admirals.* London: De Vero, 1952.

Sagnac, Philip. *Le Rhin français pendant la Révolution et l'Empire.* Paris: Alcan, 1917.

Sahlins, Peter. "Fictions of a Catholic France: The Naturalization of Foreigners, 1685–1787." *Representations* 47 (1994): 85–110.

———. *Unnaturally French: Foreign Citizens in the Old Regime and After.* Ithaca, N.Y.: Cornell University Press, 2004.

Saiffert, Freymuth. *Faits justificatifs, pour la légion germanique.* N.p., n.d.

Salerian-Saugy, Ghougas. *La justice militaire des troupes suisses en France sous l'Ancien Régime: D'après des documents conserveés aux archives de Berne et de Paris.* Paris: Jouve, 1927.

Sarmat, Thierry. *Les Ministres de la Guerre 1570–1792: Histoire et Dictionnaire Biographique.* Paris: Belin, 2007.

Sauvegarde du Capitaine des Cent Suisses, pour l'exemption du Logement des Cent Suisses dans les Maisons appartenantes à l'Hôtel-Dieu. Paris: Imprimerie royale, 1662.

Sauzey, Jean-Camille-Abel-Fleuri. *Les Allemands sous les aigles franc͵aises: Essai sur les troupes de la Confédération du Rhin, 1806–1814.* Paris: Chapelot, 1908.

Saxe, Maurice de. *Mémoires sur l'art de guerre de Maurice de Saxe, duc de Courlande et de Sémigalle, maréchal général des armées de S.M.T.C. &c. &c. &c.: Nouvelle édition conforme à l'original, et augmenté du Traité des Légions, ainsi que quelques lettres de cet illustre capitaine sur les opérations militaires.* Dresden: George Conrad Walther, 1757.

Schaller, Henri de. *Histoire des troupes suisses au service de France sous le règne de Napoléon Ier.* Paris: Microméga, 2012.

Schama, Simon. *Patriots and Liberators: Revolution in the Netherlands, 1780–1813.* London: Collins, 1977.

Scharf, Thomas. *History of Philadelphia, 1609–1884.* Philadelphia: J. B. Lippincott, 1884.

Schechter, Ronald. *Obstinate Hebrews: Representations of Jews in France, 1715–1815.* Berkeley: University of California Press, 2003.

Schreiber, Ernst. *Französische Ausweisungspolitik am Rhein und die Nordfrankenlegion.* Berlin: Reimar Hobbing, 1929.

Schwarzfuchs, Simon. *Du Juif à l'israélite: Histoire d'une mutation 1770–1870.* Paris: Fayard, 1989.

Scott, Samuel F. *The Response of the Royal Army to the French Revolution: The Role and Development of the Line Army, 1787–93.* Oxford: Clarendon Press, 1978.

Selig, Robert. "A German Soldier in America, 1780–1783: The Journal of Georg Daniel Flohr." *William and Mary Quarterly* 50 (Jul. 1993): 575–90.

Sepinwall, Alyssa. *The Abbé Grégoire and the French Revolution: The Making of Modern Universalism.* Berkeley: University of California Press, 2005.

Serrant, Henri. *Le Service du recrutement de 1789 à nos jours: Son organisation, ses cadres, son rôle.* Paris: Charles-Lavauzelle, 1935.

Servan, Joseph. *Le soldat citoyen, ou Vues patriotiques sur la manière la plus avantageuse de pourvoir à la défense du royaume.* N.p., 1780.

Sewell, William. "The French Revolution and the Emergence of the Nation Form." In *Revolutionary Currents,* edited by Michael Morrison and Melinda Zook, 91–125. Lanham: Rowman & Littlefield, 2004.

Six, Georges. *Dictionnaire biographique des généraux et amiraux 1792–1814.* Paris: Saffroy, 1934.

———. *Les généraux de la Révolution et de l'Empire.* N.p.: Bordas, 1947.

Smith, Digby. *Napoleon's Regiments: Battle Histories of the Regiments of the French Army, 1792–1815.* London: Greenhill Books, 2000.

Smith, Jay M. *Nobility Reimagined: The Patriotic Nation in Eighteenth-Century France.* Ithaca, N.Y.: Cornell University Press, 2005.

Soboul, Albert. *1789: "l'An Un de la Liberté."* Paris: Éditions sociales, 1950.

Spurr, Harry A. *The Life and Writings of Alexandre Dumas (1802–1870).* New York: Frederic A. Stokes, 1903.

Stacey, C. P. *Quebec, 1759: The Siege and the Battle.* Toronto: Macmillan, 1959.

Stanbridge, Karen. *Toleration and State Institutions: British Policy toward Catholics in Eighteenth-Century Ireland and Quebec.* London: Lexington Books, 2003.

Stauben, Daniel. *Scènes de la vie juive en Alsace.* Paris: Michel Lévy, 1860.

Stauffach, Henri-Alexandre. *Avis aux Suisses, sur leur position envers le Roi de France: Par Henri-Alexandre Stauffach, du Canton de Schwitz.* N.p., 1791.

Steenackers, F. F. *Histoire des ordres de chevalarie et des distinctions honorifiques en France.* Paris: Librarie internationale, 1867.

Stovall, Tyler. "The Color Line behind the Lines: Racial Violence in France during the Great War." *American Historical Review* 103 (Jun. 1998): 737–69.

Stovall, Tyler, and Georges van den Abbeele, eds. *French Civilization and Its Discontents: Nationalism, Colonialism, Race.* Oxford: Lexington Books, 2003.

Stradling, R. A. *The Spanish Monarchy and Irish Mercenaries: The Wild Geese in Spain, 1618–68.* Dublin: Irish Academic, 1994.

Strathern, Paul. *Napoleon in Egypt.* London: Vintage, 2008.

Sulte, Benjamin. *La guerre des Iroquois.* Ottawa: Durie, 1897.

Szajkowski, Zosa. "French Jews in the Armed Forces during the Revolution of

1789." *Proceedings of the American Academy for Jewish Research* 26 (1957): 139–60.

———. *Jews and the French Revolutions of 1789, 1830 and 1848.* New York: Ktav, 1970.

Table générale par ordre alphabétique de matières des lois, sénatus-consultes, etc. Paris: Imprimerie royale, 1816.

Taylor, George. "Noncapitalist Wealth and the Origins of the French Revolution." *American Historical Review* 72 (Jan. 1967): 469–96.

Tone, Theobald Wolfe. *The Writings of Theobald Wolfe Tone, 1763–1798.* Oxford: Oxford University Press, 1998.

Tornare, Alain-Jacques. *Vaudois et Confédérés au service de France, 1789–1798.* Yens-sur-Morges: Cabédita, 1998.

Torpey, John. *The Invention of the Passport.* Cambridge: Cambridge University Press, 1999.

Tozzi, Christopher. "Between Two Republics: American Military Volunteers in Revolutionary France." *Proceedings of the Western Society for French History* 39 (2013): 166–76.

Tremblay, Denis. *Grand détail de l'insurrection qui a eu lieu hier 27 mai 1792 au village de Courbevois, près Paris.* Paris: Imprimerie de la veuve Errard, n.d.

Turner, Frederick Jackson. "The Origin of Genet's Projected Attack on Louisiana and the Floridas." *American Historical Review* 3 (Jul. 1898): 650–71.

———. "The Policy of France toward the Mississippi Valley in the Period of Washington and Adams." *American Historical Review* 10 (Jan. 1905): 249–79.

Valynseele, Joseph, et al. *Dictionnaire des Maréchaux de France du Moyen-Âge à nos jours.* Paris: Perrin, 2000.

Van Kley, Dale. *The Religious Origins of the French Revolution: From Calvin to the Civil Constitution, 1560–1791.* New Haven, Conn.: Yale University Press, 1996.

Vanel, Marguerite. *Évolution historique de la notion de français d'origine du XVIe siècle au Code Civil: Contribution a l'étude de la nationalité française d'origine.* Paris: Ancienne imprimerie de la cour d'appel, 1945.

Vaughan, Harold Cecil. *The Citizen Genêt Affair, 1793: A Chapter in the Formation of American Foreign Policy.* New York: Franklin Watts, 1970.

Vergé-Franceschi, Michel. *La Marine française au XVIIIe siècle.* Paris: SEDES, 1996.

Viet, Vincent. *Histoire des Français venus d'ailleurs de 1850 a nos jours.* Paris: Éditions Perrin, 2004.

Wahnich, Sophie. *L'impossible citoyen.* Paris: Albin Michel, 1997.

Watteville, Baron of. *Le régiment de Watteville, une page de son histoire (1789–1792).* Paris: Émile Lechavalier, 1898.

Weber, Eugen. *Peasants into Frenchmen: The Modernization of Rural France, 1870–1914.* Stanford, Calif.: Stanford University Press, 1976.

Weber, Jacques, ed. *Les Relations entre la France et l'Inde de 1673 à nos jours.* Paris: Les Indes Savantes, 2002.

Weil, Patrick. *How to Be French: Nationality in the Making Since 1789.* Durham, N.C.: Duke University Press, 2009.

Wells, Charlotte. *Law and Citizenship in Early Modern France.* Baltimore: Johns Hopkins University Press, 1994.

Wilmin, Henri. *Forbach: La ville et le canton pendant la Révolution Française (1789–1799).* Sarreguemines: Pierron, 1980.

Wolf, Simon. *The American Jew as Patriot, Soldier and Citizen.* Philadelphia: Levytype, 1895.

Woloch, Isser. *The French Veteran from the Revolution to the Restoration.* Chapel Hill: University of North Carolina Press, 1979.

Wright, D. G. *Napoleon and Europe.* London: Longman, 1984.

Zwilling, Franz. *Discours sommaire sur la création de la compagnie des cent gardes suisses ordinares du Corps du Roy.* Paris: Langlois fils, 1676.

INDEX

Act of Mediation, 174

Africa, 17, 24–25, 27, 40, 152, 176, 218

Aix-en-Provence, 64–65

Aix-la-Chapelle, 132, 164

Allen, Ira, 153–54, 264n79, 264n85

Allobroge Legion, 97–99

Alsace, 21, 30, 33, 41, 69, 101, 124, 204, 207, 213

Alsace, Regiment of, 20, 30, 71–72, 122, 143

American Revolution, 21, 26, 27, 75, 104, 106, 117, 136, 153, 156

Americans, 26, 103, 154; legions formed by, 104–6. *See also* Allen, Ira; Eustace, John Skey; Tate, William; United States; Vermont

Amerindians, 25, 101, 103, 104

annexed territories, military recruitment within, 23, 29, 99, 162–66, 171–73, 179, 185, 191, 204

Arendt, Hannah, 7

army of France: desertion by foreigners from, 4, 57–58, 63–64; emigration from, 4, 64; reforms of, 23, 30, 50

August 10, 1792, revolution of, 50, 80–81, 85, 94, 98, 121, 129, 207

Auld Alliance, 21

Austria, 18, 21, 24, 25, 26, 28, 33, 38, 43, 73, 93, 94, 95, 100, 102, 111, 118, 123, 125, 130, 147, 156, 157, 158, 159, 161, 179, 181, 184, 186, 189, 194, 210

Avignon, 204, 209, 211

Bantry Bay, 143, 144, 146, 147

Bastille, 6, 49, 51, 54–57, 59, 65, 98, 244n18

Batavian Committee, 96

Batavian legions, 96–97, 114

Batavian Republic, 147, 149, 155

Battalion of Repatriated Frenchmen, 191

Bavaria, 43, 117, 132

Bavaria, elector of, 132

Belgian Legion, 97

Belgians, 94, 95–98, 111, 114, 135, 162, 194

Bercheny, Regiment of, 24, 63, 64

Bermuda, 145

Berwick, Regiment of, 40, 76

Black Legion, 146

Black Pioneers, Battalion of, 176, 178

blacks, 8, 11, 15, 24–26, 33, 40, 101, 106–10, 114, 152, 158, 188, 216, 220, 229–30; in Egypt campaign, 152, 158; in Napoleon's army, 175–78. *See also* Black Pioneers, Battalion of; Legion of the Americans; Royal African, Regiment of

Bloch, Marc, 199, 207

Blum, Léon, 199

Bonaparte, Joseph, 176, 177, 214

Bonaparte, Louis, 155, 172, 174, 214

Bonaparte, Napoleon, 1, 13, 14, 15, 147–52, 156, 161, 162, 168, 211, 275n61; dissolution of foreign corps by, 192–93; foreign troops under, 170–97

Bouillon, Regiment of, 25, 57, 72

Bourbon Restorations. *See* Restorations, first and second Bourbon

Boyer, Jean-Pierre, 107

Britain, 22, 26, 44, 103, 111, 137, 143, 146–48, 153, 179, 180, 237n48. *See also* England; Wales, 1797 invasion of

Cahiers de doléances, 6, 53

Campo-Formio, treaty of, 147

Canada, 13, 140, 153–55, 264n85. *See also* New France

Caribbean, 25, 26, 27, 107–9, 110, 158, 161, 174, 175, 176, 177

Carnot, Lazare, 92, 93, 110, 124, 138, 148

Castella, Regiment of, 59, 83

Catholicism, 1, 17, 22, 31, 127, 153, 185, 200, 203

Charles VII, 19, 21

Châteauvieux, Regiment of, 56, 57, 58–61, 245n46

Cincinnati, Society of the, 104

Cisalpine Republic, 157, 161

citizen-soldiers, 11, 39, 48, 53, 55, 88

Clare, Regiment of, 1, 26, 27, 45

Clark, George Rogers, 104–6, 153, 162

Clark, William, 144

Clarke, Henri-Jacques-Guillaume, 181

Cloots, Anacharsis, 52, 100, 131

Coblenz, 163, 210

colonies of France, 14–15, 26–28, 30, 37, 89, 103, 106–10, 137, 150, 151, 161, 162, 166, 175, 177, 178, 194, 195, 218, 231

Comtat Venaissin, 65, 204, 209

Confederation of the Rhine, 174, 185

conscription, 46, 67, 140, 170, 172, 173, 212; in annexed territories, 167, 172; of foreigners, 44, 120, 166–68; of Jews, 34, 200, 211, 213–14

Constitution of 1791, 4

Constitution of 1795, 13, 133, 136, 140–41, 143, 155, 206, 218

Consulate (government), 13, 139, 140, 161–62, 168, 174, 184

Coptic Legion, 151–52

Corsica, 23, 42, 172. *See also* Royal-Corse, Regiment of

Courten, Regiment of, 32, 84

Crancé, Edmond-Louis-Alexis Dubois de, 3, 67, 69, 90

Custine, Adam-Philippe de, 67–68, 77, 92, 93, 162

Dabrowski, Jan Henryk, 155–57

Diesbach, Regiment of, 53, 57

Dillon, Arthur, 45, 76, 118, 123, 124, 258–59n86

Dillon, Henri, 190

Dillon, Théobald, 123

Dillon, Regiment of, 25, 27, 40, 123, 127, 128–29, 130

Directory (government), 9, 13, 66, 86, 102, 114, 136, 139, 140–49, 153–56, 159, 161, 162, 163, 168, 171, 172, 173, 174, 184

Doppet, Amédée, 99

Dreyfus, Alfred, 198, 199, 215

droit d'aubaine, 4, 17, 44, 170

Dumas, Alexandre, 109

Dumas, Thomas-Alexandre, 109

Dumouriez, Charles-François, 73, 76, 95, 109, 128, 130, 131, 135, 137

Dutch, 34, 36, 75, 95–97, 100, 102, 112, 113, 135, 147, 155, 172, 194, 205, 214. *See also* Batavian Committee; Batavian legions; Batavian Republic; Free Foreign Legion

Edelstein, Dan, 7

Egypt, 13, 140, 151–53, 170, 188

Eickemeyer, Rudolf, 164, 166

Elizabeth I, 21, 33

émigrés, 62, 63–64, 77, 91, 127, 135, 146, 179, 190, 210; foreigners in army of, 63, 84

England, 22, 40, 112, 127, 145, 146, 181. *See also* Britain

Ernest, Regiment of, 64–66, 79, 159, 246n76

étranger, definition of, 233n9

Eustace, John Skey, 76, 118, 135–36, 248n135, 260n140

Expeditionary Legion, 151, 161–62, 177

Fishguard, landing at, 146–47

Flanders, 37, 57

Flue, Louis de, 54

Foreign Brigade, 143

Fouquier-Tinville, Antoine Quentin, 128, 133

free companies, 12, 86, 89, 93–94, 95, 96, 97, 99, 106, 113, 114, 118, 230

Free Foreign Legion, 96–97

French army. *See* army of France

French colonies. *See* colonies of France

French Foreign Legion, 14, 86, 218
Fronde, 20
Furet, François, 7, 50–51

Genêt, Edmond-Charles, 103–6
Germanic Legion, 99–103, 113–14, 141, 161, 204, 207
Germany, 7, 9, 15, 21, 25, 34, 41, 64, 74, 125, 132, 135, 165, 172, 174, 179, 181, 185, 186. *See also* Bavaria; Confederation of the Rhine; Holy Roman Empire; Prussia; Rhineland
Grand Sanhedrin, 202, 212–13
Greek Legion, 151–52
Greeks, 29, 89, 151–52, 188, 239n87
Grégoire, abbé Henri, 178, 201, 209, 274n45
Guadeloupe, 46, 101, 107, 109, 161
guest workers, 10
Guibert, comte de, 30, 50, 89

Habsburgs, 20, 189
Haiti, 107, 158. *See also* Saint-Domingue
Helvetic Confederation, 20, 37, 60, 79
Helvetic Republic, 159–60, 174
Hesse, Charles de, 76, 118, 132–33, 135
Hoche, Lazare, 143
Holy Roman Empire, 37, 38, 41, 68, 200, 202
Hundred Days, 14, 188, 194–96, 217
Hundred Swiss, Company of, 19, 21, 35, 38, 77, 194, 217
Hungarians, 19, 24, 63, 98, 164, 165, 188
hussars, 19, 24, 34, 42, 54, 62, 63, 64, 117, 126, 173

Independent Revolutionary Legion of the Mississippi, 106
India, 25–26, 27, 40, 45, 108, 148, 165
Invalides, Hôtel des, 31, 239nn88–89
Ireland, 1, 13, 21–22, 23, 27, 33, 38, 40, 46, 126, 128, 185, 218; French invasions of, 143–49, 162, 180; French recruitment in, 22–23, 42, 185
Irish, 21–23, 28, 76, 165, 179, 180, 185, 239–40n102. *See also* Clare, Regiment of; Dillon, Arthur; Dillon, Théobald;

Dillon, Regiment of; Walsh, Regiment of
Irish Brigade (British), 64, 246n75
Irish Brigades (French), 22, 45, 123, 143
Irish Legion, 180–81, 183, 186, 189, 190, 195
Italians, 23, 38, 151, 179. *See also* Royal-Corse, Regiment of; Royal-Italien, Regiment of
Italy, 23, 38, 147, 156, 157, 161, 171, 176

James II, 22, 28
Jewish Legion, purported creation of, 211, 275n61
Jews, 8, 9, 11, 14, 34, 101, 198–216, 274n45, 275n61, 276n71, 276nn80–81, 277n83
Joseph-Napoléon, Regiment of, 183, 184, 194
Jourdan Law, 166–67

Karrer, Regiment of, 27
Keating, Thomas, 133
Kellermann, François-Christophe de, 64, 73, 74, 81, 92, 93, 112, 124
Kilmaine, Charles Jennings, 126–27, 133, 147, 260n130
Kilmaine, Charles Jennings, 126–27, 133, 147, 260n130
Korps Israelieten, 214
Kosciuszko, Tadeusz, 156

Lafayette, marquis de, 94, 98, 118, 129, 131
La Marck, Regiment of, 25, 32, 33, 41, 43, 119
language, and the army, 7, 10, 34–37, 40, 69, 70, 72, 94, 100, 101–2, 111, 117, 121–22, 146, 150, 165, 183, 189, 200, 204, 210–11, 230, 231
Lauffeld, battle of, 26
légion, definition of, 251n3
Legion of the Americans, 108–9, 175, 176
Legion of Equality, 107, 176
Legion of the Franks of the North, 162–66
Legion of the Mountains, 110
legions, 9; dissolution of, 112–14; through 1794, 86–114; under Directory and Consulate, 155–58; under Napoleon, 180–82. *See also* Allobroge

legions (*continued*)
  Legion; Batavian legions; Belgian
  Legion; Black Legion; Coptic Legion;
  Expeditionary Legion; Free Foreign
  Legion; French Foreign Legion; Ger-
  manic Legion; Greek Legion; Inde-
  pendent Revolutionary Legion of the
  Mississippi; Irish Legion; Legion of the
  Americans; Legion of Equality; Legion
  of the Franks of the North; Legion of
  the Mountains; Maltese Legion; Por-
  tuguese Legion; Propaganda Legion;
  Royal Foreign Legion
Leipzig, battle of, 192
lettres de naturalité, 17, 45, 217
levée en masse, 120
Liégeois, 19, 23–24, 94; in legions,
  95–97, 111. *See also* Royal-Liégeois,
  Regiment of
Lorraine, 25, 29, 33, 41, 42, 69, 71, 213
Louis Philippe, 14, 218
Louis XI, 19
Louis XIII, 19
Louis XIV, 20, 22, 24, 29, 31, 44, 45, 76,
  166
Louis XV, 24, 29, 32, 35, 38
Louis XVI, 23, 28, 53, 65, 117, 135
Louis XVIII, 14, 181, 194, 217
Louisiana, 30, 104–6, 177
Luckner, Nicolas, 74, 81, 92, 93, 94, 95, 97,
  117–18, 124, 137, 259n95; persecution
  during Terror, 129–30, 133
Lynch, Isidore, 1–2, 134

Machiavelli, Niccolò, 30, 50
Madagascar, 25
Malta, 41, 150, 162
Maltese Legion, 150
Mamelukes, in Imperial Guard, 152, 178,
  187
Mangourit, Michel-Ange-Bernard,
  104–5, 145
Marat, Jean-Paul, 55, 59, 60, 62, 63, 78,
  80, 101, 123, 124, 129, 131, 138, 205,
  257–58n52, 273n30
Marseille, 24, 64–65, 79, 121
Mathiez, Albert, 7, 51

Mazarin, Cardinal, 23
mercenaires, definition of, 243n185
Miaczynski, Joseph, 118, 130, 131, 137
Milice royale, 166
Miranda, Francisco de, 118, 124, 130–31,
  136–37, 259n104
Mississippi Valley, 103–4, 106. *See also*
  Independent Revolutionary Legion of
  the Mississippi
Moran, Jacques, 118, 127–28, 129, 134, 137
Mughal Empire, 25, 40
Muslims, 33–34

Nancy, 58–60, 201, 202
Naples, 18, 23, 175, 176, 177, 178
Napoleon. *See* Bonaparte, Napoleon
National Assembly, 3, 12, 49, 53, 55, 58,
  60, 61, 62, 63, 73, 76, 78, 109, 117, 135,
  190, 201, 202
National Guard, 49, 57, 59, 61, 64, 65, 74,
  119; service of foreigners in, 58; service
  of Jews in, 201–8, 211
nationality, 1, 4, 8, 76–78, 100, 102, 116,
  120, 128, 132, 134, 135, 169, 194, 197, 219;
  codification of, 4, 76, 140, 168, 170
nationalization of French army, 3, 4, 5, 9,
  14, 49, 72, 78, 84, 114, 118, 119, 133, 141,
  171, 218
naturalization of foreign troops, 3, 4,
  45, 76, 106, 116, 135, 137, 153. See also
  droit d'aubaine; lettres de naturalité;
  nationality
navy, 11, 27–28, 44, 70, 75, 125, 126, 136,
  148, 186
nègre, definition of, 237n41
New France, 27
New York, 26, 76, 154
Noailles, Louis de, 3, 66
Nordon, Anselme, 101, 198, 207–8, 215,
  274n44

Ottoman Empire, 2, 24, 89, 151, 275n61

Paine, Thomas, 52, 131
Paris, 13, 31, 38, 41, 49, 53, 58, 59, 65, 76,
  95, 108, 109, 113, 120, 132, 133; foreign
  troops in, 54–57, 61, 72, 80, 101

Penal Laws, 22, 33

Piedmont, 23, 98; French annexation of, 162–63

Poland, 126, 130, 156, 157

Polish, 100, 117, 118, 155, 156, 158, 165, 179, 181, 183; legions, 155–58, 183–84, 265n101

Portuguese, 177, 194–95, 217; legions, 182, 188, 194

Portuguese Legion, 182, 194

prisoners of war, 70, 74, 111, 126, 142, 143, 146, 148, 155, 163, 175, 179, 181, 182, 183, 186, 193, 194, 197

Propaganda Legion, 111

Protestants, 22, 27, 31–33, 117, 239n88

Prussia, 21, 43, 44, 74, 78, 99, 100, 101, 102, 111, 117, 125, 156, 158, 207

Prussia, Regiment of, 179, 183, 189

Raimond, Julien, 108–9

Rapport, Michael, 7, 51

Reign of Terror, 1, 2, 6, 7, 8, 12, 13, 51, 52, 68, 138, 140; and Jewish troops, 205–6; treatment of foreign troops during, 115–33

Reinach, Regiment of, 37, 57

religion and foreign troops, 31–34, 174, 229, 239nn86–88. See also Catholicism; Jews; Muslims; Protestants

Restorations, first and second Bourbon, 5, 8, 14, 193–94, 217–18, 219

Revolutionary Tribunal, 127–31, 133, 205, 206, 232

Rhineland, 15, 71, 162–64, 167, 172, 174

Robespierre, Maximilien, 124, 132, 133, 138, 141

Rousseau, Jean-Jacques, 30, 50

Royal African, Regiment of, 175–78

Royal-Allemand, Regiment of, 54–56, 60, 63, 64; desertion from, 57

Royal-Corse, Regiment of, 23, 27, 34, 42

Royal-Deux-Ponts, Regiment of, 27, 32, 68, 142, 143

Royal Foreign Legion, 217

Royal-Hesse-Darmstadt, Regiment of, 119

Royal-Italien, Regiment of, 23, 34

Royal-Liégeois, Regiment of, 23, 49, 59, 61–62, 69, 71, 72, 79, 114, 245n58

Royal-Nassau, Regiment of, 33, 46, 62, 71

Royal-Suédois, Regiment of, 21, 63

Russia, 130, 192

Russians, 89, 156, 158, 165, 188; and French navy, 28

Saiffert, Jean-Geoffroy, 100

Saint-Domingue, 25, 107–8, 158, 161, 177, 178. See also Haiti

Saint-George, Joseph-Bologne de, 109

Salis-Samade, Regiment of, 54, 56, 57, 65

Salm-Salm, Regiment of, 33, 111, 142

San Ildefonso, treaty of, 182

Savannah, siege of, 107

Savoy, 23, 97–99

Saxe, Maurice de, 25, 28, 33, 68, 87

Saxony, 44, 56, 100, 165

Schorp, Kaspar, 163–64

Scotland, 21, 38, 40, 97, 118, 181

Senegal, 25

Servan, Joseph, 30, 31, 50, 58, 100, 110, 130

Seven Years' War, 32, 45, 117

Sheldon, Dominique, 118, 127, 134

sister-republics, 9, 13, 105, 140, 147, 149, 153, 155–59, 161, 168

slavery, 15, 103, 107–10, 175, 177, 178; abolition of, 106, 108; and enlistment of troops, 106, 152; reintroduction of, 177–78

Sonnenberg, Regiment of, 57

Spain, 18, 33, 82, 84, 99, 130, 132, 174, 177, 181, 182, 183, 196; New World possessions of, 103–5, 130

Spanish, 18, 21, 33, 103, 135; in French army, 113, 177, 179, 182–84, 188, 194–96, 217

Stengel, Henry Christian, 131–32, 134

Strasbourg, 74, 186, 189, 208, 216

Sweden, 75, 179

Swedes in French army, 21, 236n18

Swiss: demi-brigades, 158–61, 163, 174; disappearance of rosters for, 40; dissolution of regiments, 77–85, 194; in French army, 19–20, 27, 29, 31, 32,

Swiss (*continued*)
33, 35, 37–39, 44, 47, 49, 53–62, 64–65, 67–70, 72, 76, 77, 90, 91, 94, 98, 99, 114, 119, 121, 123, 141, 158–61, 163, 174–75, 178, 188, 192, 196, 207; privileges of, 37–39, 44–45, 66, 159, 174, 217
Swiss Guards, Regiment of, 19, 20, 38, 55–58, 62, 77, 79, 80, 81, 84, 85, 98, 121, 207; defense of Tuileries by, 80, 274n44
Syrians, 152

Tate, William, 104–6, 145–46, 153
Terror. *See* Reign of Terror
Thirty Years' War, 20, 23, 47
Tone, Theobald Wolfe, 144–45, 147–48, 149
Toulon, 28, 99, 128, 148, 150, 151, 152
translation, of official list of commands for drills and maneuvers, 240n116

United Irishmen, 144, 147, 165
United States, 12, 103–6, 107, 131, 135, 136, 145, 146, 153–54, 156, 181. *See also* Americans; Vermont

Valmy, battle of, 1, 73, 124, 132, 210
Vermont, 153–54
veterans, 32, 57, 76, 77, 80, 82, 83, 84, 95, 96, 98, 119, 150, 151, 160, 172, 186, 187, 190, 193, 194
Vichy France, 199, 216
Vigier, Regiment of, 59
Volontaires de Saxe, Regiment of, 2, 25, 33, 40, 188

Wahnich, Sophie, 7, 52
Wales, 1797 invasion of, 145–46
Walsh, Regiment of, 1, 27, 104, 162
Ward, Thomas, 124, 128, 130
Warsaw, 100, 130, 184
Waterloo, battle of, 4, 196, 217
Wielhorski, Józef, 155
William of Orange, 22
Wimpffen, Georges-Félix de, 68, 118, 210
women, 27, 32, 45, 93, 126, 153, 206, 219
Wyzkowski, Józef, 155

Yiddish, 34, 200, 204